Europe and the End of the Age of Innocence

Francesco M. Bongiovanni

Europe and the End of the Age of Innocence

palgrave
macmillan

Francesco M. Bongiovanni

ISBN 978-3-319-74369-1   ISBN 978-3-319-74370-7   (eBook)
https://doi.org/10.1007/978-3-319-74370-7

Library of Congress Control Number: 2018934899

© The Editor(s) (if applicable) and The Author(s) 2018
This work is subject to copyright. All rights are solely and exclusively licensed by the Publisher, whether the whole or part of the material is concerned, specifically the rights of translation, reprinting, reuse of illustrations, recitation, broadcasting, reproduction on microfilms or in any other physical way, and transmission or information storage and retrieval, electronic adaptation, computer software, or by similar or dissimilar methodology now known or hereafter developed.
The use of general descriptive names, registered names, trademarks, service marks, etc. in this publication does not imply, even in the absence of a specific statement, that such names are exempt from the relevant protective laws and regulations and therefore free for general use.
The publisher, the authors and the editors are safe to assume that the advice and information in this book are believed to be true and accurate at the date of publication. Neither the publisher nor the authors or the editors give a warranty, express or implied, with respect to the material contained herein or for any errors or omissions that may have been made. The publisher remains neutral with regard to jurisdictional claims in published maps and institutional affiliations.

Cover illustration: estherpoon/iStock/Getty; Andrew Latshaw/EyeEm/Getty

Printed on acid-free paper

This Palgrave Macmillan imprint is published by Springer Nature
The registered company is Springer International Publishing AG
The registered company address is: Gewerbestrasse 11, 6330 Cham, Switzerland

Endorsements For *Europe And The End Of The Age Of Innocence*

'The European Union's mood has improved as its economies pick up, the euro crisis fades, migration and terrorism fears pass and even Brexit no longer provokes concern. In his new book, Francesco Bongiovanni warns against complacency. The gap between Europe's elites and its citizens is glaring; north-south and east-west tensions persist; the euro and migration crises could easily return. All this makes plans to build a united states of Europe wholly unrealistic. His gloomy message should be heeded, especially in Brussels, Berlin and Paris.'
—John Peet, *Political Editor, The Economist*

'Severe but necessary. An extreme lucidity that should bring Europe, through its ever-closer union, to political initiatives able to safeguard its traditional values and new common interests in the midst of an inescapable universal revolution.'
—Georges Berthoin, *Former chief of staff of Jean Monnet—a founding father of Europe—former High Representative of the European Economic Community with the United Kingdom*

'Europe—as presently constructed—is no longer fit for purpose. With his trademark style, Bongiovanni takes an unflinching look at what led the continent to this moment. Do not read this book if you're optimistic about Europe's future—but read this book if you care about that future.'
—Ian Bremmer, *President and founder of Eurasia Group, a leading global political risk research and consulting firm*

'Francesco Bongiovanni's *The End of the Age of Innocence* presents an unsettling but coherent view of Europe's future. It is a view which is not usually heard in polite European circles but one which is often heard privately. Bongiovanni worries about what he sees as a fight for the soul of Europe.'
—George Yeo, *Former Minister of Foreign Affairs of The Republic of Singapore*

'Bongiovanni is right: the West in general doesn't seem to know anymore what it stands for or where it wants to go. Europe is particularly lost and adrift. This book provides a valuable and timely wake-up call. Europeans ignore it at their own peril.'
—Kishore Mahbubani, *Dean, Lee Kuan Yew School of Public Policy NUS*

'A brilliant reconstruction of an inevitable disaster or a doomsday interpretation of the Union's future? The analysis goes to the roots of the socio-economic European malaise that threatens our common dream, the salvation of which desperately requires acts of political bravery.'
—Leonardo Maisano, *European affairs commentator*

Endorsements For *The Decline And Fall Of Europe*:

'It has become impossible to pretend otherwise: Europe is in steep decline. The Continental dream of economic prosperity, social security and international good citizenship has given way to a nightmare of chronic unemployment, unsustainable debt, demographic decline, political paralysis and street violence. In *The Decline and Fall of Europe*, Francesco Bongiovanni offers the most perceptive account to date of a Europe that indulged too many illusions and is now awakening to bankruptcy.'
—Bret Stephens, *Foreign Affairs Columnist, Wall Street Journal*

'Provocative and alarming, a wake-up call for the twenty-first century.'
—Nils Pratley, *The Guardian*

'An important read for anyone interested in the future of Europe.'
—John Paulson, *President, Paulson & Co. Inc*

'A very lively and witty survey of Europe's ills.'
—Dominique Moisi, *author of The Geopolitics of Emotions*

'A thoughtful and provocative cautionary tale that Americans should read if they want to see how our own increasing regulatory structure, accelerating entitlements, and ballooning national debt could lead to the same decline that the author so clearly describes in Europe. Francesco Bongiovanni mixes common sense with an experienced eye for the details that show how utopianism overwhelmed the benign postwar vision of a united Europe and resulted in a nightmare. His description of the EU bureaucracy as an organization of 40,000 souls, a budget of 126 billion Euros, and the ambition to control every part of European life is lamentable proof of Kafka's vision.'
—John Lehman, *Former Secretary of the Navy in the Reagan Administration and a member of the 9/11 Commission*

'In view of the current crisis in the European Union in general and the Euro zone in particular, the arrival of this book could not be more timely. It is a comprehensive review of the way the initial favourable development of the EU has gone wrong and the range of problems it currently faces. Should be read by every MP in the Union's 27 countries!'
 —Stephen Valdez, *author of An Introduction to Global Financial Markets*

'Revealing. A valuable tool for those who are interested in understanding the roots of the current Eurocrisis and for decision-makers engaged in limiting its bitter consequences.'
 —Lucio Caracciolo, *Limes, Italian Review of Geopolitics, Editor-in-chief*

*This book is dedicated to all of you,
people of goodwill and reason, who seem to be fewer and fewer.
You have the right to know and the duty to try to understand.*

About the Author

Francesco M. Bongiovanni has lived in Europe, Asia, the USA and in the Arab world. He holds an MBA from Harvard and a doctorate in engineering. A former investment banker, he subsequently worked as an entrepreneur and as an advisor in strategy and finance. He has been made a Knight of the Order of St Charles for his contribution to humanitarian and biodiversity protection endeavours. He is an author and a composer of classical symphonic music and jazz.

Contents

1	Introduction	1
Part I	The Trilogy	11
2	The Awakening	13
3	The Tsunami	31
4	Barbarians in the City	83
5	The Rise of Alternative Politics	141
6	Ensuring the Survival of a 'Europe of Values'	191
Part II	A Brief History of How to Mess Things Up	205
7	The Island That Couldn't Get Far Enough	207
8	Uber Alles? Not So Fast!	225

9	The More It Changes, the More It Stays the Same	243
10	The Gas Wars	269
11	The Trump Card	283
12	Conclusion	293
Sources and Acknowledgements		299
Bibliography		301
Index		303

1

Introduction

> Any fool can know. The point is to understand.
> Albert Einstein

Apart from deserving my gratitude, anyone who read my first book, *The Decline and Fall of Europe*, is entitled to ask whether this sequel is really justified. Have things changed so much since the book was published in 2012 that a new one is necessary, or is this just the old dish being warmed up? To this legitimate question the returning reader needs a clear answer—as much as I needed one before deciding to embark on this new writing adventure. The fact is, sadly, that there have been dramatic new developments—most as sudden as they were unexpected—which have caused Europe to find itself today on a significantly more worrisome trajectory than the one I had anticipated in my first book. Interestingly, some of the people who, back then, suggested that *The Decline and Fall of Europe* was too pessimistic now say it was perhaps not pessimistic enough. This change in mood reflects the simple truth that, since 2012, the situation in Europe has considerably deteriorated across many dimensions and the changes are starting to directly and visibly affect a vast number of people. On top of a general worsening in ways that had largely been predicted at the time, new developments have piled up that may take the continent into uncharted, dangerous territory. I am therefore afraid that the answer to the above question is that it is high time to re-examine the situation in Europe.

The Decline and Fall of Europe was intended to be a 360 degree tour, offering a balanced description of the European 'system' and of the intractable challenges facing Europe, which were leading to inexorable decline across any dimension one cared to analyse. Among these, the transformation of the welfare state into the unsustainable 'Civilization of Entitlements' that was bound to condemn parts of Europe to gradual impoverishment (which I have at times jocularly taken to illustrate as follows in my speeches: 'you can have long vacations or you can have the money for long vacations, but you can't have both'); the crisis of a single currency built on a flawed architecture; the vast inefficiencies of the EU's Tinguely Machine and so on. The purpose of the book was to try to figure out what was really going on and where it could take Europe, concluding that 'the quality of life our children will know will be inferior to the quality of life we have enjoyed in the past half century'.[1] At the time *The Decline and Fall of Europe* was published, Europeans were still by and large in denial. Subjects such as failed immigration and integration policies, and the Islamization of Europe's open societies were still mostly considered taboo. A major publishing house I had approached about translating the book for distribution in France replied that while what the book said was true and mattered, the French were not ready to hear such truths. Similarly, publishers I approached in Germany, Italy, Spain and Scandinavia showed scant interest in translating the book for distribution in their own countries. It seemed that Europeans didn't really want to know (or perhaps they already knew everything, or the book wasn't good enough). The book therefore remained available only in its original English language and generally did much better in North America, the United Kingdom and Asia than in continental Europe. I was invited to give some speeches, lectures and TV interviews outside Europe. The point I am making here is that non-Europeans seemed far more interested in understanding the plight of Europe than Europeans themselves, whose main concern appeared to be to ensure that their privileged way of life would continue.

How much things have changed since then! Europeans have by and large woken up to the first tremors of the Titanic scraping against the iceberg. By early 2017 most of them were finally conscious of the frightening realities they were facing and recognized that there was no room left for blissful denial—a sea change from their attitude five years earlier. Something had clearly evolved in the collective European psyche, and denial had given place to bewilderment, fear and anger. These feelings translated into the recent and spectacular rise of 'alternative politics' across most of the continent, a development that could lead to dangerous territory if historical precedent is any indication. Europeans are now affected enough, worried enough, angry enough that they finally show significant interest in trying to understand what is hitting them (this will hopefully cause my books finally to be translated!). Consider, for instance, the controversial issue of the Islamization of European societies. New interest in this issue translated into the phenomenal success of Phillippe Houllebecq's 2015 book *Submission*,[2] a political-fiction novel set in 2022 in a France governed by its first president from an Islamic party. One can agree or disagree with the relevance of Houllebecq's book, but the fact remains that it sold 120,000 copies in France in five days upon its January 2015 launch, and became a top seller in Italy and Germany as well. This awakening does not, however, necessarily mean Europeans will collectively muster the will and courage to take appropriate measures to steer the ship away from the iceberg, assuming one can figure out what the appropriate measures should be. Unfortunately, I see very little chance of this happening and profess complete trust in the ability of governing political 'elites' to ensure that the ship holds its course steady to hit the iceberg, head on and at full speed. The reader will, by the way, notice that throughout this book the word 'elites' (in the context of European or Western political elites) is set within quote marks, reflecting the difficulty I encounter in associating the mediocre class of people guiding the Western world today with the very word 'elite'.

Allow me to confess something personal. Writing a book on Europe is quite demanding, particularly if one carries out one's own research, as I did for both books. This was all the more so in my case, since writing and researching takes away precious time from my interests in business and composing music. Unfortunately, not much money is to be made by writing such a book. So, my motivation had to come from some other direction. I wrote *The Decline and Fall of Europe* because of the shock I experienced when I came back from spending 15 years in the dynamic continent that is Asia only to find a Europe busy tying a rope around its own neck. I was then prompted to write *Europe and the End of the Age of Innocence* because the slow decay I had predicted in the first book appeared to have been replaced by a potentially swifter and more turbulent end game.

It seems that as Europeans are finally becoming interested in knowing more about their destiny and the reality surrounding them, they are realizing that they cannot rely on their political leaders, governments or the mainstream media to always tell the truth. Social media is not necessarily better. All of these players have been compromised, time and again caught lying, hiding facts, fabricating or manipulating information to advance their own interests or ideology-driven agendas. Having woken up from a long state of slumber and denial, the average European hungers for information but has become very suspicious of what he/she is fed, and rightly so. Written by an average European who put himself through the difficulties of trying to find out what was really going on, *Europe and the End of the Age of Innocence* is a small contribution to the need for a balanced and informative view, which I hope is laid out in a way that everybody can read and understand. To my readers, I should like to reiterate that I am no scholar, journalist, historian, political scientist or politician, nor do I harbour ambitions of becoming any of these. I am an ordinary man who decided to undertake a new journey of discovery to find out a bit more about today's Europe, put these findings on paper and share them with you. Once again, 'Trying to make sense of all the material turned out to be like one of these games where you connect the dots and slowly see patterns emerging.'[3] No one is entirely impervious to outside influence or can wholly shed his/her own education and background; yet I have attempted to write a book devoid of ideological bias, laying out the facts as well as I could given my limited research capabilities and, apart from a few instances where I can't resist venturing an opinion, I generally leave it to the reader to reach his/her own conclusions.

Had the trajectory followed by Europe been more or less in line with the findings laid out in *The Decline and Fall of Europe*, I wouldn't have bothered to write a sequel, and you wisely wouldn't have considered reading it had I done so. Yet, to name just a few of the unexpected and sudden developments that made necessary a reassessment of Europe's state of affairs, who would have predicted, just a year before Brexit, let alone back in 2012, that the UK would leave Europe—the first time since the end of the Second World War that the European integration process has been officially put in reverse? Who would have said, back in 2012, that Marine le Pen would have had a significant chance of winning France's 2017 presidential election with a programme intending to lead Europe's second-largest country down the path of far-right nationalism and outside Europe and the eurozone, potentially reducing the European project to a chapter in history books? Who would have said, even in 2016, that the German general election of September 2017 would result, for the first time since the end of the Second World War, in a far-right nationalist party entering parliament and that Germany would find itself without a government? Who would have imagined that German Chancellor Angela Merkel would suddenly and unilaterally open her country's doors to a human tsunami fleeing what American journalist George Friedman aptly calls the 'world of chaos', causing the death of Schengen, and fracturing Europe along East–West lines (just as mismanagement of the euro fractured Europe along North–South lines)? Who would have said that the placid Merkel would take actions that would contribute in no small measure to Brexit, to the rebirth of nationalism and the explosion of alternative politics across the continent? The issue of 'others' has now inserted itself prominently into the forefront of European life and politics. The 'trilogy' formed by unwanted mass immigration (UMI), by the creeping yet increasingly visible Islamization of Europe's open societies and of their Euromuslim minorities (by which I mean Muslims living in Europe), and by the daily Jihadist terrorist acts that have become Europe's 'new normal', has replaced the economy and jobs as the main topic of conversation across the continent and constitutes a key focus of this book. Will Europe's open societies and cherished way of life survive this onslaught? As I am writing these lines, I just heard on the news that another bombing took place in a London subway with dozen wounded and that yet another soldier was stabbed by a Jihadist in France. By the time you finish reading the first section of this book, it is likely that further Jihadist attacks will have taken place, that several thousand more migrants from Africa or the Middle East will have reached European shores and that a few hundred million euros of taxpayer money will have been spent dealing with UMI. The 'trilogy' is dramatically changing the broad socio-political landscape, to the great surprise of the mediocre and clueless traditional political 'elites' who, having fallen prey to a new form of seductive, multiculturalist and post-national ideology, have mostly chosen to ignore reality and the grievances of their constituencies (the fact, however, that politicians who tell the truth don't enjoy long careers means ordinary people carry their share of responsibility). Where can this sea change take Europe?

And let's not forget the Trump presidency—another unexpected development with profound implications for an increasingly fragmented Europe that may have to fend for itself more and more in an increasingly unstable world. After a long absence, geopolitics is inviting itself to Europe's table, where it is finding a reluctant, bewildered and unprepared host. As if all this were not enough, Germany has become Europe's de facto ruler, a position for which its qualifications are dubious at best. Granted, Berlin has probably not coveted this position and more likely finds itself in it as a consequence of France's not-so-slow collapse and the United Kingdom's recent estrangement. Germany's policies in relation to the euro—in particular, its misplaced insistence on fiscal austerity measures and refusal to entertain any idea of economic solidarity—have ravaged southern economies and cast serious doubts on the viability of the single currency. Since Germans see Germany first (and who can blame them?) and Germany does not deliver the 'international public goods' (by which I mean things that a nation does but that other nations perceive as being also beneficial to them) that would contribute to its legitimacy as leader of Europe and benefit the rest of its partners, the ship scrapes the iceberg with no qualified captain on deck. The very recent and surprising dose of instability injected into German politics will make things even more difficult for Europe. Some of the challenges just mentioned couldn't have been anticipated in *The Decline and Fall of Europe*, yet others could perhaps have been anticipated, constituting shortcomings of my previous analysis which it is now time to set right. To understand the plight of Europe, we are compelled to take a closer look at these and other issues in the course of the book. We shall also take a fresh look at what happened—or rather, what didn't happen—to the euro after 2012, and what it means for the future of the single currency. We shall take a look at the geopolitical impact of the USA's very recent inroads into European energy markets and the relationship with the Ukrainian crisis. Covering all issues affecting Europe today is an impossible task, so we shall focus on selected ones, among which what I call the 'trilogy' figures prominently. As stated above, this in my opinion is to a large extent responsible for Europe's very recent and dramatic political transformation.

Zooming out to look at the broader picture one can see that Europe is not alone in its predicament. The entire 'Western world' seems to have lost its compass. The West in general doesn't seem to know what it stands for anymore, or where it wants to go. Perhaps this is due to the 'fatigue' of a Western civilization on the declining slope of its life curve—it is, after all, the destiny of civilizations, to come and go, just as anything 'alive' does. Perhaps because it is fast losing the absolute and relative pre-eminence among civilizations it was used to enjoying for many centuries. Or perhaps because it is tearing itself apart between two views of society which it convinced itself are mutually exclusive: a liberal-universalist view based on a flat world, and a conservative-nationalist one that sees a world full of mountains. Whatever the causes of this loss of direction, Europe and especially the USA seem intent on reconsidering if not rejecting the basis of post-Second World War Western civilization while offering no alternative, to the delight of rising powers such as China. The mediocrity of today's political leadership on both sides of the Atlantic doesn't help and reflects the decline of a civilization that is short of breath, short of ideas and energy, and that seems, at times, intent on self-immolation. Political correctness, which appears to have become the guiding force of Western thought, is no substitute for wise policy. The late Charlton Heston's words to the effect that 'political correctness is tyranny with manners' have long been forgotten on both sides of the Atlantic. Too busy tying itself in politically correct knots and in fighting internal wars of moralization, the West seems unable to marshal the energy and will to find pragmatic solutions to its identity and existential problems and is fast losing ground in the wider context of competing civilizations. Westerners who remain indifferent should perhaps be reminded of Dante

Alighieri's warning: 'The hottest places in hell are reserved for those who maintain their neutrality in times of moral crisis.'

This book is not about the larger issue of Western civilization and its alleged decline. It is about Europe. Watching Europe fall apart is no joy, especially for a European. As the epitome of a post-modern benign power, Europe has a very useful role to play in the world and it is truly a shame that it may collapse before playing it to the end. Yet it is falling apart right in front of our eyes and the movie is not even running in slow motion anymore. Things seem to be happening faster and faster. Many dejected Europeans have been turning to unsavoury and amateurish 'alternative' politicians for hope and solutions. Granted, some of the challenges facing Europe today do have solutions, at least in theory. The mere fact that Europe has recently moved from a state of denial to the realization that it is in deep trouble would normally inject a note of optimism, since the first step to finding and implementing solutions is to accept that there are problems and try to understand them. I have implicitly and explicitly ventured some personal ideas about solutions here and there in the course of this book. Many people far more qualified than I am have been proposing solutions as well. Yet, if you allow me to define political will as the inverse of the distance between a solution and its actual implementation, I can safely say that the absence of any noticeable political will when it comes to devising and implementing concrete, pragmatic, sensible solutions remains a hallmark of a Europe that revels in 'muddling through'. Europe loves to shoot itself in the foot, then calmly reload and shoot itself in the other foot. Europe delights in being the prisoner of one ideology or another, rejecting pragmatism as intellectually and morally unworthy of interest. Europe rejoices in crossing the fine line dividing political correctness from cowardice time and again. This unfortunate state of affairs prevents me from harbouring any new feelings of optimism. To the question 'do you think Europe is in worse shape today than it was five years ago' ('in better shape' wouldn't qualify as a serious question, would it?), my response is: 'Europe is, today, in a worse shape than it was five years ago, and it is in better shape today than it will be five years from now.' Whenever someone asks me to sign a copy of *The Decline and Fall of Europe* I have adopted the habit of handwriting this little sentence above my signature: 'In the hope that I am completely wrong.' I believe I shall continue this habit if I am asked to sign copies of *Europe and the End of the Age of Innocence*. I sincerely hope that I am utterly wrong in my assessment of the state and destiny of Europe and that things will work out for the best. Let the reader form his/her own opinion in the following pages.

Notes

1. Francesco M. Bongiovanni. 'The Decline and Fall of Europe'. *Page 4. Palgrave Macmillan.* 2012.
2. Philippe Houllebecq 'Submission', *Editions Flammarion*, 2015.
3. Francesco M. Bongiovanni. 'The Decline and Fall of Europe'. *Page 4. Palgrave Macmillan.* 2012.

Part I

The Trilogy

2

The Awakening

How something changed in Europe and it is no longer just about jobs and the economy

Jolted!

The November 2015 terror attack in Paris's Bataclan theatre, during which Jihadists left 130 dead, resonated worldwide with the same intensity as 9/11 in New York, the 2004 Madrid bombings and the 2005 London Underground bombings. The year 2016 was another *annus mirabilis* with, among others, the March carnage in Brussels that left 32 dead, the 14 July massacre in Nice—perpetrated by a single truck driver, Tunisian-born French resident Mohamed Lahouaiej Bouhlel—with 84 victims, followed by a copycat attack in Berlin—carried out by yet another single truck driver, Tunisian asylum seeker Anis Amri—resulting in 12 deaths. These were among the most horrific examples from a long list of Jihadist attacks that was getting longer every day. Each time, the culprit was singled out as radical Islam; each time, social media was awash with shock and indignation; each time, governments pledged their determination to do whatever was necessary to fight this evil; each time, the enemy was portrayed as a nebula of alien religious fanatics; and, each time, additional steps were taken to tighten security and seek targets for retaliation at home and possibly abroad. Yet the succession of massacres showed that nothing was changing, no end was in sight and mayhem could happen again anywhere, anytime. By 2016 it had become clear to Europeans that, when it came to domestic security matters, this was Europe's terrifying 'new normal'.

Evidence reportedly exists that some of the perpetrators of the Bataclan massacre rode the current wave of mass migration from the Middle East to a welcoming and careless Europe and that some of their accomplices were likely radicalized French citizens free to move around after their return from 'Jihad 101' abroad. This attested to the self-destructive levels permissiveness had reached in Europe. Some French Jihadists who joined ISIS abroad were even known to have been receiving payments from French social security and the authorities' initial lame response was that they could not do much about it.[1] Evidence has shown that most terror attacks are perpetrated by people who are known by the security services to be dangerous radicals and yet remain free to move around, evidence of Europe's dramatic failure to effectively address such issues.

A mere month after Bataclan, incidents of mass sexual assaults perpetrated by migrants and refugees against women in Cologne (as well as in various other German and European cities) at the end of 2015 were, similarly, a wake-up call with regard to the masses Europe had welcomed. Cologne was the tipping point because it was too big to ignore—over five hundred complaints were filed—and it also revealed in broad daylight the extent to which the authorities and mainstream media were engaged in a conspiracy of silence.[2] The perpetrators could not have chosen a more tolerant and liberal city than Cologne, where migrants make up a third of the population.[3] The incident had the effect of a cold shower on naïve Germans, aghast to discover that these people could turn out to be so brazenly ungrateful, defiant and violent towards their hosts. Cologne police reported deliberate attempts by migrants and refugees to provoke them, including an instance when one 'tore up a residency permit with a smile on his face, yelling "You can't touch me. I'll just go back tomorrow and get a new one,"' and another who said 'I'm a Syrian! You have to treat me kindly! Mrs. Merkel invited me'.[4] According to German feminist and publisher Alice Schwartzer, 'this explosion of sexual violence on the same night in five countries and in a dozen cities is no coincidence. This is organized.'[5]

It's Not the Economy Anymore

This string of terror attacks confronted Europeans with the reality that anyone could become a victim. Citizens from all walks of life recoiled with horror, imagining what the thousands of Jihadists Europe was known to harbour could do. The proliferation of 'lone wolf' attacks caused some to fear that any Muslim, including their neighbour, could be a potential threat. In the wake of the electoral victory of the anti-immigrant right in Austria's October 2017 elections, public opinion expert Peter Hajek said that 'after initially welcoming refugees in 2015, voters grew jaded and came to see the newcomers less as legitimate asylum seekers than as economic migrants. They also began to regard Muslims in general as suspect [...] They do not really differentiate between Muslims and Islamic extremists [...] Nearly every Muslim seems to be dangerous.'[6] It dawned on Europeans that they were in a one-sided war and that the world around them was changing due to the ubiquitous presence of increasingly assertive minorities, masses of unwanted migrants, and the creeping Islamization of their societies. To a growing mass of citizens increasingly affected in their day-to-day lives by these emotionally charged issues it was all evidence that accommodation had gone too far. Many came to the conclusion that the radicals' most potent weapon was not their kamikazes, it was the naiveté and political correctness of open societies. Questions that were previously considered taboo were publicly asked with newfound alarm. To show themselves welcoming and tolerant, did Europeans need to continue bending over backwards to accommodate ungrateful and hostile minorities with incompatible values? How compatible was Islam with European values, and how much of it could be tolerated? How much national identity should be sacrificed to make space for minorities? Did Europe have to absorb, in the name of compassion, masses of migrants from societies that did not necessarily share the same values, and do so at a time of economic crisis? Wolfgang Schäuble, Germany's minister of finance and a key figure of Angela Merkel's Christian Democrats (CDU) party used words that were unthinkable just a few years earlier: 'Without a doubt, the growing number of Muslims in our country today is a challenge for the open-mindedness of mainstream society.'[7]

By the second half of 2016 it was obvious that something had changed dramatically in the collective European psyche. Wherever I travelled within the continent, the 'trilogy' of unwanted mass immigration (UMI), Islamization and Jihadist terrorism had replaced jobs and economic concerns as the main topic of conversation. The shift in priorities was as clear as it was sudden and unexpected. *The Economist* recognized that 'European voters worry more about immigration and terrorism than about economic insecurity.'[8] Surveys conducted by Eurobarometer revealed that, while unemployment was the main concern for 45% of respondents in the winter of 2014, within less than a year immigration had moved to first place (with unemployment and the economy back in second place and terrorism far back).[9] By the spring of 2016, 48% placed immigration as their main concern with terrorism now a close second at 39% and the economy far behind at 20%. Even in Sweden, traditionally one of Europe's most migrant-friendly societies, UMI had, by early 2016, become the main concern for 40% of citizens, above worries about jobs, welfare and schools. This represented the biggest opinion swing ever witnessed by the pollsters.[10] In another Swedish poll, those considering immigration as one of the top 3 social issues in the country more than doubled from 25% to over 55% between 2014 and 2016.[11] In the United Kingdom, there is little doubt that Brexit was to a large extent about the British people's desire to regain control of their frontiers. Similarly, security was a key concern of the majority of French voters before the 2017 presidential election and a large majority felt the state could not adequately protect them.[12] By mid-2017, nearly half of the Germans surveyed said refugees and integration were their biggest concerns, with social inequalities the focus of only 14%.[13] *The Economist* wrote that 'immigration has soared to first place in ranking of voters' concerns' ahead of the September general election in Germany.[14] The Alternative for Germany party (*Alternative für Deutschland*, AfD) then entered parliament: the first time a far-right nationalist party had done so in Germany since the end of the Second World War. An IPSOS survey taken that same year showed that 63% of Germans considered Islam a menace and 60% of all Europeans said immigration had had negative effects on their countries.[15] All over Europe, security was now a paramount concern, in addition to the safety of the European way of life and national identity. All of these issues concerned the relationship of mainstream populations with the 'others'. At the same time, people felt that the traditional political parties had failed to understand their new concerns, let alone address them. In Germany, for instance, 58% felt the country's established parties were failing to take concerns about radical Islam seriously enough.[16] The combination of these new challenges and people's disillusionment with mainstream political forces amounted to a game-changer for Europe.

In late 2016, Europeans woke up from a long period of denial to find that the golden era of European exceptionalism was over. The list of Jihadist atrocities grew endlessly; masses of unwanted migrants from the 'world of disorder' kept flowing in; domestic security visibly deteriorated and relations between host populations and increasingly assertive elements from Euromuslim minorities deteriorated.[17] As a result, the blissful and innocent life most Europeans had got used to, largely insulated from the instability plaguing other parts of the planet, gave way to a deeply unsettling new normal. By 2016, a palpable feeling that enough was enough, that things were spiralling out of control arose among ordinary citizens, whose day-to-day lives were increasingly affected by these issues. Disillusion and a feeling of impotence were being replaced with anger at the deep disconnect of mainstream political 'elites' unable to face reality and provide solutions. Europeans were now forcing themselves to ask a question they had done their best to avoid for a long time: were they going to continue down the path of self-immolation in the name of lofty egalitarian and humanitarian ideals, or were they prepared to compromise these ideals in order to protect their cherished way of life? Their collective response to this question would determine whether or not Europe's open societies could survive as we know them.

The Things We Talk About

These emotionally charged issues are complex to analyse. To better understand them, it is important to differentiate between two broad topics. On one hand is the current of Islamization affecting Muslim minorities in European societies (as well as the host societies themselves to some extent) and the radicalization of a subset of these minorities. This topic relates to settled minorities that are already part of Europe, and carries a significant religious component. On the other hand is the challenge posed by the masses of unwanted economic migrants and war refugees, a topic related to new immigration that has (to some extent) less of a religious component. These issues have different dynamics and implications, although they feed into each other. They both deal with the relationship between host populations and 'others'—in other words, people who are not European or are not of European descent—and touch on the challenges, real and perceived, that their presence on European soil poses to host societies.

As earlier pointed out, I aggregate UMI, Islamization and Jihadism in a box labelled the 'trilogy'. Crucially, it is their *combined* impact that has shaken Europe to the core, reshaping societies and politics in ways that were unthinkable in 2012. At that time, Islamization and immigration were not perceived by mainstream Europeans as existential threats to their societies, despite warnings from Cassandras, such as Italian journalist Oriana Fallaci back in the early 2000s. However, the three elements of the 'trilogy' combined into a powerful, combustible mixture bound to reach a critical mass and detonate at some point. Were it not for the 'trilogy' we likely wouldn't have witnessed the rise of 'alternative politics' (comprising far-right nationalism), which has the potential to take Europe back to pre-Second World War and pre-EU times: a dramatic reversal of the course of history. Were it not for the 'trilogy' we likely wouldn't have witnessed Brexit: the New York Times recognized that 'It is the flow of people into the European Union that has had the greatest geopolitical impact, and helped to precipitate the British vote.'[18]

Who imagined a few years ago that Berlin would be the object of a major terrorist attack, that more than a million refugees would reach the heart of Europe in the course of a single year, that Schengen would fall apart and that Sweden would carry out the first substantial mass deportation seen on European soil since the Second World War? This 'trilogy' has, in just a few years, become the chief driver of a profound change in today's Europe. An understanding of what is going on and where it may be heading starts with an understanding of the nature, origins and dynamics of each of its three components. To have any real value, this understanding must be based on facts, analysis and common sense, rather than ideological or religious bias. Such is the basis of the research I personally conducted and am now sharing. I have chosen to divide the study of the 'trilogy' into two parts. The first part, 'The Tsunami', deals with UMI. UMI deserves to be treated separately because migrants are not at war with Europe. UMI is the result of human tragedy on a large scale. Granted, some migrants are Muslim, some are criminals and some radicals have hitched a ride in their midst. But the reasons the vast majority of migrants undertake the perilous journey to reach Europe have little to do with Islamist, Jihadist or criminal aspirations. Economic migrants flee poverty in their own countries; war refugees flee armed conflict in their own countries. The second part, 'Barbarians in the City', discusses Islamization and Jihadism. These two faces of the same coin are directly related to the emergence on the world stage of the radical ideologies embraced by a fast-growing subset of the Euromuslim minority that considers itself at war with its host societies. Why have doors been opened to the millions of migrants Europe clearly has difficulty absorbing? Why has Islamization been tolerated to the extent it has? Why has Jihadism flourished in Europe? It is time to take a closer look at what made it possible for all this to happen as extensively as it has.

Beyond Political Correctness

Born from the ashes of the Second World War, the European Project was a clever and idealistic enterprise in which the intertwining of economic interests with freedom of movement and increased commerce combined to relegate intra-European conflicts to the dustbin of history and brought about an era of prosperity. To its credit, the Project delivered the goods.

By the dawn of the new millennium, Globalization had taken over the hearts and minds of many. It promised a 'flat world' in which barriers were removed, supranational alliances became the norm, and growing prosperity for all became a possibility due to the expansion of trade and inclusiveness. The planet was open for business. Everybody had a chance and everybody could participate on an equal footing, the only by-product would be a more peaceful world in which nations would grow more connected with each other as they busied themselves with trade. The European Project made similar promises, of removed barriers and ever-expanding cooperation and inclusiveness. It found traction with most Europeans, despite not being a grass-roots initiative and its well-publicized shortcomings. The EU, its institutions and creations—such as the euro—gained more and more power and influence in the daily lives of Europeans as a 'benign' supra-national construct. Globalization and the European Project had their discontents in Europe, but were generally perceived to be beneficial. They were pulling in the same direction, removing barriers, promoting inclusiveness, trade and prosperity. They were, however, slowly diluting the power and influence of the traditional nation-state.

With the fall of the Berlin Wall and the end of the Cold War in 1990, direct security threats from abroad were removed and, apart from the odd economic crisis, Europe entered an even more blissful age. In this safe and prosperous Europe led by the seductive ideologies of the European Project and globalization, a new post-modern, post-national and liberal paradigm emerged. Ideas spawned in the 1960s, including hostility to tradition, authority and existing power structures, found the space to fully express themselves. Soft power replaced hard power. Christianity's cherished notion of *mea culpa* was reborn under the guise of what Pascal Bruckner labelled the 'tyranny of guilt', in which the West atoned for the sins of its colonial past and centuries of pre-eminence.[19] This combined with the ideals of democracy, human rights, universalism, egalitarianism, inclusiveness, tolerance and cultural relativism to produce a new ideology akin to a new religion. It came with its own sacred dogmas, myths, rituals and internal contradictions. At its core dwelt the primacy of universal human rights, inclusiveness and moralism, making it quite seductive. These moralizing forces went global. Not content with dictating moral codes to people within one society, nations would now dictate moral codes to other nations, a far cry from the post-Westphalian order according to which what a country does within its boundaries is its own business. Crucially, within the context of a state, the identity and aspirations of any group of people were to be placed on an equal footing with every other group's, including the majority. Just as individuals should enjoy equal rights, minorities, defined by religion, sexuality or other criteria, were to be respected and protected. Every hint of inequality had to be levelled out to avoid social injustice. Europe was ruled by a new liberal paradigm. Country after country adopted a model based on a liberal free-market economy, human rights and the sanctity of diverse sociocultural identities. This construct was overseen by democratic yet increasingly technocratic, almost apolitical, governments that managed but didn't lead. A relic of the past, the traditional nation-state—in which people forged a common identity around a national narrative and shared a common culture and destiny—was giving way to post-national 'identity politics'—in which the preservation of the specific identity and aspirations of any minority group was sacrosanct. The post-modern world was to be 'flat' and egalitarian. Notions such as nationhood or the preservation of national, ethnic or cultural identity gradually became anathema because they placed the value and identity of a group—the majority, host population group—above that of the rest, or, worse, excluded 'others'. It is important to understand that this ideology has been the main force guiding Europe in recent times, particularly around issues such as immigration, the integration of minorities, and national identity.

The paradox of this post-national ideology is that, while it portrayed itself as inherently liberal, democratic and by implication pro-free speech, it couldn't help itself from being as intolerant of dissent as any totalitarian political ideology. Henry Ford's famous quip, that customers could choose any colour for the Fort T as long as it was black, was revived in the new ideology's mantra: 'You are free to have your own views as long as they are the same as mine'. Dissenting views were marginalized, ignored, silenced or demonized. At the top of the list of sins were 'xenophobia', 'Islamophobia' or worse, 'racism'—whatever these catch-all, overused labels came to mean. The punishment was damnation by intellectual 'elites' and the media, who became western society's self-appointed arbiters, 'sanitizing' it into conformity with the new dogmas by deciding what was morally acceptable and what was not. Writing on the 'Illusions of cultural universalism', essayist Leszek Kolakowski warned in 1990 that humanism had the potential to become 'moral nihilism'.[20] The resulting 'political correctness', decried by some as tyrannical, was not confined to one side of the Atlantic. It could go to amusingly absurd lengths, not even sparing the academic world. In 2016, my own alma mater, Harvard University, the USA's oldest institution of higher education, announced that it was removing the word 'master' from the denomination of degrees such as Master in Business Administration. This was because some students had protested that it amounted to an apology for slavery (in the context of master and slave) and so was offensive. One wonders whether this same process could lead to the word being removed from 'Mastercard'; whether the 'White House' should be renamed; or the US constitution discarded as it condones slavery. Harvard went a step further, removing a reference to 'puritans' from the lyrics of its ceremonial song, which dates from the nineteenth century as part of a project promoting 'inclusion and belonging'.[21] This is an interesting case of twenty-first century neo-puritans sacrificing the historical existence of their predecessors to the altar of political correctness. Not to be undone, the municipality of Oxford in England removed the word 'Christmas' from all its official documents to avoid offending non-Christian minorities. Brighton College replaced its 170-year-old traditional uniform with a gender-neutral one,[22] and in July 2017 the BBC reported that the London Underground was changing its 'Ladies and gentlemen' welcome formula in case someone not fitting either category got offended.

Westerners, who pride themselves on the freedom of their societies, have been busy tying themselves in knots to conform to their supreme moral ideals, enforced by a self-appointed 'morality police'. Debate recently raged in the USA, concerning the removal of a statue of Christopher Columbus's in New York City's Columbus Circle. The explorer was involved in slavery and the colonization process he launched was not exactly kind to natives. In the same way, debate raged in France concerning the removal of a Christian cross above the statue of Pope John Paul II in Brittany, for the sake of the separation of Church and State. One can disapprove of things that happened in the past (and one would be at a loss to find anyone who condones slavery nowadays), but does it mean that all traces of these things must be eradicated? If this logic is followed, shouldn't Italians raze the Colosseum, which was the seat of horrific games? Shouldn't Egypt get rid of the Pyramids, built with slave labour? These incidents remain isolated cases, but they are significant and symptomatic. In Western societies, some of the most extreme ideologues are striving to do away with any vestiges of Western civilization that do not conform to their moralistic, purist and egalitarian vision of the world in an orgy of revisionism. In doing so, they advocate a revision of history that amounts to nothing less than 'purification', akin to an *autodafé*. Their view is not dissimilar to that of ISIS when it blew up pre-Islamic historical artefacts in Syria and Iraq in the name of a purer vision of Islam. The Islamic State reportedly declared that 'it regarded artefacts as sacrilegious vestiges that deserve to be obliterated'.[23] History has shown that ideologies—either acting in the name of God or moved by secular or moral imperatives—taken to their extremes can morph into totalitarian forces that have few qualms about removing whatever does not conform to their paradigm, whether artefacts, writings, or people. The biggest problems arise when ideology replace common sense and pragmatism. Every time Europe has let itself be seduced by a "strong" ideology, whether from the left or the right or from some other direction, it has ended in tears. The new liberal ideology we talked about - despite its humanist roots – can be perceived, to some extent, as a totalitarian ideology in the sense that it does not tolerate competition and requires complete subservience. This ideology spawned political correctness which, to some such as writer Tom Wolfe, has turned into an instrument of social control wielded by the new dominant classes.[24] Western societies seem to have lost the sense of themselves, their values, where they come from. They seem to be seeking new, radical directions. This development is worrisome when we consider that twentieth century Europe spawned ideologies like fascism, national-socialism and communism with the disastrous results we know. Let us hope we are not witnessing the first stirrings of a new ideological beast that Europe is going to unleash in the twenty-first century.

Leaving aside these philosophical digressions, it is also important to understand that a new political model evolved in Europe in parallel with the new ideology. Differences between the traditional forces of the centre-right and the centre-left, which once dominated the political landscape, have mostly levelled themselves out since the 1980s. Both forces converged into a 'new model' of European governance, dominated by centrist technocratic governing elites. The new European political model that emerged at the dawn of the new millennium was essentially apolitical, devoid of much ideology. It borrowed economic liberalism from the right and social liberalism from the left. According to sociologist Frank Furedi, this new technocratic model rested on two fundamental elements: the de-politicization of political life, and the passivity of citizens.[25]

The Debate That Wasn't

Europe is proud of its values, and rightly so, at the forefront of which are democracy, human rights, gender equality and freedom of expression. These issues have been the object of vigorous and healthy debates within societies for some time. Such debates are what makes democratic, open societies stronger than totalitarian ones, because they involve—at least in theory—consensus-building among the general population. Yet no proper debate took place on immigration, minorities, Islamization and national identity, fundamental issues that could affect a country far more profoundly and irreversibly than any economic policy. Political correctness had it that such a debate was not allowed for a long time lest minorities be offended. In France it was illegal to produce any statistics on the basis of race while, paradoxically, radical preachers were free to spread hatred, and magazines remained free to openly insult foreign cult figures. Some subjects were considered off-limits. No mainstream European leader cared to explain to voters the realities of perhaps the most fundamental social issues defining the country they and their offspring would live in. The absence of a meaningful debate on these highly charged issues has had profound implications.

As seductive as it may be, the new ideology was not devoid of internal contradictions. Tolerance expanded to paradoxically include the tolerance of intolerance: radical preachers openly advocated violence against the very European societies they lived in and were allowed to spill their venom in the name of freedom of expression. Noam Chomsky's words—

'If we don't believe in freedom of expression for people we despise, we don't believe in it at all'—were being followed to the letter. Meanwhile, no criticism of the new ideology was tolerated. *The Economist* pointed out how unhappy people were when their discomfort with minorities was labelled as racism, and how they 'dislike the balkanisation of their countries into identity groups'.[26] For Pascal Bruckner, 'Islamophobia' had become a weapon of mass intimidation that ended up shutting down any criticism from Westerners, as well as from reform-minded Muslims.[27] The same feminists who have been quick to mobilize at the slightest hint of any infringement of women's rights by mainstream Europeans (or Americans) have been overwhelmingly silent in the aftermath of Cologne's mass sexual attacks perpetrated by migrants (likely for fear that such condemnation would smack of racism and of imposing 'our' way of life onto 'others') and by and large look the other way when confronted with the subjugation of women promoted by Islamists in Europe. In a January 21st 2016 interview by *Der Spiegel* magazine, German feminist and publisher Alice Schwartzer recognized that 'Many feminists have remained silent from the outset regarding the problem of Islamist agitation, out of fear they will be accused of racism'. In the age of the internet, this silence cannot be attributed to a lack of information, which raises the suspicion that the new moralists are only interested in instances where the 'bad guys' are Westerners. Such moral relativism is a by-product of the 'tyranny of penitence' surrounding the West's ongoing *mea culpa* and desire for atonement, that I previously mentioned. By holding non-Westerners to lower moral standards, the new ideology can be said to carry a racist element in its DNA.

According to the essayist Gilles-William Goldnadel, during the French presidential election of 2017 multiculturalist ideology and political correctness prevented any debate on the key questions of immigration and Islamic terrorism from taking place. Instead, it shifted the debate to more mundane and 'aseptic' issues, such as the economy.[28] Goldnadel believes the centre right lost the election because it didn't dare bring up the issue of immigration. As the 'elites' shied away from meaningful debate, one could have expected the fourth estate to fill the gap. A large portion of the media has, however, embraced the new ideology, perhaps seduced by the moral and progressive principles it conveys. Just like the 'elites', the mainstream media became incapable of seeing the world beyond what it wanted to see. It disqualified itself from the indispensable role it was supposed to play in a modern, open society as a neutral provider of information to voters. Without access to proper, unbiased information the ritual of voting becomes a travesty and democracy an illusion. Realities that did not match its vision of the world did not register on the media's radar, or were simply ignored as aberrations. This state of affairs was in full display during the US election in 2016. Media and pollsters alike, having ignored a large portion of the population and its grievances because they didn't fit the conventional narrative, were taken completely by surprise by the Trump victory. Often accused of being a propaganda machine for the ideas of the political and intellectual 'elites', the mainstream media is in danger of rendering itself obsolete. It has, moreover, shown surprisingly little patience for dissidence. This state of affairs is not without consequences. First, a healthy, open and vigorous debate based on unbiased information, which is what gives democracy its strength, is prevented from taking place. Second, people are no fools and, as a number of them feel let down by political 'elites' and the media, they look for alternative solutions outside mainstream politics, not necessarily a healthy development. If, however, the socio-political crisis provoked by the explosion of the 'trilogy' centre stage had a positive impact, it was that an open debate was finally launched on important issues that had been avoided for decades.

Crash Test Dummies

Ideological blindness has led Europe into: the misguided establishment of a supra-state, in which unelected, faceless Brussels-based gnomes make decisions that increasingly affect lives everywhere; the transformation of the welfare state into an unsustainable 'Civilization of Entitlements'; the launch of a flawed common currency; and the application of harsh austerity measures in a time of severe economic crisis. Ideological blindness was at work again when it came to *Willkommenskultur* (the host population's vaunted welcoming attitude towards migrants). Conventional wisdom had it that nothing bad could result from an enterprise launched for a good cause. Any problems that might arise could be dealt with later and in any case please don't be a party pooper. All of this worked for a while. Then these myths came crashing down one by one. The unsustainability of the 'Civilization of Entitlements', supposed to deliver ever-growing levels of social benefits to all forever, was bound to catch up with low-growth economies, structural inefficiencies, adverse demographics and other socio-economic realities sooner or later. It did. The unsustainability of a common currency plagued by widely divergent economies, tied to a single interest rate and currency value, which lacked a central treasury and solidarity mechanisms, was bound to hit the eurozone sooner or later. It did. The fall of these myths resulted in the mass unemployment and near-bankruptcy of the economies that line Europe's Southern belt, and in a deep cleavage between creditor and debtor nations: between the North and the South. The extreme dysfunctionalities of an EU machine impervious to reform were bound to promote the de-legitimization and disintegration of the European Project. Combined with flawed immigration policies, this resulted in Brexit and the fall of the myth of an ever-closer union. These problems, bad enough, pale in comparison to the challenges now facing Europe, as the full impact of unwanted mass immigration, Islamization, and Jihadism on the security, fabric and sustainability of Europe's open societies finally hits home. The death of Schengen, the erection of new walls separating countries and the rise of nationalism are evidence that the myth of Europe's *Willkommenskultur* was now crashing down. As usual, Europe was caught unprepared and did not have a plan.

Notes

1. '290 Jihadistes ont touché des prestations sociales en 2014'. *Valeursactuelles.com*. 17 March 2015.
2. 'Cologne attacks: New Year's Eve crime cases top 500'. *Bbc.com*. 11 January 2016.
3. Michelle Martin. 'Cologne attacks show Germany unprepared for migration challenge'. *Reuters*. 28 January 2016.
4. By Maik Baumgärtner, Markus Brauck, Jürgen Dahlkamp, Jörg Diehl, Ullrich Fichtner, Jan Friedmann, Matthias Geyer, Hubert Gude, Horand Knaup, Alexander Kühn, Dialika Neufeld, Ralf Neukirch, Ann-Kathrin

Nezik, Miriam Olbrisch, Maximilian Popp, Gordon Repinski, Sven Röbel, Barbara Schmid, Fidelius Schmid, Andreas Ulrich and Antje Windmann. 'How New Year's Eve in Cologne Has Changed Germany'. *Spiegelonline*. 8 January 2016.
5. Emma-Kate Symons. 'Cologne attacks: "This is sexual terrorism directed towards women"'. *Nytlive.nytimes.com – New York Times*. 19 January 2016.
6. Griff Witte, Luisa Beck 'For Austria's Muslims, country's hard-right turn signals an ominous direction'. *Washingtonpost.com. – The Washington Post*. 20 October 2017.
7. Caroline Copley. 'Germany's finance minister presses for a 'German Islam''. *Reuters*. 2 October 2016.
8. 'Unshrinking the continent'. *The Economist. Page 29*. 10 September 2016.
9. Eric Maurice. 'Terrorism and migration top EU public's concern'. *Euobserver*. 29 July 2016.
10. Alistair Doyle, Simon Johnson. 'Not in my backyard? Mainstream Scandinavia warily eyes record immigration'. *Reuters*. 16 February 2016.
11. 'Immigration is changing the Swedish welfare state'. *The Economist*. 8 June 2017.
12. Eric Maurice. 'Terrorism and migration top EU public's concern'. *Euobserver*. 29 July 2016.
13. Judith Vonberg. 'Merkel rules out limiting number of refugees in Germany'. *Cnn.com – CNN*. 17 July 2017.
14. 'Merkel aims for a fourth'. *The Economist. Page 34*. 23 September 2017.
15. 'Les Européens face aux migrants'. *Le Figaro Magazine. Pages 50–55*. 29 September 2017.
16. Kate Brady. 'Almost two thirds of Germans believe Islam "does not belong in Germany," poll finds'. *DW Akademie*. 12 May 2016.
17. Thomas L. Friedman. 'Order vs. Disorder, Part 2'. *Nytimes.com – The New York Times*. 15 July 2014.
18. Jim Yardley, Alison Smale, Jane Perlez, Ben Hubbard. "Brexit' provokes a caustic postwar unravelling'. *International New York Times. Page 1–4*. 27 June 2016.
19. Pascal Bruckner, 'The tyranny of guilt: an essay on Western Masochism'. *Princeton University Press, 2010*.
20. Leszek Kolakowski. 'Modernity on Endless Trial – Looking for the Barbarians: the Illusions of Cultural Universalism'. *University of Chicago Press. 1990*.

21. Sean Coughlan. 'Why is Harvard ditching the puritans?'. *Bbc.com*. 13 April 2017.
22. Olivia Rudgard. 'Skirts for boys at private Highgate School under plans for gender-neutral uniform'. *Telegraph.co.uk*. 14 May 2017.
23. Rick Gladstone, Maher Samaan. 'ISIS Destroys More Artifacts in Syria and Iraq'. *Nytimes.com – The New York Times*. 3 July 2015.
24. Alexandre Devecchio, 'Tom Wolfe: "Le politiquement correct est devenu l'instrument des classes dominantes"'. *Lefigaro.fr – Le Figaro*. 29 December 2017.
25. Frank Furedi. 'Revolte contre les technocrates'. *Courrier international Page 14*. April-May 2017.
26. 'League of nationalists'. *The Economist. Page 66.* 19 November 2016.
27. Alexandre Devecchio. 'Pascal Bruckner: "L'antiracisme est devenu un marché judiciaire"'. *Lefigaro.fr – Le Figaro*. 10 February 2017.
28. Gilles-William Goldnadel. 'La droite a perdu parce qu'elle n'a pas osé parler d'immigration". *Lefigaro.fr*. 18 June 2017.

3

The Tsunami

The challenge of unwanted mass immigration and its consequences on a naïve and unprepared Europe

After the Euro, the Great Immigration Debacle

In the autumn of 2015 German Chancellor Angela Merkel spoke about the masses of refugees she had committed Germany to take in, saying 'this immigration will change the country'.[1] Such change goes beyond the image of Munich's sprawling Theresienwiese square cordoned off during Oktoberfest a year later for security reasons, for the first time in 183 years—a shock for Germans.[2] The great immigration debacle is already changing Germany—and Europe—profoundly and irreversibly, far more than Merkel imagined. The country's economic success and demographic decline had, according to Organisation for Economic Co-operation and Development (OECD) statistics, propelled Germany to second place as a destination for migrants in 2014, with 400,000 arrivals (just behind the USA), up from ninth place in 2009. Until that point, three quarters of migrants had been from European countries, mostly Eastern Europe.[3]

Merkel's 2015 declaration resulted in a massive and very sudden change in the quantity and origin of immigrants.

A growing malaise had been palpable for some time among mainstream Europeans increasingly concerned with minorities, immigration, Islamization and national identity. According to a *National Geographic* study of how immigration is changing the face of Europe, 'The few people who are willing to throw Molotov cocktails at refugee shelters or obscenities at the chancellor are just the tip of an iceberg of peaceful and mostly silent Germans who in their hearts don't want so many migrants in Germany, especially Muslim ones'.[4] The sheer scale and suddenness the 2015–2016 refugee tsunami added a new dimension to it all. By then, a complacent Europe could no longer ignore that it was confronted with a crisis of unprecedented proportions, the consequences of which would reverberate for decades to come. Just as with the currency crisis, the refugee crisis caught European leaders unprepared and is changing the continent. It is exacerbating divisions within and between countries as well as impacting budgets, social stability and security. The mainstream was getting increasingly agitated, not buying blindly anymore into the 'elites' politically correct narrative and openly voicing, for the first time, its concerns over the previously taboo subjects of immigration and minorities. More ominously, mismanagement of these issues by largely incompetent ruling 'elites' opened the door to a return of nationalism.

The object of this section is unwanted mass immigration (UMI), a reality that had slowly been building up for some time, but suddenly exploded centre-stage as a direct consequence of the Syrian conflict and strife in Libya. Frontex (the agency established in 2004 to police Europe's external frontiers) estimates that a record 1.8 million migrants got into Europe in 2015 alone,[5] 60% of whom were 'economic migrants' (migrants who do not qualify as war refugees) in search of a better life, mostly from Morocco and Tunisia, but also from Nigeria, Pakistan and other places. This tsunami, the largest migration wave since the end of the Second World War, is a human tragedy in the face of which nobody can remain indifferent. Yet Europe's decision to open its arms and let in masses of people it doesn't know what to do with, who largely end up as a burden to society and an unhappy underclass, is likely to have dire social and economic consequences. As we shall see later, pragmatic solutions to the UMI challenge exist. They may not be perfect, but they could have gone a long way towards addressing the problem and should have been explored.

Apart from a number of radicals and Jihadists who infiltrated Europe as refugees (the number may actually not be that small according to *Der Spiegel*, who warned that thousands of Taliban and other fighters are likely to have entered Germany, hitching a ride among the refugees[6]), and given the more than 11,000 'virgin' Syrian passports ISIS is estimated to possess,[7] UMI poses a specific type of challenge: what to do with these masses of people, especially in high unemployment countries? The cost of feeding, clothing, maintaining and policing them falls on the taxpayer and, as we shall see in a later section, this cost is immense. At the very least, the migrants' ubiquitous presence causes discomfort among the mainstream population. Their origins in alien cultures that can be difficult to integrate and the disastrous conditions they live in often turn them into a restless, dangerous and dejected lot with few alternatives besides living as vagrants, partaking in criminal activities or being exploited by criminal gangs. In France, just across the Channel, the 'Calais jungle', an illegal migrant ghetto now 'dismantled', numbered close to 10,000 people[8]—95% of whom were men, 60% of whom came from Sudan[9]—living entirely outside the law and with no hope of ever becoming part of any society. The presence of great numbers of these people spread all over Europe means the problem is substantial, real and won't go away. Parking them in camps or ghettos won't make them disappear and the security situation in nearby areas is bound to worsen as they become increasingly desperate and restless. By letting so many in without a clear plan, Europe has not done itself or these migrants a favour. Merkel's unilateral initiative may have been motivated by noble humanitarian ideals, but it has been variously decried as having caused the death of Schengen; having contributed to Brexit (polls effectively confirmed that immigration was the main motive for the 'Brexit' vote);[10] and having promoted a profound East–West fracture within Europe, as countries such as Poland, Slovakia and Hungary steadfastly refuse to abide by imposed refugee quotas. 'It was the onset of more than a million refugees marching through Greece and the Balkans toward Germany that may ultimately prove to be the most destabilizing event in Europe's recent history' said the *New York Times*.[11]

How Did We Get Here? How Did *They* Get Here?

In recent times UMI into Europe mainly followed two routes. On Europe's south-eastern flank, a land route through Turkey and the Balkans has been mainly used by Syrian refugees, migrants from the Middle East and other regions. By mid-2017 this route was shut down and would likely remain so for as long as the agreement Europe reached with Turkey held. On Europe's southern flank, a sea route mainly used by migrants from North Africa's Arab countries and from deep within the African continent—embarking in Libya and landing on the shores of Italy— remained open due to the impossibility to reliably enrol anarchic, post-Gaddafi Libya in any Turkey-type agreement. For many years, European solidarity was nowhere in sight as the so-called Dublin agreement—a part of the Schengen treaty requiring illegal migrants to be kept for processing in the country where they first land—provided the perfect excuse for the rest of Europe to turn a blind eye to the plight of southern 'frontline' states, such as Italy, Spain or Greece. They were left to their own devices in dealing with the thousands of illegal migrants continuously landing on their shores. It was the explosion of the Syrian refugee crisis in 2015, and the subsequent sudden and unexpected migratory flux—on a scale that dwarfed anything Europe has previously seen—that forced all of Europe to wake up and face a reality it hardly controlled anymore.

Had European leaders paid attention, this latest crisis could have at least been anticipated and managed, perhaps even avoided altogether. Its immediate roots lay largely in the failure of the international community to provide the UN with the means needed to alleviate human tragedy and do its job in Lebanon, Jordan and Turkey, where more than 4 million refugees had found shelter.[12] The capacity to take care of these people in camps run by the UN was rapidly overwhelmed. The UN reportedly received only 1.7 billion USD of the 4.5 billion it had requested in order to provide adequate food and shelter to the refugees before they could (hopefully) safely return to their own countries.[13] Due to the lack of adequate resources, living conditions in UN camps and refugee areas deteriorated to the point where millions of people had to survive on a daily pittance. Many had little choice but to attempt a costly and perilous journey to Europe—the newly advertised Eldorado—to the delight of traffickers feeding on human tragedy. The alternative would have been for refugees to go back to their own countries, torn by war. In other words, less than 3 billion euro were reportedly needed at the time to plug the gap to make the camps viable and contain the refugee problem. This sum pales in comparison to the tens of billions of euro Germany alone is now spending year after year to deal with the masses it has taken in, as we shall see in a later section of this book. Having failed to anticipate the crisis, European leaders found themselves overwhelmed. The result was that they made precipitous and emotional decisions with profound implications in reaction to social media. Public outrage over the horrific picture of the body of 3-year-old Aylan Kurdi washed ashore on a Turkish beach hit social networks in early September 2015, instantly mobilizing governments and NGOs. It likely also played a key role in Merkel's well-publicized announcement that Germany would open its doors, a watershed event that started a stampede.

Berlin's original declaration that it would take in 800,000 refugees right away, and possibly 500,000 per year thereafter (it reportedly took in more than a million in 2015 alone) may have been motivated by commendable humanitarian considerations, but likely had also something to do with demographic decline at home.[14] A 2015 report from the Bertelsmann Foundation showed the country needed to import up to 491,000 workers per year.[15] This number is corroborated by the Berlin Institute for Population and Development's own estimate that Germany would need a net immigration of around half a million a year through 2050 to sustain its economy, its retirees and its sick, since Germans don't make enough babies (deaths exceed births by about 200 thousand per year).[16] Without this input, Germany's population, numbering around 82 million today 'is set to shrink by 15% by 2050, according to government forecasts, with the workforce falling by 30%'.[17] Given the dismally low birth rates throughout the continent, Europe's cherished 'Civilization of Entitlements' is under serious threat everywhere. This is a real challenge, as I pointed out in *The Decline and Fall of Europe*: 'the total population of Europe standing today at about 800 million, could by mid-century have shrunk to 632 million, or to a mere 480 million, or a loss of 40% by the end of the century' and 'Europe's share of world GDP could fall from 30% to under 10% by the second half of the century [...] the welfare state, pride and joy of modern Europe, is bound to fail in the coming decades'.[18] Without enough new working people to replace retiring ones, the system is simply not sustainable and there can't be economic growth. To put it crudely, the choice is between giving up generous social benefits, producing lots of offspring very fast, or importing people. This last solution is the one chosen by most European governing 'elites'. Italy may be the worst hit by demographic decline, and this has very serious implications. Istat (the Italian statistics bureau) revealed that by 2065 the Italian population will have shrunk from today's 60.7 million to 53.7 million.[19] In an alarming article, *The Economist* predicted that 'For all the political difficulties migrants can cause, Europe will need more of them if it wants to avoid shrinking.'[20]

Indian essayist Pankaj Mishra, wrote in an article:

> Too much migration has already taken place for the ultra-nationalist fantasy of ethnically and culturally homogenous populations to be realized. Yet many demagogic tendencies across Europe threaten to make the continent relive its awful past of sectarian hatred. Hating and beggaring thy neighbour for the sake of short-term political gains is no longer just confined to the usual suspects, such as Hungary's Prime Minister Viktor Orban [...] Hungary, like most European countries with declining populations, needs migrants.[21]

For all his good intentions, Mishra fails to understand that, aside from a few supremacists, what animates the many Europeans desirous of curtailing immigration today is not a desire for racial purity, or any form of hatred for others, or a desire to 'beggar thy neighbour'. Racial purity is something that was long ago relegated to the dark pages of Nazi history. Aside from the odd extremists, one would have difficulty in finding modern Europeans actually defending racial purity, or harbouring feelings of 'hatred' for boat people or Syrians, Nigerians or Eritreans. Europeans who want to send them back home or stop them coming will tell you that they don't 'hate' them. What they want is to keep them out or send them back home. One may or may not agree with the desire, expressed by most people in Hungary (and other places such as the Czech Republic, where two thirds of people oppose taking in refugees,[22] and where populist president Milos Zeman, said that it might be better to lose EU subsidies than be forced to accept Muslim migrants[23]) to curtail immigration, but who are we, as outsiders, to decide what is good for Hungarians or for Czechs? Isn't it the people's sovereign right to decide for themselves how to live their lives in their own country? Or are multiculturalists vested with a God-given mission and right to impose their view of the world on others? Cultural and moral imperialism, real or perceived, is one of the root causes of the 'anger' that is tearing Europe apart. 'This dislike for immigration has led to animosity toward EU members who favor an open immigration policy, notably Germany, and increased hostility toward the European Union itself' one journalist argued.[24] One must also keep in mind that, when countries joined the EU, they opened their doors (especially through Schengen) to the free movement of people from within the Union. They never agreed to accept migration from outside the Union. So, in what name should such exogenous migration be imposed? However noble the intention may be, it hardly makes sense to impose it in the name of human solidarity.

Demographics are not everything. With unemployment at 22% and an economy still playing catch-up, Spain's circumstances are, for instance, dramatically different from those of Germany, which has nearly full employment. So are those of France and Italy, with unemployment exceeding 12%, and economies that are barely keeping up (in all fairness, it must be noted that cheap, undeclared migrant labour is the lifeline of many small enterprises in some places). Besides, in France, labour regulations make it quite difficult for newcomers to find work, and a high minimum wage takes away the incentive to hire low-skilled labour. For these southern European countries and some in the East, taking in new migrants hardly represents an opportunity. Newcomers are likely to end up swelling the legions of the unemployed and becoming an economic and social burden. The overwhelming majority of migrants arriving in Italy are not war refugees, but young economic migrants from Africa and 90% of them are under 35 years old.[25] What sense is there in keeping them, when youth unemployment in the country is already 40%? What was arguably good for Germany was not necessarily good for the rest of Europe.

Merkel's decision may have partly been motivated by demographics, yet it was not part of a well-thought-out plan. It was an opportunistic and precipitous decision that ignored the reality of more than 20 million unemployed across Europe.[26] The 500,000 Germany needs yearly represent only about 2.5% of this total, and it is difficult to believe that Germany would not find enough jobless Europeans as qualified and willing as Syrian imports. If the European labour market functioned properly, one would logically expect to see the excess workforce from countries such as Spain, Italy or Greece, which suffer from high unemployment, flow en masse to countries that need manpower, like Germany. Nothing of the sort happens on any significant scale, so Germany will spend billions of euro trying to 'reformat' human imports from the Middle East to fill the gap, instead of tapping into the resources of its European partners. Europe is far from enjoying the USA's high labour mobility for several reasons. Aside from the obvious language barriers, the high social benefits a country bestows on its jobless perversely act as a disincentive to finding jobs elsewhere in Europe. The vast majority of the record 685,000 people from the EU who came to work in Germany in 2015 came from Poland, Romania and other Eastern European countries, where domestic unemployment benefits are very low (Germany modified regulations to ensure that these people would get very little in terms of social benefits while working in Germany).[27] It would make sense for national jobless support regulations to be tweaked to ensure that, under appropriate circumstances, a job available in another European country counts as a job offered in the home country. This may trigger the end of overblown unemployment benefits at home and promote intra-European labour mobility. Granted, some of the most ambitious young Poles, Italians and French have moved to London, New York or Shanghai to work, but the great majority prefer to remain unemployed at home if they can survive on government handouts. One would expect the EU to enact regulations ensuring that the gap be filled by a European jobseeker before labour imports from outside the EU can be considered. But the EU has been too busy legislating on the curvature of bananas and the size of condoms to think about effective intra-European labour mobility strategies. Equally important is the lack of adequate funding, incentives, or language and training programmes within the EU to effectively promote such mobility. The EU and European governments have largely failed to properly acknowledge, let alone address, the issue of intra-European labour mobility.

Eyes Wide Shut

To the most worried Europeans, current immigration trends amount to a 'replacement' of host populations in certain areas by migrants from Africa and other places. Conspiracy theories abound, particularly in some far-right political circles, to the effect that a concerted effort is under way to replace 'original' European populations with imported ones. The numbers supposedly backing such theories simply do not add up when confronted with statistics that show, for instance, that in France the aggregate population of North African, sub-Saharan African and Asian origin is officially estimated at only 5% of total population.[28] 'Replacement migration', which refers to the migration that a country would need to offset population decline and ageing, resulting from low fertility and mortality rates is, however, neither a figment of the imagination nor a secret. UN projections indicate that, over the next 50 years virtually all European countries as well as Japan will face population decline and an ageing population. The UN reportedly considered replacement migration as a solution for the most affected countries, particularly Europe.[29]

Italy is a case in point, with its fast-aging population and geography that makes it the natural arrival point for migrants coming from Africa by sea. The country has been overwhelmed by the relentless arrival of thousands upon thousands of migrants on a daily basis for decades. By mid-2017, sea arrivals of migrants were up 40% compared to the previous year. Over 50,000 migrants had arrived during the first five months, 97% of whom embarked in Libya; only 6,000 were turned back towards Libya, before reaching international waters with the help of the Libyan coastguard.[30] This prompted Italian authorities to lament that 'saturation' had been reached in Italy and that the country could not cope anymore. Accusing the rest of Europe of 'looking the other way' Prime Minister Paolo

Gentiloni threatened to prevent foreign ships carrying migrants from reaching Italian ports (ships from other European countries have been known to rescue or simply ferry migrants and dump them into Italian ports).[31] Italians complain that Europe pretends that Italy abides by the Convention for the Safety of Life at Sea and takes in the migrants, while in fact Europe subsequently prevents these migrants from crossing from Italy into other European countries. All the while, Europe provides very little in terms of economic assistance to Italy, amounting to a cheap and convenient way for the rest of Europe to buy a good conscience while confining the problem to Italy. Austria used troops and military vehicles to prevent migrants crossing the frontier from Italy in the summer of 2017. This showed that the same lack of intra-European solidarity decried in the response to the eurozone crisis was at work in the case of the migratory crisis. In other words, it was up to the troubled countries to adjust, except of course if the troubled country is Germany, in which case absorption quotas are to be imposed all over Europe.

Given current UMI trends, Italy's official statistics bureau ISTAT predicts that permanent migrants, who numbered 4.6 million in 2016 will have grown to 14.1 million by 2065.[32] By then, 37% of Italy's population will be made up of migrants, mostly from Africa, with Nigeria the principal source. And by then, Italy will undoubtedly be radically and irreversibly different from the country it is today, socially, ethnically, culturally and politically. These trends have been known for some time, yet no policies have been enacted to radically incentivize Italians to make more babies, while billions have been spent taking care of migrants. To French demographics expert Michèle Tribalat, the title of whose 2010 book translates as *Eyes Wide Shut*, European elites have chosen to blind themselves to the realities of mass migration.[33] First of all, governments make no effort to keep up-to-date and complete immigration-related statistics, and no effort to reveal to their constituencies the realities of what is going on. According to Tribalat, the notion that immigration is beneficial to the economy because immigrants take up jobs that citizens do not want and bring in new vital forces that will help sustain an ageing host population, is a dubious argument promoted by pro-immigration lobbies as has been shown by the US labour-market economist George J. Borjas. American-British writer Douglas Murray didn't mince words in his new book *The Strange Death of Europe*, predicting that, as a consequence of the delusional utopianism of its elites, 'by the end of the lifespans of most people currently alive, Europe will not be Europe and the peoples of Europe will have lost the only place in the world we had to call home'.[34] For good measure, Murray adds: 'Europe is committing suicide. Or at least its leaders have decided to commit suicide. Whether the European people choose to go along with this is, naturally, another matter.'[35]

These are controversial issues for which reliable information is lacking. Europe would do a great service to itself by examining the situation pragmatically. What are the consequences of declining birth rates and an ageing population on, among others, the sustainability of its societies and of its cherished 'Civilization of Entitlements'? If sustainability is in serious doubt and a slow-motion catastrophe looms, what radical measures can be taken to incentivize Europeans to procreate? If such measures involve very high costs, how do these costs compare to the economic and social costs of letting in and taking care of masses of migrants from Africa and other places? Are there any other solutions? If migration from outside the EU is the only solution, are Africa and the Middle East the best sources or should Europe not also look at Asia and other places with, perhaps, more compatible values and reputations for hard work and industriousness? Once more, a proper debate is lacking and without a proper debate there can be no consensus on effective solutions, so Europe finds itself lacking leadership and direction and reacting to events instead of shaping them.

Realities on the Ground

According to scientists, you and I—and all human beings—are descendants of migrants from Africa. Migration has always been a part of human history. Populations have been moving and mixing all over the globe for eons. Today no culture or society can claim to be 'pure' and, according to the UN, in 2015 the world held 244 million migrants—people living in a country where they weren't born.[36] There is nothing unusual in the notion of migration and the mixing of populations, just as there is nothing unusual or new in the notion of territoriality, likely hard wired in humans since bands of wandering foragers gave way to settled societies during the Agricultural Revolution tens of thousands of years ago. States, kingdoms and other polities organized themselves to keep outsiders out of their territories to safeguard people, chattel and their way of life. The 1648 Treaty of Westphalia, which followed the 30 Years War, is widely regarded as having enshrined the modern notion of the 'nation state'. A nation-state is made up of people who share a common culture, religion and history—identity—who live within internationally recognized borders—territoriality—and whose actions inside these borders is nobody else's business—sovereignty. After the World Wars, the fall of empires, said to be great amalgamators of nations, released a plethora of such nation-states. Throughout history, immigration was viewed in many different ways with, at one extreme, a country like the USA defining itself through immigration and, at the other, a country like Japan defining itself by keeping others out. Not all migrants settle in a country because they wish to morph into clones of locals. Some settle because of convenience, economic or otherwise, others because circumstances leave them no other choice. Thus goes human history. American journalist Thomas L. Friedman divides today's world between a 'world of disorder' and a 'world of order', with people naturally flocking from the first to the second, as per a sort of second law of human thermodynamics.

Writing for the Foreign Policy Research Institute, Naweed Jamali,[37] a second-generation Muslim–American migrant from Pakistan, explored why the USA does not seem to have a problem with its Muslim population as Europe does. 'It's not the influx of Muslims; rather, it's Europe's inability to welcome and assimilate migrants', Jamali wrote. He pointed out that American Muslims are the second most educated population group after American Jews and that 80% of American Muslims are happy with their life in the USA (a subsequent Pew Research Center survey actually showed 89% of them to be 'proud to be American and Muslim' despite growing feelings of discrimination).[38] Jamali provides a relevant personal example: some of his family emigrated to Europe and some to the USA. The second generation does not really feel assimilated in Europe but feels assimilated in the USA. So, there is effectively a difference, which he attributes to the difference in the welcome host societies give to new migrants. There is undoubtedly some truth to this, due to cultural-historical differences. The USA is, after all, a nation of migrants, while European nations have traditionally defined themselves by keeping others out, so they may be less naturally welcoming. Discrimination on the basis of ethnicity or religion certainly exists in Europe and it may even be on the rise, yet there is much less of it than perceived. Sociologist Philippe d'Iribarne used data from a 2017 survey by the European Union Agency for Fundamental Rights (FRA) to show that 75% of Muslims in France said there is discrimination against their religion in their country, yet at the same time only 20% of them said they have personally been discriminated against on the basis of their religion in the previous five years. The gap between perception and reality was just as wide elsewhere. In Sweden the numbers were respectively 72% and 30%, in Belgium 59% and 19%, and in Spain 26% and 10%.[39] In any case, Jamali ignores a few important points: Muslims represent 1% of the population of the USA, against 5% or more in some European countries where they constitute a far more ubiquitous minority. Second, unemployment in many European countries is about double the rate of that in the USA and much more when it comes to youth unemployment, and since Euromuslims are generally the poorest, youngest and least educated, they are more likely to remain unemployed. Third, social benefits are much more generous in Europe than in the USA. If you settle in the USA you need to have already 'bought into the system' and be willing to work hard to survive and by doing so you become part of the system, whereas in Europe a migrant can more easily survive on government handouts and has less incentive to become part of the system. The other point is that Europe is geographically much closer to the Middle East and North Africa, so its Euromuslim subset is more easily subject to cultural, political, ideological and other influences from these regions.

Another interesting comparison between European and US integration of Muslim communities comes from US journalist Richard C. Longworth. He describes a journey he took to the depressed city of Bradford, in England's North, as London bureau chief for the *Chicago Tribune* in 1991. He found a sub-community of Muslims 'who were so isolated from the city around them that they might as well have been living in a walled ghetto', remaining 'poor and inbred'.[40] Mostly originating from two towns in Northern Pakistan, they had come a couple of generations before to work in Bradford's textile mills, then settled and were forgotten as the local economy declined. Their community centred on the local mosque where the Imam preached fundamentalist Wahhabism. 'Discriminated against in Bradford and shut off from the wider community, the Bradford Muslims, and especially their youth, took their reality and their religion from the mosque.' Longworth was, 25 years ago, witnessing 'the first signs of the radicalization of younger Muslims born and raised in the West. Their parents were glad to be in Bradford. The sons, alienated from the society around them, absorbed hatred wrapped in fundamentalism [...] The same thing was going on elsewhere in Europe'. Longworth feels that the USA does a better job at integration than Europe because the USA rides 'roughshod over native cultures, insisting that the new immigrants become Americans' and adds 'It may be forced integration, but it works.' Longworth's view on forced integration can be contrasted with that of Mariam Shahin, author of a 2007 short film about Muslims in Berlin (she is one of them), who said that the new generation of Arab-Germans 'is fully versed in the multicultural mindset which developed in the past 50 years in dozens of societies around the globe'. 'Unlike many of their predecessors', says Shahin, 'they don't accept the dominance of one culture over the other. They seek parity—they insist on it.' And that, while the new refugees will need to conform to the German way of doing things, 'they are unlikely to be forced to assimilate culturally, like those who came before them. In cultural terms, they will remain Arabs in Europe's largest country and strongest economy.'[41]

External factors such as politics (as in the case of the German–Turks we are exploring in the following section) or ideologies imported from abroad (such as Islamism) can affect the already difficult process of the integration of an imported minority in a modern host society. Ghettoization and apartheid—voluntary or imposed—and ethnic enclaves are no substitutes for full integration which, in many cases, remains utopic. A young Muslim who seemed perfectly integrated and was doing well at school tried to butcher a Jew wearing a *kippa* in Marseille in the name of the Islamic Caliphate.[42] Similarly, the London underground bombers of 2005 seemed perfectly integrated in British society, yet they murdered 56 innocents in the name of Jihad. Living side by side with a host population is not necessarily proof that a minority is fully integrated. Something far more complex and elusive is at play, that can lead some individuals far astray. Yet immigration and diversity can undeniably enrich life and inject vital new energy into a country. The Turkish *gastarbeiter*, or guest worker, played an important role in building up the German economy. In 2015, close to half of new businesses in Germany were created by non-Germans, many of them migrants from the Middle East.[43] The industrious Chinese diaspora, for one, has played a key role in the dynamic development of local economies in Southeast Asia (this, however, didn't prevent tensions from developing in Malaysia between the majority Muslim Bumiputra and the ethnic Chinese minority). More recent examples of success include the wave of Russian Jews into Israel (who are no strangers to the recent transformation of Israel into a tech powerhouse), or the Polish, French and Italian migrants who followed Pakistanis and Indians in turning London into a leading world hub city, not to speak of migrant success stories in Silicon Valley, epitomized by one Steven Jobs, who was the biological son of a migrant from, of all places, Syria.

In modern times the absorption of large numbers of imports from alien cultures by a mature host society is, nevertheless, a complex issue which impacts a country's social fabric and identity and there is no proven model of integration that works seamlessly. In *The Decline and Fall of Europe* I pointed out that, in Europe,

> 'Different countries have tried different models (of integration) so far with dubious results [...] at one end of the spectrum the politically correct laissez-faire model of 'multiculturalism', championed by the U.K. [...] in the name of generosity, tolerance and universal freedom of choice for the newcomers the British renounced the primacy of their own values or cultural heritage in their own home and ended up promoting fragmentation instead [...] The end result of such a process [...] is bound to be two communities subjected to two different sets of laws within a country, institutionalizing cleavage and further diluting the essence of the nation-state' and at the other end of the spectrum in France 'the government wouldn't recognize that there were minorities in the country [...] requiring immigrants to make an effort to integrate [...] Is there a right way after all? [...] How justified is the growing anxiety of the European public with regard to the assimilation of Muslims in their societies?'[44]

The problem of integration is not merely European. Turkey, which is Muslim and arguably not really part of Europe, has had great difficulty integrating the more than 3 million Syrian refugees that it absorbed (and has been taking care of since 2011 reportedly at an aggregate cost of 25 billion USD). They are dependent on aid since the local job market is closed to them, so these refugees are increasingly resented by the host population and are becoming a permanent underclass in Turkey, a recipe for social trouble.[45] While minorities have generally been accepted and integrated into modern Europe in the past, problems with host populations are naturally compounded when the minority's assertion of a separate identity becomes too ubiquitous and is in direct opposition to the values and customs of the host society, or when its actions go beyond self-ghettoization and directly affect the host population. Singapore, the epitome of a multicultural society, seems to be an exception. Its very strong central government tightly controls the proportions of Chinese, Malays, Indians and others, keeping a close tab on the relations between them. Singaporeans are encouraged from early on to be very disciplined and respectful of each other, a situation that does not, however, prevent tensions from existing under the surface, especially with newcomers from Indonesia and China. Broadly speaking, it is only logical that the more numerous, culturally alien, conspicuous and assertive an imported minority is, and the weaker the response from the political establishment in upholding the national identity as the glue keeping everybody together, the higher the chance of tensions between host society and minority.

When the Sultan Comes Calling

Whatever reasons push them to settle abroad, most migrants wish to retain some degree of attachment to their roots. Germany's Euromuslim minority is different from that of France and consists of 3 million Turks (of which half are now German citizens) and more than a million newcomers from the Middle East and other areas, recently added as a consequence of Merkel's policies. This brings the total Muslim population to over 4 million. Many Turkish families who settled in Germany decades ago still do not speak German, only watch Turkish TV and most get their information from the Turkish language media. Decrying Turkish 'ghettos' in Germany, migration researcher Joachim Schulte said that 'nationalism is strongly conserved and the contacts to Germans and Austrians are reduced to a minimum [...] everyday communication occurs only in the home community [...] Turkish brides are imported [...] and they never learn German', yet, to be fair, 51% of first and second generation Turks surveyed feel that 'No matter how hard I try, I am not accepted as part of German society'.[46] Back in 2006, a study by the Essen Centre for Turkish studies found that 83% of German Turks described themselves as religious or strictly religious. 'Religiousness has increased', the authors of the study wrote at the time.[47] In 2009, *Der Spiegel* pointed out that 'many Turks who came to Germany as guest workers decades ago didn't want to become part of German society, they wanted to earn money there and return home after a few years. That didn't happen, though. The Turks stayed on, but it seems that their original attitude hasn't changed. They formed ghettos and didn't establish much contact with Germans, and all that made it harder for their children to find a place in German society.'[48] To paraphrase Max Frisch, Germans asked for workers, and they got people instead. Back in 1992 the percentage of mixed marriages by girls of Turkish origin, which can be a measure of integration, was only 2%, (compared with 24% at the time for girls of Algerian origin in France),[49] a very low rate that by 2006 had only gone up to 8%.[50] In 2012 *Der Spiegel* pointed out a paradox: on the one hand more and more Turks wanted to integrate into German society, while on the other an increasing proportion said they were religious and only 15% said that Germany was more their homeland than Turkey.[51] While many German Turks live in separate communities, their relationship with the host population has historically been good, although many German Turks feel like second class citizens. How integrated are they?

In France, host-minority relations are close to disastrous. This difference has variously been attributed to the absence of a colonial legacy in Germany, the fact that Germany's Turks are the product of Turkey's secular Kemalization (i.e. westernization), the abundance of jobs in a full employment economy. Unlike the French, Germans have not been actively debasing their own culture and identity so there is not the profound identity crisis in Germany that exists in France. Germany's blissful situation may be changing however, and from an unexpected quarter. It was already known that over the past decades the Turkish government was making efforts to influence people of Turkish descent via the ministry of religious affairs, which delivers Friday sermons from Ankara to mosques all over Germany.[52] Ahead of his 2008 visit to Germany, Turkish leader Recep Tayyip Erdogan, always ready to stoke the fires of Turkish nationalism at home and abroad, publicly labelled the assimilation of Turks in German society a 'crime against humanity'. This was a clear call for non-integration that alarmed Germany's politicians, all the more since the message was well received by many German Turks.[53] Following the aborted coup in Turkey in 2016, over 40,000 German Turks answered a call from the pro-Erdogan Union of European-Turkish Democrats (UETD) to take to the streets.[54] The fact that Erdogan, perceived today by most Europeans as a maverick nationalist-Islamist dictator with interests increasingly diverging from those of Europe, could mobilize and send to German streets legions of Turks was not lost on German leaders. In early 2017, things got more heated as Erdogan tried to mobilize Turks living in Germany and other European countries to vote in Turkey's April referendum, designed to grant him extended powers at home. Likely worried about tensions developing among its Turkish community between Erdogan's supporters and those against him (thousands of Kurds also living in Germany had, in the past, taken to the streets to protest Berlin's rapprochement with Erdogan), Germany (followed by the Netherlands and Austria) refused to let high officials from Ankara address Turkish crowds in Germany. Interestingly, after the south-western city of Gaggenau prohibited Erdogan's envoys from addressing German-Turkish crowds on the Turkish referendum issue, the city hall had to be evacuated due to a bomb alert.[55] According to sociologist Necla Kelek, mosques in Germany have been turned into voting stations for Erdogan's AKP party. An infuriated Erdogan publicly labelled the leaders of these countries 'Nazis' and went on to call Europe 'racist, fascist, cruel [...] anti-Islam and anti-Turkish'.[56] This escalating war of words bodes ill for EU–Turkish relations, for NATO–Turkish relations and for the agreement signed to stem the flow of migrants arriving by land, which Erdogan has used (to no avail) to push Europe into granting visa-free access to Turkish citizens lest he sent masses of Syrian refugees across the border (while hinting at granting Turkish nationality to masses of Syrian refugees living in Turkey—who would then have free access to Europe). Surprisingly, 63% of Germany's Turks able to vote did so in favour of Erdogan in the referendum, a substantially higher percentage than in Turkey itself. According to Munster University's Detlef Pollack, this showed that integration has not worked and that for second and third generation German-Turks, Islam and Turkey have become key identity markers.[57]

Germany's leaders were bound to wonder how many of its 3 million Turks would be likely to answer calls from Erdogan, and the extent to which the Turkish community could be polarized. Besides, could Erdogan (or someone else) play the religious card at some point with Germany's Turks? In the aftermath of the referendum, Erdogan accused Europe of provoking 'a struggle between the cross and crescent', redefining the episode as a dispute between Christendom and Islam, and issued warnings on the safety of westerners.[58] Serious allegations that imams had been spying on Erdogan's opponents in Germany for Ankara's had, in the past, driven Interior Minister Thomas de Maizière to ask for Turkey's Ditib, who controls 970 mosques in Germany—the largest network in the country—to become independent from Diyanet (*Diyanet İşleri Türk-İslam Birliği*, the Turkish–Islamic Union for Religious Affairs, Turkey's state controlled directorate of religious affairs).[59] This was a clear sign of growing concern. German daily *Die Welt* revealed the existence of a network of 6000 informers from MIT (*Milli İstihbarat Teşkilatı* ,Turkey's national intelligence agency) operating in Germany. Their main focus is dissidents, in particular sympathizers of Hizmet, the political movement of US-based Fethullah Gulen, whom Erdogan accused of having engineered the failed July 2016 putsch.[60] It was further revealed that MIT operated 800 agents in Western Europe, and that Turkey's spying operations covered the Netherlands, Austria and Switzerland.[61] An EU country sharing a 270 km border with Turkey, Bulgaria has been at the receiving end of Turkey's renewed efforts to meddle in European affairs. This prompted Bulgarian president Rumen Radev to accuse Ankara of supporting his country's Dost party, the new party of Bulgaria's Turkish minority (which constitutes just under 10% of the country's 7.4 million population).[62] Should the EU–Turkish agreement on containing migrants at the Turkish frontier fall apart, Bulgaria would find itself on the frontline of a new wave of migration. As relations between Turkey and Germany steadily worsened following the arrest of several German citizens in Turkey, Erdogan—not one to shy away from stirring trouble abroad—urged German Turks to vote against Germany's main parties in the September 2017 elections. This drew sharp rebukes from Germany's establishment, who accused him of meddling in Germany's affairs. Hostility between the two countries was turning into a serious affair. Under Erdogan's rule, Turkey's newfound assertiveness has resulted in German Turks and Turkish domestic politics becoming factors that can no longer be ignored in the question of Germany's domestic stability.

The Turkish problem is, in truth, much broader and deeper than this. Relations between Turkey and the EU have been deteriorating on a daily basis. Erdogan's Turkey—which less than a decade ago was said to be on its way to becoming part of the EU—has, for all intents and purposes, morphed into what many in Europe (and in the USA) now increasingly perceive to be an out-of-control—if not outright hostile—Islamo-nationalist dictatorship. Having turned into a wanton 'one man show', Turkey has now become a major source of concern to its European neighbours. Erdogan's declarations and personal ambitions to assume the mantle of a new sort of Ottoman Sultan and revive Turkey's power in the Middle East make him a loose cannon in the eyes of Europe. Granted, his foreign policy adventures and constantly shifting alliances have not gotten Erdogan anywhere, but the reliability and stability of this NATO ally, which happens to field the largest army in the region and is supposed to guard the alliance's southern flank, is more than ever in doubt.

The 100 Billion Euro Gamble

Chancellor Merkel, who recognized in 2010 that Germany's '*Multikulti*' experiment 'utterly failed' subsequently advocated '*Willkommenskultur*'.[63] She took the view that millions of newcomers from societies with value systems light years away from that of Europeans could promptly and smoothly be reformatted *en masse* into good German citizens. The chancellor's new slogan became '*Wir schaffen es!*' ('We can manage!'). If the Cologne mass sexual assaults were any indication, it amounted to a reckless gamble, one that comes with a 100 billion euro price tag as we shall see in a later section. The authorities had assumed that the newcomers, grateful for the open-arms welcome they had received, would be on their best behaviour and blend in. Blinded by a mix of ideology and naiveté, German 'elites' ignored cultural differences. They disregarded the possibility that the reformatting of legions of young, mostly male newcomers (70% were single males) from socially and politically dysfunctional regions, where intolerant and violent societies are the norm, and where uncovered women are considered fair game, may not work out as expected. Cologne was the consequence of underestimating socio-cultural differences, just as Berlin would later be the consequence of underestimating the Jihadist threat.

After Cologne, leading German magazine *Der Spiegel* asked whether Germany was really sure that it could handle the influx of refugees and whether it had the courage and the desire to become the country in Europe with the greatest number of migrants.[64] It pointed out that the consequences of Cologne made it impossible to continue as before, echoing the view of Gunther Krichbaum, Chairman of the Bundestag's Committee on European Affairs, who warned that 'Cologne has the quality of changing the entire debate over refugees'.[65] In the aftermath of the 'Maria' affair—in which a young Afghan refugee raped and killed a 19-year-old social worker who was helping refugees—Rainer Wendt, the head of German police union DPolG lamented: 'This victim and many others could have been avoided if our country had been prepared for the dangers that come together with massive immigration.'[66] Incidentally, the killer had previously been jailed for ten years in Greece for attempted murder but was released after serving just over one year, due to the authorities' decision to free space in over-crowed prisons.[67] This provides proof, once more, of the cavalier attitude and lack of any serious coordination by authorities all over Europe in the face of dangerous radicals and unruly migrants. In the case of Cologne, to some observers, 'Police evidence of a heavy Moroccan and Algerian criminal gang presence in the assaulting hordes suggests this is a problem of longer-standing migrant populations and not exclusively, or even mostly, of newer arrivals like

Syrians or Iraqis.'⁶⁸ Ergo, Germany's migrant problem was not confined to these recent arrivals. Its roots were now discovered to be wider and more established. If the newcomers don't properly integrate—because of cultural incompatibility or because the German economy slows down and can't provide enough jobs—what then? Berlin's line of thought was that it may all be looked at as an investment in the future, once the newcomers became productive. If one gave up on the idea that, with the right financial and other incentives, the host population may actually start making more babies, then importing people to plug the deficit had some merit, except that it ignored qualitative aspects, such as what sort of people should be imported and what would happen if things didn't work out as planned?

Before 1990, migrations were mostly intra-European. Subsequently, migrants came from all over the world. While there is some historical precedent for the absorption of large numbers from foreign cultures, the behaviour of many new migrants and refugees is decidedly more aggressive today than during these past migrations, on top of which is the new dimension of militant Islam. Aside from the odd Jihadists hitching a ride in the midst of migrants, to what extent does UMI generate increased risks for the population at large? While asylum seekers represented 1% of the population of the German state of Baden–Wurttemberg, during the first nine months of 2015, they were involved in 5% (or 27,255) of all registered crimes—that is, they were five times more likely than locals to commit crimes—and took part in 1000 cases of grievous bodily harm, 22 of attempted murder, and 700 of domestic burglary. The highest numbers of offenders were Syrian refugees.⁶⁹ By late 2016 figures, from Germany's Federal Criminal Police Office (Bundeskriminalamt) reportedly pointed to a worsening situation: migrants had committed 142,500 crimes in just six months, equivalent of 780 crimes a day, an increase of nearly 40% over 2015.⁷⁰ This prompted many citizens to wonder why migrants convicted of a crime had not immediately been sent back home, instead of continuing to enjoy support from taxpayers. The total number of rapes and sexual assaults recorded in Germany in 2016 rose 12.8 percent compared to 2015, an increase blamed on an influx of asylum-seekers, many young and male.[71] On the other hand, following Cologne, anti-immigration campaigners and right wingers have been accused of exaggerating the threat posed by migrants concerning sexual assaults. A report showed that 82% of offences by migrants were non-violent, mostly theft, counterfeiting and travelling on public transport without a ticket, that only one victim in 28 recorded killings was German and that most incidents were between migrants of the same nationality.[72] Data on criminality can be manipulated and the fact that many migrants fail to officially register means the picture is likely to be incomplete anyway. Migrants in general may or may not be more likely to commit crimes than German citizens, but what is certain is that the proportion of crimes they commit in absolute terms grows as they start to make up a larger share of the population.[73] Out of the 1.1 million migrants reaching Germany at the time, only 476,000 had applied for asylum by January 2016, which means another 600,000 or so, likely ineligible for asylum, were roaming around Germany or elsewhere in Europe (some were using different identities) as authorities could not account for them.[74] In September 2017 German authorities lost track of another 50 alleged Iraqi immigrants whom they had just freed from human traffickers.[75] In Sweden, another country very welcoming and generous to migrants and refugees, foreigners went from 1% to 15% of the total population in less than a century and 80% of asylum seekers obtained the status of political refugees. Sweden suffered its own Cologne moment when bands of young refugees, mostly from Afghanistan, assaulted scores of young Swedish girls at the 'We Are Stockholm' music festival in 2014, and at other festivals in 2016.[76] Similar attacks took place in Switzerland and other countries and Europeans were, time and again, caught unprepared. While anti- and pro-immigration campaigners have often manipulated data and put a spin on stories, it is not possible to ignore the reality that UMI has affected the security and well-being of host country citizens in many places. One just has to talk to ordinary citizens to understand this. If integration is, under normal circumstances, not a given, more and more Germans came to realize that the rapid integration of masses of aliens from cultures based on incompatible value systems was an unrealistic utopia. By then it was too late.

If the driving force behind this *Willkommenskultur* was not economic but humanitarian, where should it all stop? In 2017, over 65 million people have been displaced by conflicts around the world.[77] What is Europe's fair share? Five million, 10 million or maybe 20 million? Given that Europe is already at breaking point, can it realistically afford more bouts of generosity *à la* Merkel? In 2016, German Development Minister Gerd Mueller warned that only 10% of Syrian and Iraqi migrants had reached Europe so far, that 8 to 10 million were still on the way, and that millions more were coming from Africa.[78] Unsurprisingly, Chancellor Merkel's legendary resilience showed signs of abating. An Insa poll in January 2016 showed that 40% of Germans wanted her to quit over the refugee crisis.[79] The four Jihadist attacks perpetrated in Germany by mostly migrants and refugees over a single week during the summer of that same year made things worse. The CSU party head, Horst Seehofer, threatened to blow the ruling coalition to pieces if Merkel did not close the doors. The wind had changed.

'Wir Schaffen es'! ... or Maybe We Can't

Merkel did not have a Plan B, so when things started to look as if they wouldn't work out, having realized she may have gone too far too fast, the *Kanzlerin* tried to extricate herself from a difficult position by launching two initiatives. Her volte-face started with a trip to plead with Turkey's Erdogan to slow down the flow of refugees in exchange for billions of euro, free Schengen visas for Turks and a face-saving resumption of EU accession talks. This costly initiative had the merit of reducing refugee inflows through Turkey, by then the main land route to Europe. It must be said to the *Kanzlerin*'s credit that her plan worked. By 2017, the flow of refugees from inland routes through the Balkans had been considerably reduced and the line of defence held, despite a general worsening of German–Turkish relations. Secondly, previously deaf to calls for assistance from European frontline states, Germany suddenly rediscovered a penchant for European solidarity. It used its hegemonic position to turn its own refugee fiasco into a European problem by pushing other countries to absorb part of the masses it had unilaterally let in. German Finance Minister Wolfgang Schäuble warned at a meeting of EU finance ministers in Brussels that 'Many think this is a German problem but [...] we'll see that it's not a German problem—but a European one.'[80] This was a prelude to the 'absorption quotas' which Germany promoted, pursuant to which European countries had to take their own share of refugees. By September 2017, only 24,000 of the 160,000 refugees supposed to be resettled by EU-mandated quotas agreed in 2015 had been resettled. The European Court of Justice rejected demands by Hungary and Slovakia to be excused from making good on these quotas.[81] This decision was promptly applauded by German Foreign Minister Sigmar Gabriel, who reiterated that these quotas had to be swiftly implemented by all countries.[82] Perceived by some as German 'moral imperialism', this stance had already been decried by Hungary's hard-line Prime Minister Viktor Orban,[83] attesting to the cleavage the refugee situation had created, in particular between socially conservative Eastern European countries such as Poland and Hungary and Western Europeans. According to *Bloomberg* 'The real political tension between the EU's east and west started two years ago during Europe's worst refugee crisis since World War II. While Merkel allowed them in, political parties in Hungary, Poland, and the Czech Republic joined in an anti-Islamic chorus that boosted their popularity. A July survey showed 57 percent of Poles would rather leave the EU than let in refugees.'[84] There is little doubt that Merkel's migration policies fuelled the rise of populist governments in Eastern Europe's socially conservative countries (just as they did in the rest of Europe). With this populism came authoritarian regimes that, today, put Eastern Europe increasingly at odds with Western Europe. This new East–West fracture was reflected in a Pew Research Centre study evidencing wide variations of opinion about Muslims in Europe. The most unfavourable were found in Eastern and southern Europe (with the notable exception of France). These opinions also varied along political lines with, as could be expected, people on the right generally more inclined to give Muslims an unfavourable rating—by a substantial margin—than leftists.[85]

In early 2015, Doris Akrap, the daughter of a guest worker in Germany, wrote about the admirable initial attitude of Germans towards refugees:

thousands of Germans have pitched in; they take food and clothes to the camps, take refugees to meetings with the authorities in their own cars, pay their fares, foot their medical bills, teach German, translate forms, share couches and bikes, act as nannies, open up soccer clubs, schools and kindergartens for refugee kids, and go on demonstrations against right wing attacks across the country.[86]

Germany has indeed been trying hard to integrate the refugees it takes in, with community homes being built, children attending school within three weeks of arrival, and compulsory integration courses that include 600 hours of German language and 100 hours of civics. Yet, 'it will be many years before Germany can fully assess how well it has integrated its newcomers' warned *The Economist*.[87] Akrap feared it would not last, and she was right. Having become the first country to open its doors wide, Germany ironically became, in September 2015, the first Schengen country to close its borders.[88] Some of Europe's most tolerant and welcoming countries followed in Germany's footsteps and made their own well-publicized moves designed to discourage newcomers. Denmark cut assistance benefits by half and required refugees to hand over any assets in excess of 1400 euro (the infamous 'Jewellery bill' passed by parliament).[89] Sweden—the most generous in Europe, having taken in 3424 asylum seekers per 1 million inhabitants in 2014, compared to Britain's 218[90]— carried out the first mass deportation seen on European soil since the Second World War, sending 80,000 migrants back home.[91] Sweden was known for having one of the most generous immigration policies but now has one of the most restrictive ones. These measures were a very visible admission of failed policies implemented by incompetent and naïve governments blinded by ideology. The damage was, however, already done and these measures were just attempts to prevent a bad situation from getting worse. In early 2017, Hungary's parliament adopted by a very large majority a law establishing detention camps along its frontiers, in which all migrants would systematically be kept until decisions were made on their status—not unlike Australia's much decried policies.[92]

A change in mood was palpable all over the Western world. By early 2017, even in Canada, which had been proud of its welcoming approach to migrants, 40% of citizens surveyed wanted illegal migrants from the

Middle East and Africa, now crossing from the US to Canada, to be deported.[93] Their views aligned with those of half of US citizens. In Germany, where half of the 700,000 requests for asylum made in 2016 had been rejected,[94] the issue was now how to send these refuseniks back home as fast as possible. Merkel took steps to accelerate deportations. At the end of 2016, 207,000 migrants were facing deportation from Germany (only 25,000 of them were actually deported and another 55,000 left voluntarily).[95] This number was supposed to increase to 450,000 by the end of 2017 with the acceleration of repatriation programmes estimated to cost over 90 million euro. According to a December 1st report by the Daily Mail, November 2017 saw the industrial city of Salzgitter, in Lower Saxony, become the first German city to officially ban the arrival of new refugees among 'growing complaints about newcomers draining resources and benefits'. As much as 91% of refugees in this city had no job and were on welfare. Europeans were starting to realize that the sustainability of their cherished Civilization of Entitlements was incompatible with the welcome given to the human tsunami from the world of chaos. The Salzgitter ban started a trend for more such bans in Germany, which elicited a reminder from the UN refugees agency that they were illegal.[96] At the same time, however, a government report estimated that over 400,000 new Syrian refugees would be arriving in Germany in 2018 because of a 'family reunification policy'.[97] The nationalist party AfD was quick to capitalize on this fact in its successful bid to enter parliament in the September 2017 elections. Having publicly confessed to the failure of *Multikulti*, but then praised *Willkommenskultur* and unilaterally opened the immigration floodgates, Merkel had, by 2017 completed her volte-face, saying 'We must put repatriation right at the top of the agenda.'[98] Yet the new drive to deport masses of unwanted economic migrants speaks volumes as to the failure of European policies in addressing the recent UMI crisis. Europe let these people in and now couldn't get rid of them fast enough. But deportations are often difficult to organize, because the countries of origin of illegal immigrants often refuse to take them back. What to do, then? The 'open door policy' often turns out to be a costly 'revolving door' policy. In mid-2017 Merkel's steadfast refusal to put a cap on new refugee arrivals, despite 47% of Germans being in favour of doing so, was yet another case of aloof European governing 'elites' dismissing the will of the people.[99] Governments that have long been in denial of realities are now going so far as to pay migrants to incentivise them to go back home. In 2012, I warned that 'Instead of Dutch society changing these immigrants for the better, it was the immigrants that had changed Dutch society for the worse, causing it to shed its tolerance',[100] a sad reality affecting most of Europe today. Why were these people let in in the first place if they are now to be sent back home? Shouldn't Europe's so-called elites have thought about it all before rolling out the welcome mat? Had the 'elites' done their job properly, they would have spared the world the tragic spectacle of the first mass deportations from Europe since the Second World War.

The Cost of Good Conscience

If things don't work out and if not enough jobs can be found for the newcomers and they remain in Europe, will taxpayer money be used to feed and shelter large numbers of migrants forever? However noble humanitarian motivations may be, UMI carries substantial economic and social costs that Europe's governing 'elites' and pro-immigration lobbies have mostly chosen to ignore (if not actually hide) to the detriment of their constituencies who, after all, end up bearing these costs. Douglas Murray's assertion that 'the economic benefits of immigration accrue almost solely to the migrant', and that the problems presented by incomplete integration dwarf the benefits of diversity,[101] imply that the cost–benefit analysis of immigration is biased towards the migrant. This is not easy to determine, and perhaps Murray is wrong and great economic benefits will accrue sooner or later to the host country from this immigration. At the very least, immigrants represent a reservoir of manpower and there is little doubt that those who manage to integrate, work and pay taxes constitute a market and a force that contributes to a country's economic life. It is especially difficult to quantify the benefits side of the equation, so we shall content ourselves with exploring the costs side. However, in all fairness, the benefits side deserves to be quantified and compared to the costs side. Estimating the costs is a difficult task for two reasons. First, pro-immigration governments often attempt to hide or manipulate information in a pretence that these costs are minimal.

Former French Finance Minister Michel Sapin famously declared that these costs would amount to just a few million euros while they were known to be several hundred times higher.[102] Second, cost calculations are complex, as one needs to take into account not only the direct costs of welcoming, feeding and housing migrants, but also indirect costs such as processing, mobilizing rescue and police forces, infrastructure, health and education, and so on. Qualitative elements such as the impact of UMI on the well-being and stability of host societies can't be quantified, but the results are plain enough for all to see.

'People seeking refugee status in European countries are generally entitled to food, or money to buy it, plus shelter and medical attention, schooling for their children and access to interpreters and lawyers'; in addition, they generally receive cash allowances and other benefits.[103] The resulting total package varies a lot from country to country, and is difficult to estimate. In Germany, for instance, the cash allowance for a refugee reportedly started at 143 euros per month, rising to 216 euros per month after three months, and became 400 euros per month after 15 months if the asylum application was accepted, according to a Reuters report in 2015. This is in addition to free housing and an allowance of 92 euros per month per child. In France, the cash allowance was 343 euros per month.[104] Moreover, these people need to be processed, transported, housed, fed, clothed, their health taken care of and their kids sent to school. Various studies have been made and one figure German and French estimates seem to agree on is that it cost more or less 12,500 euros to welcome, maintain and process a migrant up to the time his or her request for asylum is accepted or rejected, which takes on average a year. This figure explains to some extent the 10 billion euro budget announced by Germany for first 800,000 migrants the country initially took in. To care for refugees, Germany's finance minister, Wolfgang Schäuble, budgeted 10 billion euros in 2016, set to rise every year and reach 20 billion euros per year in 2020 (by which time the aggregate cost of taking care of the wave of refugees is expected to have risen to 93.6 billion euros in Germany alone).[105] When the costs of 'Immediate relief to states and municipalities' in relation to refugees is factored in, Germany's Federal Ministry of Finance puts the total bill for Germany at an average of 20 billion euros per year for the next four years.[106] This prompted *Der Spiegel* to wonder 'how it [the government] intends to raise this money. Will it do so through borrowing? Or will the country have to raise taxes?'[107]

Illegal immigration is another challenge which carries its own specific costs estimated to be in excess of 4.6 billion euros per year in France alone.[108] All these costs are only part of a larger total bill. For instance, the number of migrants claiming benefits in Germany soared from 363,000 to 975,000 from 2014 to 2015. Total benefits paid to them are estimated to aggregate over 5 billion euro per year, to the great displeasure of many Germans, in particular from the poorer Eastern half of the country.[109] It is estimated that teaching them to speak German will cost another 5.7 billion euros.[110] Health coverage of unwanted migrants is estimated at over 800 million euro per year in France.[111] In the UK, the health and education costs of illegal migrants were reportedly in excess of 3.7 billion pounds per year.[112] In Italy, over 133,000 migrants were housed in hotels and other structures in 2015, at an estimated cost of 918 million euros. This figure went up by at least 60% in 2016. The total cost of unwanted migrants for the year was estimated by the government to exceed 3.3 billion euros.[113] In Italy, the cost of saving migrants at sea, providing first assistance, and protecting and educating more than 20,000 unaccompanied children was estimated at over 3 billion euros in 2016 and was expected to jump to 3.8 euros in 2017.[114]

As governments have to take care of migrants until they find a job or are sent back home, the faster they can find work and contribute to the economy, the better. Two difficulties arise with this. The first is obviously the difficulty of finding jobs in high unemployment economies and the second is the learning of languages and basic skills in the absence of which a migrant remains 'unemployable'. In this respect a study by Germany's Institute for Employment Research showed that only 8% of refugees aged between 15 and 64 found a job within a year of arrival, and it took five years for half of them to find a job. In Oberhausen, a town in North Rhine-Westphalia, for instance, out of 1902 refugees, only 42 (about 2%) found a job or were learning a trade.[115] In other words, even in Germany where unemployment is low,[116] the state needs to take care of migrants for several years before they become productive, at a substantial cost. In Sweden, statistics showed that less than 500 of 160,000 arrivals managed to secure jobs. It is no wonder that the Swedish Government started offering migrants up to the equivalent of 3500 pounds each to go back home.[117] Despite its well-performing economy, Sweden has been feeling severe budgetary strains in its generous domestic welfare system,[118] due to the costs of taking care of the 163,000 refugees which *Migrationsverket*, the Swedish Migration Agency, says the country welcomed in 2015.[119]

What happens when a migrant's request for asylum is rejected? According to regulations, the migrant is supposed to be deported. Of the 700,000 asylum requests made in Germany in 2016, close to half have been rejected,[120] a proportion similar to Italy's.[121] How many of these refuseniks are actually deported? (The word refusenik used to refer to Jews denied permission to emigrate from the Soviet Union. I beg the reader to forgive the extreme freedom I am taking in using it in a sort of reverse mode for migrants denied permission to settle in Europe). In France, for instance, 96% of migrants who are refused asylum actually remain in the country instead of being deported, at an estimated additional cost to taxpayers of over 500 million euros per year.[122] French authorities have reportedly offered up to 4500 euros per person to incentivize some of these refuseniks to leave, to little avail.[123] In Germany, resisting deportation is not difficult at all, pro-immigration groups even offer tips on how to thwart a deportation.[124] A lot of refuseniks from Germany actually end up in Paris. The vast majority of migrants reaching Italy are supposed to be deported because they are not war refugees but economic migrants mainly from Nigeria and Pakistan. 90% of the Pakistanis' requests for asylum are rejected, since their country is not at war, but they can ask for a legal recourse and thus remain in Italy for another year or two. More than 100,000 of them remained in 2016:[125] idle, fed, sheltered and clothed by taxpayers. For the entire, EU only 39% of those refused asylum were actually sent back home in 2013.[126] Europe keeps and supports, in other words, 60% of the ineligible migrants it is supposed to send back home. What is the sense of keeping them in Europe since they inevitably end up as an economic, social and security burden on societies which have no use for them?

Europe is not the only one bearing the cost of UMI. Jordan, for one, has taken in 650,000 Syrian refugees according to the UN Refugee Agency UNHCR and claims to have spent more than 10 billion USD in the past five years, or so, to take care of them. Yet, unlike Europe, Jordan has, according to Amnesty International, not shied away from sending groups of refugees back home, into conflict zones.[127] In Europe, in any case, the aggregate costs of UMI appear to be very substantial, in the tens of billion euros per year, year after year, with no clear end in sight. Nobody has carried out an exhaustive analysis of these costs and pro-immigration governments and lobbies are likely in no hurry to do so. Yet Europeans would do themselves a favour by facing reality and thoroughly quantifying the aggregate financial burden of these policies at the national as well as the European level, especially at a time when austerity is the norm and citizens are asked to tighten their belts. Are ordinary Europeans prepared to pay the bills? In 2016 Angela Merkel's CDU party suffered its worst ever electoral defeat in Berlin.[128] In the autumn of 2017 the far-right, nationalist, anti-immigrant party AfD gathered enough votes to enter parliament for the first time, a clear sign of voters' discontent. A German citizen interviewed by AFP summed it up: 'Now many people are asking: "Where does all the money come from for the refugees? [...] All of a sudden? That's just not on!"'[129] In France an IFOP poll showed 73% of citizens did not want to pay for migrants,[130] attesting once more to a profound disconnect between Europe's governing 'elites' basking in pro-immigration ideology, and their constituencies. Ordinary Italians have been resentful of the cash handouts and other benefits migrants get from the state, at a time when pensions are being slashed and taxes continuously raised. Italy's economy is nearly bankrupt, yet legions of refugees are seen to receive a daily cash allowance from the state (without having to work) in addition to free housing, food and clothing. Some Italians complain this is more than what they get from their pensions or unemployment benefits. The fact that some of these migrants have been seen throwing food they don't like on the floor and trashing the places where they are housed does not exactly endear them to the local population.[131] Former Italian premier Matteo Renzi, echoing Angela Merkel, advocated the welcoming of even more migrants, declaring that they represented an 'opportunity' for Italy. He was booted out of his job at the end of 2016 as angry Italians pointed out that the only opportunity these migrants actually represented was to the Mafia, which was involved in lucrative human trafficking. They were not wrong: among others a police inquiry showed that in Isola di Capo Rizzuto the mafia had been awarded a government contract to run a migrant centre for ten years, siphoning off government funding while starving the migrants.[132]

To the above mentioned costs must be added the more than 3 billion euros in aid to Ankara to provide for Syria's refugee camps in Turkey, of which the EU itself pledged to provide a third in 2016, with the remainder to be provided bilaterally by EU countries.[133] In addition to costs at the national level, UMI generates expenses at the EU level, such as the aid mentioned and the billions of euros spent so far by Frontex on policing Europe's external frontiers (300 million euros in 2017 alone).[134] More than 400 million euros of EU aid was given to Greece to increase the number of refugees living in apartments to 30,000 by the end of 2017, as well as over 57 million euros to refugees for monthly cash stipends, food and medication (i.e. free housing, cash allowances and benefits for refugees at a time when most Greeks can't make a living). This was part of a 1.3 billion euro package of EU aid to Greece alone for refugees.[135] And then there are costs associated with UMI which cannot be quantified, such as those related to the worsening social and security situation. How to evaluate the social cost of Cologne? Of Calais? Of Berlin? These costs cannot be quantified, yet they are part of the bill which Europeans continue to pay in relation to UMI. Despite all of this, some Europeans remain surprisingly adamant that more migrants should be welcomed. This was obvious at a demonstration in February 2017 in Barcelona, where over 160,000 people chanted 'Our home is your home'.[136] Meanwhile, Spain is a country reeling from very high unemployment. Less surprisingly, the demonstration was organized by the leftist mayor of the city.

Welcome to the Ghetto

The life of a migrant is a human tragedy. Striving to improve one's lot is a natural impulse for any human being and, however misguided one's steps may be in undertaking a long and perilous journey to reach what is wrongly advertised as an Eldorado, the drive to do so is human. The decision to leave one's land and family likely comes after all other options have been exhausted and one has decided to do whatever it takes to leave poverty, dejection, corruption and other scourges in the hope of finding something better. To undertake the journey, the migrant first needs to find ways to assemble what represents a vast sum of money to pay human traffickers and the like. And then the adventure, most of the time hellish, starts. A UN report revealed that 77% of children and young adults are subjected to some form of abuse during their journey to reach Europe.[137] Having reached Europe after a costly, terrifying and dangerous journey by sea or on land, some migrants end up in comfortable shelters, but the vast majority (in particular illegal immigrants) ends up in camps or parked in ghettos, or as vagrants with few alternatives but to start a life on the margin of society. The consequence of bad UMI policies was epitomized by the so-called 'jungle of Calais' in France. Calais was not a refugee camp, but a settlement of illegal migrants. For years a festering sore of desperate souls from everywhere—from Africans (43% of people in the camp were from Sudan) to Afghani Pashtuns—mostly economic migrants in search of a better life.[138] For them, Calais was the end of a hellish journey, a squalid, makeshift village of close to 10,000 people left to their own devices, with no hope, no income, no laws and no support except from a few NGOs. 'We are literally trying to get drinking water to people. We don't have water, we don't have food—and no sanitation', Clare Moseley, the founder of Care4Calais, an aid organization active throughout France said at the time. 'There's skin disease, gum disease. It really, really is the absolute basics of life here.'[139] By the end of 2016, the Hollande government had seemingly taken Calais off the radar by 'cleverly' reallocating its inhabitants in small groups to various cities and villages across France (with scant regard for the opinion of citizens living in those places), potentially transforming one big Calais into dozens of small Calais. Large and small Calais exist everywhere in Europe (there are more than 100 migrant shantytowns just in the area around Paris), sometimes in the form of camps, other times as pockets of migrants living in neighbourhoods alongside a better-off mainstream population.[140]

Life in these lawless camps is as squalid as it is dangerous. As many as 70% of women in migrant camps are reportedly the object of sexual violence and rape by migrant males.[141] Different migrant communities and gangs within these camps compete for scarce resources and, from time to time, violently confront each other. In these camps, Europe has not merely imported these people but also their intra-communal problems. Fights frequently erupt between Ethiopians, Eritreans, Afghanis and Kurds, for instance. In Germany's camps, an average of ten attacks a day on migrants were reported in 2016.[142] Hundreds of asylum seekers and refugees were injured in more than 3,500 attacks on them and their shelters.[143] Migrants are preyed upon and subjected to violence by other migrants, as well as by far-right hooligans and other predators. In Germany, some security agents working in shelters have been exposed by the media for having encouraged the prostitution of young migrants, boys and girls.[144] Too little has been said about the issue of children and very young migrants, a tragedy within the tragedy. Close to 10,000 of these very young migrants have disappeared in Europe between 2014 and 2016. In 2015 Sweden, the most generous in Europe, welcomed 35,000 very young people, representing 40% of the total that reached Europe. A Stockholm police spokesperson admitted that many of these youngsters without a family end up becoming criminals or victims exploited by criminal networks active in drugs, robberies, the sex industry and the like.[145] In July 2017, well after the Calais Jungle was officially closed, migrants came back, coalescing in Calais. An estimated 700 of them were now living in forests around the city.[146] Fights, which used to take place inside the Jungle, were now taking place in the city of Calais itself, pitting hundreds of Ethiopians against Eritreans in violent confrontations in the city's industrial zone, leaving scores of injured.[147] Such evidence shows that, together with misery, Europe has been importing tribal and other conflicts from Africa.

What sense is there in letting so many migrants in, if all Europe has to offer them is a life of danger, crime and squalor? Yet Europe kept welcoming them, and not content with waiting for boatloads of migrants to reach its shores, it took to sending its own boats all the way to the coast of North Africa to actually fetch and ferry them across the Mediterranean, doing human traffickers a great favour and incentivizing more economic migrants to come.

Bye Bye Schengen (and the Rest)?

Launched at the dawn of the new millennium, the euro single currency and the Schengen free-travel area initiatives were heralded as the two pillars that would cement European unity. The opposite happened, both have generated acute crises. Political 'elites' chose to ignore the inherent architectural flaws of the euro just as they chose to ignore that secure external borders were necessary for Schengen's viability. Europe has managed (so far) to keep the flawed currency construct alive at the cost of massive chronic unemployment in the south and serious tensions. Schengen's days were numbered when Merkel unilaterally announced Germany would open the doors to masses of migrants from outside Europe.

Schengen was designed to allow the free movement of Europeans within treaty areas. It was not designed to deal with masses of extra-Europeans invited by one country who, by virtue of being let in, could then freely circulate within the free-travel area. Austrian Chancellor Werner Faymann warned that, since the EU failed to protect its external borders, individual countries had no choice but to take matters into their own hands.[148] A victim of its own flawed open-door policy, Germany was, as we pointed out, the first to reinstate border controls, starting a domino effect. Austria, France (where 80% of citizens were favoured a return to border controls—something that was not lost on Marine Le Pen's far right Front National party).[149] Belgium and other countries did the same, and even non-EU member Macedonia closed its border with Greece. Many countries introduced checkpoints and took steps, some of which were controversial. Supposed to be temporary, these moves will likely last longer than expected. Barbed wire walls, such as the 150 km fence Hungary built on its border with Serbia and Croatia,[150] are not likely to come down soon. Following European criticism of the harsh new border and refugee control measures enacted by the Danes in 2016, Danish Minister of Integration and Immigration Inger Stojberg snapped 'Danish immigration policies are decided in Denmark, not in Brussels', after border controls had been in place for a while, he added 'Denmark will have border controls for as long as it is necessary.'[151] Sadly, physical borders have once more sprung up all over Europe. By mid-2017 it was clear that the European Commission's efforts to force countries to cease controlling their frontiers were falling on deaf ears. Danish Prime Minister Lars Løkke Rasmussen stated that his country was ready to defy the Commission and would not stop controls at its own border as long as the EU didn't properly control its external frontiers.[152] This position was effectively, and silently, taken by most European countries, and who can blame them? In the autumn of 2017, Germany itself, together with

France, Austria, Denmark and Norway asked for article 25 of the Schengen code to be modified to allow individual countries to extend the period during which they can enact temporary border controls from six months to two years (extendable to four years in special cases).[153] Against the ropes, Merkel found herself with no choice but to limit the number of refugees Germany would take in henceforth to 200,000 per year and to extend border controls for another six months. If Schengen survives, there will be likely remain some sort of internal border controls and/or a reduction of the travel-free area. In a sense, the same lack of intra-European solidarity that made the euro unsustainable has made Schengen unsustainable. A complete shutdown of intra-European frontiers is not impossible, although unlikely, and would deal a fatal blow to the European integration project, aside from carrying heavy costs to the European economy, estimated at 100 billion euros by 2025 for just the Schengen area.[154]

The consequences of the UMI debacle did not stop at Schengen. Both Merkel and the EU Commission President Jean-Claude Juncker warned in 2015 that nationalist reactions to the refugee crisis were threatening the entire edifice of common European market achievements as well as the common currency. They ominously warned that Europe was facing its 'last chance'.[155] Merkel went further, stating that the fate of the euro was 'directly linked' to a resolution to the migration crisis, to which Juncker added 'Without Schengen [...] the Euro has no point.'[156] In an interview with German newspaper *Die Welt*, former European Parliament President Martin Schultz issued his own warning: 'The European Union is in danger. No one can say whether the EU will still exist in this form in 10 years [...] the alternative would be a Europe of nationalism, of borders and walls [...] which led the continent to catastrophe in the past.'[157] The urgency of the situation was reflected by European Council President Donald Tusk's January 2016 warning that Schengen would break apart if the immigration situation wasn't sorted out within two months. His view was echoed by a German high official in early 2016: 'We have until March, the summer maybe, for a European solution.'[158] The danger of what a collapse of the EU would really mean was highlighted again in early 2017 by Juncker, with a dire warning: 'If the European Union collapses, you will have a new war in the western Balkans'.[159] The amazing thing in all this was why, if the stakes were clearly so high, had Europe done nothing for years to protect its external frontiers? How could a German Chancellor unilaterally invite millions of aliens into the Schengen space? Why had the EU turned a blind eye for years to what was happening in its frontline states in the south and refused to assist them? Blinded by the integrationist principles of the post-national ideology and, as always, in chronic denial of the realities of the world, European governments found themselves unable to take effective measures to curb the flow of UMI and unable to think in strategic terms, condemning Europe to be overwhelmed by events.

Gaddafi Blues

By mid-2017 one could say that the main UMI inland route to Europe had, to a great extent, been successfully constricted and controlled, thanks to the cooperation of Turkey. However costly the agreement may eventually be to Europe, Turkey turned out to be a surprisingly reliable and effective partner in blocking access. Inland routes and Aegean Sea routes on Europe's south-eastern flank that had mainly been used by war refugees and migrants from the Middle East were mostly shut down (not before close to a million and a half migrants had got in, as we already pointed out). At the same time, however, the situation concerning the other main UMI route, the sea route mainly used by economic migrants from the African continent embarking in Libya en route to southern Italy, had noticeably worsened. Given the anarchy and chaos reigning in post-Gaddafi Libya, the idea of a reliable Turkey-type agreement to curb migration flows emanating from Libya remained a pipe dream. Any thought, by the way, that European governing 'elites' had learned their lesson following the Libyan debacle and would thereafter think twice about launching partial military adventures abroad, was disproven by Europe's subsequent involvement in the Syrian war. This was another military adventure with no clear strategic objective and no serious thought given to the chaos that would ensue in Syria and the region should Syria's strongman, Assad, be removed. As bad a dictator as Gaddafi had been, the question of whether Europe was better off with him at Libya's helm or with the new anarchy and chaos can be answered by taking measure of the reality that migration from Libya into Europe has exploded in the post-Gaddafi era.

By mid-2017 sea arrivals to Italy were up 40% compared with the previous year, and it was expected at the time that close to 250,000 migrants would land in Italy over the course of the year compared with over 181,000 the previous year.[160] An overwhelmed and desperate Italy found Europe as uninterested as ever in sharing the burden, prompting alternative political party M5S to increase its anti-immigrant rhetoric with its MP Luigi di Maio publicly complaining of a Europe 'dying' over its handling of the migrant crisis and its lack of solidarity. As Austria was moving troops and armoured vehicles to block migrants from crossing over from Italy, AFP reported that 'The pressure on Italy's refugee system has been exacerbated by its EU partners reneging on promises to take in asylum seekers under a scheme aimed at relocating 160,000 people from Italy and Greece to other EU states. As of June 5, only 5,694 people had been relocated from Italy and several eastern European countries are refusing point blank to comply with the scheme.'[161] Frans Timmermans, the European Commission's deputy head, decried the work of NGOs running rescue operations off the coast of Libya as counterproductive and in need of control. He said they were a 'pull factor' encouraging migrants to take the journey and risk their lives in flimsy dinghies in the hope of being picked up and then ferried over to Italy (NGOs have, among others, been accused of coordinating with people-smugglers by phone or using lights to signal the location of their rescue boats). The difficulty of working out any effective UMI-control agreement with the Libyan authorities, the lack of solidarity among European nations in sharing the burden of migrants having reached Italian ports, the lack of decisive action in the high seas to turn back migrant boats, the lack of concrete action against human trafficking networks and the action of NGO rescue operations all contributed to encourage UMI. By the end of the summer, however, something seemed to have changed. The *Washington Post* spoke of a 'mysterious' drop in migrants crossing the Mediterranean just when warm waters should have resulted in a peak in crossings. According to Elizabeth Collett, founding director of Migration Policy Institute Europe, interviewed by The Washington Post on September 1st, 2017, the decline was not necessarily long-term and was likely due to a combination of factors such as 'a recently revamped Libyan coast guard or changes in border operations in Niger, which traditionally has been a starting point for many migrants en route to Libya and then Europe'. In addition to this was the cooperation of Libyan militias who had previously helped human traffickers, but were now attracted by financial incentives backed by the Italian government. These arrangements led a migration specialist to say 'I question how sustainable this dip is. I don't expect it to be a long-term decline.'[162] Whether or not the decline in crossings would last, it showed that at last European authorities had woken up and were finally trying to do something to curtail the flow. Collett's doubts were proven right: within a few months it was clear that, while arrivals to Italy from Libya (which used the sea route in 92% of cases) had decreased by 25% due to the abovementioned measures, the slack was being taken over by other sea routes. Tunisia saw a threefold increase compared to the previous year, Algeria a twofold increase and Turkey a 63% increase. Migrants were simply using alternative routes, but the flow continued, relentless.[163] By 2017, the across-the-board failure of European policies concerning UMI had become very visible. The damage was done. Schengen was on the ropes, various small and large Calais-style camps plagued the continent, intra-European political tensions due to UMI were rising, unsustainable costs were hitting national budgets, tensions between masses of dejected and increasingly assertive migrants and increasingly agitated host populations were on the rise in many places. There was little hope that these problems would go away. The UMI challenge has always been made of two parts: how to prevent more migrants from coming in and what to do about the masses already here. Concerning the first part, the EU was, by the summer of 2017, finally moving to a 'hard borders' approach, with tough action against migrant-source countries unwilling to cooperate with repatriations, including withholding development aid and visa restrictions. In striving to deal with the problem closer to its source, Europeans found themselves confronted with African realities. According to a report by Foreign Policy, 'Efforts to train and equip local security forces and militias have empowered gunmen known to torture, enslave, and kill civilians. Intentionally or not, European taxpayers are now funding a massive deterrence and interdiction effort that is largely invisible in Europe but profoundly damaging to Africa. It's also futile: Despite the billions of dollars being spent, the current efforts won't resolve the causes of Africa's exodus or stop its flow.'[164] Concerning what to do with migrants already in Europe, an unexpected decision by the European Court of Justice stated that Dublin rules applied. This means that migrants who end up in countries other than those where they landed (the 'border states' such as Italy and Greece) could be deported back to border states. This ignored the advocate-general's warning that the system could leave border states 'unable to cope'.[165] It was not helpful. At the breaking point, Italy started implementing previously unthinkable measures such as 'to return migrants to detention camps on Libyan soil where inmates face forced labor, torture and rape; imposing tough new rules on charity-run rescue ships, thus making their missions more difficult; and pursuing administrative action against Italians [...] who help under-the-radar migrants'.[166] Would the deal with Turkey (said to cost the EU over 6 billion euros by 2018) hold at a time of rising tensions between Ankara and the EU? Would agreements with unruly parties in Libya and other places also hold? This was by no means certain. Assuming these deals did hold, the question remained as to what to do with the masses already in Europe. Blinded by ideology, led by mediocre 'elites' of dubious competence and in chronic denial, Europe had, once more, only itself to blame for the predicament it found itself in.

Notes

1. 'Migrant crisis: Influx will change Germany, says Merkel'. *BBC News*. 7 September 2015.
2. Hélène Kohl. 'Compte à rebours pour Merkel'. *Le Journal du Dimanche*. Page 13. 18 September 2016.
3. Nicolas Barotte. 'L'Allemagne, nouvel eldorado de l'immigration'. *Lefigaro.fr – Le Figaro*. 26 May 2014.
4. Robert Kunzig. 'With the worst history of xenophobia, Germany has taken in the most refugees of any European country. The stakes of the experiment are high.' *Nationalgeographic.com*. 2016.
5. 'Risk analysis for 2017'. *Frontex*. 15 February 2017.

6. Andrea Shalal, Helen Popper. 'Thousands of ex-Taliban fighters may have entered Germany: report'. *Reuters.com*. 22 April 2017.
7. 'L'EI détient plus de 11.000 passeports syriens vierges'. *Lefigaro.fr – Le Figaro*. 10 September 2017.
8. 'La 'Jungle' de Calais passe le cap des 10.000 migrants, selon deux associations'. *Lepoint.fr – Le Point*. 19 September 2016.
9. E.M. 'Migrants: à Calais, les tensions demeurent'. *Le Figaro. Page 9*. 24 October 2017.
10. Robert Kunzig. 'With the worst history of xenophobia, Germany has taken in the most refugees of any European country. The stakes of the experiment are high.' *Nationalgeographic.com*. 2016.
11. Jim Yardley, Alison Smale, Jane Perlez, Ben Hubbard. "Brexit' provokes a caustic postwar unravelling'. *International New York Times. Page 1–4*. 27 June 2016.
12. 'Syria's refugee crisis in numbers'. Based on sources from UN Refugee Agency (UNHCR), Office for the Coordination of Humanitarian Affairs (OCHA), International Organization of Migration (IOM). *Amnesty International*. 20 December 2016.
13. 'Funding shortage leaves Syrian refugees in danger of missing vital support'. Leo Dobbs, Jonathan Clayton. *UNHCR News*. 25 June 2015.
14. 'Germany welcomed more than 1 million refugees in 2015. Now, the country is searching for its soul.' Rick Noack. *The Washington Post*. 4 May 2016.
15. 'The labour market will need more immigration from non-EU countries in the future'. *BertelsmannStiftung*. 27 March 2015.
16. Robert Kunzig. 'With the worst history of xenophobia, Germany has taken in the most refugees of any European country. The stakes of the experiment are high.' *Nationalgeographic.com*. 2016.
17. Joseph Nasr. 'Germany needs migrants as workforce dwindles, but must pay for them'. *Reuters*. 10 December 2015.
18. Francesco M. Bongiovanni, The Decline and Fall of Europe (Palgrave Macmillan, 2012).
19. 'The demographic future of the country'. *Istat.it*. 26 April 2017.
20. 'Why Europe needs more migrants'. *The Economist*. 12 July 2017.
21. Pankaj Mishra. 'Europe's Migrant Crisis Isn't Over'. *Bloomberg.com*. 5 September 2017.
22. Bill Wirtz. 'Forget Frexit, the EU's next threat comes from the East'. *Newsweek.com – Newsweek*. 5 February 2017.

23. Leonid Bershidsky. 'How Western Capital Colonized Eastern Europe'. *Bloomberg*. 12 September 2017.
24. Bill Wirtz. 'Forget Frexit, the EU's next threat comes from the East'. *Newsweek.com – Newsweek*. 5 February 2017.
25. 'Gian Maria De Francesco. 'L'ondata dei migranti cresce Ma non ha diritto di rimanere'. *Il Giornale. Page 13.* 4 February 2017.
26. 'Unemployment statistics'. *Eurostat* – Statistics Explained. 31 January 2017.
27. 'Allemagne: immigration record de pays de l'UE'. *Lefigaro.fr – Le Figaro*. 2 July 2016.
28. Frédéric Joignot. 'Le fantasme du 'grand remplacement' démographique'. *Lemonde.fr*. 12 August 2014.
29. 'Replacement Migration: Is It a Solution to Declining and Ageing Populations?'. *Un.org. Department of Economic and Social Affairs – Population Division*.
30. 'Italie/migrants: 50.000 arrivées depuis janvier'. *Lefigaro.fr – Le Figaro*. 22 May 2015.
31. 'Migrant crisis: Italy threatens to shut ports'. *Bbc.com*. 28 June 2017.
32. 'Il future demografico del paese. Previsioni regionali della popolazione residente al 2065'. *Istat.it*. 26 April 2017.
33. Michèle Tribalat. 'Les Yeux Grands Fermés'. *Editions Denoel*. March 2010.
34. Dominic Sandbrook. 'Is Europe committing suicide? Controversial book claims elites in UK and the Continent are encouraging mass immigration because they've lost faith in historic Christian values'. *The Daily Mail*. 20 May 2017.
35. Michael Rosen. "The Strange Death Of Europe' Says Europe's Decline Is A Choice'. *Thefederalist.com*. 29 September 2017.
36. Robert Kunzig. 'With the worst history of xenophobia, Germany has taken in the most refugees of any European country. The stakes of the experiment are high.' *Nationalgeographic.com*. 2016.
37. Naweed Jamali. 'Why the US doesn't have a Muslim problem, and Europe does'. *Foreign Policy Research Institute*. 3 Avril 2016.
38. Adelle M. Banks. 'US Muslims believe in American dream despite discrimination'. *USA Today*. 26 July 2017.
39. Philippe d'Iribarne. 'Les musulmans sont-ils discriminés'. *Le Figaro. Page 22.* 27 November 2017.

40. Richard C. Longworth. 'Commentary: The decades-long smoldering of England's Muslims'. *Chicago Tribune*. 5 June 2017.
41. 'The New Germans'. *Aljazeera.com*. 24 May 2017.
42. 'Marseille: l'inquiétant profil du jeune agresseur de l'enseignant juif'. *BFM TV*. 12 January 2016.
43. 'Startup-Kultur'. *The Economist. Page 21*. 4 February 2017.
44. Francesco M. Bongiovanni. 'The Decline and Fall of Europe'. *Palgrave Macmillan*. 2012.
45. 'The new neighbours – Turkey is taking care of refugees, but failing to integrate them'. *The Economist*. 29 June 2017.
46. George Jahn. 'High Turkish support for Erdogan in EU worries Europeans'. *The Seattle Times*. 4 May 2017.
47. Katrin Elger. 'Survey Shows Alarming Lack of Integration in Germany'. *Spiegel.de – Spiegel Online*. 26 January 2009.
48. Katrin Elger. 'Survey Shows Alarming Lack of Integration in Germany'. *Spiegel.de – Spiegel Online*. 26 January 2009.
49. Eric Zemmour-Emmanuel Todd: globalisation ou retour des nations?'. *Le Figaro. Page 18*. 12 September 2017.
50. Diana Fong. 'Low Rate of German-Turkish Marriages Impedes Integration'. *Dw.com – Deutsche Welle*. 24 February 2008.
51. 'Young Turks Increasingly Favor Integration and Religion'. *Spiegel.de – Spiegel Online*. 17 August 2012.
52. Alex Gorlach. 'To Integrate the New Refugees, Germany Must Avoid Its Mistakes With Turkish Migrants'. *Huffingtonpost.com – The Huffington Post (TheWorldPost)*. 2016.
53. Jeanette Seiffert. 'Erdogan visit polarizes Germany's Turks'. *Dw.com – Deutsche Welle*. 20 May 2014.
54. Cédric Ferreira. 'Des dizaines de milliers de Turcs d'Allemagne manifestent leur soutien à Erdogan'. *France24.com*. 1 July 2016.
55. 'Alerte à bombe dans une mairie allemande'. *Lefigaro.fr – Le Figaro*. 3 March 2017.
56. 'Erdogan vows Turkey will 'review relations with EU''. *Bbc.com*. 21 March 2017.
57. Nathalie Versieux. 'Pour les jeunes des 2e et 3e générations, l'Islam et la nation turque sont devenus des repères identitaires'. *Le Temps online*. 19 April 2017.
58. Susan Fraser, Christopher Torchia. 'In Europe spat, Turkish president warns Westerners on safety'. *ABC News, Associated Press*. 22 March 2017.

59. 'L'Allemagne veut des mosquées indépendantes de la Turquie'. *Lefigaro. fr – Le Figaro*. 14 March 2017.
60. Nicolas Barotte. 'Soupçons d'espionnage en Allemagne'. *Le Figaro Page 9*. 7 April 2017.
61. 'Turkey's Influence Network In Europe Is Leading To Tension'. *Huffingtonpost.com*. 5 June 2017.
62. 'Le président bulgare accuse la Turquie d'"ingérence' dans les prochaines élections'. *Lefigaro.fr – Le Figaro*. 17 March 2017.
63. Stephen Evans. 'Merkel says German multicultural society has failed'. *BBC NEWS*. 17 October 2010.
64. 'Where I'm From, This is Handled By Men'. *Spiegelonline – Der Spiegel*. 2 January 2016.
65. See note 22 in Chap. 2.
66. Nicolas Barotte. 'Migrants: cette affaire Maria qui bouleverse l'Allemagne'. *Le Figaro. Page 10*. 8 December 2016.
67. 'Refugee on trial for rape, murder of German student'. *AFP.* 5 September 2017.
68. Emma-Kate Symons. 'Cologne attacks: 'This is sexual terrorism directed towards women". *Nytlive.nytimes.com – New York Times*. 19 January 2016.
69. Sue Reid. 'Why Germany can't face the truth about migrant sex attacks: SUE REID finds a nation in denial as a wave of horrific attacks is reported across Europe'. *Mail online (The Daily Mail)*. 9 January 2016.
70. Julian Robinson. 'Angela Merkel under more pressure over refugee policy as it is revealed migrants committed 142,500 crimes in Germany during the first six months of 2016'. *Mail online (The Daily Mail)*. 1 November 2016.
71. Frank Jordans. 'German police union chief slams NYE "safe zone" for women'. *Associated Press*. 30 December 2017.
72. Lizzie Dearden. 'Refugees responsible for tiny proportion of sex crimes in Germany despite far-right claims following Cologne attacks'. *Independent.co.uk*. 19 February 2016.
73. Frank Jordans. "German police union chief slams NYE 'safe zone' for women". *Associated Press*. 30 December 2017.
74. Sam Tonkin. 'Exclusive: German government admits it cannot account for 600,000 of its 1.1million asylum seekers—and many could be using multiple identities to travel across Europe'. *Mailonline (The Daily Mail)*. 22 January 2016.

75. 'Allemagne: sauvés des mains de passeurs, des migrants disparaissent'. *Lefigaro.fr – Le Figaro*. 18 September 2017.
76. Dan Bilefsky and Christina Anderson. 'Swedish Police Investigate Over 40 Reports of Rape and Groping at 2 Music Festivals'. *New York Times*. 5 July 2016.
77. Adrian Edwards. 'Global forced displacement hits record high'. *UNHCR*. 20 June 2016.
78. James Dunn. 'Only 10% of migrants have reached Europe so far, claims German development minister as he warns up to ten million people are 'still on the way''. *Mail Online – The Daily Mail*. 11 January 2016.
79. Paul Carrell, Noah Barkin. 'Forty% of Germans say Merkel should resign over refugee policy: poll'. *Reuters*. 29 January 2015.
80. Alastair Macdonald, Noah Barkin. 'End of Europe? Berlin, Brussels' shock tactic on migrants'. *Reuters*. 18 January 2016.
81. 'EU court rejects Hungary, Slovakia appeal in refugee case'. *Associated Press*. 6 September 2017.
82. 'Germany Says EU States Must Implement Court Ruling on Migrants Swiftly'. *Reuters*. 6 September 2017.
83. Ruth Bender. 'Orban Accuses Germany of 'Moral Imperialism' on Migrants.' *The Wall Street Journal*. 23 September 2015.
84. Peter Laca, Wojciech Moskwa, Zoltan Simo. 'The 'Dark Past' in Merkel's Backyard'. *Bloomberg.com*. 26 September 2017.
85. Conrad Hackett. '5 facts about the Muslim population in Europe'. *PewResearchCentre*. 19 July 2016.
86. Doris Akrap. 'Germany's response to the refugee crisis is admirable. But I fear it cannot last'. *Theguardian.com – The Guardian*. 6 September 2015.
87. 'Hearts and minds'. *The Economist. Page 22*. 16 September 2017.
88. Luke Harding. 'Refugee crisis: Germany reinstates controls at Austrian border'. *The Guardian*. 13 September 2015.
89. Arwa Damon, Tim Hume. 'Denmark adopts controversial law to seize asylum seekers' valuables'. *CNN*. 26 January 2016.
90. Nicole Chang. 'Two graphs that show how many asylum seekers Britain really accepts'. *Independent*. 13 May 2015.
91. David Crouch. 'Sweden sends sharp signal with plan to expel up to 80,000 asylum seekers'. *The Guardian*. 28 January 2016.
92. 'Migrants: la Hongrie adopte la détention systématique'. *Lefigaro.fr*. 7 March 2017.

93. Rod Nickel, David Ljunggren. 'Exclusive: Almost half of Canadians want illegal border crossers deported – Reuters poll'. *Reuters.com*. 20 March 2017.
94. Erik Kirschbaum, David Stamp. 'Germany aims to deport record number of rejected asylum seekers in 2017'. *Reuters.com*. 19 February 2017.
95. 'Merkel seeks to ramp up failed asylum seeker deportations'. *Bbc.com – BBC News*. 9 February 2017.
96. Soraya Sarhaddi Nelson. 'A German City, Citing Pressure On Services, Gets Green Light To Ban New Refugees'. *NPR*. 29 November 2017.
97. Noah B. Strootte. 'The German Election Is a Christian Civil War'. *Foreignpolicy.com – Foreign Policy*. 11 September 2017.
98. Josh Lowe. 'Germany's Angela Merkel 'to announce migrant crackdown''. *Newsweek.com – Newsweek*. 9 February 2017.
99. Judith Vonberg. 'Merkel rules out limiting number of refugees in Germany'. *Cnn.com – CNN*. 17 July 2017.
100. Francesco M. Bongiovanni. 'The Decline and Fall of Europe'. *Palgrave Macmillan*. 2012.
101. Michael Rosen. '"The Strange Death of Europe" Says Europe's Decline Is A Choice'. *Thefederalist.com*. 29 September 2017.
102. Jean-Paul Gourévitch. '30 000 Migrants supplémentaires en deux ans: ce que va nous couter la décision de Hollande'. *Contribuables Associés*. 13 Mai 2016.
103. 'Which European countries offer the most social benefits to migrants?'. *Euronews.com based on research by Reuters Compiled by Mark Trevelyan; Editing by Gareth Jones*. 16 September 2015.
104. Compiled by Mark Trevelyan, edited by Gareth Jones, 'Factbox: Benefits offered to asylum seekers in European countries'. *Reuters*. 16 September 2015.
105. Michelle Martin and Andrew Heavens. 'German government plans to spend 93.6 billion euros on refugees by end 2020: Spiegel'. *Reuters*. 14 May 2016.
106. Andreas Becker. "Can we do this?' – The costs of the migrant crisis'. *DW-Deutsche Welle*. August 23 2016.
107. Markus Dettmer, Christian Riermann. 'Budget Battle Begins over Germany's New Residents'. *Spiegel Online*. 29 February 2016.
108. Arnaud Folch. 'Immigration: ce que coûtent vraiment les clandestins'. *Valeurs Actuelles*. 30 June 2011.

109. Michelle Martin, Gareth Jones. 'Number of migrants claiming benefits in Germany surges by 169%'. *Reuters*. 5 September 2016.
110. David Crouch. 'Sweden sends sharp signal with plan to expel up to 80,000 asylum seekers'. *The Guardian*. 28 January 2016.
111. Jean Marc Leclerc. 'Aide médicale aux étrangers: la facture explose'. *Lefigaro.fr*. 7 November 2013.
112. Jack Doyle. 'Our £3.7bn a year bill for illegal migrants' health and education: Huge cost emerges as ministers admit controversial 'go home' vans led to just 11 people leaving the country'. *The Daily Mail*. November 1, 2013.
113. Vladimiro Polchi. 'Immigrati, ecco quanto ci costa davvero accoglierli'. *Repubblica.it*. 29 October 2016.
114. Vladimiro Polchi. 'Immigrati, ecco quanto ci costa davvero accoglierli'. *Repubblica.it*. 29 October 2016.
115. Bruno Boelpaep. 'Is Germany's migrant crisis over? One city put to the test'. *Bbc.com*. 8 September 2017.
116. By Matthias Bartsch, Jan Friedmann, Hubert Gude, Horand Knaup, Ralf Neukirch, Conny Neumann, René Pfister, Christian Reiermann, Michael Sauga, Christoph Schult and Wolf Wiedmann-Schmidt. 'Germany Shows Signs of Strain from Mass of Refugees'. *Spiegel Online*. 17 October 2015.
117. Charlotte England. 'Sweden sees record numbers of asylum seekers withdraw applications and leave'. *The Independent online*. August 2016.
118. Daniel Dickson, Johan Ahlander 'Soaring asylum numbers force Sweden to cut costs, borrow more'. *Reuters*. 22 October 2015.
119. 'Nearly 163,000 people sought asylum in Sweden in 2015'. *Migrationsverket*. 12 January 2016.
120. "Chez nous, c'est chez vous': Barcelone dans la rue pour accueillir les réfugiés'. *Lefigaro.fr – Le Figaro*. 19 February 2017.
121. 'Gian Maria De Francesco. 'L'ondata dei migranti cresce Ma non ha diritto di rimanere'. *Il Giornale*. Page 13. 4 February 2017.
122. Ludwig Gallet. "96% des demandeurs d'asile déboutés restent en France', vraiment?'. *L'Express*. 21 October 2015.
123. Delphine de Mallevoue. 'Asile: déboutés outre-Rhin, ils affluent à Paris'. *Le Figaro. Page 10*. 9 March 2017.
124. Date Brady. 'Hundreds of migrants resisting deportation from Germany at the last minute'. *DW-Deutsche Welle*. 19 August 2016.

125. 'Allarme Pakistan; troppe richieste d'asilo sospette'. *Il Giornale. Page 3.* 21 December 2016.
126. Laurence Peter. 'Migrant crisis: Who does the EU send back?'. *BBC News.* 9 September 2015.
127. 'Jordanie: l'accueil des réfugiés syriens coûte 10 mds de dollars'. *Lefigaro.fr – Le Figaro.* 10 October 2017.
128. Kim Hjelmgaard. 'Germany's Merkel admits migrant policy cost votes'. *USA TODAY.* 19 September 2016.
129. Isabelle Le Page. "Merkel understood nothing': AfD's fury in east Germany'. *AFP.* 22 October 2017.
130. '73% Des Français opposés à assumer fiscalement le cout de l'accueil des migrants'. *Contribuables Associés.* 9 October 2015.
131. Giuseppe De Lorenzo. 'Eraclea, profughi protestano per il cibo e lo buttano in strada'. *Ilgiornale.it.* 27 July 2015.
132. 'Mafia controlled Italy migrant centre, say Police'. *Bbc.com.* 15 May 2017.
133. Eszter Zalan. 'EU finalises €3bn fund for Turkey refugees'. *Euobserver.com.* 3 February 2016.
134. 'Europe, la fin?'. *Courrier International. Page 20.* April-May 2017.
135. 'EU announces new emergency support for Greek refugee crisis.' *Washingtonpost.com – The Washington Post.* 27 July 2017.
136. 'Chez nous, c'est chez vous': Barcelone dans la rue pour accueillir les réfugiés'. *Lefigaro.fr – Le Figaro.* 2 February 2017.
137. 'Un rapport pointe les abus subis par les jeunes migrants'. *Lefigaro.fr – Le Figaro.* 12 September 2017.
138. Marion Mourgue. 'Sarkozy refuse que la France soit 'submergée''. *Le Figaro. Page 4.* 22 Septembre 2016.
139. James MacAuley. 'The Calais 'Jungle' is gone, but France's migrant crisis is far from over'. *washingtonpost.com – The Washington Post.* 10 June 2017.
140. 'Migrants: "plus de 100 bidonvilles en Île-de-France" (Pécresse)'. *Lefigaro.fr – Le Figaro.* 26 September 2017.
141. 'France: 70% des migrantes ont été violentées'. *Lefigaro.fr – Le Figaro.* 8 March 2017.
142. 'Germany hate crime: Nearly 10 attacks a day on migrants in 2016'. *Bbc.com – BBC News.* 26 February 2017.
143. Simon Cullen, Susannah Cullinane. 'Germany: Thousands of migrants targeted in attacks last year'. *Cnn.com – CNN.* 27 February 2017.

144. 'Allemagne: des agents de sécurité incitent des migrants à la prostitution'. *Lefigaro.fr* – *Le Figaro*. 25 October 2017.
145. Stéphane Kovas. 'En Suéde, l'épineuse gestion des mineurs étrangers'. *Le Figaro*. Page 15. 7 April 2017.
146. E.M. 'Migrants: à Calais, les tensions demeurent'. *Le Figaro*. Page 9. 24 October 2017.
147. 'Seize blessés après une bagarre entre migrants à Calais'. *Lefigaro.fr* – *Le Figaro*. 1 July 2017.
148. Nina Lamparski. 'Austria to cap asylum-seeker claims, deepening EU migrant rift'. *Yahoo News*. January 20, 2016.
149. '80% des Français favorables au retour des contrôles aux frontières'. *BFM TV*. 16 September 2015.
150. 'Hungary starts building fence on Croatian border'. *Dw.com* – *Deutsche Welle*. 18 September` 2016.
151. Lizzie Stromme. 'Denmark snubs EU as Government vows border controls will REMAIN to halt migrant influx'. *Express.co.uk*. 27 January 2017.
152. 'Schengen: le Danemark s'apprête à défier l'UE'. *Lefigaro.fr* – *Le Figaro*. 16 May 2017.
153. 'Paris et Berlin veulent des règles plus souples pour rétablir des contrôles frontaliers'. *Lefigaro.fr* – *Le Figaro*. 12 September 2017.
154. Richard Vainopoulos. 'Le prix de la fermeture de l'espace Schengen'. *Lesechos.fr*. 25 April 2016.
155. Peter Foster, Matthew Holehouse. 'State of the Union: Europe in the last chance saloon, warns EU president Jean-Claude Juncker'. *Telegraph.co.uk* – *The Telegraph*. 8 September 2015.
156. Alastair Macdonald, Noah Barkin. 'End of Europe? Berlin, Brussels' shock tactic on migrants'. *Reuters*. 18 January 2016.
157. Michelle Martin, Jeremy Gaunt. 'EU is in danger and can be reversed: European Parliament's Schulz'. *Reuters*. 8 December 2015.
158. 'Donald Tusk warns EU has TWO MONTHS to get migrant crisis under control or Schengen will fall'. *Mail Online, Associated Press*. 19 January 2016.
159. Lionel Barber. 'Juncker warns Trump to stop praising Brexit'. *Financial Times* – *FT Weekend*. Page 1. 25 March 2017.
160. Angus MacKinnon. 'Rome seeks migrant moratorium, warns of social tensions'. *AFP*. 13 June 2017.
161. Angus MacKinnon. 'Rome seeks migrant moratorium, warns of social tensions'. *AFP*. 13 June 2017.

162. James MacAuley. 'The mysterious drop in the number of migrants crossing the Mediterranean'. *Washingtonpost.com* – *The Washington Post.* 1 September 2017.
163. 'Italie: augmentation des arrivées de migrants'. *Lefigaro.fr* – *Le Figaro.* 10 October 2017.
164. 'Europe slams its gates'. *Foreignpolicy.com.* 4 October 2017.
165. Justin Huggler. 'EU court rejects 'open-door' policy and upholds right of member states to deport refugees'. *The Telegraph.* 26 July 2017.
166. Michael Birnbaum. 'In once-welcoming Italy, the tide turns against migrants'. *Washingtonpost.com* – *The Washington Post.* 25 August 2017.

4

Barbarians in the City

Islamization, Jihadism and their impact on Europe's open societies

The Archipelago

Europe is made up of mature, populated countries with clear identities and developed economies. Despite the substantial population flows and various invasions that took place through the ages, the presence of large Muslim minorities within Europe is something new. Allow me to recall relevant words from *The Decline and Fall of Europe*: 'Immigration into Europe is a very recent phenomenon [...] It is easy to forget that these are recent arrivals and that, before then, Europe had already had problems with nationalism and the issue of non-Muslim intra-European minorities [...] intra-European minorities have been the object of much suffering and of mass transfers of population through the ages [...] During the reconstruction efforts that followed the end of WWII, workers were imported and [...] these workers were considered a necessity and were naturally assumed to be a temporary phenomenon [...] yet as intra-European migration didn't suffice, employers started looking abroad [...] Eastern European countries were stuck on the wrong side of the iron curtain [...] Europe was compelled to look elsewhere, and that meant mainly the Muslim countries of the Maghreb to the south and Turkey to the east, as well as former colonies in Africa and elsewhere [...] when economies started slowing down in the 1970s, attitudes towards immigration started to change for the worse'. And yet, 'Europe continued to keep its doors open to immigration [...] Contrary to America's melting-pot philosophy which acted as a motor for integration, immigration into Europe created from the outset two separate classes of people [...] Social, cultural and religious alienation was the natural and unfortunate outcome of this state of affairs [...] it is the new generation (of immigrants) that uses religion to gain an identity of some sorts'.[1] In France for instance, immigration stemmed from other European countries until the beginning of the twentieth century and was mainly related to temporary work until 1950, after which permanent immigration started.

The total number of Muslims in the EU is now estimated at over 19 million,[2] making 'Euromuslims' (the reader will, I hope, forgive the use of this term, which I coined for purposes of convenience in this book) by far the largest minority, spread throughout Europe as an archipelago. If integration is defined as acceptance of and adherence to the values and behavioural codes of the host society in which they settle, it is undeniable that the vast majority of Euromuslims are integrated and wish nothing more than to lead a good life within the European context. Their contributions to society are just as commendable as anyone else's. In France, home to Europe's largest Muslim population (on a par with Germany's), an IFOP survey for Institut Montaigne published in the *Journal du Dimanche* in September 2016 showed that 46% of them are totally secular (or on the way to complete integration) and 25% are a bit more religious—'Islamic pride' types—who still reject the veil.[3] The real problem, as we shall see, lies with the remaining 29%.

In 2011, the Pew Forum published a report predicting that Europe's Muslim population would reach 57 million by 2030, or 7.8% of Europe's total,[4] growing to 10% in 2050. Working from a baseline estimate of a total Muslim population in Europe of 25.6 million in 2016, a Pew report issued at the end of 2017 placed 2050 estimates as ranging from 7.4% of the total population in Europe (or 30 million Muslims in total) under a 'zero migration' scenario; 11.2% (or 58.8 million) in a moderate migration scenario; and a little over 14% (reaching 75 million) in the case of a sustained high migration scenario (i.e. at the 2015–2016 levels).[5] According to these statistics, the demographic domination of Muslims in Europe is simply not going to happen despite the apocalyptic predictions that have been heard from some quarters. Yet all scenarios point to significant growth of this minority population. The impact of this will be uneven, with Germany the most affected, under a high migration scenario. Here, the Muslim minority could reach 20% of the population by 2050, and in Sweden it could reach 31%. Nevertheless, complacency led modern Europeans to ignore for a long time the emergence of a current of Islamization that started to affect not only the lives of minorities but those of ordinary Europeans as well. It also had profound implications for the future of Europe's open societies. To Harvard historian Niall Ferguson, Europe is undergoing a process not unlike that which caused the fall of the Roman Empire: 'Uncannily similar processes are destroying the European Union today [...] Let us be clear about what is happening. Like the Roman Empire in the early fifth century, Europe has allowed its defences to crumble. As its wealth has grown, so its military prowess has shrunk, along with its self-belief. It has grown decadent in its shopping malls and sports stadiums. At the same time, it has opened its gates to outsiders who have coveted its wealth without renouncing their ancestral faith'.[6] The current of Islamization, increasingly aggressive and conspicuous, reached levels that were bound to provoke a reaction from host societies, particularly when assertiveness occurred in direct opposition to core European values. To many Europeans, the absurd levels of accommodation occasionally reached by liberal political 'elites' in confronting these challenges smacked of submissiveness and decadence. Small but well publicized incidents here and there added oil to the fire, such as the decision of some European authorities to forbid crucifixes in some places to avoid offending Muslims. Or when, after the Cologne incident, the mayor advised women not to walk alone to avoid provoking migrants, prompting some Germans to ask whether they should perhaps start wearing the *burka*.[7] Or when Italians covered nude works of art,[8] during the visit of Iranian President Rouhani in January 2016 (Iranians reportedly didn't even ask for this and Indonesia's Balinese did not cover statues showing nudity during the March 2017 visit of King Salman from Saudi Arabia and the Saudis didn't complain).[9] These examples attest to the extent to which some Europeans appeared ready to go in order to satisfy themselves that they are not offending Muslims. Or when some drivers from RATP (the French public bus company) reportedly refused to drive women.[10] Or when young Muslim students in Switzerland refused to shake the hand of their female teachers.[11] Many Europeans went from being indifferent to such instances to being annoyed by them, to feeling a visceral rejection of anything that had to do with Islam. The rise of popular anti-Islam movements such as Germany's Pegida ('Patriotic Europeans against the Islamization of the Occident')—which, after being founded in October 2014, rapidly proved its ability to mobilize thousands of supporters for demonstrations across Europe—was a direct consequence of these trends.

While the vast majority of Euromuslims are integrated in their host societies and are moderate or barely interested in religious matters, a minority of them subscribes to a radically different agenda. As a consequence of this Europe is confronted by Islamism and Jihadism. Before going any further, let us define what we are talking about. As Lotfi Maktouf puts it in his essay 'The separation of church & state under the Islamist protocol', Islamism is 'an ideology that is all about governance: conquering and maintaining political power'.[12] According to the Brookings Institution, 'Islamist groups believe Islamic law or Islamic values should play a central role in public life. They feel Islam has things to say about how politics should be conducted, how the law should be applied and how other people—not just themselves—should conduct themselves morally.' Moreover, 'the point of Islamism is to advocate for a privileged social and political role for Islamic belief'.[13] Ismail Yusanto, spokesman for Indonesia's radical Islamist group Hizbut Tahrir made it even clearer: 'From the Islamic perspective, the state should exist for only one purpose: how to implement Shariah'.[14] Wikipedia defines Islamism as referring 'to diverse forms of social and political activism advocating that public and political life should be guided by Islamic principles, or more specifically to movements which call for full implementation of sharia. It is commonly used interchangeably with the terms political Islam or Islamic fundamentalism.' and points out that 'In Western media usage the term tends to refer to groups who aim to establish a sharia-based Islamic state, often with implication of violent tactics and human rights violations and has acquired connotations of political extremism.' For clarity's sake, let us argue in this book that 'Islamism' is the political ideology pushed by 'Islamists'. It is an ideology that seeks its legitimacy in 'Islam'—the religion—of which it advocates an uncompromising, literal and extreme interpretation. Islamism seeks to expand and rule, that is, to 'Islamicize' any available space it can find. 'Islamization' is the consequence of the application of the ideology of Islamism to a society, a neighbourhood or a community. In this book we shall refer to 'radicals', 'fundamentalists' and 'Salafists' as extreme Islamists, and 'Jihadism' as the military movement: the violent strain rooting itself in Islamist ideology that expresses itself in terrorist acts perpetrated by 'Jihadists', in our case EuroJihadists.

The Bad and the Worse

The creeping Islamization of Europe's open societies is a political project deliberately carried out by Islamists, the subset of the Euromuslim community that is the least interested in integrating with European society or in the Europeanization of Islam, but promotes instead the Islamization of Europe. In *The Decline and Fall of Europe*, I pointed out that 'this ideology found in Europe a tolerance, a liberty of expression, a freedom of networking and recruiting it could not even dream to find in repressive Islamic countries'.[15] Melissa Crouch, senior lecturer at the University of New South Wales in Sydney, Australia, similarly said that 'Democracy gives a greater space to everyone, including a greater space for radical Islam'.[16] In Europe, Islamism is a long-term enterprise by which, as a starting point, Islamists systematically and relentlessly assert their cultural differences and aspirations, essentially a request for apartheid. According to writer Kamel Daoud—himself a moderate Muslim who has been accused of Islamophobia—Islamists position themselves as the only legitimate representatives of Islam, thus monopolizing religion within their community.[17] Taking advantage of the weakness, tolerance and openness of their host societies across Europe, they first of all aim to carve out within the host country a separate social, legal and physical 'space' in which to live in accordance with what they perceive should be the ways of Islamic society. On their way to securing their own 'space', Islamists strive to coerce the rest of the Euromuslim minority (i.e. the moderates who constitute the majority of the minority) in order to swell their own ranks and openly split mainstream society into *Ummah* (the community of the faithful) and *kaffir* (infidels). Their tactic is to relentlessly probe, push, provoke and extend their 'space'. They apply it with deliberate patience, cleverly using the weaknesses of open societies to their advantage. The vast number of mosques dotting Europe constitutes a prime target for Islamists, a fast-growing, ready-made network. They strive to infiltrate and co-opt them, reformatting them into ideal bases from where to spread radical views. A November 2016 report from 'Organe de Coordination Pour l'Analyse de la Menace' (OCAM), a Belgian antiterrorism watchdog, warned of a growing number of mosques falling into the hands of Salafists who, with their relentless drive and funding from the likes of Saudi Arabia, succeeded in displacing moderate imams.[18] Attempts by the French government to try to regulate, let alone control, France's 1800 imams in order to better control radicalization have proven futile. Many of them come from abroad and do not even speak French (they preach in Arabic in France) and imams are effectively under the control of Islamic institutions.[19]

We are not going to examine here the historical roots of Islamism, contenting ourselves with pointing out the interesting viewpoint of Algerian-born writer Boualem Sansal. For him, the recent wave of Islamization is a direct result of the recently failed 'Arab spring', which swept away dictatorships and competing societal projects (such as pan-Arabism, socialism or democracy in the Arab world), creating a void that, instead of being filled by progressive and democratic forces, was immediately filled by Islamists. Emboldened by the pre-eminence they had just recovered in their own turf, Islamists now intended to impose themselves on the rest of the world, starting with the weakest link: Europe.[20] Let us briefly examine what motivates Islamic fundamentalists, which is simple in its complexity. Contrary to popular belief, theirs is not really a peculiar or deviant 'interpretation' of religious scriptures but an uncompromisingly 'literal' one. They wish to apply to the letter today what the Koran says (what it says is considered an absolute, since it is believed to be the actual word of Allah written down), as well as what the *Sunna* and *Hadiths* (guiding rules and traditions derived from the observation of the Prophet's life and deeds) say, with no regard to the fact that they are precepts of life dating from the seventh century. Fundamentalists are profoundly convinced that the validity of these scriptures transcend time and place and that any interpretation, any compromise, smacks of impurity and is intolerable. Since the scriptures are supposed to cover and regulate all aspects of human life, society, law and politics, fundamentalists do not see the need for and reject any other law, in other words the secular laws of the countries they happen to live in. For them the only valid law is sharia and the only acceptable behaviour is that dictated by the scriptures. The endgame for the most ambitious and hard-core Islamic fundamentalists (groups such as Islam4UK or Sharia4Holland) goes way beyond simple apartheid or ruling the entire Euromuslim community and includes dreams of an Islamic future for Europe, in line with the old dreams of the conquest and conversion of *kaffir* lands. For the most hardcore fundamentalists, scriptures are clear and unequivocal: the entire world should be converted to Islam, by force if necessary, and those who don't convert should become *dhimmis* (protected non-Muslim minorities who pay the *djizya* tribute tax), or be killed. There is little ground for compromise with such people. De Villiers is not far from reality when he states that the Islamists' global strategic project is to physically liquidate Christians in the Orient (where they went from 20% of the population a century ago to 2% today) and wipe out any trace of Christianity in the West.[21] In 1999, Giuseppe Bernardini, archbishop of Izmir (Turkey) warned of a 'clear program of expansion and re-conquest' of Europe in a letter to the Synod of European Bishops. He reported the ominous words of a high Muslim representative at an interreligious conference: 'Thanks to your democratic laws we will invade you; thanks to our religious laws we will dominate you',[22] not unlike the warning radical Egyptian preacher Youssef al-Qardawi's issued to Europe in 2002: 'With your democratic laws, we shall colonize you'.[23]

The second challenge, Jihadism, is of a distinctly 'kinetic' nature. Islamization is a long term, mostly non-violent enterprise, a 'soft conquest' that uses the welcome mat of open societies as its weapon of choice, leverages on the sympathies of the liberal left and patiently aggregates gains. Jihadism is universally recognized as a clear and present danger: an uncompromisingly violent enterprise seeking immediate and highly visible results. It expresses itself though lethal force, violence and terror tactics to indiscriminately kill people (including Muslims and the perpetrators themselves if necessary) in order to visibly destabilize, destroy and inflict physical damage. The target of Jihadists is not just open European societies but just about any society they dislike in the world including Muslim societies abroad. They set no limits in what they are willing to do. In Europe, Jihadism works mostly through home grown or infiltrated cells as well as through self-radicalized 'lone wolves' who are mostly losers and petty criminals seduced by a simplistic Islamofascist ideology. Surprisingly, EuroJihadists also include well-educated, well-to-do Euromuslims who are above suspicion (the perpetrators of the 2005 London bombings were perfect examples). This phenomenon is difficult to explain and, in the eyes of many Europeans, it could to turn any Muslim into a potential suspect. Just as with Islamization, the spread of Jihadism has been encouraged by the feeble response of Europe's open societies led by weak governments and judiciaries.

The notion that a clear consensus exists on the evil of Jihadist terrorism needs to be tempered by the reality that there is no clear consensus on its causes. These are many and complex, and yet some Western 'leaders' manage to find a way to pin the blame on Western societies. After the Manchester massacre, French President Macron tweeted that terrorists thrive on poverty.[24] This simplistic statement ignored the fact that many perpetrators are not poor and implies that this is not a religious-ideological struggle but a simple question of income disparity. After the London Bridge massacre a former US Secretary of State reportedly blamed the problems the United Kingdom faces with extremists on its treating Muslims worse than they are treated in the USA.[25] This simplistic and inaccurate statement flies in the face of the reality of permissiveness in the United Kingdom. Such statements also serve to muddy the waters and amount to excusing the perpetrators by accusing the victims of malignant neglect. Controversial Algerian writer Boualem Sansal sees no big difference between Islamism and Jihadism: to him Jihadism is just another face of Islamism.[26] Sansal sees Islamism as a political movement devoted to the 'soft' conquest and transformation of neighbourhoods and territories into sharia-formatted lands, while Jihadism aims at 'punishing' and destroying the hated western civilization. To Sansal, the facts that the Taliban has been routed from Kabul, ISIS is militarily defeated, the Muslim Brotherhood is banned and Al-Qaeda is a shadow of its former self do not change anything. Like the Phoenix, Islamism will always undergo rebirth and transformation, finding a new life and means of expression elsewhere. According to the Algerian writer, multiculturalism— the idea that all cultures, including Islam, have an equal place and can peacefully coexist in a society—is actually perceived by Islamists as an insult rather than a concession. Nothing, in their eyes, can equal Islam, therefore Islam should be pre-eminent, even in multicultural societies.

And the Winner Is...

To Yuval Noah Harari, 'Radial Islam poses no serious threat to the liberal package, because for all their fervour, the zealots don't really understand the world of the twenty-first century [...] radical Islam may appeal to people born and raised in its fold, but it has precious little to offer unemployed Spanish youths or anxious Chinese billionaires.'[27] Harari is right in that, however tolerant Europeans may be in letting the ideology flourish in their midst, a scenario in which scores of non-Muslim Europeans would convert and follow that ideology is unthinkable. Yet Islamism is the strongest ideological current to sweep Europe in a long time and is not going to just disappear any time soon. It is changing Europe, and for the worse. In fact, it is spreading fast within Euromuslim communities mostly due to the 'benign neglect' of European authorities. Sharing her own experience after a friend was seriously injured during the London bombings in September 2017, American (conservative) actress Julienne Davis wrote 'My husband and I saw Britain changing before our eyes. The final straw was during the 2006 Danish Embassy Muhammad cartoon protest, when hundreds of Islamists holding signs like "Behead Infidels" and "Prepare for a New Holocaust," marched unopposed to the Danish Embassy in London.'[28] Europe needs to understand Islamism and its implications and urgently decide what to do about it.

Between the challenges of Islamism and Jihadism, Islamism is actually the more dangerous. It is the more difficult to address within the context of democratic, egalitarian, rule-based European societies. First of all, Islamists do not necessarily openly break laws. They simply operate within existing laws or in grey areas to further their aims. For instance, a German court ruled that the seven Salafist radicals who carried out 'Sharia patrols' in the streets of Wupperthal in 2014 had not broken any laws and they were released.[29] France's Conseil d'Etat (State Council) ruled that the *burkini* (the swimsuit version of the *burka*) was legal, overturning a French mayors' ban. Secondly, every individual gain Islamists make here and there is not life threatening in itself. Patrick Calvar, head of France's domestic security agency (DGSI), stated that he feared radicalization 100 times more than terrorism because of radicalization's potential to disrupt the equilibrium of the country's society.[30] Wearing Islamic garb, illegally blocking traffic on a city street for a group prayer, requesting more mosques or Koranic schools, and demanding the removal of crucifixes are not life threatening per se or clearly outlawed acts. While more and more Europeans are increasingly disturbed by them, feel they are opposed to integration and that they are mostly provocations that fit into a logic of agitation and self-apartheid, they are at a complete loss on how to deal with the challenge they represent. The response of European society is also systematically weakened by its egalitarian principles. In order to outlaw the display of Islamic signs in certain places for instance, the authorities prohibited the display of *any* religious signs—including Christian ones such as crucifixes, despite their having been part of European cultural heritage for two millennia—something that Islamists are likely to interpret as some sort of victory, further emboldening them. In dealing with these delicate issues Europeans have often chosen the path of self-immolation, trampling on their own culture, history and values, oblivious to the fact that, by doing so, they encourage further assertiveness from Islamists.

The Euromuslim population is relatively young and it is paradoxically in the younger generation of Euromuslims that Islamic assertiveness is found to be more intense. In France, an IFOP survey showed the average age of Muslims to be 35.8 against 53 for the rest of the population. Of these, 28% are religious 'ultras'—which, by the way, amounts to more than a million ultras!—and of these radicals half are under 25 years old.[31] Older generations of Muslim migrants, born outside Europe, generally kept their heads down, were content to make a living and practiced a 'light' and inconspicuous version of the faith (if at all). New generations are, by contrast, born on the continent and feel they are just as entitled as any other Europeans to be in Europe, that it is their land too. Yet they often don't feel accepted and form an underclass that does not feel attached to traditional European culture, roots and history. They are paradoxically much more assertive of their faith as a marker of identity than their parents were. It is within this younger generation, men and women, some as young as 16, that radical Islam finds the most traction.

Europe's open societies have had great difficulty recognizing the danger posed by the process of radicalization that affects its Euromuslim minority, let alone doing anything concrete to contain or reverse it. When it comes to dealing with the assertion of separate identities by minority communities, the United Kingdom chose a course that was completely 'laissez faire' while France insisted (or at least pretended to insist) on *laïcité* (secularism). Both policies have been failures in preventing the growing Islamization and estrangement of their Euromuslim communities. Europeans are at a complete loss in dealing with these issues

With a Little Help from My Friends

To the question of why Islamism the ideology has been so successful, Kamel Daoud provides a simple explanation. Just as is the case with other totalitarian ideologies, he explains, Islamism is an all-inclusive system that offers comfortable and simple answers to all questions of existence, from sexuality to business to politics. It offers the illusion of a spiritual life and a place of refuge from rejection by society.[32] To explain Islamism's tactical prowess, the Middle East expert Daniel Pipes gives the example of Turkey in a summer 2013 article for the *Middle East Forum*: 'Although spawned as a totalitarian model, Islamism has shown much greater tactical adaptability than either Fascism or Communism. The latter two ideologies rarely managed to go beyond violence and coercion. But Islamism, led by figures such as Turkey's Premier Recep Tayyip Erdoğan and his Justice and Development Party (AKP), has explored non-revolutionary forms of conquest. Since it was legitimately voted into office in 2002, the AKP gradually has undermined Turkish secularism with remarkable deftness by working within the country's established democratic structures.' When it comes to Europe, Pipes might have added that Islamism makes inroads not so much because it is strong, but because European open societies are weak. The July 2014 Trojan Horse inquiry's report ordered by the British government on radical Islamists' infiltration of Birmingham schools in the United Kingdom uncovered evidence of an attempt to takeover schools and indoctrinate children. It described a 'coordinated, deliberate and sustained action to introduce an intolerant and aggressive Islamist ethos into some schools in the city' and shed light on how radicals operate to extend their influence. An anonymous letter leaked to councils and teaching unions claimed radicals were forcing out non-compliant teachers and governors and that the attempt, 'Left unchecked [...] would confine schoolchildren within an intolerant, inward-looking monoculture that would severely inhibit their participation in the life of modern Britain.' Commenting on the official report on the situation, the *Guardian* wrote 'It will also make uncomfortable reading for Birmingham city council as it accuses local politicians and officials of ignoring evidence of extremism for years, repeatedly failing to support bullied head teachers and putting the need to soothe community tensions ahead of all else.'[33] This was yet another example of how radicals are left free to pursue their agenda. The former head of the Metropolitan Police's counterterrorism command, Peter Clarke, stated that he had not found evidence of terrorism. However, he said there was 'very clear evidence that young people are being encouraged to accept unquestionably a particular hard-line strand of Sunni Islam that raises concerns about their vulnerability to radicalisation in the future [...] Essentially the ideology revealed by this investigation is an intolerant and politicised form of extreme social conservatism that claims to represent and ultimately seeks to control all Muslims. In its separatist assertions and attempts to subvert normal processes it amounts to what is often described as Islamism.' Dame Louise Casey, who led the Trojan Horse Enquiry, recognized that, in the name of diversity, Britain had entirely neglected integration. She also decried the status of many Muslim women in the country, who she said found themselves effectively at the mercy of their husbands and deprived of their basic rights as British citizens.[34]

The tremendous gains made by Islamists in the recent past cannot be explained without the realization that a large proportion of the 'elites' and of the mainstream population of most European countries is made of people (including but not limited to the liberal left) who strongly believe in a very open and multicultural multi-ethnic society and do not necessarily perceive Islamization as a threat. In fact, to some of them such as Jade Lindgaard, co-president of French online news outlet Mediapart, the real menace to society is not Islamism but Islamophobia.[35] Many from Europe's liberal left have been advocating a quasi-complete opening of frontiers to immigration and some such as Zoe Desbureaux (member of parliament for France's far-left movement, France Insoumise) consider Jihadists as martyrs and are openly apologists for their actions.[36] To French journalist Judith Waintraub, there exists in France a very influential and successful 'Islamosphere' made of 'agents of influence' including intellectuals, politicians and journalists. For these people, the Muslim is the new oppressed, whom they have a duty to defend against the white man, his oppressor.[37] Not always, but in some cases, these agents of influence help spread Islamism even among the youth. How else can we characterize the following examples provided by former French headmaster Bernard Ravet? First, authorities in Marseille inaugurated a new mosque of 'tabligh obedience', the stated objective of which is to re-islamicize the people. Secondly, the state contracted for the creation of a private Islamic college in order to make it easier for families to put their veiled daughters in an Islamic school environment?[38] The popular perception that ruling elites are biased in favour of minorities is not helped by the callousness these elites sometimes show their own citizens: bereaved families of victims of the December 2016 terror attack in Germany were reportedly aghast at their 'bureaucratic' treatment by the German authorities and furious that it took one year for Chancellor Angela Merkel to decide to see them.[39]

In the absence of a clear national consensus on the nature and extent of the threat posed by Islamism, there can result little political will to actually contain the ideology, let alone roll back its gains. The threat of Jihadism is, on the other hand, paradoxically 'easier' to address in terms of political will, because the Jihadists' use of violence as their chosen means of expression makes them natural outlaws in everybody's eyes.

Contrary to what happens with Islamization there is a national consensus to do something about Jihadism although the effectiveness of the response is greatly curtailed by restrictive self-imposed rules of the game and an over-lenient judiciary. In Europe, Jihadists can win battles but at the end of the day, as horrific as terror attacks may be, the aggregate number of victims on European soil so far remains minuscule. In Europe, Jihadists can't defeat an army or occupy a city, so they can't possibly win the war because, as bad as it gets, their action will consist of isolated incidents (although the threat of biological and other weapons of mass destruction is real and ISIS reportedly advocated the poisoning of food in grocery stores in Europe and the USA).[40] Jihadists win in capturing the headlines, in terrorizing the population and forcing it to change its way of life, and in destabilizing society. As I wrote in 2012, 'an exasperated mainstream comes to associate all immigrants with the radicals, threatening the future cohesiveness of Europe's multi-ethnic societies'.[41] Islamism, on the other hand, can score far more substantial victories since a lack of any consensus recognizing it as a serious threat means Europeans may continue doing nothing or very little about it. Yet, according to Daniel Pipes, it can be defeated: 'The Islamists are on the march today, but their ascendance is recent and offers no guarantees of longevity. Indeed, like other radical utopian ideologies, Islamism will lose its appeal and decline in power. Certainly the 2009 and 2013 revolts against Islamist regimes in Iran and Egypt, respectively, point in that direction.'[42]

Allons enfants...but Where?

France deserves special consideration as it holds an unenviable position, together with the United Kingdom, at the top of the radicals' Islamization drive and the Jihadists' target list. More arrests for religion-inspired terrorism took place in in 2015 in France than in the next five most affected EU countries combined.[43] A 2016 Ipsos poll showed that a majority of French people considered that they don't feel as much at home in France today as they used to.[44] A similar poll taken a year later showed the situation had distinctly worsened, with 65% of the respondents saying that there are too many foreigners in France, 60% stating that Islam as a religion is incompatible with France's values and 61% complaining that immigrants do not make efforts to integrate into French society.[45] For Patrick Calvar, who headed France's domestic intelligence agency, the writing on the wall was clear: 'We are on the verge of a civil war. I think this confrontation is going to happen.'[46] The *Wall Street Journal* reported the presence of an estimated 15,000 Salafists among France's 7 million or so Muslims, 'whose radical-fundamentalist creed dominates many of the predominantly Muslim housing projects at the edges of cities such as Paris, Nice or Lyon. Their preachers call for a civil war, with all Muslims tasked to wipe out the miscreants down the street.'[47] According to leading daily *Le Figaro*, France has emerged from 70 years of peace and an increasingly large number of citizens do not see a clear separation between Islam (the religion) and Islamism (the radical ideology).[48] To many observers, this makes a civil war in France inevitable at some point.[49] Such dark predictions will hopefully not come true but they cannot be taken lightly. In Eric Zemmour's view, the history of France is first of all a history of civil wars and the recent massive influx of Islam, opposed to the existing order, will inevitably lead to a civil war-type conflict.[50] To some analysts, the causes for this sorry state of affairs are found in a combination of the country's colonial past, its ubiquitous presence at the forefront of the West's projection of military power in the Middle East and Africa and its failed integration policies. This simplistic view does not entirely convince in light of the fact that other European countries that don't meet these criteria, such as Germany, Sweden or Finland, have also been the target of Jihadists.[51] Other causes have been variously cited, such as the passivity of French authorities, the sheer size of the Euromuslim minority (Europe's largest, variously estimated to number close to 4, 6 or 7 million—reflecting the fact that in France statistics based on religion or ethnicity have been illegal),[52] and the fact that this minority is mostly of North African origin, allegedly a more restless lot than, say, Germany's Turks.[53] The question of why some European countries, such as Ireland or Switzerland, are much less at risk of terror attacks than Portugal, for instance, itself much less at risk than, say, France or the United Kingdom, kept nagging journalist Bonnie Kristian.[54] According to Robin Simcox, a national security expert at the Heritage Foundation who probed for answers, the likelihood of terror attacks directly correlates with the relative and absolute size of the minority Muslim population in a country. Switzerland, Ireland, Portugal, and Norway's combined Muslim population is probably something just over 600,000, while in the United Kingdom, France, and Germany the combined figure is around 13 million. According to Bonnie Kristian's July 2017 article in *The Week*, 'there is a very large disparity in the number of people groups like ISIS can target for potential recruitment, as compared with somewhere like Portugal, where the Muslim population is nominal'. Kristian added that according to The Brookings Institution's Jonathan Laurence the key 'is whether or not you have second-, third-generation migrant-origin communities large enough for there to exist some kind of critical mass, where the kind of subculture could develop that at the very margins you find teens or young men in their 20s willing' to fight for ISIS at home or abroad. Kristian reported that The Cato Institute's Trevor Thrall favoured instead the idea that 'the pattern of attacks by ISIS, or ISIS-inspired attacks, follows reasonably closely with how involved those European countries have been in the U.S.-led coalition's counter-terrorism efforts in the Middle East [...] the countries that have suffered the most recently are the countries that had the most troops'. A Colonial past, an interventionist foreign policy, the size of the minority population: all of these factors play a role to some extent. Yet, in the case of France there is also something more fundamental at play that has to do with how the French view themselves and their country today, a case that holds a lesson for the rest of Europe.

Driven by the new post-modern ideology that considers 'national identity' a sin that contravenes its universalist and egalitarian principles, the French themselves have, in the recent past, embarked on a systematic debasement and dismantling of their own culture and national identity. In accordance with the egalitarian principles of multiculturalism, all cultures, indigenous as well as imported, need to be held on an equal footing, ergo the pre-eminence of French culture *in France itself* needs to be toned down in order to make place for the minority's culture. A by-product of this is the process of 'reverse integration' by which it is the host society itself that undergoes changes in order to adapt to the requirements of the minority. The pride bordering on chauvinism the French used to display for their immense historical and cultural heritage has largely given way to a feeling of rejection, if not shame, conveyed by 'elites' from the mainstream left and right alike. Eric Bésson, former minister of national identity under Nicolas Sarkozy's centre-right government, stated that France was neither a people nor a language, nor a territory: it is an aggregate of peoples who want to live together.[55] This view was echoed by Emmanuel Macron, former minister of the economy in the socialist Hollande government. As a top contender in France's 2017 presidential election (which he won), he said 'There is no French culture. There is a culture in France, and it is diverse.'[56] French essayist Eric Zemmour laments that France is the country that has been the most methodically destroyed as a nation.[57] Under attack from the French themselves, the country's national historical narrative has lost its traction with the population and may soon become a museum curiosity. History has been the object of manipulation by the authorities in an effort to de-nationalize the country's identity and pretend that the minority has always been part of the country's history, culture and social fabric. In other words, some French themselves, at the highest level, from right and left alike, are telling you there is no such thing as French culture and identity anymore and that France does not have any Christian roots. This implies that the country is reduced to a geographic area in which various communities happen to live, administered by a technocratic government. 2017 presidential candidate and former minister of national education, François Fillon, lamented that 'ideologues' have been rewriting history books to 'impose their view of society',[58] so that the new official historical narrative becomes, in the words of De Villiers 'Islamo-compatible'. This accommodating revisionism can take almost comical forms. In one example, complaints were made about the removal from history schoolbooks of, among others, the name of Charles Martel, who defeated the moors in Poitiers in 732.[59] In another, socialist Paris mayor Anne Hidalgo declared that Ramadan was a traditional French celebration,[60] oblivious to the fact that Ramadan, one of the five pillars of the Islamic faith, is not a celebration but a personal fasting sacrifice and has never been part of French cultural heritage. Tariq Ramadan, a famous preacher and professor, who happens to be the grandson of Hassan al-Banna (founder of the Muslim Brotherhood), provided a clear indication of where French culture and society may be heading under the impulse of its 'elites': 'France's culture is now Muslim. Islam is a French religion and the French language is a language of Islam.'[61] To De Villiers, two societies are now contending

French soil, one made of the old, disintegrating nation, and the other made of the newcomers who are carrying their own civilization with them and do not intend to cede anything.[62] While one cannot talk of cultural self-immolation in Germany to nearly the extent it exists in France, a debate regarding the pre-eminence of *Leitkultur* (host society's dominant culture) is ongoing in the country. *Leitkultur* was advocated by the likes of Interior Minister Thomas de Maizière, who famously said 'We don't "do" the burka'. The liberal left establishment, including Greens and SPD (Social Democrats), flatly oppose the concept of *Leitkultur*, despite the fact that more than half of Germans think their country is in need of a *Leitkultur*, as evidenced by a Focus newsmagazine survey.[63] France is not the only place were Europeans place egalitarian principles ahead of the host society's cultural pre-eminence.

Instead of promoting social cohesiveness, the systematic self-immolation of the country's national identity has had the opposite effect. It is an important and overlooked cause of the disintegration of French society. The country is fragmenting into various separate groups, says essayist Emmanuel Todd.[64] France may, sadly, be the leading candidate in Europe for a serious breakdown of law and order. Violence, especially at school and against police, firemen and the military, is on the rise. The country was subjected to waves of demonstrations by its over-stretched police forces. They were fed up with arresting the same perpetrators time and again only for them to be released once more by an over-lenient judiciary and fed-up with seeing their patrol cars systematically ambushed and attacked—sometimes with deadly force—in some neighbourhoods. This is testimony to how fast the imprint of the state is receding. 'Everything that represents state institutions [...] is now subjected to violence based on essentially sectarian and sometimes ethnic excesses, fuelled by an incredible hatred of our country. We must be blind or unconscious not to feel concern for national cohesion', said Thibaud de Montbrial, a lawyer and expert on terrorism.[65] Unsurprisingly, suicides have been on the rise among overstretched, overworked and underpaid police and security forces in France. During a single week in November 2017, a total of seven officers committed suicide.[66]

It all boils down to a simple question: why should the minority aspire to French identity and culture if the mainstream French themselves despise this identity and culture? The result of this effort by the French themselves to discredit their own heritage perversely promotes the self-ghettoization of the minority, which has no option but to look within itself and its own origins to seek identity and cultural markers: an open invitation to the Islamists. In light of all this, can one be surprised that the French national anthem was booed a few years ago at the main stadium in Paris by French citizens of Arab origin? The more France loses its sense of itself and its self-respect, the more an identity vacuum is created, which the most assertive elements of its Islamist subset strive to fill with their own alternative identity and values which are clear, simple and uncompromising, and so particularly appealing to the simple minds of the young. According to political journalist Ed West, 'Radical Islamism thrives in the absence of other identities, which is why it is especially prevalent among second-generation migrants, who are more likely to feel alienated and torn between cultures [...] Religion provides the comfort of certainty, something politicians have failed to see because they have assumed that particular Western values are universal or inevitable, when they are actually quite unusual and fragile.'[67]

The excessive tolerance and leniency shown by French authorities towards the *dérives communautaristes* (misdeeds perpetrated by communities) further encourages the assertion of this separate identity, driving a vicious spiral. Kamel Daoud decries the short sightedness and complacency of French elites towards Islamism, adding that they ignore or minimize the totalitarian dimension of this ideology.[68] Making room for a minority is one thing but the self-destruction of a country's national identity is another. This will logically lead to a profound identity crisis and perversely promote cleavage between host society and minority. Interestingly, the European Project has also contributed to the weakening of national identities. Broadly speaking, the supra-national and integrative nature of the European Project, together with the globalization drive that followed decades later, inevitably came at the expense of the national identity of individual countries. While the appeal of national identity broadly declined everywhere, a strong European identity failed to materialize, resulting in a vacuum that lowered any defence mechanisms countries had against encroachments on their individual national identities. No wonder the Islamist narrative, with its strong and simple identity markers and philosophy, has taken so well within minorities in Europe, especially among the young.

The Price of Moderation

Euromuslims in general are increasingly perceived by many Europeans as ambivalent about, if not siding with radicals, a dangerous development. Granted, nobody knows for sure where the *banlieues* stand regarding Bataclan or Nice and nobody dares to openly ask. A 2016 survey by Institut Montaigne showed that the percentage of Muslims in France who consider Sharia law to be above the country's secular laws is a significant 29%.[69] Yet, as earlier pointed out, Euromuslims are by and large moderate. Most of them are genuinely unhappy about Europe's accommodating stance towards radicals and would be the first to cheer a clear toughening of governments' attitudes. Asked what he thought of the French authorities' decision to start shutting down Salafist mosques in the aftermath of the Paris attacks, Tareq Oubrou, the moderate Imam of Bordeaux, replied 'What have they been waiting for?'[70]

Among my own friends are Muslims, who are perfectly integrated in European mainstream society. They are doctors, teachers, bank employees etc., they work hard, pay taxes and contribute to society, just like any other European. They dress like any European and want their children to have a good education and a good future. Their main concern is employment.[71] They do not renege on their roots and take pride in their ancestry, yet they embrace the society they chose to live in. They are moderate in that they hold little interest in religious matters (if any) or practice a light and apolitical version of their faith, without assertiveness. Make no mistake: most Muslims in Europe are like that. In fact, 76% of them are like that, according to a Europe-wide poll taken in 2016.[72] These people are, however, caught between a rock and a hard place. 40% of them say they are regularly confronted with discrimination or even violence, but there is more. On one side the mainstream European population is increasingly suspicious of them, on the other the community they belong to is getting increasingly radicalized. Sonia Mabrouk speaks of moderates being trapped: if they keep quiet then they are perceived by mainstream Europeans to be sympathizers of radicalism and if they make their voices heard these same Europeans don't pay attention to what they say and radicals within their own community vilify them.[73] The tragedy for these moderates is that they, and especially their children, constitute prime targets in the eyes of Islamists, who consider moderates a flock gone astray, in need of 'reformatting', if not outright 'traitors' to the Islamic cause. Within Euromuslim communities, such as in the French *banlieues*, peer pressure to join the ranks of the Islamicized is real and relentless.[74] European authorities, as usual in denial, do not recognize the danger and do little to protect moderates from contagion or enlist them in the struggle against radicals. Moderates, who could have been Europe's best asset in the common struggle against Islamism and Jihadism because they form, after all, the community in which the radicals have to live and operate, are essentially left to their own devices in facing Islamists. To Middle East expert Daniel Pipes, 'Non-Muslims should support moderate and Westernizing anti-Islamists. Such figures are weak and fractured today and face a daunting task, but they do exist, and they represent the only hope for defeating the menace of global Jihad and Islamic supremacism, then replacing it with an Islam that does not threaten civilization.'[75] On the other hand many Europeans feel that moderate Muslims have been pretending for too long that they are not concerned by the worsening radicalization or that they are just victims. Moderates need to show that they are part of the solution lest they be perceived as being part of the problem. They need to take a visible and firm stand and become active partners in finding solutions, ideally taking the lead in eradicating religious extremism from their midst. For Hakim El Karoui, a consultant with Institut Montaigne, Muslims should mobilize against religious fundamentalism and promote the development of a spiritual Islam that frees itself from political Islam.[76] Yet, for moderates to undertake this difficult and dangerous task by themselves without the full support of governments is unrealistic.

Conversations with moderate Muslims attest to the scary reality of their lives within their communities. Their coercion is a high priority on the agenda of the Islamists. A girl who does not wear a veil is often ostracized and will have difficulty marrying within her community. Islamists have actually been paying women to wear the veil and I know of one receiving a hefty 700 euros per month from her mosque's imam to wear it at all times when outside home: the type of offer few can afford to refuse. The young son of another Muslim friend, who eats pork and does not practice Ramadan has been ostracized by fellow Muslim students. Malleable children remain primary targets. The biggest fear of moderate Muslim parents in Europe today is not the ascent of far-right political parties: it is that their children will fall prey to radicals. Nadia Remadna is a Muslim mother and author of *How I Saved My Children*, a book that provides 'a harrowing account of her struggle to raise her children alone in a French suburb where she says ultra-religious groups are trying to "take power"'.[77] She summarized the tragic situation in no uncertain terms: 'Before, we mothers were afraid of our kids getting into juvenile delinquency, but now we are petrified they will become terrorists.'[78] Sadly, concerned parents such as Remadna expect little help from local government officials whom she accuses of turning a blind eye… Tunisian-born Samia Maktouf, a Paris-based lawyer, seeks government aid for the families of victims of terrorism and recently published a book the title of which translates as 'I shall defend life as much as you preach death' has been called an apostate by Islamists and has been the object of death threats.[79] Everywhere moderate Muslims, even moderate religious leaders, are under pressure and worried about radicals

Islamists make inroads because they are organized, ruthless, relentless and because the authorities by and large let them do what they please. Islamists are in the driving seat and often successful in reaching out to moderates and turning them into Islamicized Euromuslims, if not radicals. Former French Prime Minister Manuel Valls recognized publicly that radical Islamists were winning the ideological and cultural battle in France.[80] As a consequence of these gains, the cleavage between the mainstream population and the minority gets wider and the proportion of Islamists and radicals within the minority increases, a vicious cycle that bodes ill. Jews have recently been emigrating from France, their *Alyah* often motivated by security concerns for themselves and their families. This is understandable, considering that violent incidents against Jews have been on the rise in France and all over Europe in recent years, perpetrated by hooligans, far-right and far-left extremist, as well as by radical Muslims.[81] Islamization inevitably begets anti-semitism. You can have Islamists or you can have Jews, but you can't have both. In an article entitled 'Muslim Anti-Semitism Threatens France's Democracy', Newsweek reported that the brother of Mohamed

Merah (who killed three Jewish schoolchildren, as well as soldiers and a teacher in France in 2012) said that 'In the Merah household, we were brought up with hating Jews, the hatred of everything that was not Muslim.' He added that, when the medical examiner brought to his family the body of his brother, 'People came over. They cried tears of joy. They said that he had brought France to its knees. That he did well. Their only regret was that he had not killed more Jewish children.'[82] According to this report, 'The Merah trial exposed a reality in France: anti-Semitic roots run deep within some elements of the French Muslim community [...] the problem is spreading' and 'French anti-Semitism is distinguished in Europe by its level of violence, ranging from attacks to abductions and even to murders.' In France's *banlieues*, more than one anti-Semitic incident a day has taken place on average between 2005 and 2015.[83] Virulent anti-semitism is to be expected from Islamists, encouraged by 'elites' who have turned a blind eye. What I didn't expect at all, though, was to find out in conversations with some moderate *Muslim* families that they are now considering France to be too far down the path of Islamization, and spoke of emigrating to countries where their children would not be at risk of being preyed on by radicals. While still rare, such instances are a signal of the predicament some moderates find themselves in.

Wrong Question

Questions have been raised as to whether there is a fundamental incompatibility between Islam and modern Europe. At one end of the spectrum is De Villiers, for whom there may be moderate Muslims but there is no moderate Islam. He believes Islam itself cannot be modified or reformed, it is simply incompatible with and cannot adapt itself to Europe's open societies and a Muslim considers his religion (and not the country he lives in) as his homeland.[84] This view is echoed by the likes of Zineb El-Rhazoui whose controversial manifesto 'Destroy Islamic Fascism' stated that 'those that think that Islam has nothing to do with terrorism are ignorant.'[85] For the likes of Portuguese master storyteller José Rodrigues dos Santos—who, all the way back in 2009 gave a realistic overview of the causes and effects of Islamic radicalism in his thriller *The Wrath of God*—the notion of the forceful conquest and conversion of infidel lands is historically part of Islam the religion and embedded in its scriptures. Dos Santos pointed out in an interview for news agency Lusa that '60% of the Koran are orders for war and recalled words from the prophet Muhammad: "I declare war on everyone until everyone says Allah is the only God and I am His prophet".' He recognized that 'there is also a side to it [Islam] that is never shown to us, Westerners. That unknown side, the calls for war.'[86]

It is historically undeniable that Islam expanded by conquest, motivated by a desire to bring the entire world under its fold. But didn't Christianity do the same centuries ago? Today's increasingly popular narrative according to which Islam as a religion is, in the context of the twenty-first century, inherently violent, rests in large part on the idea that, since the perpetrators of Jihadist terrorist acts and the promoters of radicalization are Muslim, then all Muslims are Jihadists or radicals: a flawed logic. This simplistic narrative is also counterproductive because it precludes the possibility of any dialogue, even with the millions of moderate Muslims living in Europe. It is also a reductive fallacy (a visit to Indonesia, the world's largest Muslim country, home of some of the nicest people one can meet, will convince anyone of this) that ignores the centuries-long horrors Europeans inflicted each other during the Inquisition or perpetrated in faraway lands in the name of Christ, as well as the history of endless and bloody intra-European wars of religion, some of which took place in our lifetimes in the Balkans and Ireland. According to this yardstick the Christian religion would also be a violent cult, even if Christian scriptures don't call for violence. Anyway, this book is not about theology, nor is it about the comparative merits of various religions. I am not naively saying here that Islam is a peaceful religion that happens to be hijacked by violent deviant radicals. My aim is to try to understand what is going on around us and whether solutions can be found to the challenges confronting us today. The truth is that religions have, throughout millennia of human history, been interpreted in many ways and used and abused by zealots and by the power-thirsty, devoid of scruples.

The question of the compatibility of Islam with Europe's open societies is not particularly useful. First of all, it ignores realities on the ground. Not only are there moderate Euromuslims but the majority of them, as we pointed out earlier, is actually moderate. Consequently, the problem cannot logically be Islam itself despite its 'content'. Some other forces must be at work. Secondly, the question amounts to useless speculation because, assuming one 'demonstrates' that Islam is incompatible with modern Europe, then what? Would all Muslims be deported? Would they be forced into mass apostasy? Let us instead take a pragmatic approach. The real issue is instead Islamism, the radical ideology sweeping through the Euromuslim population, due in great part to the carelessness of weak European societies and their hopeless and derelict 'elites'. The question should instead be: 'Is Islamism compatible with Europe's open societies?' And the answer, this time, is clearly 'no'. 'Radical Islam is the problem, but moderate Islam is the solution', says Daniel Pipes. More importantly, he adds that, 'the Islamists are on the march today, but their ascendance is recent and offers no guarantees of longevity. Indeed, like other radical utopian ideologies, Islamism will lose its appeal and decline in power.' Pipes warns that non-Muslims should resist 'all forms of Islamism—not just the brutal extremism of an Osama bin Laden, but also the stealthy, lawful, political movements [...] Whoever values free speech, equality before the law, and other human rights denied or diminished by Sharia must consistently oppose any hint of Islamism.'[87] Quanta A. Ahmed, an American Muslim engaged in the fight against Islamism in the USA complained that: 'We have failed to dismantle Islamism, the ideology that delivered 9/11, because we have been unable to examine and disable Islamism through frank speech. Dismantling Islamism demands we distinguish Islam the religion, from Islamism the totalitarian ideology.'[88] If no distinction is made between Islam—the religion—and Islamism—the ideology of conquest—then the ultimate outcome can only be total confrontation or submission, not particularly desirable outcomes, to say the least. The distinction between Islam and Islamism may seem to be a mere question of semantics but it is not. The distinction is central to the search for solutions aimed at ensuring the peaceful coexistence of established Euromuslim communities with western societies in the long term.

If, as we are saying here, it is the Islamist ideology that should be fought tooth and nail, the response from a weak Europe in denial has been wanting. The response of the Euromuslim community in general has also been wanting. Following the Manchester terror attack, British Prime Minister Theresa May issued a famously tough statement:

> There is [...] far too much tolerance of extremism in our country. So we need to become far more robust in identifying it and stamping it out across the public sector and across society. That will require some difficult, and often embarrassing, conversations [...] The whole of our country needs to take on this extremism, and we need to live our lives not in a series of separated, segregated communities but as one truly United Kingdom.

to which the Muslim Council of Britain responded with words thus paraphrased by *The Economist*:

> If you want a broad conversation about ideology and culture, even an embarrassing one, let's have one. But it won't be the sort of conversation that you want or expect. You want to talk about imams with hardline ideas about gender, sexuality and self-segregation by Muslims, because you think all that is a gateway to terrorism. Well, we want to talk about Muslim grievances, including those over British foreign policy.[89]

Such references to alleged foreign policy misdeeds by European governments are counterproductive and contribute to the mistrust the mainstream population feels towards the minority. These references are inevitably interpreted as attempts at justifying extremism at home in the name of disagreements over government actions abroad. They inevitably smack of allegiance to a foreign, inimical cause or community rather than to the home country. However right or wrong the views of the minority may be when it comes to the actions and policies of European governments abroad, in most of Europe the absence of prompt, highly visible and unqualified condemnations of terror attacks by the Euromuslim community—or the qualifications attached to such condemnations—contribute to the distrust felt by most Europeans towards the minority.

Free Radicals

Europe has for a long time looked the other way while forces of radicalization have been at work within its societies, enabling the emergence of a radical 'minority of the minority'. Blinded by an ultra-liberal ideology, governments, the judiciary and the media have seen to it that astonishing levels of passivity and leniency have been reached in facing Islamists. *The Economist* pointed out that 'most British Muslims abhor extremism, but a distinct minority is ambivalent'—an alarming statement—and decried the 'blind eye turned by local authorities to the recent infiltration of some Birmingham schools by Islamists'.[90] Demands by some Islamists to be subjected to sharia law rather than to the secular laws of the host country, perhaps the most extreme instance of a drive for a separate *de jure* status, have been generally resisted. Yet, in Britain more than 85 sharia courts are now officially attached to mosques, dealing mostly with family rights. This has prompted 'growing concerns that Britain's sharia courts are fostering extremism, undermining women's and human rights and creating a parallel justice system whose basic principles conflict with the law of the land.'[91] It has been pointed out that 'as elements of Sharia crept into the legal framework of various European countries', a trend implicitly recognized even by the archbishop of Canterbury, 'it suddenly seemed as though some of the absolute bases of Western civilization were being offered up for negotiation.'[92] In Germany, courts have tolerated some child marriages among refugees despite serious misgivings, though a law was subsequently debated to prevent them.[93] In France sharia effectively rules certain neighbourhoods. The veil, *burka*, and more recently the controversial *burkini*—the swimwear version of the *burka*—are increasingly perceived to be political statements, markers of a separate identity in the quest for a separate community space. Germany recently adopted a law prohibiting government employees to wear the veil at work, yet, like other European countries, could not bring itself to prohibiting it in public spaces.[94] As earlier pointed out, the drive by various French mayors to prohibit the *burkini* in the summer of 2016 was overturned higher in the government by the Conseil d'Etat.[95] This granted Islamists an easy victory, despite Prime Minister Manuel Valls himself having declared that the *burkini* and the veil were symbols of the 'enslavement of women',[96] and despite the opposition of 64% of the French population to the authorization of the *burkini*.[97] This same State Council, by the way, shot down a proposed law that would have made it illegal to consult Jihadist websites.[98] To French philosopher Luc Ferry, the *burkini* was not the result of any religious obligation but a recent invention by Islamists to push the limits in their drive to Islamicize society and, as such, should be prohibited.[99] Ferry decried a

'Munich pacifism' which hides 'hatred for liberal democracies' under the guise of tolerance.[100] In Strasbourg, the European Court of Human Rights decided in 2017 against Muslim women who had appealed to it in in their fight against a Belgian law prohibiting them from wearing the *niqab* in public areas, perhaps a sign that the limits of tolerance had been reached.[101] The judiciary has similarly shown great reluctance to act decisively. Leniency towards radicals has often been the norm. For instance it took 20 years for British authorities to decide to arrest Anjem Choudary, a notorious hate preacher who had been openly advocating Jihadism in the United Kingdom.[102]

Thousands of mosques exist all over Europe, many of which have, for years, been known to be financed by Islamic regimes abroad. Some have been known for a long time to be hotbeds of radicalization, a reality that continues thanks to the cavalier attitude of European authorities. As earlier pointed out, known radical preachers have often enjoyed a degree of freedom in Europe that they wouldn't dream of in their original countries. Paraphrasing former French Prime Minister Manuel Valls, President Emmanuel Macron stated that, in France, radical Islam has made inroads because the state has effectively stepped down.[103] Everywhere in Europe, institutional weakness has willingly and knowingly enabled a hostile ideology to flourish. Prisons have become recruiting and indoctrination grounds for Jihadists with little response from the authorities. In Brussels, about one kilometre from the seat of Europe's parliament and 500 metres from the stock exchange building, an entire city district called Molenbeek was known for a long time as 'Jihad central' because it harboured legions of radical Islamists, free to move around and proselytize. Among others, all of the following came from Molenbeek: Hassan El Haski, mastermind of the 2004 Madrid bombings that left 194 people dead; Mehdi Nemmouche, who killed four at the Jewish Museum in Bruxelles; Amedy Coulibaly, who killed a policewoman and four people at a Jewish market in Paris; and some of the perpetrators of the November 2015 massacre in Paris.[104] Salah Abdeslam, one of the perpetrators of the November 2016 Paris, attacks hid in Molenbeek for more than four months before he was arrested.[105] In France, more than 10,000 radicals labelled 'S' by the authorities—the famous '*fichés S*' who are recognized as posing a security threat—remain, by and large, free to move around. The police acknowledges that it does not have the means to keep a constant eye on them. Astonishingly, central authorities have so far refused to inform any mayors of the identity of *fichés S* radicals living in their areas.[106] A known dangerous radical could be working in a school, in public transportation or at the post office: a ticking human bomb in the midst of the local population. Yet, the government deems that neither the local authorities nor the population are entitled to know about it in order to protect the civil liberties of this known radical. Karim Cheurfi, was known to France's security services from 2016 as a radical who did prison time. He was seeking weapons to kill policemen and reportedly sought to get in touch with ISIS operatives and was interrogated and released in January 2017 and again in April for lack of proof. Two weeks later he did exactly what he had promised to do: he killed a policeman on the Champs Elysées.[107] Cheurfi was not a *fiché S* but had the dubious distinction of being on a list of 15,000 individuals that the DGSI security services kept of radicals susceptible to becoming terrorists. He was, in other words, a known serious potential threat yet remained free. Adam Djaziri—who died in a failed terrorist attack on the Champs Elysées in June 2017—was not only another *fiché S*, a known dangerous radical free to roam around, he also had a valid licence to carry firearms (which was renewed in February 2017) and actively practiced at a shooting range, a fact known by the police. It was later established that more than 100 *fichés S* radicals actually possessed valid licences to carry firearms. It was only in August 2017 that a law was passed allowing officials who grant firearms permits to access information as to whether the person asking for one is a *fiché S*.[108] Not that the absence of a licence would deter a radical from carrying weapons but this shows, once more, the cavalier attitude and astonishing level of carelessness and incompetence among the authorities. Since most radicals enjoy freedom of movement and can't be kept under surveillance at all times, preventing a terrorist incident sometimes boils down to sheer luck. One of the five suspects arrested for placing gasoline doused gas canisters connected to a mobile phone-activated detonator at the entrance of a building in Paris in October 2017 was (once more) a radical known by security services, who nonetheless was free.[109] The canisters, which could have created a huge explosion with many victims, were discovered by pure chance by a person living in the building.

In the United Kingdom a documentary entitled *The Jihadis Next Door* was aired on Channel 4 in 2016, showing bearded radicals praying besides a black ISIS flag in the manicured Regent's Park in central London. They admonish a policemen who asks them questions. This would be astonishing in itself were it not for the fact that among the radicals was one Khuram Butt, a 27-year-old British citizen of Pakistani origin who was subsequently killed while participating in the London Bridge terror attack that left seven dead and 48 wounded.[110] British security services were reportedly warned five times (including by people from his own community) about the danger posed by Salman Abedi, who perpetrated the attack in Manchester that left 22 people dead in June 2017, yet the authorities chose to do nothing.[111] This is despite the fact that the British security services (MI5 for domestic intelligence, MI6 for foreign intelligence, and Scotland Yard and other police forces) are considered among the best and most integrated in Europe as well as possibly the most advanced when it comes to the detection and prevention of radicalization. The United Kingdom's interior ministry estimates that there are more than 3000 dangerous radicals in the country, of whom 500 are estimated to be ready to attack at any time, according to a 2014 report by The Guardian. Scotland Yard's anti-terrorism boss, Mark Rowley, spoke of 20,000 radicals having been on the police's radar screen.[112] In Germany, the Bundesverfassungsschutz domestic intelligence agency estimates the number of Islamists in the country at 40,000, of which over 9000 are ultra-radical Salafists. Among these, those estimated to pose a serious threat of terrorism range from 500[113] to more than 1600[114] (in May 2017, Germany's Federal Criminal Police Office (BKA) revealed that the number of people in Germany believed to be capable of carrying out a terror attack had quadrupled since the start of the war in Syria).[115] Yet these people remain by and large free to move around while the number of policemen tasked to keep an eye on them remains wholly inadequate at fewer than 3000. Absurdly, inside the German security service, the man responsible for monitoring Islamists turned out to be a mole: a convert to Islam who had reportedly been warning radicals of police operations until his arrest in late 2016.[116] German security services had, for a while, been keeping an eye on Anis Amri, a young Tunisian who had done jail time in Italy, was labelled a 'dangerous Islamist', moved to Germany, was arrested on possession of false documents, then released. Subsequently re-arrested, his deportation procedure could not be completed since Tunisian authorities did not provide necessary documents for his deportation in a timely fashion. Constrained by legal regulations limiting preventive detention time, German police released him and security services lost track of him.[117] He subsequently killed 12 people and wounded 48 at the Breitscheidplatz Christmas market in Berlin on 19 December 2016. All this shows how sadly inadequate the system can be in confronting known serious threats. The cavalier attitude of German authorities towards security threats has been variously attributed to the fact that the country thought itself immune from Jihadist violence (its well-publicized *Willkommenskultur* and the absence of German military intervention in the Middle East probably fed this illusion) to the fact that Germans place individual freedoms above anything else, thus acting as a restraint on security forces (German security services notoriously depend in great measure on the help of their foreign counterparts). These weaknesses are nothing new. The 'Hamburg cell' played a key role in preparing the 9/11 attack in New York and in recent times more than 800 German radicals went to join Jihad in Syria.[118] That Salafism had largely contaminated Catalonia, the Spanish region where car ramming attacks took place in Barcelona and Cambrils leaving 15 dead and 120 injured, was a widely known fact for years. A 2007 report written by the US ambassador to Spain, Eduardo Aguirre, leaked by Wikileaks warned that: 'Spanish and American authorities have identified Catalonia as the largest Mediterranean centre for Islamist radical activity.'[119]

In most of Europe not only are known dangerous radicals free to move around, they are sometimes astonishingly free to publicly boast their allegiance to known terrorist organizations and to proselytize. Their numbers are, moreover, simply overwhelming and are increasing every day. In France, the number of radicals is estimated to have grown by 60% in less than two years.[120] To these one must add the most radical, dangerous and foreign-trained elements. In the summer of 2017, the Interior Ministry estimated that 217 combat-trained French Jihadists had come back from Syria and Iraq.[121] Jihadist terrorism in Europe is worsening and will not disappear overnight. According to Yves Trotignon, former Jihadism specialist with the French security service (DGSE)—DGSE, or *Direction Generale de la Sécurité Exterieure* is the French security service dealing with threats from abroad while DGSI, or *Direction Generale de la Sécurité Interieure* deals with internal threats—more and more terrorist attacks will escape being detected by the authorities and the menace from Jihadist terrorism is not likely to subside in Europe for two or three generations at the very least.¹²² Europe is in for a rough ride. Given the seriousness of the situation, it is difficult to characterize the attitude of European authorities in confronting domestic terrorism as something other than a mix of denial, irresponsibility, carelessness and incompetence. It is too easy to just blame security forces, who are overstretched and tasked with an impossible job under increasingly severe budget constraints. The fault mainly resides in the lack of political courage among the ruling classes to admit the extent of the problem, let alone confront it. Yet, in a democratic system, politicians need to listen to the people in order to keep their jobs. Notably lacking here is any political pressure from a general population too comfortable in its apathy. Following the August 2017 terror attacks in Barcelona and Cambrils, a large demonstration was organized in Barcelona to 'protest against terrorism'. Neither the authorities nor the people could bring themselves to call the enemy, radical Islam, by its real name. There was no demonstration against radical Islam. To them, the enemy was terrorism—which is a form of warfare—and not the ideology moving people to use the weapon of terrorism. They could just as well have organized a demonstration against explosives, bullets or knives. Complaining that no politician or media outlet had dared call Barcelona an Islamist attack, former French anti-terrorism chief Alain Marsaud warned that fear of naming the enemy will make it impossible to win this war.¹²³

The Devil You Know

Pure 'lone wolf' attacks perpetrated by individuals operating on their own, entirely absent from the radar screen of the authorities can occur and are nearly unstoppable but they remain rare. The vast majority of the perpetrators of terror attacks in Europe have been known to the authorities before they acted. They have operated with accomplices or facilitators and networks within their communities. Consider the last three attacks which took place before April 2017, in which vehicles were driven into innocent crowds. Khalid Masood, who killed 12 people in Westminster, was a Muslim convert whom the authorities knew had been radicalized.

He had been previously arrested and released for violence and weapons possession (after Westminster, the police arrested some of his accomplices and facilitators). Anis Amri, who carried out the attack in Berlin, had also been identified as a radical. He had been arrested and released in Italy and Germany (German police reportedly falsified a document showing that he could have been rearrested before the Berlin attack).[124] The author of the April 2017 attack in Stockholm was reportedly an Uzbek known to Swedish security services as an ISIS sympathizer. Yet he was free and was only arrested after he had killed five people and injured 15. In Finland, 18-year-old Abderrahman Mechkah, a Moroccan who killed two people and wounded eight in a knife attack in Turku after his demand for asylum was rejected, was already known by security services to harbour radical extremist ideas. Yet he was under no surveillance whatsoever.[125] In Spain, following the August 2017 terror attacks in Barcelona and Cambrils, it emerged that the radical Moroccan imam, Abdelbaki Es Satty, had indoctrinated the perpetrators at a mosque in the small town of Ripoll. He had served time in prison for drug trafficking and had nearly been deported from Spain. However, the Spanish judge had decided that he was not a grave enough menace to society to justify his expulsion.[126]

The overwhelming majority of terror attacks are perpetrated, organized or facilitated by people such as these, known by the authorities beforehand as potentially dangerous radicals and more often than not in possession of a criminal record. It seems the authorities are in denial about the fact that a subset of the Muslim minority is at war with society and that any radical, especially one with a criminal record, however petty, constitutes a serious danger. The authorities have so far decided that these known ticking time bombs can continue to mingle with an unsuspecting population. They are free to move around in their countries and, in the context of Schengen, remained free to cross European frontiers, unless caught preparing or perpetrating an attack or doing something unlawful. The selective complacency of authorities is a general phenomenon that has been in evidence in Sweden, Germany, Greece and other countries. Some refugees convicted of rape or assault were simply expelled or released (some of them went on to commit further mayhem).[127] In other instances, convicted radicals were released early (some of them went on to commit further terrorist acts), while any mainstream European citizen failing to pay his taxes would be mercilessly hunted down and punished to the full extent of the law.[128] It took the 130 corpses from the November 2015 Paris massacre to convince French authorities to remove security passes from 70 employees at Charles De Gaulle airport known for a long time to harbour radical views. These employees were privy to sensitive areas such as baggage handling.[129] Meantime, the Swiss only then took a similar measure with 30 employees at the Geneva airport (inscriptions such as 'Allah Akbar' were subsequently found on some Air France planes, meaning the threat remained real).[130] There is also the issue of illegal, jobless immigrants who are known by the authorities to be petty criminals, yet remain free. While not known as radicals, they can potentially radicalize and perpetrate acts of terror at any time. Case in point: the young Tunisian immigrant who was known by French authorities for years to be in the country illegally, as well as a petty criminal and who had seven different identities. He had been arrested and released in the past for drug offences and in 2015 was again arrested for illegal possession of a firearm, then released once more. On a Friday in late September 2017 he was arrested yet again for theft in Lyon and almost immediately released yet again by a judiciary that didn't want to bother, having decided that his crimes were not bad enough to warrant prison or deportation. Two days later, he stabbed two young students to death at the Marseille train station while shouting 'Allah Akbar'.[131] Interestingly, some French left-wing politicians called this perpetrator a 'martyr'.[132]

In refusing to physically remove all known radicals from society, in keeping in Europe scores of migrants who are known to be illegals—and some who are known criminals—the European political class and authorities are effectively guilty of dereliction of duty and criminal negligence. Not only do dangerous radicals remain free to move around, but those who possess European citizenship continue to enjoy the full rights and benefits that come with it. Of the 290 known Jihadists who had left France for Syria and Iraq, 20% received their payments from French social security up to the time it was revealed they were doing so (payments were subsequently stopped).[133] Ineffectual calls made in Germany to strip convicted Jihadist bi-nationals of German nationality got no traction. Similarly, even after the Paris carnage the French liberal establishment couldn't bring itself to strip convicted bi-national terrorists of their French nationality, although this measure exists elsewhere in Europe (where examples of its application remain rare). It exists in Britain, as well as Denmark, where two radicals were stripped of Danish nationality.[134] In Australia, it was applied in the case of Khaled Sharrouf;[135] in the Netherlands, four Jihadists lost their nationality;[136] and in Israel, 20 Arab-Israelis who went to fight for ISIS lost their Israeli passport.[137] In France, a convicted terrorist can continue enjoying all the advantages of French nationality, from social security to legal support. The push to strip convicted terrorists of French nationality was, however, supported by 85% of French people.[138] This attests once more to the growing disconnect between the views of the governing 'elites' and the new popular reality on the ground. Yet, while Merkel's approval ratings dropped in the aftermath of two terrorist attacks in Germany in the summer of 2016, they had recovered to pre-refugee crisis levels by the end of that year, proving the resilience of liberal views among the general population, and the ambivalence of Europeans when facing such issues.[139]

Asymmetric War

Open societies equipped themselves with armies to fight enemies abroad and police forces to deal with unruly citizens at home. But these forces and the laws of the land were never meant to deal with significant minorities at home who did not subscribe to the societies' core values and who actively seek to impose alien customs in opposition to existing ones or to carve a separate physical and legal space for themselves—let alone with radicals intent on physically harming or replacing the host societies with one based on alien values and customs. It was unthinkable in the first place that anyone in their right mind would prefer any form of society to an open, liberal, democratic one. Despite close calls involving communist parties in Western Europe during the Cold War, the democratic ballot was expected to naturally marginalize any such deviants from the political scene, with those flushed out simply fading into oblivion. Europe was generally centre-right or centre-left. It was accepted that the pendulum would periodically swing and the odd unruly extremist was dealt with by police forces. The rules of the game were made by 'reasonable' people for 'reasonable' people and were equally applied to everybody since everybody was supposed to have bought into the system. In *Homo Deus*, author Yuval Noah Harari reminded us that 'Democratic elections work only within populations that have some prior common bond, such as shared religious beliefs and national myths. They are a method to settle disagreements between people who already agree on the basics.'[140] The laws that are supposed to maintain social peace among citizens that generally subscribe to such a construct are, however, wholly inadequate when dealing with a significant number of people who reject the system, the rules, the values and everything they represent.

Prevention and the degree to which it can be tolerated should be one of the core elements of the debate on fighting terror but it is not. After the July 14, 2016 terrorist attack in Nice that left 87 dead, President Francois Hollande reiterated that his government would not change any laws for a few months (the government's most notable measure was to extend the State of Emergency, which had clearly failed to stop anything in the first place). The message from the top was, at the time, essentially a lame one of impotence and abdication: nothing much could be done. People would have to learn to live with increasing levels of threat in their daily lives and fatality played a role. This message was not unlike that of German authorities who advised people to stockpile food and water in response to a string of Jihadist attacks during the summer of 2016. A leading US conservative magazine the *National Review* complained that 'Western countries would rather accept a certain level of threat than do what it takes to mitigate it.'[141]

Hard-line Europeans feel that the standard arsenal of democracy and its existing rules of the game are inadequate in the fight against radicals and terrorism. If adequate responses cannot be found within the existing constitutional or judiciary framework, they believe extra constitutional solutions should be found. Or the rules of the game should be tweaked to specifically address the issue of a separate class of people, barbarians, living within the walls of the city and hell-bent on its destruction. The delicate question that arises is, naturally, that of abuse and how to prevent it. In Australia, pursuant to the arrest of lone wolf Faheen Lodhi, caught in 2003 in the early stages of planning a terrorist act, a New South Wales court commented that, in enacting preventive legislation, Parliament intended 'to create offenses where an offender has not decided precisely what he or she intends to do'.[142] The book, *Critical Debates on Counter-Terrorist Judicial Review*,[143] in which these topics have been discussed at length, recognizes that while exceptional counter-terrorist policy justifies itself from the exceptional nature of the threat and the high stakes involved, the risk is one of 'entrenchment', or, the 'normalization of emergency measures'. Yet it is reasonable to think that appropriate safeguards can be put in place to prevent abuse. Risks of terrorist incidents cannot be entirely eliminated. But solutions exist to reduce them. However, the failure to muster any political will to vigorously address such issues means open societies are condemned to fight what I label an 'asymmetrical war of wills'. One side is shackled by rules of its own making and the other sets no limits in what it can do, how far it will go or what weapons it can use, including self-sacrifice. In his book "*Ever Wonder Why?: and Other Controversial Essays*" Thomas Sowell predicted that 'If the battle for civilization comes down to the wimps versus the barbarians, the barbarians are going to win.' As long as this asymmetry persists, the response of the open society will remain ineffective.

The Illusion of Accommodation

The attitude of European authorities towards Islamization and radicalization has ranged from denial to accommodation. Journalist Céline Pina pointed out that in France Islamization didn't figure at all in the 2017 presidential debates despite being a key preoccupation of the electorate. This reflects the 'elites'' denial as well as that of unions, political parties, associations and businesses. Pina pointed out that the United Kingdom has pushed complacency to new extremes. The authorities have proudly announced that policewomen can wear the *burka*. Multiculturalism has permitted separatist ideologies and practices to flourish, a fact that has not spared the country from terror attacks.[144] The old accommodation policy by which British authorities had allowed London to become a sanctuary for Islamist leaders from around the world (earning the capital the nickname 'Londonistan' at the time) in the hope of avoiding Jihadist attacks was shattered by the 2005 London bombings.

In recent years this policy gave way to yet another policy of accommodation, in which entire English neighbourhoods were effectively abandoned to the rule of Salafists with the same objective of buying social peace. The illusion that this new form of accommodation would work was once more shattered by the spectacular Westminster terror attack carried out in March 2017 by one Khalid Masood who, adding insult to injury, lived in Birmingham: a city which had been at the forefront of this policy of accommodation. Germany and Sweden's illusions that their own moderation on the international political scene, their absence from military operations in the Middle East and their well-publicized tolerance and *Wilkommenskultur* would spare them major terrorist attacks on their soil, were similarly shattered. The Berlin and Stockholm attacks, incidentally, heralded a new wave of low-cost, highly visible and effective attacks during which a vehicle is driven into a crowd. Victims of their own naiveté and denial, these countries are slowly realizing that their 'exceptionalism' is rapidly coming to an end. To Pina, accommodation is cowardice and cowardice does not pay in confronting totalitarianism as the twentieth century and its millions of dead taught us.

Mister Rogers' Neighbourhood

How bad is Islamization after all? Should a minority not be allowed to live the way it wants to live? What would an Islamicized area or neighbourhood (i.e. one mostly peopled by Muslims who, by choice or coercion, follow rules imposed by radical Islamist ideology in their daily lives) actually look like? Can an Islamicized community live side by side with the mainstream and how stable would the result be?

A leading French daily published a report describing Trappes, a small city 35 km from Paris, where 70% of its population of 30,000 is Muslim, and unemployment runs high.[145] According to the report, Trappes has fallen into the hands of Salafists and has been thoroughly Islamicized, providing a good example of how this process works. Religion now defines this place with its five mosques, the proliferation of Koranic schools and Halal shops and the omnipresence of the Islamic veil on the streets. Fifty of its people went to fight Jihad in Syria. French security services have taken to calling the place 'Trappistan' while others label it the 'French Molenbeek'. The Muslim Brotherhood controls this city and has effectively achieved 'self-apartheid' for the community, which now lives as a virtual 'Bantustan': a separate mini-state within the French territory where young people refuse to be labelled 'French'. Islamists do not take kindly to the state intervening in their affairs: in 2013 Trappes exploded with riots after police tried to control the ID of a woman wearing the veil. In Brignais, another neighbourhood, religious observance was reported to have taken over social life. Women are covered from head to toe and social habits have changed to the extent that some people won't even talk about music anymore.[146] An undercover report that aired on state-owned television channel France 2 in December 2016 showed Sevran, an area in the north-east of Paris near Charles de Gaulle airport, also ruled by Islamists (at least 15 people left Sevran to join Jihadists in Syria and Iraq). Here, women are clearly discriminated against and are not admitted into bars. This attests to the point made by Pascale Boistard in a January 2016 interview by French weekly *Marianne* when she was minister for women's rights: 'There are areas in our country where women are not accepted.' The report also revealed that some women in Lyon were adapting their dress to avoid being threatened by Muslim extremists.[147] *Laïcité*, the French version of secularism, supposed to be one of the core principles of the republic, is hardly enforced in *banlieues*, which the state has mostly abandoned to Islamists. According to François Pupponi, deputy mayor of Sarcelles, in such neighbourhoods the situation is even worse than police reports say. The police do not patrol these neighbourhoods anymore and do not know what goes on: they are overwhelmed.[148] The problem of gender regression is not limited to the *banlieues*. In the centre of Paris itself, some areas have reportedly become essentially off-limits to women, partly because of a worsening of overall delinquency and partly due to Islamization.[149] Algerian writer Boualem Sansal points out that in many Islamicized neighbourhoods in France you won't find a Christian or a Jew, a homosexual, a free thinker, an artist or a woman wearing trousers.[150] De Villiers' book *Les cloches sonneront-elles encore demain?* depicts with vivid and alarming detail a France much further down the path of Islamization than anyone would have expected.[151]

In Islamicized neighbourhoods in the United Kingdom, and other places in Europe the story is the same. The city of Birmingham has been known for some years as a hotbed of radicalization and arguably the most Islamicized city in England. Here, loudspeakers ensure that the Birmingham Central Mosque *muezzin* calling the faithful to prayer every day is heard loud and clear by everybody. The Birmingham schools scandal of 2014, mentioned earlier, in which some city schools were reportedly being taken over by Islamists, gives an idea of what schools would be like in such environments. There were 'claims that boys and girls were segregated in classrooms and assemblies, sex education was banned, and non-Muslim staff were bullied. In one case it was alleged that the teachings of a firebrand al Qaida-linked Muslim preacher were praised to pupils.'[152] In the city's Small Heath district where 95% of inhabitants are Muslims, certain schools prohibit the teaching of drawing and music—considered sinful activities—to children; women are covered from head to toe and also usually wear black gloves in public; pubs—which were part of vibrant traditional British life—are closed or walled; curtains separate women and families from men in most restaurants; bookstores are religious; and school education has a decidedly religious orientation.[153] Duisburg, in the heart of Germany's Ruhr, is a different case. Its northern district of Marxloh, where people mostly live in squalor and poverty, is known as a no-go-area for the police.[154] It is not really an Islamicized area because many of its 20,000 inhabitants—60% of which have foreign origins—are Rom and Eastern European illegals, yet Salafists thrive in such environments and are able to maintain their networks. It is in the Marxloh jungle that Anis Amri, the perpetrator of the Berlin massacre, managed to escape all surveillance.

The pressure exerted by radicals is not limited to families (or their favourite target, women within their communities) but extends, wherever possible, to all aspects of community life. This includes economic and social life, with the takeover of mosques from moderates followed by their control and radicalization, the 'buyout' and control of shops and small commercial enterprises. The full Islamization of a city, village or neighbourhood amounts to a comprehensive conquest and re-formatting of the physical, spiritual, legal, commercial, cultural and social space. Wherever the Islamist ideology finds space to freely express itself within a community, De Villiers reports that it does so in an uncompromising fashion. It embarks on a process of self-ghettoization, pushing as far as it can to replace the host society's 'civilization' with the 'purist' Islamist paradigm. It imposes the primacy of religion in all affairs. Relations between the sexes would be marked by gender segregation and the subjugation of women. Crimes of honour, forced marriages, child marriages and polygamy would be likely. Homophobia would be a given while relations with other religious communities would be marred by intolerance and anti-semitism. In many mosques taken over by radicals, preachers are known to exhort the faithful to discard state laws in favour of the Koran and sharia. They condone violence against women, Christians and Jews.

We pointed out earlier that the younger generation is a target of choice for Islamists. One does not need to go very far to get a taste of the impact of this ideology on youth education. The march of Islamism in the French school system is relentless. Its consequences were depicted in a new, controversial book by Bernard Ravet, a former headmaster of schools in Marseille.[155] Inevitably, he was labelled an Islamophobe. It is not just the fact that students refused to have a minute of silence to honour the victims of the 2015 terror attacks in France. In colleges where 90% of the students are Muslim, Ravet describes a transformed environment in which more and more girls are veiled. There is a deepening fracture and segregation between boys and girls. Students dispute Darwin's theory of evolution. In the canteen, students refuse to eat any meat that is not Halal. Students who do not fast during Ramadan often get beaten up (the proportion of students practicing Ramadan went up from about half in 2005 to 90% or 95% by 2013, testimony to the progress of Islamization among the young). Students maintain that men and women are not equal and that an adulterous woman should be stoned and a thief should have his hand cut off.[156] This is increasingly the reality in many of France's state schools. As the state places few obstacles in the way of the Islamists' efforts to indoctrinate malleable youth it comes as no surprise that the radicalized are increasingly younger. It is a little more surprising that the proportion of girls among radicalized youth is steadily increasing, attesting to the Islamists' success in spreading their ideology.[157]

Needless to say, Islamicized communities provide the most fertile ground for the recruitment and concealment of Jihadists. The perpetrators of the Paris attack were able to hide in the Islamicized neighbourhood of Molenbeek in Belgium for four months. One of them hid just a few blocks from his family home before he was caught. According to De Villiers, interviewed by France's RTL in October 2016, some of this conquest and re-formatting is already happening in France. Others lament that it is also happening here elsewhere in Europe. In the physical space they control and at its boundary with the host society and sometimes beyond, Islamists pretend that the *kaffir* respect—if not adapt to—their customs. In Cannes, France, a sportsman was attacked by radical hotheads because he was taking a shower naked in the male changing room after a soccer game.[158] In September 2015, Muslim radicals patrolled the streets of Wuppertal, Germany, declaring the area to be a 'Shariah-controlled zone' where alcohol, music and pornography were prohibited.[159] Many similar cases attest to the radicals' desire to impose their vision of the world, even outside their own communities.

A Question of Choice

Europeans take their open, democratic societies, their individual freedoms and gender equality for granted today. They forget that they are not the natural default setting of any human society. They forget that they are enjoying a degree of well-being and peace that no generation before them has ever known. These benefits have been earned through centuries of struggles, revolutions and sacrifices. Their continuation in the future is by no means a given. Democracy, which has been dubbed 'the worse form of government—except for the alternatives' has its shortcomings but it has by and large delivered unprecedented levels of peace and prosperity to modern Europe. In essence it is a rules-based system concocted by citizens who share a set of basic values and accept that they are collectively better off following rules set by elected representatives even if they don't always like these rules. While such a system does not preclude the presence of minorities, it is logically more likely to come into existence and sustain itself as a stable political and social construct in a context where a large majority shares a common history, language, culture and core values—or at the very least a common vision. Common sense has it that the stability of such a system is not threatened by the presence of minorities as long as they are not too widely divergent and as long as they collectively buy into the system, the vision and wish to maintain it. Addressing the question of diversity, philosopher Philippe Bénéton, author of an essay on the moral unhinging of the West,[160] reminded us that—while diversity can enrich a society—the more diverse a society is the less the people who compose it have in common.[161] If people have very little in common then the only thing left that binds them together is adherence to the rules of the game. In other words multiculturalism assumes that differences between people don't really matter and everybody will get along with everybody else as long as they follow mechanical rules (what if they don't?). Yet, according to Bénéton, evidence taken from very diverse societies around the world shows that rules are not sufficient to enable them to live under the same roof in a stable and peaceful way. Following this line of thought, since Islamists reject the rules of the host society and strive to rewrite their own, there is really nothing that would bind an Islamicized community (i.e. a community that lives by the Islamist ideology) to a mainstream European community. They would live side by side in different worlds, with very little linking them to ensure the stability of the construct.

However annoying and unappealing this may all be to Europeans, none of this is a priori life threatening. In countries with large Muslim communities Europeans could, after all, pursue the trajectory of accommodation they have been following so far. This is likely to lead to their living side by side with Islamicized communities here and there, such as those we just described, in a kind of apartheid. This is the direction things were taking until recently. Perceptions changed due to the combination of the recent explosion of Jihadist attacks, with corpses lining the streets of European capitals, and the UMI tsunami with its conspicuous masses of aliens. In the minds of increasingly larger numbers of Europeans, Jihadism, Islamism and UMI were suddenly perceived as facets of one same—'us' versus 'them'—coin. They sensed that their children would end up living in a world where their cherished European way of life would be at risk and may, in some areas, be replaced by something that they viscerally rejected because it clashed with everything they stood for. Indifference over broad trends of Islamization slowly gave way to annoyance and then to alarm in a post 9/11 context in which the narrative of a conflict of civilizations gained traction. In Europe some countries timidly started to take concrete measures to contain the Islamization of their territory. But most remain transfixed, in denial or simply unable to do anything about it. The Swiss, for instance, drew some red lines. They decided that there would be no minarets built on their territory[162] and that any Muslim student refusing to shake the hand of a teacher of the opposite sex would be subjected to a heavy fine.[163] In Switzerland these decisions became the law of the land and are enforced. In France, on the other hand, the law said the *burka* was prohibited, but has not been seriously enforced for fear of provoking riots. Some places in France now look like replicas of villages from another world. In ambivalent Germany new regulations were enacted in early 2017 prohibiting government employees to wear the veil while allowing it in the rest of the public sphere.[164] Pieter-Jaap Aalberberg, Amsterdam's Chief of Police, proposed to let Muslim policewomen wear the veil and planned to recruit more Muslims to the police force (to reflect the evolution of a population that was by then 52% of non-Netherlands origin). However, his ideas were badly received by the population and political parties.[165] In other places, such as the United Kingdom, regulations governing such issues don't even exist. What Europe will be in the future depends on what Europeans want it to be. If the current trajectory is followed, more and more pieces of Europe may be turned into neighbourhoods such as the ones we just described. If Europeans wish to prevent this from happening, a debate needs to take place, a consensus needs to be reached by the host population on the limits of a minority's assertion of its own separate identity and the country needs to stand firmly by its decision and enforce it. This goal remains mostly elusive.

An Ounce of Prevention…

Not a day goes by without a terrorist act taking place somewhere in Europe: a driver ploughing his car into a crowd, a lone attacker stabbing a passer-by or a terrorist plot thwarted by security forces. It has become a terrifying feature of daily life. As we pointed out earlier, in the vast majority of cases the perpetrators have been known beforehand by the security establishment as potentially dangerous radicals. Yet they largely remain free to move around until they act, a Damocles sword hanging over the head of each and every European citizen. If the first duty of any government anywhere should be to do whatever it takes to ensure the safety of citizens, European governments have largely failed. At fault are not police forces who have been doing a commendable job, mostly behind the scenes, in very difficult circumstances. Ordinary citizens would be aghast if they knew the high number of attacks stopped by security services every month. Europol reported 211 foiled, thwarted or completed attacks in 2015 alone for six EU countries (almost half took place in the United Kingdom).[166] The number of instances investigated by France's UAVMT (the security unit tasked with analysing terrorist's movements in France, staffed by a mere ten people) exploded from 5000 in 2015 to over 165,000 for just the first nine month of 2017.[167] The main problem in ensuring that whatever can be done is actually done is lack of political will, which translates into the cavalier attitude of most European governments, political 'elites' and the judiciary.

A first issue arises with the leniency of a judiciary prone to hand down light sentences and release convicted perpetrators early. The illusion that a bout of prison life will reform a Jihadist and remove the threat he or she poses after release flies in the face of evidence. After their release from prison, some radicals have perpetrated acts of terror, such as Richard Reid, the 'shoe bomber' and Muktar Ibrahim, the leader of the London 2015 bomb plot. It also naively ignores that some prisons have become hotbeds of radicalization and even some prison guards have been suspected to be Islamic radicals.[168] According to a *Washington Post* report, 'France's prisons have a reputation as factories for radical Islamists, taking in ordinary criminals and turning them out as far more dangerous people.'[169] Early releases and light sentences, bad enough in the case of common criminals and gangs, amount to dangerous gambles in the case of Jihadists capable of perpetrating terrorist acts. The second, bigger, problem is, as previously pointed out, a lack of consensus in relation to *preventive* measures, in other words locking up individuals who are deemed to represent a serious potential threat, but are not yet there. As described earlier, democratic societies by and large reject the subjective judgement of harsh preventive measures, considering that they smack of arbitrary rule leading to abuse. The price to pay for this good conscience is that legions of potentially dangerous radicals remain free to move around and not much can be done until it is too late. In this way, the population is expected to rely on the state to keep an eye on all dangerous extremists and stop them on time in case they are about to commit a terrorist act: an impossible job. First of all, when it comes to intervention the old rules of the game do not apply. Long gone are the days when terrorists took people hostage in order to make demands and open negotiations. Today's Jihadist does not make requests. He or she just wants to slaughter, unfazed by the knowledge that he or she will be killed too. Rapid, decisive and lethal intervention on the spot is therefore necessary in order to minimize the number of victims. Secondly, when it comes to prevention, round the clock surveillance of one single individual requires a great deal of manpower. Keeping thousands of dangerous radicals under 24/7 control while remaining ready to intervene anywhere within minutes would require the deployment of tens of thousands of additional security forces at a time when they are already overstretched and budgets are slashed: an impossible task.

European leaders from left and right alike have repeatedly proven their delusional view of the situation and their incompetence by trimming police budgets at a time of exponentially growing threats from domestic terrorism. 'Since Theresa May became home secretary in 2010 the number of police officers has fallen by 21,500' lamented the *Guardian*.[170] Under former French President Nicolas Sarkozy thousands of police jobs were similarly eliminated. May and Sarkozy were, by the way, both centre-right. At the European level, cooperation on internal security matters remains far from satisfactory. According to experts it is 'the fragmentation and inaccessibility of security data that can actually paralyze the fight against terrorism'.[171] Created in 1995, Europol (the European agency in charge of police cooperation among EU countries) has been suffering from an initial lack of data and the reluctance of member states to share sensitive information with the agency. The situation improved following the 2015 attacks in Paris, in particular with regard to efforts to boost the inter-operability of databases.[172] Given these realities it is not surprising that terrorists can slip through the net from time to time.

Relying on surveillance and rapid intervention once a crime is under way will never bring the threat down to acceptable levels, let alone remove it. Prevention is thus key. The ultimate preventive measure would be to round up all radicals deemed to be potential threats and preventively imprison them, a solution that Europeans won't contemplate. Common sense has it that these Jihadists, *de facto* enemies of the nation, should not enjoy the same freedoms and should not be subjected to the same laws and due process that apply to ordinary citizens. 'Lone wolves' are another matter, unknown to be dangerous until they randomly act, and no prevention is possible in their case. Yet, allowing individuals who are known to be threats to mingle with a population they intend to slaughter at the first opportunity is tantamount to subjecting that population to a game of Russian roulette. More and more people feel that if the constitutional framework does not allow for proper preventive measures, the rules should be tweaked. The application of these measures is nevertheless difficult. What are the criteria for preventively imprisoning somebody? Who decides and for how long should a preventively imprisoned radical be held for? Let's keep in mind Benjamin Franklin's thoughts on the matter: 'Those who would give up essential Liberty, to purchase a little temporary Safety, deserve neither Liberty nor Safety.' Essentially, Europeans need to decide the level of threat they are willing to live with and how far they are willing to compromise their ideals to reach that level. Just after the November 2015 attacks in Paris, an Ifop survey showed that 84% of those surveyed were willing to trade some of their civil liberties for better security.[173] The real question is how far they are willing to go down this route.

The vast majority of citizens understand and accept that exceptional measures need to be taken in relation to an emergency situation and that some freedoms need to be traded for security. Yet two issues arise. The first is that, instead of being temporary and reversed once the emergency is over, exceptional measures historically tend to remain part of the system because of legal 'inertia'. In this way, citizens get stuck with draconian laws even in 'normal' times. Legal experts such as Mireille Delmas-Marty are also afraid that modifications allowing the law to intervene earlier pave the way for a 'predictive justice' system that is no longer based on the traditional custom of accusing someone of a crime which has been committed and doing so on the basis of proof.[174] Instead, it opens the way for suspicions over crimes that may be committed in the future. The fear, in other words, is that it could lead to abuses, which is a reasonable concern. If, however, preventive measures are a necessary evil in the prevention of massacres, it would be absurd and remiss to simply disregard them all together on grounds that they could lead to abuse. There is no ideal or perfect system and safeguards can be put in place to ensure that such measures will disappear once the threat has been removed. In addition, the level of 'suspicion' which triggers legal action needs to be well understood and measures introduced that will prevent abuse. If the current situation is deemed to be unacceptable, and if harsh measures such as the preventive locking up or neutralization of known radicals can substantially reduce the threat level, Europeans owe it to themselves to seriously consider this route.

Notes

1. Francesco M. Bongiovanni. 'The Decline and Fall of Europe'. *Pages 155–187. Palgrave Macmillan*. 2012.
2. Ian Drury. 'The number of Muslims in Europe reaches 44m: Serious concerns raised about the challenges of integration following attacks on Paris'. *Mail Online*. 16 November 2015.
3. 'Musulmans de France: pour 29% des sondés, la charia est plus importante que la loi de la République'. *BFM TV and AFP*. 18 September 2016.
4. 'The Future of the Global Muslim Population'. *Pew Research Centre – pewforum.org*. 27 January 2011.
5. Kirsten Grieshaber. 'Study: Europe's Muslim population to grow, migration or not'. *Associated Press*. 29 November 2017.
6. Ferguson, Niall (16 November 2015). 'Paris and the fall of Rome'. *The Boston Globe*. Retrieved 31 May 2016.
7. Melissa Eddy. 'Cologne Mayor's 'Arm's Length' Advice on Sexual Attacks Stirs Outcry'. *The New York Times*. 6 January 2016.
8. Piera Matteucci. 'Rouhani: "Statue coperte? Grande ospitalità italiana". Franceschini: "Scelta incomprensibile"'. *Repubblica.it*. 27 January 2016.
9. 'Bali: pas de statues camouflées pour le roi saoudien'. *Lefigaro.fr – Le Figaro*. 8 March 2017.
10. Eugénbie Bastié. 'La RATP confrontée à la poussée du communautarisme Islamiste'. *Lefigaro.fr*. 17 November 2015.

11. 'Switzerland: Muslim students must shake teacher's hand'. *BBC News.* 25 May 2016.
12. Lotfi Maktouf. 'The separation of church & state under the Islamist protocol'. *Turkish Policy Quarterly.* Fall 2015.
13. Shadi Hamid, Rashid Dar. 'Islamism, Salafism, and Jihadism: A primer'. *Brookings.edu.* 15 July 2016.
14. Richard C. Paddock. 'Governor's defeat in Indonesia shows rise of Islamists'. *The International New York Times. Page 2.* 8 May 2017.
15. Francesco M. Bongiovanni. 'The Decline and Fall of Europe'. *Palgrave Macmillan.* 2012.
16. Richard C. Paddock. 'Governor's defeat in Indonesia shows rise of Islamists'. *The International New York Times. Page 2.* 8 May 2017.
17. Alexandre Devecchio. 'Kamel Daoud: 'La culture française? J'en suis amoureux". *Le Figaro. Page 16.* 7 April 2017.
18. Isabelle Ory. 'Le fondamentalisme Islamique gangrène les mosquées belges'. *Le Figaro. Page 11.* 10 February 2017.
19. Jean Marie Guénois. 'La formation des imams se révèle presque impossible à encadrer'. *Lefigaro.fr – Le Figaro.* 17 March 2017.
20. Alexandre Devecchio. 'Boualem Sansal: 'Pour les islamistes, l'épisode Europe touche à sa fin'. *Lefigaro.fr – Le Figaro.* 13 October 2017.
21. Philippe De Villiers. 'Les cloches sonneront-elles encore demain?'. *Editions Albin Michel. Page 21.*
22. 'We will dominate you'. *Middle East Forum – The Middle East Quarterly.* December 1999.
23. Ivan Rioufol. 'Une guerre civile menace la France somnolente'. *Blog. lefigaro.fr.* 29 August 2016.
24. Ivan Rioufol, 'Ce que dit le theatre muet de la Macronie'. *Le Figaro. Page 19.* 2 June 2017.
25. Graham Lanktree. 'John Kerry says the U.K. faces problems with extremists because it treats Muslims worse than the U.S.'. *Newsweek. com.* June 2017.
26. Vincent Tremolet de Villers. 'Boualem Sansal: «Il faut combattre l'Islamisme dans toutes ses dimensions". *Lefigaro.fr – Le Figaro.* 29 May 2017.
27. Yuval Noah Harari. 'Homo Deus'. *Harvill Secker. 2016. Pages 268–269.*
28. Julienne Davis. 'London bombing shows danger of Islamification in Britain and Europe. Is the US next?'. *Foxnews.com.* 16 September 2017.
29. 'Sharia Police' street patrols did not violate law, German court rules'. *Theguardian.com – The Guardian.* 21 November 2016.

30. Assemblée Nationale. Compte rendu, Commission de la défense nationale et des forces armées. *Page 10.* 10 May 2016.
31. Hervé Gattegno. 'Qui sont vraiment les musulmans de France'. *Le Journal du Dimanche. Page 2.* 18 September 2016.
32. Alexandre Devecchio. 'Kamel Daoud: 'La culture francaise? J'en suis amoureux". *Le Figaro. Page 16.* 7 April 2017.
33. Patrick Wintour. 'Leaked report reveals 'aggressive Islamist agenda' in Birmingham schools'. *Theguardian.com – The Guardian* '. 18 July 2014.
34. Laure Mandeville. 'Les failles de l'intégration 'made in England". *Le Figaro. Page 14.* 22 June 2017.
35. Eugenie Bastié, Alexandre Devecchio. 'Edwy Plenel, le procureur au banc des accusés'. *Le Figaro. Page 20.* 27 November 2017.
36. 'Terrorisme: Mélenchon et Ruffin se désolidarisent des propos d'une députée suppléante LFI'. *Leparisien.fr.* 4 October 2017.
37. Judith Waintraub. 'Politiques, journalistes, intellos: enquête sur les agents d'influence de l'islam'. *Lefigaro.fr – Le Figaro.* 7 October 2017.
38. Marie-Estelle Pech. 'Islamisme à l'école: les vérités sans fard d'un ancien principal de collège'. *Le Figaro. Page 2.* 31 August 2017.
39. Cyril Sauvageot. « Attentat de Berlin: après un an d'attente, les proches des victimes sont reçues par Angela Merkel ». *Franceinfo.* 18 Decembre 2017.
40. Jack Moore. 'ISIS Supporters Call For Poisoning of Food in Grocery Stores Across U.S. and Europe'. *Newsweek.com – Newsweek.* 7 September 2017.
41. Francesco M. Bongiovanni. 'The Decline and Fall of Europe'. *Palgrave Macmillan.* 2012.
42. Daniel Pipes. 'Can Islam be reformed?'. *Danielpipes.org.* July/August 2013.
43. 'French election explained in five charts'. *Bbc.com – BBC News.* 8 March 2017.
44. Matthieu Chaigne. 'France: déjà la guerre civile?' *Lefigaro.fr – Le Figaro.* 21 June 2016.
45. Esther Paolini. 'L'immigration et l'Islam crispent de plus en plus les Français'. *Lefigaro.fr – Le Figaro.* 3 July 2017.
46. Peter Allen, Sam Tonkin. 'France is 'on the verge of a civil war' which could be sparked by a mass sexual assault on women by migrants, intelligence chief warns'. *DailyMailMailonline.* July 13, 2016.
47. John Vinocur, 'Averting France's War of All Against All'. *The Wall Street Journal.* July 18, 2016.

48. Marie-Amélie Lombard-Latune. 'La France est sortie de 70 ans de paix'. *Le Figaro*. 15/11/2015.
49. Matthieu Chaigne. 'France: déjà la guerre civile?'. *Lefigaro.fr – Le Figaro*. 21 June 2016.
50. Eugènie Bastié, Alexandre Devecchio, 'Eric Zemmour-Emmanuel Todd: globalisation ou retour des nations?'. *Le Figaro. Page 18*. 12 September 2017.
51. Erik Bleich. 'France has had more than its share of terrorist attacks. These 3 factors explain why.'. *Washingtonpost.com – The Washington Post*. 18 July 2016.
52. Hervé Gattegno. 'Qui sont vraiment les musulmans de France'. *Le Journal du Dimanche. Page 2*. 18 September 2016.
53. Islam en France. *Wikipedia*.
54. Bonnie Kristian. 'Many European countries have no terrorism problem. Why?'. *Theweek.com – The Week*. 18 July 2017.
55. 'Identité nationale: visite surprise de Besson à La Courneuve'. *Leparisien.fr*. 5 January 2010.
56. 'Fillon juge 'indigne' les propos de Macron sur la colonisation'. *Lefigaro.fr. – Le Figaro*. 15 February 2017.
57. Eugènie Bastié, Alexandre Devecchio, 'Eric Zemmour-Emmanuel Todd: globalisation ou retour des nations?'. *Le Figaro. Page 18*. 12 September 2017.
58. 'Fillon: 'On enlève Clovis, Jeanne d'Arc, Voltaire' des livres d'histoire'. *Publicsenat.fr*. November 24th, 2016.
59. Donatien. 'Clovis et Charles Martel virés des manuels d'histoire'. *Agoravox.tv*. 7 September 2010.
60. RMC / BFM TV interview of Anne Hidalgo. July 8, 2015.
61. Alexandre Devecchio. 'Tariq Ramadan se rêve-t-il en héros de Houellebecq?'. *Lefigaro.fr – Le Figaro*. 11 February 2016.
62. Philippe De Villiers. 'Les cloches sonneront-elles encore demain?'. *Editions Albin Michel. Page 131*.
63. Stephanie Kirchner. 'The arrival of hundreds of thousands of migrants is fueling a German identity crisis'. *www.Washingtonpost.com – The Washington Post*. 1 June 2017.
64. Eugènie Bastié, Alexandre Devecchio, 'Eric Zemmour-Emmanuel Todd: globalisation ou retour des nations?'. *Le Figaro. Page 18*. 12 September 2017.
65. Alexis Feertchak. 'Thibault de Montbrial: 'Il y a clairement une population qui est en guerre contre la Police'. *Figaro.fr Figaro Vox*. 19/10/2016.

66. 'Suicide de l'ancien chef de la lutte contre le hooliganisme, Antoine Boutonnet'. *D3*. November 2017.
67. Ed West. 'Europe, Islamism and some uncomfortable home truths'. *Blogs.spectatort.co.uk – The Spectator*. 22 March 2016.
68. Alexandre Devecchio. 'Kamel Daoud: 'La culture francaise? J'en suis amoureux''. *Le Figaro*. Page 16. 7 April 2017.
69. 'Musulmans de France: pour 29% des sondés, la charia est plus importante que la loi de la République'. *BFM TV and AFP.* 18 September 2016.
70. S.C. 'Tareq Oubrou favorable à la fermeture des mosquées au discours radical'. *BFM TV.* 16 November 2015.
71. Hervé Gattegno. 'Qui sont vraiment les musulmans de France'. *Le Journal du Dimanche. Page 2.* 18 September 2016.
72. 'Europe: les musulmans attachés au pays dans lequel ils vivent'. *Lefigaro.fr – Le Figaro*. 22 September 2017.
73. Violaine De Montclos. "Sonia Mabrouk: 'Les musulmans de France sont piégés'". *Le Point. Page 64.* 2 March 2017.
74. Louise Couvelaire. 'Ces musulmans des quartiers sous la pression de l'Islam radical'. *Lemonde.fr – Le Monde*. 22 February 2017.
75. Daniel Pipes. 'Can Islam be reformed?'. *Danielpipes.org.* July/August 2013.
76. Marie-Christine Tabet. 'L'Islam est le support de la révolte de certains musulmans'. *Le Journal du Dimanche. Page 5.* 18 September 2016.
77. David Chazan. 'This isn't Paris. It's only men here' – Inside the French Muslim no-go zones where women aren't welcome'. *The Telegraph*. 18 December 2016.
78. Emma-Kate Symons. 'Meet the founder of the French Jihad-busting Mothers' Brigade'. *NYTimes.com.* 21 September 2016.
79. Samia Maktouf. 'Je défendrai la vie autant que vous prechez la mort'. *Michel Lafon*. Novembre 2017.
80. Maité Hellio. Malek Boutih: "Les responsables musulmans français sont sous la pression des salafistes'". *Le Nouvel Observateur-L'OBS.* 7 April 2016.
81. Marianne Meunier. 'Pour les juifs européens, l'antisémitisme s'aggrave'. *La Croix*. 20 Fevrier 2015.
82. Simone Rodan-Benzaquen. 'MUSLIM ANTI-SEMITISM THREATENS FRANCE'S DEMOCRACY'. *Newsweek.com.* 198 November 2017.
83. Stéphane Kovacs. 'Ces Français juifs qui fuient la violence des banlieues'. *Lefigaro.fr – Le Figaro*. 24 October 2017.

84. Philippe De Villiers. 'Les cloches sonneront-elles encore demain?'. *Editions Albin Michel*. Page 221.
85. Emma-Kate Symons. 'Zineb el Rhazoui, Charlie Hebdo survivor, discusses why the world needs to 'Destroy Islamic Fascism'". *Nytlive.nytimes.com – The New York Times*. 18 November 2016.
86. *Joserodriguesdossantos.com. Interviews*.
87. Daniel Pipes. 'Can Islam be reformed?'. *Danielpipes.org*. July/August 2013.
88. Quanta Ahmed. 'Mr. Trump, you have a unique opportunity to defeat Islamism. As a Muslim I'm ready to collabourate'. *FoxNews.com*. 5 December 2016.
89. 'Why Europe's Muslims do not chant in unison, as its politicians would like'. *The Economist*. 18 July 2017.
90. 'Bagehot – Battlefields of the mind'. *Economist.com from the print edition of The Economist*. 7 January 2016.
91. Guy Adams. 'Inside Britain's Sharia courts: There are now EIGHTY-FIVE Islamic courts dispensing 'justice' across the UK. This investigation into what really goes on behind their doors will shock you to the core'. *Mail online – The Daily Mail*. 15 December 2015.
92. Michael Rosen. '"The Strange Death of Europe" Says Europe's Decline Is A Choice'. *Thefederalist.com*. 29 September 2017.
93. 'Germany polygamy: Minister says migrants must abide by the law'. *Bbc.com – BBC News*. 15 June 2016.
94. Damien Stroka. 'L'Allemagne interdit partiellement le port du voile intégral'. *AFP*. 28 April 2017.
95. 'Le Conseil d'Etat met un terme aux arrêtés 'anti-burkini'. *LeMonde.fr – Le Monde*. 26 August 2016.
96. Anne-Sylvaine Chassany. 'Islam and the state'. *Financial Times. Page 11*. 16 September 2016.
97. 'L'interdiction du burkini sème la zizanie à gauche'. *Le Figaro. Page 1*. 25 August 2016.
98. 'Le délit de consultation de sites djihadistes de nouveau censuré'. *Lefigaro.fr – Le Figaro*. 15 December 2017.
99. Luc Ferry. 'Burkini, et puis quoi encore?'. *Le Figaro. Page 19*. 25 August 2016.
100. Luc Ferry. 'Burkini, et puis quoi encore?'. *Le Figaro. Page 19*. 25 August 2016.
101. 'Belgique: La cour de Strasbourg confirme sa position sur le niqab'. *Reuters*. 11 July 2017.

102. Jamie Grierso, Vikram Dodd, Jason Rodrigues.' Anjem Choudary convicted of supporting Islamic State'. *The Guardian*. 16 August 2016.
103. 'Valls: La République a reculé face à la radicalisation'. *Lefigaro.fr – Le Figaro*. 15 Novembre 2017.
104. 'Attentats à Paris: Molenbeek, foyer de Jihadistes malgré lui'. *RFI*. 16 November 2015.
105. Ian Bremmer. 'These 5 Facts Explain Why Europe Is Ground Zero for Terrorism'. *Time*. 22 March 2016.
106. Jean-Marc Leclerc. 'Les maires réclament les noms des fichés S de leur ville'. *Lefigaro.fr – Le Figaro*. 7 October 2016.
107. Ségolène Allemandou. 'Attentat des Champs-Élysées: les zones d'ombre'. *France24.com*. 22 April 2017.
108. 'La liste des fichés S accessible aux agents autorisant la détention d'armes'. *Lefigaro.fr – Le Figaro*. 4 August 2017.
109. Christophe Cornevin, Valérie Malvoue, Delphine Samson. 'Engin explosif à Paris: l'un des suspects était fiché pour radicalisation"'. *Lefigaro.fr – Le Figaro*. 3 October 2017.
110. Florentin Collomp. 'L'un des auteurs de l'attentat du London Bridge figurait dans un documentaire sur l'Islamisme. Un de ses complices avait été signalé par la Police italienne.'. *Lefigaro.fr – Le Figaro*. 6 June 2017.
111. Robert Mendick, Gordon Rayner, Martin Evans, Hayley Dixon. 'Security services missed five opportunities to stop the Manchester bomber'. *Telegraph.co.uk*. 6 June 2017.
112. Josselin Debraux. 'Attaque terroriste: pourquoi le Royaume-Uni est-il autant visé?'. *Francetvinfo.fr*. 4 June 2017.
113. Caroline Copley, Madeline Chambers. 'Germany bans Islamist 'True Religion' group, raiding mosques and flats'. *Reuters*. 15 November 2016.
114. David Philippot. 'Berlin va faciliter les expulsions d'immigrés illégaux'. *Le Figaro. Page 8*. 23 February 2017.
115. Matty Zuvela. 'Number of potential terrorists in Germany on the rise, report says'. *Dw.com – Deutsche Welle*. 4 May 2017.
116. Guy Chazan. 'Islamist mole found in German intelligence agency'. *Ft.com – Financial Times*. 30 November 2016.
117. David Philippot. 'Berlin va faciliter les expulsions d'immigrés illégaux'. *Le Figaro. Page 8*. 23 February 2017.
118. Nicolas Barotte. 'Comment la menace Islamiste a grandi en Allemagne'. *Le Figaro. Page 2*. 22 December 2016.

119. Ben Kentish. 'Barcelona attack: CIA warned Spanish authorities of possible Las Ramblas terror two months ago, reports suggest'. *Independent. co.uk – The Independent.* 18 August 2017.
120. Jean Chichizola. 'En France, le nombre de radicalisés a augmenté de 60 % en moins de deux ans'. *Lefigaro.fr – Le Figaro.* 18 August 2017.
121. 'Collomb: 217 Djihadistes sont rentrés en France'. *Lefigaro.fr – Le Figaro.* 6 August 2017.
122. Pierre Godon. 'Attentats en Europe: "De plus en plus de projets d'attaque passent à travers les mailles du filet"'. *Francetvinfo.fr.* 19 August 2017.
123. Anne-Laure Deparis. 'Clash: Alain Marsaud, ex-chef de la lutte antiterroriste, quitte le plateau de BFMTV en plein direct'. *Programmetvnet.fr – teleloisirs.fr.* 19 August 2017.
124. 'Attentat de Berlin: la Police mise en cause'. *Lefigaro.fr – Le Figaro.* 17 May 2017.
125. Finlande: l'agresseur au couteau connu des renseignements'. *Lefigaro.fr – Le Figaro.* 21 August 2017.
126. 'Catalogne: deux suspects remis en liberté, deux autres écroués'. *Lefigaro.fr – Le Figaro.* 24 August 2017.
127. Lizzie Dearden. 'Asylum seeker convicted of attempted murder in Greece was released before raping and killing German student'. *The Independent.* December 2016.
128. Philip Johnston, 'Radical Muslim terrorist released from prison early to ease overcrowding'. *The Telegraph.* 28 March 2008.
129. Caroline Piquet. 'Radicalisation: près de 70 badges retirés à des agents de Roissy et Orly'. *Lefigaro.fr – Le Figaro.* 14 December 2015.
130. 'Around 30 Geneva airport staff banned from the tarmac for security reasons'. *Le News.ch from Tribune de Geneve.* 13 January 2016.
131. Christophe Cornevin. 'Clandestin et multi-récidiviste: le parcours sidérant du terroriste islamiste de Marseille'. *Lefigaro.fr – Le Figaro.* 2 October 2017.
132. Marc de Boni. 'Le terroriste de Marseille qualifié de «martyr»: la polémique atteint Ruffin et Mélenchon'. *Lefigaro.fr – Le Figaro.* 5 October 2017.
133. En 2014, 290 dJihadistes ont touché des prestations sociales. *Lepoint. fr – Le Point.* 17 March 2015.
134. 'Un Djihadiste turc né au Danemark déchu de sa nationalité danoise'. *Lefigaro.fr – Le Figaro.* 31 March 2017.

135. 'Djihadisme: un Australien déchu de sa nationalité'. *Lefigaro.fr – Le Figaro*. 12 February 2017.
136. 'Pays-Bas: 4 Djihadistes déchus de leur nationalité'. *Lefigaro.fr – Le Figaro*. 13 September 2017.
137. Israël: 20 membres de l'EI vont perdre leur nationalité'. *Lefigaro.fr – Le Figaro*. 23 August 2017.
138. '85 % des Français seraient favorables à la déchéance de nationalité'. *Lemonde.fr – Le Monde*. 4 January 2016.
139. Philip Oltermann. 'Deadly attack on German soil is worst fear for Angela Merkel'. *Theguardian.com – The Guardian*. 20 December 2016.
140. Yuval Noah Harari. 'Homo Deus'. *Harvill Secker, 2016. Page 249.*
141. David French. 'The World Is Too Comfortable with Terror'. *Nationalreview.com – National Review*. 23 May 2017.
142. Waleed Aly. 'Stopping the lone wolves'. *The International New York Times. Page 9*. 3 May 2017.
143. Edited by Fergal F. Davis and Fiona De Londras. 'Critical Debates on Counter-Terrorist Judicial Review'. *Cambridge University Press*. 2014.
144. Céline Pina. 'Les attentats de Londres et le déni des candidats à la présidence française face à l'Islamisme'. *Lefigaro.fr – Le Figaro*. 24 March 2017.
145. Angélique Négroni. 'Trappes confrontée au communautarisme Islamique'. *Le Figaro. Page 15*. 5 Février 2017.
146. Marie-Christine Tabet. 'A Lyon comme ailleurs, quequechose a changé'. *Le Journal du Dimanche. Page 4*. 18 September 2016.
147. David Chazan. '"This isn't Paris. It's only men here" – Inside the French Muslim no-go zones where women aren't welcome'. *Telegraph.co.uk – The Telegraph*. 18 December 2016.
148. Jean-Marc Leclerc. 'Une note décrit l'infiltration des salafistes dans les quartiers'. *Le Figaro. Page 10*. 7 April 2017.
149. Stephane Kovacs and Service Infographie. 'Reportage – Insultées et harcelées, des riveraines qui refusent de se retrancher chez elles interpellent le chef de l'État.'. *Lefigaro.fr – Le Figaro*. 19 May 2017.
150. Vincent Tremolet de Villers. 'Boualem Sansal: 'Il faut combattre l'Islamisme dans toutes ses dimensions'. *Lefigaro.fr – Le Figaro*. 29 May 2017.
151. Editions Albin Michel.
152. Helen Pidd. 'Twenty-five Birmingham schools inspected over Islamist 'takeover plot''. *Theguardian.com – The Guardian*. 14 April 2014.

153. Rachida Samouri. 'Birmingham à l'heure Islamiste'. *Lefigaro.fr – Le Figaro*. 24 February 2017.
154. Nicolas Barotte. 'A Marxloh, les habitants prisonniers de leur zone de non-droit'. *Le Figaro. Page 13*. 15 May 2017.
155. Bernard Ravet, Emmanuel Davidenkoff. 'Principal de collège ou imam de la République'. *Editions Kero*. August 2017.
156. Marie-Estelle Pech. 'Islamisme à l'école: les véritéssans fard d'un ancien principal de collège'. *Le Figaro. Page 2*. 31 August 2017.
157. Jean Chichizola. 'Des radicalisés de plus en plus jeunes'. *Le Figaro. Page 3*. 31 August 2017.
158. A.C. 'Un sportif se fait agresser parce qu'il était nu sous la douche'. *Nice Matin – nicematin.com*. 22 February 2017.
159. 'German court lets off 'Sharia Police' patrol in Wuppertal'. *BBC News*. 10 December 2015.
160. Philippe Beneton, 'Le Déreglement Moral de l'Occident', *CERF,* 2017.
161. Philippe Beneton, 'Le monde occidental ne sait plus qui il est', *Le Figaro.fr, Vox Politique*, 10 February 2017.
162. Nick Cumming-Bruce, Steven Erlanger. 'Swiss Ban Building of Minarets on Mosques'. *Nytimes.com – The New York Times*. 29 November 2009.
163. 'Switzerland: Muslim students must shake teacher's hand'. *BBC News*. 25 May 2016.
164. Damien Stroika. 'L'Allemagne interdit partiellement le port du voile intégral'. *AFP*. 28 April 2017.
165. 'Pays-Bas: tollé contre le port du voile ou de la kippa dans la Police'. *Lefigaro.fr – Le Figaro*. 19 May 2017.
166. '211 terrorist attacks carried out in EU member states in 2015, new Europol report reveals'. *Europol press release*. 20 July 2016.
167. Christophe Cornevin. 'Plongée au cœur de la traque antiterroriste'. *Le Figaro. Page 2*. 26 October 2017.
168. 'À la prison d'Arles, des surveillants soupçonnés d'être radicalisés'. *Lexpress.fr*. 29 April 2016.
169. Michael Birnbaum. 'French prisons, long hotbeds of radical Islam, get new scrutiny after Paris attacks'. *Washingtonpost.com*. 28 January 2015.
170. Alan Travis. 'Simple numbers tell story of Police cuts under Theresa May'. *Theguardian.com – The Guardian*. 5 May 2017.
171. Pierre Berthelet. 'Europe is winning the fight against terrorism'. *Newsweek.com – Newsweek*. 9 August 2017.
172. Pierre Berthelet. 'Europe is winning the fight against terrorism'. *Newsweek.com – Newsweek*. 9 August 2017.

173. 'EXCLUSIF – Les Français prêts à restreindre leurs libertés pour plus de sécurité (sondage)'. *Lefigaro.fr – Le Figaro.* 17 November 2015.
174. 'Mireille Delmas-Marty: 'Le caractère global du terrorisme appelle une justice globale'. *Lemonde.fr – Le Monde.* 1 Avril 2016.

5

The Rise of Alternative Politics

Origins and impact of the recent wave of alternative politics on the future of Europe

Angry Birds

While the 'trilogy'—UMI, Islamization and Jihadism—carries a great responsibility for the recent, rapid, unexpected and dramatic rise of alternative political movements in Europe, it is by no means the only cause of this rise. Populist, nationalist and other unconventional political movements, which we shall collectively label here as 'alternative', were bound to raise their heads at some point. In 2012, I wrote that 'today's political correctness could rapidly give way to intolerance' and warned of 'the rise of a right riding a wave of discontent with immigration, globalization, the EU and perceived loss of national identity [...] we are witnessing the first stirrings of a "reaction".'[1] A few years later this reaction was clearly visible. Traditional political forces have effectively been elbowed out in some cases, and in others have been seriously shaken by an exasperated electorate. Alternative political forces that were previously considered marginal, or which didn't even exist or register as meaningful contenders back in 2012 have benefitted. The change in the European political landscape has been as sudden as it is profound.

Emerging alternative political forces are not confined to the far right. They include far-left movements such as Alexis Tsipras's Syriza party in Greece or Podemos in Spain. They include a new breed of political animal such as Beppe Grillo's Movimento Cinque Stelle in Italy, which is neither really right nor left and not even centre. It is a truly 'de-ideologized' party 'made of everything and its opposite' in the words of European affairs commentator Leonardo Maisano. They include brand-new centrist and pro-EU movements such as Emmanuel Macron's En Marche! in France. The rise of this party is a paradox—its pro-globalization, pro-EU and pro-immigration stance embodies everything that is rejected by unhappy citizens across Europe—that had more to do with fear of the far-right's outlandish economic programme than with an endorsement of Macron's policies. What these political forces have in common is that their arrival at the forefront of the political scene has been as swift as it was unexpected and impactful. These parties and their leaders are, by and large, brand new, inexperienced and untested. Generally labelled 'populist', they arose as the result of citizens rejecting traditional political structures. In some countries they have assumed power, while in others they have the potential of doing so. At the very least, they have the potential to exercise influence by participating in government coalitions or simply capturing significant numbers of votes. They also have the power to take Europe into uncharted territory. The very visible impact of the 'trilogy' and its high emotional charge undoubtedly played a key role in this transformation by acting as a catalyst. It increased the velocity of a reaction that was bound to take place at some time. Yet, as earlier pointed out, the reasons for this new political paradigm are not confined to the 'trilogy' alone. The reasons citizens came to look for answers beyond the traditional political landscape include the usual suspects of globalization and austerity but also the nature of the European project itself.

The Changing Soul of Europe

The paradox of globalization is that, culturally, it tends to flatten the world. It promotes the socio-cultural homogenization of the planet. Economically it can 'unintentionally' promote cleavages which have, for a long time, escaped the attention of observers and governments in the Western world. For all the good it has brought to many worldwide, globalization has created a new class of discontents in the West. The grievances of this class have not been addressed by traditional political forces, when they have not been being totally ignored or dismissed as unworthy of attention. Some, such as essayist Natacha Polony, feel that globalization and freetrade have alleviated the poverty of millions of Indians and Chinese while ruining the middle classes in Western countries.[2] American economics Nobel Prize Laureate Joseph Stiglitz pointed out that in the USA the 'real income of a typical full-time male worker is lower than it was more than four decades ago'. For him, the big winners of globalization are 'the global 1 percent—the very rich around the world—and the new middle classes in emerging markets such as China and India' while 'the group that did the worse of all—seeing virtually no growth in their incomes in a span of two decades—was the working class in Europe and America.'[3]

In the Western world, globalization's impact has without doubt been uneven. It has favoured those living in well-connected large cites, who are plugged-in to the world at large and able to enjoy its newfound flatness, who can travel, who have a higher education. These people had the ticket to join the train as it was departing the station. Many others, however, living in smaller cities, in the countryside, poorer areas, or places much less 'connected' to the fast moving globalized world didn't have the right ticket in their hand. People depending on activities and jobs rendered obsolete by globalization (or its by-product, delocalization) were in the same position. They ended up watching the train leave the station. They have found themselves at the wrong end of the growing income disparity gap. They are the losers of globalization which they perceive as a scourge and its advocates as the enemy. Many of them value their roots and identity and are deeply unhappy with the liberal elites who dominate politics and culture and dismiss these notions as 'passé'. In one of the best characterizations of the issues at hand, British essayist David Goodhart frames this ideological struggle affecting the Western world at the dawn of the twenty-first century as one pitting on one side the 'Anywheres' and on the other the 'Somewheres'. 'Anywheres' are a class of well-educated, open, mobile people, who are at home anywhere in the world. They can create start-ups, sustain immigration and EU integration and thrive in a globalized context (the most extreme of whom he labels 'Global Villagers'). 'Somewheres' are a class whose identities are more 'prescribed', they are middle-class and working-class people who are less mobile and more attached to their socio-cultural roots. For them globalization means job losses and closed factories that benefit unfair competitors abroad who have taken advantage of open trade and were not subjected to the same cumbersome domestic rules and regulations (Goodhart labels the most extreme of these 'Somewheres' as 'High Authoritarians').[4] To Goodhart, since the 1990s the right has championed economic openness and market liberalism, while the left has championed socio-cultural liberalism. In both cases this was to the delight of the 'Anywheres', who also conquered the high ground in the realms of politics and media. In the 1970s 90% of Americans aged 30 earned more than their parents, a proportion that has fallen to 50% today, with the white middle lower class bearing the brunt of this decline.[5] In the USA, the 'Somewheres'—mostly middle aged whites with limited education, whose life expectancy has been declining as proof of their 'obsolescence' (as pointed out by economics Nobel Prize winner Angus Deaton)—took their revenge voting for Trump.[6] The spectacular rise of the far-right Alternative für Deutschland (AfD) party during the September 2017 general election in Germany—a country that was supposed to be immune to extremism—resembles what happened with Trump. The AfD 'won support from voters struggling to make ends meet in one of Europe's richest countries and frustrated with mainstream parties that, they felt, ignored their concerns'.[7] The popular daily *Bild* spoke of a 'vote of anger' that would profoundly change Germany while the conservative daily *Frankfurter Allgemeine Zeitung* warned of the advent of a new era, rougher and more conflictual.[8] In Europe, the 'Somewheres' gravitated towards alternative politicians who advocated protectionism, a halt to immigration, or leaving the EU and the euro. In both cases, electoral geography shows clear voting patterns in accordance with these considerations. Political scientist Jean-François Schira noted that, as a consequence of the schism between those who benefited from the new liberal order and those who were left behind, the physical 'de-construction of nations' splitting the centre from the periphery can now be observed everywhere in the West. In the United Kingdom, Brexit pitted Greater London against the rest of the country. In the USA the division is between coastal and central states. In France the 2017 presidential election's first round showed a clear political division between larger and smaller cities.[9] According to Schira, the cleavage is no longer an ideological one between right and left but a sociological one between the winners and losers of liberalism. The risk is that the absence of guiding ideologies will fuel anger and extreme violence. This thesis relates, to some extent, to that of Indian essayist Pankaj Mishra, who believes we now find ourselves in an 'Age of Anger', as per the title of his important and challenging book.[10] He explores the causes for the irrational anger that seems to animate a plethora of actors today, from ISIS to far-right nationalists, in a historical perspective. To Mishra, anger animates the discontent of those left behind. It has gone mainstream in response to the globalization movement and to the Western ideals of individualism, free enterprise and secularism, which have become the new normal all over the world, leaving many without a clear compass.

Just as globalization generated a new class of discontents, the harsh austerity policies imposed by creditor nations on debtor nations in the aftermath of the eurozone crisis created unhappiness at both ends of the spectrum. In creditor nations many angry citizens were hell-bent on refusing to pay for what they perceived as the profligacy and lack of discipline of 'others' (i.e. debtors such as Greece). This popular theme was championed by far-right parties in creditor nations and was naturally in sync with nationalist feelings. At the other end of the spectrum angry masses from affected debtor countries complained of being hopelessly and forever stuck in an austerity prison imposed by 'foreigners'. They believed they had lost control of their economic destinies to the benefit of rich countries, yet another theme that fuelled nationalist feelings. In addition, the European project itself—with its supra-state, its pan-European integration agenda and its implied dilution of national sovereignty—had for a long time been a target of nationalist sentiment everywhere. This targeting was in addition to the broadly popular anti-EU feelings fuelled by austerity measures perceived as imposed by Brussels.

Centrifugal and nationalist forces have undeniably been at work in Europe for quite some time. Yet, by themselves, these forces were never able to provoke a truly popular agitation and an extensive revival of nationalism in Europe, let alone cause the rapid demise of the European project. Most people, at least on the continent, felt that on balance the European project, the euro and open trade had been beneficial. They were wary of throwing it all away. Polls taken in the Netherlands, Germany and France in 2016 showed majorities wanted to stay in the EU. In Italy, despite serious misgivings about the single currency, a solid majority wanted the country to remain in the eurozone.[11] This is not to say that there could not be surprises if a far-right party such as France's Front National (FN) takes power and organizes a referendum (as Marine Le Pen pledged to do). Yet it is highly unlikely that a mainstream or non-radical party in power anywhere would take the risk of organizing a referendum on exiting the EU or the eurozone. Referenda have a tendency to become an occasion for people to vent all sorts of grievances besides those related to the subject matter and can easily get out of hand, as David Cameron and Theresa May learned a bit too late. The 'trilogy' of UMI, Islamization and Jihadism was something entirely different and took it all to a different level. The 'trilogy' may have been a latecomer in stoking the fires of nationalism but its high-impact effects were highly visible to all. It carried a tremendous emotional charge, making it the catalyst of Europe's very sudden and profound shift to the right. The far-right parties of Germany, France, the Netherlands or Sweden (and the rest) could never have got as far and fast as they recently did merely on their traditional anti-Europe platforms. By co-opting the highly emotional and personal issues of security, immigration and national identity that fuelled popular anger in recent years, and adding these issues to their traditional platforms they changed everything. As the *Telegraph* reported: 'Thanks to the failure to keep control over the migration crisis and escape austerity-economics in the eurozone, the far-Right drumbeat has now become the constant knocking in the pipes of Europe's politics at a time when the plumbing looks increasingly fit to burst.'[12]

It has been obvious from the eurozone crisis that Europe's governing 'elites' have mastered the art of muddling through. In dealing with the 'trilogy' it is in their nature to also try to muddle through. Europe's response to it has thus fallen short on every count. Not only are the challenges posed by the 'trilogy' neither receding nor contained: they are actually becoming more acute by the day. Driven by their 'elites', Europeans have, for a long time, chosen accommodation. There is, however, now palpable fear among citizens that things have gone too far and nobody is doing anything about it, least of all governments. People feel that a battle is taking place that could imperil their way of life for the benefit of undeserving 'others'. A sea change has been taking place across Europe as the liberal left, which until recently imposed its pro-minority agenda, is no longer in sync with a dejected mainstream population. If radical measures to address the issues are not taken by democratic governments, they may soon be taken by undemocratic governments put in place by a fed-up electorate.

Farewell Nation-State, Hello Nations' State

In the aftermath of the surprising 2016 US election, Columbia University professor Mark Lilla pointed out that the American left had, for a generation, been 'obsessed by diversity, celebrating ethnic and other differences to the point of collective hysteria'. According to him, it had 'focused on the rights of minorities instead of on what united the American people: appealing explicitly to the black, Latino, LGBT (lesbian, gay, bisexual and trans) electorates, to the detriment of working classes whites and of those with religious convictions, who felt left out and cost Hillary Clinton the election'.[13] This line of thought was not dissimilar to that of French political essayist Eric Zemmour for whom the left—which, in the USA as well as in Europe used to be the mouthpiece of the people—changed its position, reinventing itself as the mouthpiece of minorities.[14] The trend identified by Lilla and Zemmour can be traced to the 1980s, when leftist politicians turned their attention away from the working class and traditional issues of equality and redistribution of wealth and re-focused instead on issues of race, gender, religion and sexuality.

When it comes to minorities, not all Euromuslims are happy with what they resent as the left's patronizing attitude. Tunisian author and French resident Sonia Mabrouk laments that the Islamo-leftists' portrayal of Euromuslims as a minority exploited by society and in need of protection and assistance deprives it of a much needed debate on religion and other matters.[15] According to author Philippe De Villiers, clientelism on the left (but not only on the left) plays an increasing role in France.

Having lost the vote of blue collar workers the left now looks for votes within the minority communities of the *banlieues* (perhaps a sensible electoral strategy given that birth rates there are double the rate of the rest of the country). De Villiers says this situation leads politicians to make deals with minority leaders and close their eyes to Islamization in exchange for votes.[16] Some, such as controversial philosopher Michel Onfray (who has been called an Islamophobe and was the object of warnings by ISIS) have gone much further, arguing that the left is as fascinated by Islam as it used to be by twentieth-century dictators.[17] According to Zemmour, US and European 'elites' came to share the same ideology and the same belief, in the name of antiracism, human rights and universalism, that national identity did not exist anymore. One may or may not agree with these views but it is widely accepted that the political left and the 'elites' became the main vector of the new, post-modern ideology described earlier in this book. The main by-product of this ideology became the negation of the traditional identity of nations and, as we shall see in a later section, provoked a reaction which has influenced the very recent rise of alternative political forces in the West.

In its early days at least, any new ideology or religion carries a vital energy that drives it to conquer more and more hearts and mind. Modern Europe is not immune from this impulse and has spawned totalitarian ideologies with planetary impacts and ambitions. British historian Mark Mazower reminded us that national socialism and communism are examples of ideologies that fit 'uncomfortably well' with Europe's history.[18] As a consequence of the ideological bias embedded in the European project, Europe came to perceive itself—not without reason—as a force for good and moderation in the world: a warm-hearted universalist. Europe's national anthem sounded increasingly like Hare Krishna and less and less like a passage from Beethoven's Ninth Symphony. On a broader scale, universalist principles forming the bedrock of the new ideology fuelled a never-ending expansion of external borders. Europe was happy to proselytize and welcome into its heavenly bubble any neighbouring country that would embrace its ideology and rules, with scant regard for the manageability of an enlarged construct.

Not content with absorbing nations on its immediate periphery, Europe welcomed with open arms masses of people from places far away from its borders fleeing the 'world of disorder',[19] many of whom came to share the benefits of Europe's generous 'Civilization of Entitlements'.[20] In this noble enterprise, little thought was given to the implications for social stability (and budgets) of continuing to import masses of people who, for the most part, would probably end up swelling the legions of the unemployed and would inevitably become an alienated, dejected, if not hostile, underclass. No thought was given to the possibility that, wherever minorities became very significant and long for a separate identity and space, the relatively known and stable 'nation-state' format might give way to the relatively unknown post-modern format of a *'nations'* state'. That is, a geographic area in which anyone from anywhere in the world, friend or foe, rich or poor could come to live. Whether or not they had a place or fitted in, shared local values or didn't, whether they melted into the mainstream or wanted to carve their own separate tribal space, they were welcome. The tested idea of a nation-state with a dominant culture and ethnic group was giving way to the notion of the state as a patchwork of separate, auto-defined 'communities'. Each defended its right to be different and lived under the same roof, governed by a technocratic, apolitical government: a construct for which there was no political precedent. Everybody was welcomed to the party. Ideas such as national cohesiveness, shared identity, shared values, shared language and history were considered passé. *P*olitical essayist Ivan Rioufol lamented the post-nationalism that transformed the previously indivisible nation into an 'open space' in which minorities would be protected by positive discrimination.[21] The potential instability of a construct in which society was divided into discrete elements with little in terms of glue to keep them together was not questioned. To more and more Europeans, multiculturalism, initially praised as the living proof of European tolerance, has become the vector for this communitarianism, i.e. a system of social organization based on small communities, which carries the risk of the disintegration of the dominant national culture, potentially leading to anarchy.

Threats to the cohesiveness of the nation-state may not only stem from socio-cultural or ethnic factors, such as those we just explored. Economic and other forces favouring smaller 'regions' over the geographically larger 'nation-state' can, perversely, also play a centrifugal role. Globalization is, to some extent, such a force. The world is now so interconnected that some dynamic regions are directly plugged into the larger world market, a reality that may beget the perception that the central state is not that useful after all. Due to its smaller size, a region can be more cohesive and reactive. In the twenty-first century, the large nation-state may not always appear to represent the optimal configuration for social and economic life, particularly if one conveniently choses to ignore items such as defence and infrastructure. The more a region is successful in its direct dealings with the world; the more it is able to fend for itself; the more historically and culturally homogeneous it is; the more the central state burdens it to support economically less successful areas in the country; the more independent the region will naturally aspire to be. To some extent in Europe the nation-state ends up sandwiched between, under it, smaller regions (or states in a federal state) and, over it, supranational entities such as the EU. It is logical that citizens feel closer to local and regional authorities than national ones, let alone supranational ones, or that they are more attached to their city or region than to the wider state, let alone all of Europe. This can perhaps explain to some extent the Brexit vote and the attempt by separatist forces in Catalonia to break away from Spain in 2017, perhaps the forerunner of a yearning for smaller independent regions—such as those the continent's landscape was riddled with for many centuries.

Vox Populi

Europeans have, in recent times, been subjected to a trio of highly seductive and dynamic forces—globalization, the European project and the new post-national ideology—working in concert, pulling in the same direction to remove all sorts of barriers. These combined forces promoted international cooperation, supra-national alliances, social inclusiveness (which morphed into the sacrosanctity of minorities) and the moralization of life. At the same time, however, they brought about the deconstruction and slow death of the traditional notions of 'a people' (with its unique identity and roots) and 'nation-state' (with its sovereignty). Not everybody was happy with this trend. Post-national political 'elites' made the mistake of underestimating the powerful reality that still constituted the nation-state and the depth of its appeal, compared with the limited appeal of Europe among ordinary citizens. As we have already pointed out, resentment had been building up among those who felt left out or threatened by globalization; among those unhappy with the loss of national sovereignty to faceless and unelected EU bureaucrats; and among those uncomfortable with the moralism of the new ideology and the growing presence and assertiveness of minorities its inclusiveness brought about. Western societies were divided in the past between communist and capitalist visions of the world. This time the fight was between a progressive and seductive view that embraced universalism, multiculturalism and globalization, and a conservative view attached to traditional values of sovereignty and national identity. It is a shame that the extreme polarization of Western societies over these two views has obfuscated the fact that they were not necessarily mutually exclusive. An open debate might have led to a workable compromise but this debate never took place, weakening the cohesiveness of Western societies.

Flaws in the new ideology led to the questioning of some of its dogmas. British essayist David Goodhart argues that multiculturalism became a symbol of the abandonment of the working class by liberal and leftist elites who espouse the cause of minorities. This multiculturalism was 'asymmetrical', Goodhart writes, because it only championed the cause of the cultural identity of ethnic minorities, while ignoring the cultural traditions and way of life of host societies: something not lost on the 'Somewheres'.[22] Leading French daily *Le Figaro* complained of an anti-racism that had become militant, increasingly driven by identity markers, increasingly communitarianist and increasingly destroying freedom.[23] *The Economist* pointed out that, in some places, the police or social services have indeed failed to act against 'pathologies in Muslim communities', fearful of being tarred with racism.[24] A closer look at how selectively the new ideology's principles were applied at times should raise doubts about the universality of some of its moral claims. Feminists, by and large, remained silent following the Cologne mass sexual assaults perpetrated by migrants. The same people who defended the pro-minority agenda and condoned the Islamization of European societies in the name of inclusiveness, remained overwhelmingly silent to the persecution of Arab Christians by Muslims in the Arab world. The same occurred—

until very recently—in relation to the plight of the Rohingya (the 1.1 million Muslim minority reportedly persecuted by the Buddhist majority in Myanmar, said to be the most persecuted minority on earth);[25] to the lynching of minority-Indian Muslims accused of killing sacred cows by Hindu purists in India;[26] to measures by China to ban certain baby names with religious connotations in its predominantly Muslim Xinjiang Province;[27] to the plight of African migrants ransomed or sold in slave markets in Libya;[28] to the more than 100,000 Nigerians fleeing violence from Jihadist group Boko Haram who have been forcefully sent back home by Cameroon since 2015;[29] to the increase in xenophobic violence perpetrated in South Africa by locals on migrants from other African countries.[30] The plight of minorities seemed to be worthy of the attention of the Western 'intelligentsia' only when the perpetrators of misdeeds were Westerners.

In his book *Who are we?* Harvard's Samuel P. Huntington describes a USA unable to integrate the millions of new migrants from Mexico with the same success with which it integrated previous waves of migrants. This is because Mexicans continued to speak their own language, he argues, go to their own schools and watch their own TV: living in the USA in essentially the same way they were living back home. In this situation, the old, established nation is slowly replaced by a nation of newcomers. In a November 2000 article published by the *Center for Immigration Studies*, Huntington states that 'Mexican immigration poses challenges to our policies and to our identity in a way nothing else has in the past'. Zemmour recognizes this situation as similar to that in Europe, with the difference that Europe's migrants are not Catholic, but Muslim. Few people will deny that recent mass migration is changing Europe. Yet the absence of a real debate has prevented any meaningful analysis. While the new ideology met great success in conquering the hearts and minds of many people, the rest of them resented the changes in social and cultural norms that resulted from massive immigration. They felt abandoned by traditional political 'elites', that seemed more interested in upholding the moralist universalist doctrine of the new ideology and defending minorities and newcomers, rather than protecting the roots and the historical and cultural assets of the established society.

The stage was therefore set for the comeback of the 'people' and, since traditional channels rejected the people, its comeback could only happen outside traditional channels. Brexit and Trump triumphed without the assistance of mainstream institutional support and despite the media (and everybody else it seemed) giving them very little chance of winning. According to essayist Ivan Rioufol, Trump positioned himself as the champion of the fight against the tyranny of minorities who were perceived as sapping the cohesion of the free world. He was against the doctrine of diversity promoted by the left, and, coming after Brexit, his election was proof that 'nations' were back in the business of history.[31] To political philosopher Chantal Del Sol, Trump and Clinton were caricatures of their respective camps, 'populists' and 'globalists'. Populist currents are, says Del Sol, attached to roots (such as family and country) and these roots are anathema to the liberal universalist elites that govern Western societies today. Whatever credence one may give to Rioufol and Del Sol's arguments, there are similarities and differences between the USA and Europe concerning the causes behind the recent rise of the nationalist far right. They are similar because wages have stagnated for decades in the USA,[32] and more recently in Europe,[33] leading many voters on both sides of the Atlantic to feel left out and betrayed by liberal globalist ideologies which they hold responsible for the loss of jobs to foreign shores. They are also similar because the left has, in both cases, moved from defending the cause of workers to championing the cause of minorities, compelling the lower classes to abandon the left. They are different because the 'trilogy' has not hit the USA as it has Europe. Since 9/11, Jihadist incidents have been extremely rare in the USA and its Muslim minority amounts to only 1% of the population. It is far more integrated into the US system than Europe's own, so one can't seriously speak of a palpable Islamization trend in US society as in Europe. The only significant element of the 'trilogy' to hit the USA is UMI. This concerns, by and large, Mexican migrants, who are variously reviled by some dissatisfied voters for stealing jobs; causing downward pressure on wages; freeloading or failing to integrate into the US mainstream; and threatening national identity and cohesion because of the very visible and growing trend of Latinization of certain areas of the USA.

The strategy adopted by mainstream political forces and the media in confronting the far right is to label it a bunch of dangerous lunatics, a strategy that hasn't exactly worked well given the spectacular gains made by the far right in recent years. Conventional wisdom sees populism as a pathology, as the reaction of nonentities who deserve contempt for ruining the party. Within societies the democratic debate is confined to discrediting and excluding populist ideas, sometimes hysterically, with no explanation provided other than that populism is attached to the darkest pages of European history. 'Elites' side with the people, according to Del Sol, as long as the people defend universal socialism, but once they start defending their own roots and identity, the 'elites' vilify them.[34] These observations are, to some extent, shared by French philosopher Vincent Coussedière, who believes the 'elites' have turned away from the people and that what we call populism is simply the 'old peoples'' resisting their dissolution in globalization. Rioufol sees the success of France's far right FN as the direct consequence of a political sphere that has cut itself off from the people. To Coussedière the elites' simplistic vilification of populism saves them a truly democratic debate and allows them to disregard the reality that peoples want to continue being peoples. They want to retain their way of life, their identity and sovereignty and their power to decide on matters which concern them. These prerogatives are threatened by forces such as mass immigration, supra-national institutions such as the EU and post-national alliances. To Coussedière, populism is neither from the right nor from the left, it is the manifestation of a desire to maintain roots and identity against the forces of globalization and multiculturalism.[35] In his mind voters are not defined anymore by the economy, but by culture. Just as populism from the left positioned itself in the past as the defender of the people against elites and the establishment, now populism from the right positions itself as the defender of the people against an elite which protects the 'others': migrants and Muslims.[36]

In a speech on 14 July 2016, just a few hours before the Jihadist massacre in Nice, president Hollande said that the main threat in France was the rise of populism, disregarding what actually caused the rise of populism and nationalism. One may or may not agree with historian Jacques Bainville's definition of nationalism as an attitude of defence made necessary by the weakening of the State; or with writer Romain Gary's characterization of patriotism as love for your kin while nationalism is hatred for others; or Albert Schweitzer's description of nationalism as patriotism which lost its nobility. Today's popular nationalism is not an ideology and does not find its roots in xenophobia: it is the embodiment of fear. The fear of losing socio-cultural identity in the era of multiculturalism and the fear of losing one's job and future in the era of globalization. Ruling elites should make an effort to understand the reasons why voters actually flock to alternative politicians and modify their programmes accordingly. They should not mimic them but address their issues. In its June 2017 review of Douglas Murray's book *The Strange Death of Europe: Immigration, Identity, Islam*, *The Economist* reminds us of the author's remark that the policy of isolating anti-migrant parties tended to make them even more popular and that when the Sverigedemokraterna (Sweden Democrats) were first elected into parliament with 5% of the vote in 2010 other politicians 'treated the new MPs as pariahs', not a very effective strategy given that the party subsequently became one of the most popular in Sweden, scoring 24% of the vote.[37] For all their shortcomings, Europe is better off being governed by traditional parties co-opting some ideas from the far right or involving it in coalition governments, rather than reaching the point of no-return and risking finding itself governed by fiercely nationalist parties.

Not only have ordinary citizens felt abandoned by out-of-touch mainstream political 'elites' unable and unwilling to provide effective solutions, but these same 'elites'—the mainstream governments and media—have been found time and again to hide, suppress and manipulate information in order to promote a false, self-serving narrative. The bond of trust between traditional governing 'elites' and ordinary citizens has consequently been broken, remarkably, even in Nordic countries. The subsequent disenfranchising of citizens from the system has greatly contributed to popular migration towards the nationalist far right. It is time to explore the role of this institutionalized *omertà* in the recent change to the soul of Europe.

A Conspiracy of Silence

It took almost a week for German authorities and media to reluctantly acknowledge the mass sexual assaults committed by migrants and refugees in Cologne during the 2015 year-end celebrations.[38] Before Cologne a priority of Germany's political class had been to show that it was the most tolerant country in Europe and that nothing bad could come from its *Willkommenskultur*. As a result the victims of the attacks were, to some extent, an inconvenience that was better ignored. For similar reasons it was only in January 2016 that most Swedes (and the world) learned that similar incidents had occurred in their country in 2014. 'It is absolutely clear—with the publication of internal memos by the newspaper *Dagens Nyheter*—that the Stockholm police failed to report the sex assaults at the music festival for fear of worsening ethnic tensions' reported the *Guardian*.[39] 'Instead of a frank and open discussion, an Omertà has been imposed. Its leading backers are mostly younger European women's activists, cultural relativists and anti-racists, who are accused of being more concerned about not offending migrant communities and Muslim men than standing up for the women subjected to the marauding gropers, and group rapists.'[40] Violent incidents involving migrants and refugees preying on Europe's 'target rich environment', abusing their welcome and encouraged by the permissiveness of the system are plenty. In fairness, they are perpetrated by a tiny minority of migrants and refugees. Yet citizens are mostly kept in the dark as, in most of Europe, authorities and pro-immigration forces have, with the complicity of a subservient mass-media, deliberately downplayed and often actively covered-up the extent of such incidents and continue to do so. Top German public broadcaster ZDF refused to air a segment about a rape on its 'Crime-watch' show because the 'dark-skinned' suspect was a migrant, with the following justification: 'We don't want to inflame the situation and spread a bad mood. The migrants don't deserve it'.[41] Their attitude was shared by public television chain ARD which didn't bother to report the arrest of a young Afghan migrant who raped and killed 'Maria', a young German student who was helping at a refugee welcoming centre. Former German interior minister Hans-Peter Friedrich spoke of a 'cartel of silence' in the mainstream media. He added that 'There's suspicion that they believe they don't have to report on such assaults, especially involving migrants and foreigners, for fear of unsettling the public' and decried a cover-up by the media and politicians that 'led to an illusion about an idyllic world that never existed'.[42] His view was reinforced by André Schulz, head of Germany's criminal police association who bluntly declared: 'The policy has been to leave the German population in the dark [...] ordinary citizens are being played for fools'.[43] In early 2016, the writing was on the wall with polls showing that over 80% of Germans felt the Merkel government had lost control of the refugee situation,[44] and that 40% mistrusted the press.[45]

The Western media has also been accused of failing to reporting on the plight of minority Arab Christians mistreated by Muslims in refugee camps and on board refugee boats or on the ransacking of some hotels in which refugees were hosted and similar incidents.[46] Authorities and the media are often very quick in depicting perpetrators of 'lone wolf' terrorist attacks as mentally ill, implying that their deeds have nothing to do with Jihadism and are merely random acts of folly that any 'normal' society can statistically expect. This deceitful spin amounts to lumping the truly ill together with terrorists. It was decried by the vice president of the Austrian Society of Psychiatry, Dr Georg Psota, who lamented that 'too often and too quickly atrocities and the frequently perpetrated attacks in Europe are mixed with mental illness'. He added that 'the acts of political extremists and religious fanatics are not the result of depression or other mental illness, but of the highest criminal energy'.[47] According to Daniel Zagury, an expert in psychiatry, terrorists never try to pretend they are demented.[48] This is not to say that mental illness and Jihadism are mutually exclusive; it may be that in some cases some mentally ill people are prone to commit Jihadist acts. Nevertheless, in their desire to defend the narrative according to which the problems of radicalization and Jihadism in Europe are minor and under control, the authorities are not beyond masking obvious Jihadist crimes as 'normal delinquency'. The stabbing of a French farmer by a known *fiché S* radical who was supposed to be under house arrest was a case in point. The perpetrator shouted 'Allahu Akbar' during the attack but French courts initially considered the crime to be of a 'common' criminal nature as opposed to terrorism.[49]

In recent times, anyone who interfered with the illusion that all was well with migrants and refugees risked being labelled a racist or a Nazi: the modern version of being burned at the stake. Journalist Matthias Matussek was allegedly fired from German newspaper *Die Welt* after he dared establish a link between the terrorist attacks in Paris and the refugees, despite such a link having been proved to exist.[50] German publishers and bookshops reportedly stopped distributing the best-selling books of right-winger Akif Pirincci, a writer of Turkish origin who warned that Germany was becoming Islamic.[51] This was allegedly the first time such self-censorship had occurred since the Nazi era. Aside from the resignation of the Cologne Chief of Police, there was no hint that anyone involved in any cover-ups would be denounced anywhere in Europe. Former French anti-terrorism judge Alain Marsaud spoke of *omertà* among elected politicians on issues related to Islamization, as they fear being called Islamophobic.[52] Democracies pride themselves on the idea that an open debate is healthy and that the truth is supposed to set you free. They should have added an exception for inconvenient truths.

The motivation behind institutionalized self-censure and *omertà* is variously painted as a desire to refrain from stoking intra-community tensions or from offending minorities. According to Michel Onfray, the press is not free, has never been free, will never be free and its motivations are also driven by economic realities. In France, for instance, the mainstream media survives thanks to government handouts to the tune of 400 million euros per year, so it is not surprising that the media would promote the governing elites' dominant liberal ideology.[53] Yet, aside from the fact that it smells suspiciously like the mantra of totalitarian regimes—according to which people should be kept in the dark for their own good—it is difficult to not see behind these manipulations a desire to hide failed immigration policies and to push a liberal political agenda. Stockholm Police Chief Peter Agren—in charge of the 2014 music festival mentioned earlier—admitted as much when he confessed that 'Sometimes we dare not tell how it is because we think it plays into the hands of the Sweden Democrats' (the far right party in Sweden).[54] Laurent Bouvet may be a political scientist who comes from the French left but he had the courage to point out that the media has become the promoter of its own self-proclaimed view of how society should be. In other words, it espouses a 'neo-colonial' leftist view in which the migrant has replaced the worker as a victim of oppression and in which multiculturalism is sacred. The media is ready to exonerate anyone who adheres to these ideas, he says, and condemn anyone who does not, without consideration for facts.[55] Contrary to the mainstream media, which is so often suspected to be subservient to governments, online media (which has its own share of spin-doctors and fake news) has generally remained out of reach, to the great chagrin of some authorities. Sure enough, a new law was passed by the German parliament in the summer of 2017 imposing up to 50 million euros in fines on social media networks with, the excuse of curtailing hate speech and 'fake news'. This law prompted the German journalist Jochen Bittner to wonder 'Why is Berlin cracking down on free speech online?', adding that 'a chilling effect on freedom of expression can already be felt: Twitter is now blocking accounts in Germany that have even the slightest whiff of hate speech'.[56] The *Guardian* to warned that the measure 'could have drastic consequences for free speech online'.[57] There may be good intentions behind this new law, but the fact remains that in Germany at least, social media will no longer be able to stray too far from the government's ideological line. This brazen institutionalized suppression and manipulation of information by governments and media alike achieves the opposite effect to the one intended. It fosters a climate of mistrust that has profound implications which traditional political 'elites' have failed to grasp.

The first implication is that a proper debate is prevented from taking place on important issues. This stands in the way of any proper analysis of problems and attempts to find solutions. In addition, it perverts the idea of an open, democratic society. Institutionalized *omertà* also discredits the political establishment, giving ammunition to extremist parties, such as when Germany's AfD adopted the slogan "Lügenpresse" ('lying press'), which has echoes of the Nazi era'.[58] Another consequence is that people will rely more and more on non-mainstream 'people media', such as internet posts and videos. These can be just as manipulated, and they have the power to rapidly mobilize masses of citizens, adding another layer of instability to the European social equation. Finally, *omertà* fuels a growing feeling among the mainstream population that minorities have become a new sacrosanct class and that the authorities are on their side. People are no fools and, as they feel that the authorities are not adequately protecting them; that traditional political parties provide no effective answers; and that they cannot trust their governments and media, many gravitate towards alternative politicians, if only out of spite. The cover-up of sex assaults in Sweden for instance, was rightly recognized by some observers from the media itself as 'a gift for xenophobes'.[59] Centre-right parties have been surprisingly unable to fill the gap because they are either pro-immigration themselves, such as in Germany; divided and weak, such as in France; or perceived by voters as not going far enough to protect security and national identity. The irresponsible behaviour of mainstream political forces, their failure to recognize, let alone address issues in earnest and their growing disconnect with a dejected mainstream population are important causes of the recent and dramatic rise of the nationalist far right in Europe. Right after the Cologne incident, German magazine *Der Spiegel* commented that 'voters, if they don't feel like their concerns are being taken seriously by Merkel's conservatives or her Social Democratic coalition partners, will search for answers from other, more radical groups'.[60]

The Future of the Past

Germany was a latecomer to the popular shift to the nationalist, anti-migrant right already underway in many parts of Europe. In Sweden, two people were reportedly stabbed to death in an Ikea store in the summer of 2015 by an asylum seeker on the verge of being deported. Soon after, the popularity of the far right Sweden Democrats—intent on reducing immigration by 90%—made a dramatic jump. They became the country's largest party,[61] and were still the country's second largest political force in early 2017, polling at 18%.[62] The Sweden Democrats were closely following the footsteps of Denmark's far-right Dansk Folkeparti (Danish People's Party) and Finland's far-right Perussuomalaiset (True Finns) and their successes a few months earlier. These successes were evidence that even in traditionally welcoming Nordic countries anti-immigration nationalist parties were now making substantial and swift gains. The decision by the authorities in Randers (Denmark) to make it *mandatory* for menus to offer pork in 2016,[63] remained an isolated case. Yet it was a telling example of a dramatic change in mood across Europe. In Finland, the True Finns became a solid second and its leader Timo Soini became Foreign Minister. In Denmark, the centre-right government couldn't govern without the support of the Danish People's Party. Governing coalitions including far-right parties which weren't even on the radar a few years before, now became a reality. In France, the far-right

FN had remained a fringe party with limited clout for a long time following its founding in 1972 (although its then leader Jean Marie Le Pen came in second, behind Jacques Chirac in the 2002 presidential election). Its dramatic success in 2017 can be attributed in great part to Marine Le Pen's shrewd use of the wave of discontent that carried her to the position of a front runner in the presidential election. This would have been unthinkable just a few years ago. In the Netherlands, Partij voor de Vrijheid (Party for Freedom), the anti-Islam, anti-EU nationalist party of Geert Wilders—who pioneered far right populism in Europe more than a decade ago—made substantial gains over just a couple of years to become the country's largest party by late 2016. Its ability to actually win enough seats in the 2017 elections to govern alone was never seriously considered, given the country's proportional representation system. Founded as recently as 2013, Germany's far right anti-migrant AfD party, whose then-boss Frauke Petry suggested shooting migrants at the border, effectively became the third largest political force in Germany, polling just a few points behind the SPD (the coalition partner of Merkel's CDU party) in early 2018. The AfD attracted voters who were 'anti-establishment, anti-liberalization, anti-European, anti-everything that has come to be regarded as the norm', *The New York Times* reported Sylke Tempel of the German Council on Foreign Relations as saying in October 2017. With 46.7% of the votes, Norbert Hofer, the presidential candidate for Austria's far right anti-migrant party Freiheitliche Partei Österreichs (FPO) narrowly lost the 2016 presidential election.[64] One notable exception was Italy, where Beppe Grillo's MoVimento Cinque Stelle (M5S) became, by the end of 2016, the country's driving political force. While clearly populist and fed by disenchantment with traditional politics, it started as an ambiguous political animal, not really nationalist, not openly anti-migrant or anti-EU (although by 2017 it had very visibly hardened its positions on these issues), neither truly from the far right or the far left. M5S's views on welfare, austerity and the environment are decidedly leftist, while its views on the euro, immigration and Russia had by 2017 decidedly moved to the right.

What all this shows is that Europe's political landscape has, in the course of just a few years, been turned surprisingly upside down. Far-right parties, which had remained for a long time small, fringe political forces burst onto centre-stage, in great part because of the impact of the 'trilogy' on the European psyche. For the first time since the end of the Second World War 'Nationalists and Populists (were) Poised to Dominate European Balloting'.[65] They will not disappear tomorrow because the causes of their recent successes are likely to linger for a long time, if not worsen. Their rise is not a temporary phenomenon. Traditional political parties all over the continent are now fighting for their survival. What does the nationalist far right want, and what could happen if it came to power?

Grapes of Wrath

The European far right comes loaded with heavy historical baggage. It is not just that it is openly xenophobic or, as some fear, that populist authoritarianism may be spreading everywhere.[66] It is not just that the far right is anti-semitic—a feature it shares with many Muslim immigrants as well as many European leftists (who, according to Stefan Schuster, head of Germany's Central Council of Jews, disguise their anti-semitism as criticism of Israel)—causing anti-semitism to be on the rise in many places in Europe. In Germany. '90 percent of Jews perceive anti-Semitism as a very big problem and [...] 70 percent avoid carrying any Jewish symbols in public'.[67] There could be very drastic consequences to a comeback of the far right on other fronts, such as the economy and European cohesion. A report by Morgan Stanley economists warned that 'the protest parties promise to turn back the clock' on free-market reforms while leaving 'sclerotic' labour and market regulations in place.[68] Conventional wisdom has it that the various European far-right parties are in sync with each other, not only on issues related to national identity, immigration and law and order, but also on conservative socio-economic policies. However, the picture that emerges when taking a closer look at what these parties stand for is far from monolithic, reflecting the specific situation of each country, political opportunism at the local level and lack of a shared core economic doctrine. 'Politico-economic ideas of far right parties', wrote the University of Bremen's Jan Rettig, 'do not so much orientate on coherent economic paradigms but rather on the different contexts they are active in'.[69]

In France, for instance, the FN's populist platform is in favour of an agenda of anti-capitalism and social welfare, with measures such as maintaining the 35 hours working week, increasing the minimum wage and bringing down the retirement age to 60 (a plainly unworkable measure that would probably have disastrous economic results). The FN favours nationalizations and upholds the complex and costly labour rules that are in large part responsible for France's chronically high unemployment. This programme can be said to be left-leaning, reflecting French citizens' supreme desire to cling to their cosy (and unsustainable) welfare culture and the high importance they (especially the working class) give to social protection in an increasingly uncertain economic context. Le Pen's philosophy sometimes echoes US President Donald Trump's calls for 'economic patriotism'. Among other policies, she would punish companies who manufacture abroad and reimport into France with a 35% tariff.[70] This philosophy is in contrast to the more neoliberal philosophies of Germany's AfD, who give economic competitiveness a high priority, to be achieved by a leaner bureaucracy and fewer regulations. Austria's FPO pushed for a sharp reduction in the welfare state (as did Norway's right-wing Progress Party), labour costs and whatever shackled free enterprise. England's UK Independence Party advocated deregulation, less public expenditure and cuts in welfare. With the rise of the far-right, protectionism would return, tariffs would rise and the free flow of goods and people across Europe would probably be curtailed. Broadly speaking, the populist and nationalist bias of the economic policies of the European far right raises doubts about the viability of its social and economic policies. From a global perspective questions arise about 'populism and what it means for the liberal economic order' in the words of R. Glenn Hubbard, a former economic adviser to US President George W. Bush.[71]

If there is one area par excellence in which all of Europe's far right parties concur it is that they are all anti-migrant, pro-law and order and all firmly defend national identity. In this the far right is far more in sync with public opinion than mainstream political 'elites' are. The other topic that finds far-right parties in broad agreement is their profound dislike of anything that results in loss of economic or political sovereignty. Rooted in nationalism, their doctrines pit them against the integrationist raison d'etre of the European project and its supra-national institutions. They are thus naturally anti-EU, anti-Schengen and anti-euro, but to varying degrees. According to *The Economist*, 'Compared to other Europeans, French voters are strikingly opposed to globalisation and international trade'.[72] When Germany's AfD was launched in 2013, its hostility to eurozone bailouts was its main mantra, resting on the highly popular argument that Germany should not 'pay for others' (read: Greece). The party subsequently latched on to popular discontent with Merkel's pro-immigration policies, broadening its platform to include issues related to immigration and national identity, which propelled it to some spectacular electoral victories. At the same time the AfD remains fiercely nationalistic, anti-euro and anti-EU. It is a typical far-right party that wants to recover sovereignty from Brussels and promote Germany's own interests first. Granted, the AfD is highly unlikely to assume power and—due to internal squabbling among rival factions—saw votes in its favour collapse from 15% in autumn 2016 to only 7% by March 2017.[73] Yet, the AfD revived itself under new leadership, recovered spectacularly and gathered close to 13% of the vote during the 24 September 2017 general election. In some poorer eastern parts of the country it reached over 21%, becoming the second political force after Merkel's CDU.[74] This was enough for it to enter the federal parliament as Germany's third largest political force. The sudden rise of the far right in Germany was a political earthquake in Europe's largest country which is used to atone for its troubled past and was supposed to be immune from the populist waves affecting the rest of Europe.[75] To those who attribute a great part of the empowerment of Germany's far right to Merkel's immigration policies, some experts say 'not so fast!' reminding us that 'German nationalism is an abiding force that had been artificially suppressed for decades but never fully stamped out [...] Nationalism was taboo as were any overt displays of patriotism' yet 'This was not the case in East Germany, where the Communist Party pretended that it represented a nation victimized by the Nazis and again by the West [...] There was no admission of guilt for the Holocaust in the East, no attempt to face the full significance of Germany's past nationalism' consequently 'When West Germany swallowed up East Germany in 1989, it was almost inevitable that some form of nationalism would resurface.' This view also explains how the AfD achieved its highest scores in the eastern part of the country.[76] What will be remembered from this election is not that Merkel won a fourth term, but that for the first time since the Nazi era a far right nationalist party entered the *Bundestag*. In a near replay of the meltdown of France's two main traditional parties during the 2017 presidential election, Germany's CDU and CSU—the two bulwarks of traditional German politics—achieved their worse electoral score since 1949 in the 2017 elections. The turnout of nearly 76% of voters left no doubt as to the legitimacy of the result. The country's traditional political forces were not impervious to the new trend in European politics. Germany's new ruling coalition was now longer able to ignore the AfD's success with voters. Merkel will have to contend with a new, vociferous opposition that has not hesitated to call her a 'traitor' and is out to get her. 'We're going to take back our country [...] We're going to be hunting Merkel wherever she goes', said Alexander Gauland, an AfD leader.[77] Political scientist Lothar Probst then warned that 'A very difficult period is beginning for the chancellor'.[78] Geopolitical experts at Stratfor commented that 'Germany's new political landscape is one in which the vital center has shrunk'. They added that, when it came to international challenges: 'if French President Emmanuel Macron seeks an ally in reforming the European Union or navigating the Brexit, if Trump searches for a new approach to settling the Israeli-Palestinian conflict or if tension with Russia continues to rise, the Continent's leading power will probably be less decisive, less committed and less able to influence others in its response'.[79]

Jumping Without a Parachute

France deserves our special attention once more, if only because it is the largest country where the far right might have a distinct probability of assuming power outright; it is the second largest economy in Europe; and the FN's programme is particularly drastic. If the FN assumes power in France one day, there are likely to be serious implications for the country, for Europe and for the world. Florida International University's Remi Piet said before the 2017 election that 'If Le Pen wins the elections, it would clearly mean the end of the EU as we know it, as a Frexit vote would leave Germany as the only major global economic and political actor. The EU would then be limited to a greater Germany, without any potential power to balance it out'.[80] The FN's position on the single currency was radical: it wanted France to abandon the euro in order for the country to recover the old franc, and with it its economic sovereignty. IMF boss Christine Lagarde warned that abandoning the euro would give rise, in the short term, to a period of great uncertainty and impoverishment.[81] Well-publicized catastrophic scenarios have been depicted by experts. *Le Figaro* compared the dramatic consequences for France itself to jumping without a parachute.[82] It said capital would flee; foreign investors, who held 60% of France's debt, would dump it; borrowing costs would rise; budget deficits would probably explode, as big-spender France would no longer be bound by Maastricht deficit criteria; interest rates would go through the roof; French banks would be under tremendous pressure; and there might be a bank run. The country would find itself suddenly exposed to vast amounts of foreign debt—payable in what would now really be a foreign currency—totalling more or less the size of its GDP, which it would have to repay it with a franc that could be devalued by up to 15%. GDP could decrease by 2.3–3.2% in the first year and up to 4–13% in the longer term.[83] The aggregate cost of the FN's proposed measures was estimated at 85 billion euros.[84] According to the think tank Fondation Concorde, the total bill, once indirect costs were added—such as the lowering of the retirement age—could reach 145 billion euros.[85] In addition, France would be likely to get out of the EU or, if Le Pen had it her way, ask for special status.

Most of Europe's far-right parties advocate leaving European institutions, a menace that has to be taken seriously, especially post-Brexit. Displeasure about the EU and the euro may be understandable, but for a major power to ditch these institutions carries profound consequences. The thought scares off many voters, even FN voters. While many French citizens are ambivalent about the EU, an Elab survey taken in March 2017 showed that a solid 72% wanted France to keep the euro.[86] The FN's core demand to abandon the single currency is clearly out of sync with the French public (especially the elderly and working classes, who make up its core constituency), damaging its chances to win the presidency. The EU and the euro would not be likely to survive a full-blown Frexit. The far right's viscerally nationalist agenda, its protectionist and anti-Europeanism could turn the clock back to a time when Europe was made of a bunch of competing nations in perpetual conflict. Should a major country fall prey to the far right, a rolling back of everything Europe has built in the past 70 years could ensue. If such a scenario came about, there would be a serious risk of the European Project moving into dismantlement mode, following which a chaotic period would ensue for Europe, with serious geostrategic consequences. Such outcomes, unthinkable just a few years ago, are still not the most likely but have become distinctly possible. Unsurprisingly, at the beginning of 2016 foreign investors holding euros (the currency constitutes a sizeable 25–30% of the portfolio of major foreign central banks) were moving into pre-panic mode as the likelihood of a Le Pen presidential victory increased.[87] Interestingly, by July 2017 the leopard seemed to be changing its spots. Reflecting an intense internal debate, some FN officials hinted that the party would drop its core requirement that France should get out of the euro, conscious that this position greatly contributed to the loss of the 2017 presidential election. Would the far right be nimble enough to modify some of its core policies to improve its chances?

Outcomes

While the far right has undeniably been on the rise almost everywhere in Europe, it does not necessarily follow that it will enjoy a smooth ride or that it will have the wherewithal to actually take power outright in a major country. Any thought that it can do so everywhere in Europe is a fantasy. Conventional wisdom has it that all bets are off as far as Eastern Europe is concerned. But, aside from the special case of France—to which we shall return—in most of Western Europe the most the far right can hope for is to become a coalition partner in some governments or use its newfound clout to influence governments from the side-lines. In most countries, a sharp turn in governments' agendas to the right is generally considered inevitable and is likely to remain so for years to come. This will surely be the case with regard to national identity, minorities and immigration, resulting in a toughening of positions towards 'others' across the board: a realignment that has already broadly started across the continent. In the

Netherlands, for instance, under the influence of Geert Wilders' far-right Party for Freedom (Partij voor de Vrijheid; PVV, few of the other political parties 'dare mutter a positive word about Europe or refugees'.[88] With regard to European institutions, it is unlikely there would be dramatic moves to leave them, but here, too, governments will not be able to ignore the far right's complaints about loss of sovereignty anymore. It is likely that any moves towards the further integration of the European project will be cast aside and that an increasing number of countries will, under the influence of nationalists, attempt to renegotiate conditions to recover some sovereignty from Brussels. In Germany, the far right will probably not become a coalition partner let alone win elections, but the governing coalition cannot afford to ignore the grievances of the AfD's constituency anymore. In this way, Germany is likely to have even less propensity to apply softer terms to countries like of Greece, or agree to anything that smacks of a transfer union or a softening of austerity measures. As a result, eurozone tensions are likely to be exacerbated in coming years. In late 2016 warnings were issued to the effect that 'Europe's new far right is poised to transform the continent's political landscape—either by winning elections or simply by pulling a besieged political centre so far in its direction that its ideas become the new normal.'[89]

While Europeans increasingly look to alternative political forces to address their concerns about sovereignty, security, immigration and identity—and while many have misgivings about the EU and the euro—many instinctively feel that the European project has, on balance, brought good things. It is therefore not clear how far they are willing to follow alternative politicians in actually ditching the European project and European institutions. Even in France, a referendum on the EU and the euro hypothetically called by Le Pen would not necessarily result in citizens actually voting to leave these institutions. Similarly, it is difficult to imagine that the Netherlands, this historically pro-free trade country, would enact harsh protectionist or economically patriotic policies *à la* Le Pen. Yet Wilders made clear that: 'If I become prime minister, there will be a referendum in the Netherlands on leaving the European Union.' He specified that 'we want to be in charge of our own country, our own money, our own borders, and our own immigration policy'.[90] His words may well have scared off many voters. In another example, the failed presidential bid of the far right's Norbert Hofer in Austria probably suffered from his anti-EU stance. According to Carnegie scholar Stefan Lehne, 'Trump and Brexit had a reverse effect in Austria'. He said that 'The idea of Austria's possible EU exit scared them and made them choose a candidate who is not from the establishment per se but mainstream and much more pro-European.' In Lehne's view, the election cast doubts on the 'inevitability of the triumph of populism'.[91]

We must not lose track, however, of the fact that the main reason behind the spectacular rise of the far right in the last few years is the profound dissatisfaction of an important portion of the European electorate with the response of their governments to issues of security, immigration, sovereignty and national identity. With UMI, perhaps the most visible and emotionally laden of these issues, Europe will—under the indirect influence of the far right—probably take concrete measures to tighten its external frontiers and cooperate with the governments of countries from where migrants embark to strive to curtail the flow at the origin. It is likely that the influx of new migrants, refugees as well as economic migrants, will be substantially reduced. Schengen may well remain but with new barriers and/or a reduced footprint. Tolerance of illegal migrants will probably take a hit and the numbers of deportations accelerate. Nevertheless the masses already in will, by and large, remain. It is unlikely that any European government will muster the will to round up and deport masses of migrants, especially genuine refugees. Granted, an end to the Syrian conflict may result in many refugees choosing to go back home, but many will find ways to remain, seduced by the lure of Europe's Civilization of Entitlements. It is highly unlikely that the European economy will suddenly be able to provide more jobs for established and newly imported minorities than it is already. The integration of minorities will probably not take a miraculous turn for the better. The current of Islamization in certain communities is unlikely to abate. As a result, intercommunal tensions will probably continue to rise for the reasons we have already discussed. When it comes to creeping Islamization, the challenge will persist. The underlying causes of the spread of Islamist ideology will remain and, as we previously pointed out, consensus for tackling this particular challenge remains elusive.

In an extreme case such as that of France, one scenario that has been imagined, and which may come true, includes the effective 'Bantustanization' of the country. The term 'Bantusan' refers to the mini-states the apartheid regime in South Africa established to corral non-white ethnic groups with their own economies and laws. The difference between this and our case is that we are talking about virtual mini Bantustans resulting from the voluntary apartheid of an ethno-religious group. National authorities embracing this path could save face by arguing that significant minorities are, after all, part of the nation and country and should be entitled to their own physical space. In such spaces, they could add, they can live their lives according to their customs, if that is what they really want and if this will prevent confrontation. This much can be inferred from the likes of Philippe De Villiers for whom the question is not whether this sort of scenario will happen. He believes it is already happening in some parts of France and the question is how much territory will be ceded in this way over time. Author Christian de Moliner goes much further than De Villiers. He advocates the partitioning of the country from a legal standpoint between Islamists and the host population as the only viable option left to avoid civil war.[92] For de Moliner there are two nations living in France, one of which rejects the secular system and values. According to him, the 'war for France' has already started and areas already exist that are effectively outside the rule of the Republic. Short of mass expulsions, he believes it will be impossible to get rid of the 30% of French Muslims who want to live under sharia. The current policy of French governments is one of appeasement, which he thinks results in more and more space being ceded to Islamist practices in daily life. The authorities have become increasingly severe with anyone either accused of disrupting this apparent peace, he argues, or Islamophobia. This appeasement will provoke a virulent nationalist reaction sooner or later that will end up in a civil war, de Moliner adds. As civil war should be avoided and an archipelago of geographically disconnected Islamic areas is not economically viable, de Moliner proposes that the two nations could live under the same roof and the same government but be governed by two different sets of laws. These could be the secular laws of the country, in the case of Christians, and sharia in the case of Muslims. Besides the fact that such a solution would be unworkable from a practical standpoint, de Moliner ignores the reality that true Islamists would be emboldened by this partial victory. They are moved by an ideology of limitless conquest and conversion and would probably not be content with just a portion of the pie. Going back to the issue of Bantustanization, it must be noted that France is not alone: it is also already happening in other parts of Europe. UK authorities have, as we have already seen, transferred effective control of some neighbourhoods to Islamists

(Small Heath, a Birmingham neighbourhood, is one example). In France, the imposition of radical measures affecting the minority is unlikely as it would carry a serious risk of civil strife due to the size and assertiveness of the minority. The reasons behind the shift to the right of a good portion of the mainstream population are likely to remain, if not worsen.

Deteriorating domestic security will be part of most of the European landscape for a long time. The political importance of this issue cannot be ignored. A single major terrorist incident in France just a couple of months before the May 2017 presidential election could have propelled Le Pen to win the presidency. Given the number of radicals and the progress of radicalization, the likelihood of terrorist attacks will remain quite high. Many plots will be stopped in time but the security apparatus cannot stop them all. One single event perpetrated by just a few Jihadists can result in hundreds of casualties. In some urban areas, life for ordinary Europeans could increasingly come to resemble that of Israelis who live with the knowledge that a random act of violence or terrorism can happen at any moment, anywhere. Unlike Israel, Europe's demilitarized and unarmed societies are not mentally or physically prepared for this scenario. Others may want to take the law unto their own hands. It is not surprising that militias have started springing up although they remain confined to a few packs of hooligans and far-right activists looking for a fight. For instance, Finland's neo-Nazi Soldiers of Odin (25,000 Facebook likes),[93] or Britain First's 'Christian Patrol' initiative in Luton's Muslim neighbourhood.[94] Unlike in the USA, people can't easily buy firearms in Europe. But the fact that purchases of basic defensive items such as pepper spray, exploded in Germany after Cologne speaks volumes.[95] Some of this may seem a bit extreme, and speculation about what may happen can take many forms but one thing is sure: post-2015 Europe is not going to be the same as before and nobody knows where it is heading.

The Show Is Not Over Yet…

Immediately after the Dutch election of March 2017 in which incumbent centre-right Prime Minister Mark Rutte defeated far-right firebrand Geert Wilders, *Forbes* ran an article entitled 'European elections: Are voters rejecting far-right populism?'[96] Like the Austrians the Dutch had, after all, decided against the far right assuming power. Germany's far-right party, the AfD, surged in popularity in 2016 but fell back by early 2017 as we saw earlier. The same thing happened in Finland as the True Finns (renamed the Finn's Party) saw its popularity collapse from 17.7% in 2015 to 8.2% in 2017.[97] It must be kept in mind, though, that Rutte had cleverly robbed Wilders of his anti-Islam themes; that the AfD's temporary collapse was mainly due to squabbling internal factions; and that the True Finn's collapse was actually down to its support base lamenting that the party had gone too soft on issues such as immigration after it had joined the government, prompting voters to elect hard-liner Jussi-Halla-aho in June 2017 to head the party.

Alternative political forces have several major weaknesses. First of all, whenever they advocate getting out of the EU and/or the euro they scare off the large number of voters who, after all, prefer to stay in (as happened in Austria and France). Second, when they join a government as a coalition partner they become more institutionalized and lose their virulence, to the great displeasure of many from their core constituencies (as happened in Finland). Third, most alternative parties are young and inexperienced, lacking institutional backbone. Those who have been around longer have usually always operated on the fringe so it is not surprising that they lack credible government experience and solid, credible management teams (as is the case with Germany's AfD or France's FN). Alternative political forces are amateurish. Even Macron's new party was not entirely immune from this weakness at least in its early days. Fourth, they are usually incoherent and amateurish in the programmes they propose, which are long on ideology but short on realism, especially in the more arcane domain of the economy. Fifth, alternative movements are not monolithic. They experience frequent infighting among factions which can rapidly destabilize and re-marginalize them. In the case of Germany, infighting resulted in the AfD moving even more to the right after the repudiation of leader Frauke Petry's 'softer' line. More extremism results in further marginalization.[98] The last major weakness may be the most important and was evidenced in the Netherlands. Wherever the centre right moves shrewdly to the right to capture some of the far-right's narrative, it jerks the carpet from under the far right, leaving it with little to offer.

However, the realistic answer to *Forbes'* question whether populism is disappearing as fast as it appeared is an unequivocal 'no'. Following the success of pro-EU candidate Emmanuel Macron in the first round of the 2017 French election, a *Washington Post* article stated that 'the populist wave may be ebbing' and that it paid for a politician to be pro-EU. These assessments were incorrect, reflected short term trends and led to complacency. One only needs to look at the AfD's spectacular September 2017 electoral success in Germany's general election to understand that, far from being tamed, the far right is alive and kicking. The fact that, of all places, it is in Germany—the epitome of stability, multiculturalism, Europeanism and soft power—that the far right made its most spectacular comeback is an extraordinary development. 'What is the political norm in many other European countries was considered unthinkable in post-war Germany. Not any more', said the BBC.[99] The victory of 31-year-old Sebastian Kurz's right-wing People's Party (OVP) in Austria's October 2017 election is another case in point. The OVP—which won 31.7% of the vote—was expected to form a government with the election's runner-up, the far-right FPO, which won 26.9% of the vote (this party's first leader was reportedly a former SS officer and its current leader a onetime neo-Nazi youth activist). The Social Democrats came third with 25% of the vote.[100] The resulting coalition would be markedly anti-immigration—to say the least—and dead-set against further EU integration. Noting that the election was 'shaped by immigration', the *Washington Post* conceded that 'The Austrian results reflected anti-immigrant and anti-Muslim sentiment that has been rising across Europe in recent years'. The article pointed out that the FPO had 'campaigned on the proposition that Islam is incompatible with Austrian values and an existential threat to Europe'.[101] In the autumn of 2017, the Czech Republic elected billionaire Andrej Babis, a right-winger dead-set against the EU, who had said that his country should not have to accept a single refugee. Austria and the Czech Republic were joining Hungary, Poland and other Eastern European countries in a decisive shift to the right that would give Brussels bureaucrats sleepless nights and run against Macron's pro-European plans. In another instance, the most radical fringes of Europe's extreme right were in full display at a November 2017 rally in Poland. More than 60,000 demonstrators, comprising some of the most virulent neo-Nazis, nationalists and white supremacists, gathered with the not-so-tacit support of the Polish government.

A few important considerations emerge from all this. First is the confirmation of a key thesis of this book, that the 'trilogy' has been the catalyst behind a rapid transformation of nationalist, anti-immigration, anti-EU movements from fringe alternatives into forces that can garner enough support to seize power or at least play an increasingly visible role in many countries. Naive observers thought these forces would vanish as fast as they had appeared, ignoring the realities that underpinned them. Far from being spent, the most virulent elements of these forces are only now starting to make themselves heard and felt. It is a tragedy that the likes of Merkel do not understand what they have started in Europe, a tragedy for which all Europeans may pay a heavy price in future. Another key conclusion is that, in the past few years, differences between Eastern and Western Europe on matters of identity, values, civilization and immigration have evolved into a fracture that runs deep and possibly represents the most dangerous challenge to European cohesion today. It is not entirely surprising that in most Eastern European countries, Russian President Vladimir Putin, perceived as a defender of traditional values, was found to be more popular than German Chancellor Angela Merkel, seen as the champion of liberal multiculturalism.[102]

The fundamental reasons for voters to flock to populist parties are still there and is likely remain for the foreseeable future. Among these reasons, the 'trilogy' stays in the lead, as already pointed out, but it is not alone. In the first round of the French presidential election, a majority of voters opted for candidates who were clearly against globalization, for instance. The causes of this discontent will remain largely unchanged. The legions of workers who attribute wage stagnation to globalization are still there and they will still be seduced by politicians exhorting the virtues of protectionism. The causes of discontent with the EU and the euro are not going to disappear tomorrow, nor will the impact of the 'trilogy' on social life, security and identity. There is no reason to believe that the 'elites' in power will suddenly change their DNA and work on concrete solutions, let alone solve these problems. There are no clear solutions on the table for these burning issues, so the situation may very well worsen. Alternative forces have now become a feature of the European political landscape and retain the potential to assume power in some countries or to carry great influence. Political uncertainty in Europe is the new reality.

As long as the far right stays on the side lines or stays part of coalition governments, political agendas will be pushed to the right but nothing extremely drastic is likely to happen. The assumption of outright power by the far right in a country such as France or the Netherlands cannot be dismissed outright, particularly given what happened in Austria. Wilders, Hofer and Le Pen's losses in the latest elections do not mean the far right will disappear from their countries' political lives. To the contrary, they are now established political forces. Commenting on the then upcoming French election in April 2017, philosopher Alain Finkielkraut—who claims he does not belong to any political faction—decried the liquidation of national heritage, roots, or the elements of national identity that kept people together in the past by a movement that replaces them with a patchwork of diverse ethno-racial and sexual categories. Especially at a time, he said, when the nation is disintegrating.[103] To Finkielkraut this movement limits itself to dire warnings against the danger of the far right, without much in terms of a debate. He thinks it abandons all markers of national identity to the far right, making the victory of the FN at some point 'inevitable'. To philosopher Michel Onfray, the constant demonization of the far right is an excuse for the left to avoid any changes. It has the perverse effect of actually strengthening the far right, he believes.[104] These warnings may sound outlandish, but they need to be taken seriously. And then there is the unknown and non-negligible factor we mentioned before of a terrorist incident taking place just before an important election. As a consequence, the risk of the far right taking over is likely to linger for many years to come.

King of the 'Anywheres'

Alternative politics in Europe reflect the rise of protest voters and come in all shapes and sizes as earlier pointed out. Just when we thought we had seen it all, out of nowhere came one Emmanuel Macron who rose from virtual anonymity to become Economics Minister in Hollande's socialist government within a couple of years. Then, against all the odds and in a little more than a year, he went on to create his own En Marche! party and win the French presidency in May 2017. He towered over the smouldering ruins of the centre-right and centre-left parties which had traditionally governed the country. This was a new political force that unexpectedly exploded centre-stage, claiming to represent a clean break with the past and to embody a desire for change. Macron's movement can indeed be labelled 'alternative'. Yet it represents a 'conventional alternative' (forgive the oxymoron), in that none of the policies it proposes are radically new or represent a profound break from the past. It is, after all, a centrist party whose programme has been criticized by some as a 'collage of diverse and contradictory ideas',[105] a sort of hodgepodge with little in terms of clarity of purpose and substance. Macron himself is, after all, a product of France's elite ENA (École nationale d'adminstration) school—alma mater of most high officials including Hollande—who rose, albeit rapidly, within the socialist establishment. 'En Marche!' shrewdly made minced meat of traditions and absorbed politics and politicians from the centre left and centre right alike. The only new element in it is perhaps its youth and optimism.

The clever and unconventional 39-year-old Macron is a former socialist and former Rothschild investment banker. His pro-EU, pro-globalization and pro-multiculturalism views are well known (he renamed the foreign minister 'Minister for Europe and Foreign Affairs' and declared during his campaign that there was no such thing as French culture, while in Algeria he said that French colonization had been a 'crime against humanity'). He dated his school teacher while underage, and then married her. He embodies centrism, liberalism, post-nationalism and Europeanism. He seems a mix of Obama, Trudeau and Renzi. In him, the media, the 'Anywheres', the liberal left and the post-nationalists found their ultimate champion. There couldn't have been a more perfect fit. Youth, energy, optimism, a big smile, embracing the world. The media couldn't have enough of him and the media hype in his favour has no precedent in France's presidential campaigns. Macron was the antithesis of Trump. If Trump was elected by the 'Somewheres', Macron could count on 'Anywheres' and post-nationalists alike: he fulfilled their expectations and gave them hope. He pledged to reform Europe, reform France and fight labour rigidity in order to make the French economy more competitive and open it even more to the rest of the world. Can he deliver? What happens if he doesn't?

First of all, one must keep in mind that, during the first round of the French presidential election centre-right candidate François Fillon was neutralized by corruption allegations and a shrewd smear campaign. The extreme-right and extreme-left parties of Maine Le Pen (FN) and Jean Luc Mélanchon (France Insoumise) then grabbed 43% of the votes. The grievances of these discontents centred around issues of national identity, immigration and security as well as the perception of a victimhood caused by globalization-led job losses, social inequalities and an EU-induced dilution of sovereignty. During the second and last round of voting Macron trounced Le Pen, gathering 65.9% of the vote against her 34.1%. Yet, 60% of his 65.9% was reportedly made of voters who voted for him only to block Le Pen, and over 16 million voters abstained to choose a candidate in the last round.[106] At the end of the day, 1 in 3 voters were still backing the far right in the final round. This is despite the constant demonization Le Pen was subjected to and her dismal performance during the last televised debate in which her amateurish grasp of economic issues was plain for all to see. It must also be noted that one third of the young people who voted in the presidential election voted for Le Pen.[107] Moreover, the meteoric rise of Macron's political movement came at a time when the two traditional political forces of the centre left and centre right had committed *seppuku* and were utterly discredited in the eyes of the public. Any claim that Macron won a solid mandate from French voters for his pro-EU, pro-globalization, pro-multiculturalism programme is grossly incorrect. Macron was not elected because of what he stood for. He was elected in spite of what he stood for. Granted, Macron's party (formerly known as *En Marche!* and subsequently renamed *La République en Marche* (LREM)) won an absolute majority by a wide margin during the June 2017 legislative elections. However, during the first round a majority of French voters (a historical record) abstained from voting, confirming that most citizens simply gave up on the process. A Cevipof survey showed that the vast majority of LREM candidates in this legislative election were from France's upper class—basically the 'Anywheres'—whereas the lower classes of workers and employees—basically the 'Somewheres'—amounted to only 8.5% of these candidates.[108] To French essayist Emmanuel Todd, Macron's election represented the triumph of the arrogance of the upper classes trampling on the lower classes.[109] All this is not exactly good news for the moral legitimacy of the new assembly in representing the entire country. One can only wish that, with his exceptional political acumen, his energy and enthusiasm and his message of hope, Macron will do a good job of pulling the country together. That he will reform it and concretely address the issues of concern to the dissatisfied majority. Yet, post-election, reality has pitted a majority of dissatisfied citizens—who want less Europe, less exposure to globalization, more sovereignty and less multiculturalism—against a new governing elite whose platform rests on views diametrically opposed to theirs. Macron's warm embrace of Germany, for one, is anathema to the many who found solace in the virulently anti-German electoral tirades of Le Pen and Mélanchon. These people constituted, after all, a majority in the first round of the election: a majority for whom the EU and the austerity measures imposed by Germany are the sources of most evil. How will these contradictions play out?

The new French president may be deeply pro-EU but, according to the *Wall Street Journal*, his vision of Europe is 'old fashioned [...] more in line with France's traditional approach to governance: top-down and animated by protectionist instincts'. This is shown by his desire for a 'Europe that protects' and his proposal for a 'Buy European Act'. He is 'inclined to see unfettered Europe-wide competition as a liability, not an asset'.[110] While he is profoundly convinced that the EU needs to be reformed—and rightly so—any substantial reforms are subject to the modification of EU treaties, which needs the consent of each and every one of the 28 countries that make up the club. Given that it took many years to negotiate the current treaty, that renegotiating it means opening a Pandora's box in which every country will want to protect what it got so far and maximize what it can get from new talks, and given the deep cleavages dividing Europe today, what is the chance of his achieving something concrete? First of all, Macron needs to convince Germany. His embrace of Germany comes at a time when the two countries' economies and prospects have widely diverged. France's industrial production remains 10% below its 2007 level and its public deficit is more than double the 1.5% eurozone average, the second worse in Europe after Spain. Its pro capita GDP decreased to the extent that France now ranks a paltry 28th in the world.[111]

France has fallen too far behind Germany to consider itself a peer. In the aftermath of the French election, Merkel welcomed Macron's call for a strengthening of the Paris-Berlin axis. She politely listened to his call for EU reform while making it clear that they needed to determine what reforms they wanted before treaty renegotiations could be considered. Macron's proposal for a eurozone common budget and finance minister are viewed with suspicion by Germans who are worried that these measures and others such as common banking deposit insurance may result in Germany having to shoulder common debts. A eurozone budget means a pool of money which may at times be allocated to assist countries which are having problems, and that is what Germany is afraid of. German Finance Minister Wolfgang Schäuble expressed serious doubts about the viability of Macron's proposal for a eurozone budget. He wondered first of all where the funding would come from: 'New Taxes? Be serious!'[112] When it comes to the allocation of these funds, Schäuble favoured the idea of an EU budget with an important caveat: access by countries to a European stabilization fund would be conditioned on 'the bailout fund having more say over national debt and budgets'. This would be tantamount to giving Germany 'practical control over the budgets of all the euro-zone countries'.[113] In other words, Germany will only play ball if Germany is in charge of the purse's strings. *Bloomberg View* columnist Clive Crook recognized that 'Germany's enthusiasm for Macron won't last' and that the new French president 'has talked about an EU budget ministry and centrally coordinated public investment financed with eurobonds, presumably with an EU guarantee. He's right – but that's exactly what Germany doesn't want'.[114] He added that 'Macron is pro-Europe in the traditional French way: He wants a deeper European Union, with closer integration of fiscal policy in particular. Germany is pro-EU as well, of course, but has generally preferred making the union broader rather than deeper'. Moreover, the French have traditionally favoured a more social Europe with more protections for workers, higher minimum wages and other measures which are anathema to Germans. Macron's top down and protectionist vision of Europe is not shared by Germany. Given Berlin's suspicions of France's structural rigidities, government spending habits, dirigisme and aversion to reforms, there is little chance of Berlin budging on issues of substance regarding the EU and the eurozone.

Except, perhaps if France is able to thoroughly reform itself structurally as Germany did, in which case Merkel could try to make a case to the German people. Should France fail to deliver on internal reforms, Macron's last card may be to convince Berlin that, in the Trump era, France is Germany's most valuable ally, and that, should Macron fail in addressing French concerns such as austerity, Germany is likely to find itself dealing with Le Pen in 2022 and face the end of the EU.

The next question is: will Macron be able to push through structural reforms in France? Macron himself said that the French hate reforms and France can't be reformed.[115] I beg to differ and prefer to say that the French love reform, as long as it does not result in any change. On a less jocular note, change is badly needed in an economy that lost its ability to grow steadily a long time ago and delivers a chronic unemployment level of 10% (more than double Germany's). National resources are diverted to protecting the Civilization of Entitlements, reducing what is available for investment and resulting in the obsolescence of France's industrial machine. The French economy is less and less able to compete internationally (evidenced by commercial deficits reaching 2.2% of GDP and a record 60 billion euros by the end of 2017, compared with Germany's huge surpluses). The share of industry in the country's GDP has fallen to a mere 12.6% (compared with Germany's 22.8%). French companies are less and less able to produce goods that satisfy even the internal market, causing imports to grow faster than exports.[116] The 2017 industrial production index is worse than in 2010.[117] Public deficits stand at 3.5% of GDP—more than double the eurozone average—and debt ballooned to over 2 trillion euros at a time when interest rates are picking up. This dismal performance comes despite the simultaneous low levels of interest rates, oil prices and the euro. These levels will inevitably go up sooner or later and the consequences could be dire. Reducing public spending and in particular the number of civil servants of which France which holds record numbers in Europe (with 5.64 million civil servants, and a bloated public sector spending 55% of GDP against 44% in Germany) is no easy task.[118] Of France's GDP, 34% goes to public spending for social services, to fund the entitlements which French citizens firmly believe they should receive as a birth right. Where Fillon had proposed to chop off 500,000 civil servants, Macron proposed a far more modest 120,000 during his campaign. Macron's tax cuts are not matched by savings in public spending (in particular reductions in civil servants), resulting in ever larger deficits that are financed by increases in the country's debt, hardly a recipe for sound finances. In other words, France keeps accruing more and more debt to fund its bloated civil service. French labour laws remain among the most rigid and arcane in Europe, the labour code famously comes to 3000 pages. The French work less than their German or British counterparts. According to the OECD, the average level of qualifications among French workers is lower than that of other developed countries.[119] How likely is it that the new president will be able to substantially reform France's dysfunctional labour market in the face of virulent unions and opposition from the left and the working classes who mostly voted for the FN? Under Chancellor Schroder, Germany was able to effect deep labour reforms that transformed it from the sick man of Europe into the world's lead exporter. Key components of these reforms were increased labour flexibility and the effective freezing of wages, measures which the French are very reluctant to stomach. Against all expectations, in autumn 2017 Macron shrewdly and successfully rammed through labour reforms concerning the negotiation of contracts with minimum fuss. But what would happen if he tried to substantially reform key items such as retirement age, the 35-hour working week and the number of civil servants? Retirement age in France stands at an unsustainable 62 against Germany's 65. Any hint at increasing it in France would likely result in social unrest given how the French are attached to their *retraites*. The same thing may happen with other key issues. While Macron shrewdly co-opted traditional centre-left and centre-right politicians, he does not have a mandate from the people to carry out structural reforms of this sort, however badly needed they may be. What the political class wants is one thing, what citizens will tolerate is quite another. Given France's volatile sociopolitical environment all bets are off. The reality is that, without deep structural reforms, there is little chance of France reversing its economic decline and little chance of Germany agreeing to deep changes to the EU and the eurozone. With Germany's agreement, something may happen. Without Germany's agreement, nothing will happen.

When it comes to France's growing social inequalities, economic growth is, in theory, a solution. But will the wunderkind Macron be able to deliver high growth in an economy that has not really grown for a few decades and has to contend with 3.7 million unemployed? That has consistently been losing competitiveness due to the high cost of manpower, lack of innovation and worsening demand for its products, resulting, as we have seen, in a record 60 billion euro commercial deficit in 2017?[120] What about eurozone reforms proposed by Macron, such as deeper fiscal integration, a eurozone budget and a eurozone finance minister? Martin Wolf—associate editor and chief economic commentator at the *Financial Times*—recalled a Macron adviser, who wisely pointed out that the euro's survival rests on fears of the dire consequences of a break-up, rather than on the expectation that the single currency could deliver prosperity and stability.[121] To the question of whether Macron could manage to push through his eurozone reforms, Wolf responded 'probably not', a diplomatic understatement given German intransigence. For one, France's proposed 'fiscal federalism' has little chance of being accepted by a Germany that remains opposed to solutions such as eurobonds or countercyclical fiscal policies (i.e. making use of individual countries' budgets to adjust in times of crisis). According to Wolf, the biggest problem of the eurozone is that it lacks a mechanism for 'symmetric adjustment', a position we shall explore in a later section of this book. In confronting crises, all painful adjustments are left to troubled countries. This position satisfies German Finance Minister Wolfgang Schäuble, for whom eurozone problems would not be resolved by 'weakening Germany'.[122] Germany greatly improved its competitiveness relative to the economies of France and Italy by keeping its workers' wages down, it was the only one among the three countries where wages rose less than productivity gains. Combined with a high savings rate, these 'falling unit labour costs' resulted in Germany's chronically huge current account surpluses, which are a problem for its southern European partners (Wolf could have added that the euro, undervalued for Germany, played a role in boosting its exports and making all this possible). Germany's proposed cure for this chronic structural divergence is simply that everybody should follow the German model. In other words, Germany is not going to adjust, it is up to others to do so. Wolf points out that, in a sense, this has effectively happened as the eurozone's aggregate current account went from a deficit of 1.2% of GDP in 2008 to a surplus of 3.4% in 2012. But at what cost? Wolf fears that the burden of asymmetrical adjustments carries political risks and that prolonged competitive deflation (i.e. pressure on wages) in a country such as France will likely help Le Pen become president next time.

According to essayist Nicolas Baverez, Macron's presidency may be the last chance France has to thoroughly reform itself failing which the far right is likely to come to power.[123]

To some observers, the most critical issue plaguing France today is, however, not the economy, the EU or the eurozone, and not even the deepening socio-economic inequalities. The mother of all issues in today's France is the profound identity crisis translating into a deepening fracture between host population and minority, a fracture that may lead to social instability and/or the effective Bantustanization of national territory discussed earlier. This issue was totally ignored by the 2017 election's presidential candidates and doesn't seem to be bothering Macron. Given his public declarations on French culture and minorities, there seems to be little in this quintessential multiculturalist's DNA indicating that he will address the grievances of the increasingly large numbers of French citizens concerned by the 'trilogy'. This young limelight-addicted president is the darling of the liberal establishment and of the French (as well as international) media who have been packaging him as a sort of new John F. Kennedy and best hope for France, for Europe and for the world. Expectations were running dangerously high and would sooner or later be confronted with grim French economic and social realities. Not entirely surprisingly, the disillusion started soon. During the first summer of his presidency, Macron's popularity sank to a mere 39%, the lowest of any 5th Republic president at the same time in his presidency, and well under president Hollande's 55%.[124] It is easy to forget that this president was not elected for his pro-European agenda. He does not have a mandate in that sense. He was elected because people were more afraid to elect Le Pen. Yet this wunderkind should not be underestimated, and the coming years will be interesting to watch. What happens if Macron fails to deliver? The traditional centre-right and centre-left parties, previous pillars of French politics, have been thoroughly discredited and are in ruins. They will perhaps find the energy to reconstitute themselves in the coming years—albeit most likely as shadows of their former selves—and win back the hearts and minds of the French and pick up the pieces. But if they don't, the only opposition left to succeed Macron may, by default, be the parties of extremism. Le Pen could, despite her amateurism, find in 2022, or in the following election, the same electoral highway open in front of her as Macron found in 2017.

Notes

1. Francesco M. Bongiovanni. 'The Decline and Fall of Europe'. *Palgrave Macmillan*. 2012.
2. Natazcha Polony. 'Merci pour ce quinquennat'. *Le Figaro. Page 19.* 7 May 2017.
3. Joseph E. Stiglitz. 'The Euro and its threat to the future of Europe'. *Allen Lane. Pages 309,331.* 2016.
4. Alexandre Devecchio. 'David Goodhart 'Le peuple de quelquepart s'oppose aux gens de n'importe ou'. *Le Figaro Magazine. Pages 32–35.* 5 May 2017.
5. Eric Zemmour. 'Le cauchemar américain'. *Le Figaro. Page 17.* 26 October 2017.
6. Jeanna Smialek. "Deaths of Despair' Are Surging Among the White Working Class'. *Bloomberg.com.* 23 March 2017.
7. Erik Kirschbaum. 'Merkel wins another term in Germany, but she has a newly empowered far-right foe'. *Latimes.com – Los Angeles Times.* 24 September 2017.
8. 'Les médias allemands sous le choc des élections législatives'. *AFP.* 25 September 2017.
9. Paul-François Schira. 'La gauche a assumé l'abandon du peuple, la droite doit assumer celui des élites'. *Lefigaro.fr – Le Figaro.* 6 October 2017.
10. Pankaj Mishra. 'The Age of Anger'. *Allen Lane.*
11. Kate Lyons, Gordon Darroch. 'Frexit, Nexit or Oexit? Who will be next to leave the EU'. *Theguardian.com – The Guardian.* 27 June 2016.
12. Peter Foster. 'The rise of the far-Right in Europe is not a false alarm'. *Telegraph.co.uk – The Telegraph.* 19 May 2016.
13. Mark Lilla. 'La gauche américaine prise au piège de la diversité'. *Le Monde. Page 21.* 19 December 2016.
14. Eric Zemmour. 'Pourquoi les peuples ne veulent pas mourir'. *Le Figaro Magazine. Pages 52,53,54.* 18 November 2016.
15. Violaine De Montclos. "Sonia Mabrouk: 'Les musulmans de France sont piégés". *Le Point. Page 64.* 2 March 2017.
16. Philippe De Villiers. 'Les cloches sonneront-elles encore demain?'. *Editions Albin Michel. Pages 153–154.*
17. Nicolas Ungemuth. 'Michel Onfray: 'La gauche est fascinée par l'Islam comme elle l'était par les dictateurs au XXe siècle". *Lefigaro.fr – Le Figaro.* 21 April 2016.
18. Mark Mazower, 'Dark Continent' *Penguin*, 1999.

19. Thomas L. Friedman. 'Order vs. Disorder, Part 2'. *Nytimes.com – The New York Times*. 15 July 2014.
20. Francesco M. Bongiovanni. 'The Decline and Fall of Europe'. *Page 121.* Palgrave Macmillan.
21. Ivan Rioufol. 'L'election de Macron, farce démocratique'. *Le Figaro. Page 17.* 12 May 2017.
22. Alexandre Devecchio. 'David Goodhart 'Le peuple de quelquepart s'oppose aux gens de n'importe ou'. *Le Figaro Magazine. Pages 32–35.* 5 May 2017.
23. Alexandre Devecchio. 'L'affaire Bensoussan ou la dérive inquiétante de l'antiracisme'. *Lefigaro.fr – Le Figaro.* 10 March 2017.
24. 'Fearing the 'suicide' of Europe'. *The Economist.* 15 June 2017.
25. 'The Rohyngias – The most persecuted people on earth?'. *The Economist.* From the print edition Asia. June 13 2015.
26. Tommy Wilkes and Malini Menon. 'After lynchings, India's Modi condemns violence in name of cow worship'. *Reuters.* 29 June 2017.
27. Eleanor Ross. 'China bans Muslim baby names in Xinjiang region'. *Newsweek.com.* 25 April 2017.
28. 'African migrants sold in Libya 'slave markets', IOM says'. *BBC.com.* 11 April 2017.
29. 'Cameroun accusé d'avoir expulsé 100.000 réfugiés'. *Lefigaro.fr – Le Figaro.* 27 September 2017.
30. 'What's behind attacks on foreigners in South Africa?'. *Aljazeera.com.* 25 February 2017.
31. Ivan Rioufol. 'Donald Trump, l'aubaine d'une révolution'. *Le Figaro. Page 17.* 16 September 2016.
32. Drew Desilver. 'For most workers, real wages have barely budged for decades'. *PewResearchCentre – Factank.* 9 October 2014.
33. 'Wage Stagnation. The big freeze.' *Theeconomist.com.* 6 September 2014.
34. Vianney Passot. 'Chantal Delsol: 'Le populisme est attaché à des enracinements que détestent les élites''. *Lefigaro.fr – Le Figaro.* 10, March 2017.
35. Alexandre Devecchio. 'Vincent Coussedière: 'Le populisme, c'est le parti des conservateurs qui n'ont pas de partis''. *Lefigaro.fr – Le Figaro.* 18 March 2016.
36. Vincent Coussedièere. 'Fin de partie. Requiem pour l'élection présidentielle.' *Editions Pierre Guillaume de Roux.*
37. 'Fearing the 'suicide' of Europe'. *The Economist.* 15 June 2017.

38. Emma-Kate Symons. 'Cologne attacks: 'This is sexual terrorism directed towards women". *Nytlive.nytimes.com – The New York Times*. 19 January 2016.
39. Andrew Brown. 'This cover-up of sex assaults in Sweden is a gift for xenophobes'. *Theguardian.com – The Guardian*. 13 January 2016.
40. Emma-Kate Symons. 'Cologne attacks: 'This is sexual terrorism directed towards women". *Nytlive.nytimes.com – The New York Times*. 19 January 2016.
41. Sue Reid. 'Why Germany can't face the truth about migrant sex attacks: SUE REID finds a nation in denial as a wave of horrific attacks is reported across Europe'. *Mailonline*. 9 January 2016.
42. Michelle Martin. 'Cologne attacks show Germany unprepared for migration challenge'. *Reuters*. 28 January 2016.
43. Sue Reid. 'Why Germany can't face the truth about migrant sex attacks: SUE REID finds a nation in denial as a wave of horrific attacks is reported across Europe'. *Mailonline*. 9 January 2016.
44. Damien Sharkov. 'Over 80 percent of Germans think Merkel has lost control of refugee crisis.' *Newsweek.com*. 2 April 2016.
45. 'Germans Lose Faith in the Fourth Estate'. *Spiegel on line*. 24 February 2016.
46. Hada Messia, Livia Borghese and Jason Hanna. 'Italian Police: Muslim migrants threw Christians overboard'. *CNN*. 19 April 2015.
47. Oliver J.J. Lane. 'Prominent Psychiatrist Blasts Mainstream Media For Blaming Mental Health For Attacks'. *Thementalhealthminute.net*. 5 August 2016.
48. Stéphane Durand-Souffland. 'Terrorisme: «La maladie mentale est influencée par l'air du temps". *Lefigaro.fr – Le Figaro*. 22 August 2017.
49. Edouard de Mareschal. 'Agriculteur poignardé: le juge renvoie le dossier au parquet pour enquête'. *Lefigaro.fr – Le Figaro*. 20 July 2017.
50. 'Journalist Fired for Refugee/Terror Tweet'. *Newobserveronline.com*. 19 November 2015.
51. Sue Reid. 'Why Germany can't face the truth about migrant sex attacks: SUE REID finds a nation in denial as a wave of horrific attacks is reported across Europe'. *Mailonline*. 9 January 2016.
52. Angélique Négroni. 'Trappes confrontée au communautarisme Islamique'. *Le Figaro. Page 15*. 5 Février 2017.
53. Michel Onfray. 'La parole au people'. *Page 111. Editions de l'Aube*. 2017.

54. Sue Reid. 'How Europe's most liberal nation gagged its own people on migration attacks: The Swedish conspiracy to hide the truth about the refugee influx'. *Dailymil.co.uk – Daily Mail*. 5 March 2016.
55. Laurent Bouvet. 'Réflexions sur la sidérante affaire Mehdi Meklat'. *Lefigaro.fr – Le Figaro*. 21 February 2017.
56. Jochen Bittner. 'In Germany, a curtain on social media'. *The New York Times. Page 1*. 22 June 2017.
57. 'Germany approves plans to fine social media firms up to €50m'. *Theguardian.com – The Guardian*. 30 June 2017.
58. 'What does Alternative for Germany (AfD) want?'. *Bbc.com*. 25 September 2017.
59. Andrew Brown. 'This cover-up of sex assaults in Sweden is a gift for xenophobes'. *Theguardian.com – The Guardian*. 13 January 2016.
60. 'How New Year's Eve in Cologne Has Changed Germany'. *Spiegel online*. 8 January 2016.
61. Richard Milne. 'Anti-immigration Sweden Democrats become country's largest party'. *Ft.com – Financial Times*. 20 August 2015.
62. Stéphane Kovacs. 'En Suède, l'épineuse gestion des mineurs étrangers'. *Le Figaro. Page 15*. 7 April 2017.
63. Zoie O'Brien. 'Pork made mandatory on menus to 'preserve food traditions' amid migrant influx'. *Express.co.uk*. 24 January 2016.
64. 'What next for Austria's Freedom Party?'. *Thelocal.com*. 5 December 2016.
65. Carol Matlack. 'Nationalists and Populists Poised to Dominate European Balloting'. *BloombergBusinessweek*. 20 October 2016.
66. Moira Weigel. 'Political correctness: how the right invented a phantom enemy'. *Theguardian.com – The Guardian*. 30 November 2016.
67. 'Jewish leader says anti-Semitism growing in Germany'. *The Associated Press Berlin*. 29 November 2017.
68. Carol Matlack. 'Nationalists and Populists Poised to Dominate European Balloting'. *BloombergBusinessweek*. 20 October 2016.
69. Jan Rettig. 'Economic policies of the european far right: Suitable pluralism or cumulated inconsistencies?' *EuroMemo Group, 22nd Conference on Alternative Economic Policy in Europe*. 15–17 September 2016.
70. Tim Worstall. 'Marine Le Pen's Absurdly Nationalistic Economic Plans'. *Forbes.com*. 4 March 2017.
71. Nelson D. Schwartz, Patricia Cohen. 'A warning shot on globalization'. *International New York Times. Page 16*. 27 June 2016.

72. 'League of nationalists'. *The Economist. Page 63–64*. 19 November 2016.
73. Nicolas Barotte. 'Allemagne: les populistes de l'AfD au plus bas'. *Le Figaro. Page 8*. 2 April 2017.
74. Yannick Pasquet. 'Allemagne: la droite nationaliste brise un tabou avec une percée historique'. *AFP.* 25 September 2017.
75. Gregor Aysch, Adam Pearce, Bryant Rousseau. 'How Far Is Europe Swinging to the Right?'. *Nytimes.com – The New York Times*. 5 December 2016.
76. Jacob Heilbrunn. 'Don't blame Angela Merkel for the rise of the right in Germany'. *Latimes.com – Los Angeles Times*. 28 September 2017.
77. Erik Kirschbaum. 'Merkel wins another term in Germany, but she has a newly empowered far-right foe'. *Latimes.com – Los Angeles Times*. 24 September 2017.
78. Deborah Cole, Hui Min Neo. 'Weakened Merkel wins fourth term, hit by nationalist 'earthquake''. *AFP*. 25 September, 2017.
79. Cameron Munter. 'Clouds Gather On The Horizon Of Germany's New Political Landscape'. *Forbes.com – Forbes*. 28 September 2017.
80. Remi Piet. 'Why the French elections will change the face of Europe'. *Aljazeera.com*. 7 March 2017.
81. 'Trois Français sur quatre sont opposés à une sortie de l'euro'. *Lefigaro.fr – Le Figaro*. 10 March 2017.
82. Anne Bodesco, Bertille Bayart, Cécile Crouzel, Danièle Guinot. 'Sortie de l'euro: l'engrenage infernal'. *Le Figaro. Pages 1-2-3*. 9 March 2017.
83. Jean-Pierre Robin. 'L'Europe ne survivrait pas si la France sortait de l'euro'. *Le Figaro. Page 4*. 9 March 2017.
84. David Bensoussan. 'Front national: la facture délirante du programme économique de Marine Le Pen'. *Challenges.fr*. 11 February 2017.
85. Michel Rousseau. 'Les énormes trous financiers du programme économique du Front national'. *Fondationconcorde.com*. 14 February 2017.
86. 'Trois Français sur quatre sont opposés à une sortie de l'euro'. *Lefigaro.fr – Le Figaro*. 10 March 2017.
87. 'Central bank diversification strategies: rebalancing from the dollar and euro'. *World Gold Council*. 13 March 2013.
88. 'Act 'normal' or get out'. *The Economist. Page 17*. 11 February 2017.
89. Sasha Polakow-Suransky. 'The ruthlessly effective rebranding of Europe's new far right'. *Theguardian.com – The Guardian*. 1 November 2016.
90. Pieter Cleppe. 'What Geert Wilders winning the Dutch elections would mean for the EU'. *International Business Times*. 13 March 2017.

91. 'EU leaders rejoice at Alexander Van der Bellen in Austrian election'. *Deutsche Welle – DW.com.* 5 December 2016.
92. Christian de Moliner. 'Pour éviter la guerre civile, divisons la France'. *Causeur.fr.* 17 Novembre 2017.
93. Jack Wallis Simons. 'EXCLUSIVE – Nazi daggers, SS hats and a hangman's noose: On night patrol with the 'Soldiers of Odin', neo-Nazi led vigilantes vowing to 'keep Europe's women safe from migrant sex attacks". *Mail online.* 7 February 2017.
94. Chris York. 'Britain First Denounced By Every Major Christian Denomination In The UK'. *The Huffington Post UK.* 30 January 2016.
95. Caroline Copley. 'Germans stock up on pepper spray and blank guns after attacks'. *Reuters.* 8 January 2016.
96. Shellie Karabell. 'European Elections: Are Voters Rejecting Far-Right Populism?'. *Forbes.com.* 16 March 2017.
97. Tatu Ahponene. 'True Finns, false hopes'. *Jacobinmag.com.* 8 April 2017.
98. 'Germany AfD: Right-wingers set to move further right'. *Bbc.com.* 22 April 2017.
99. Jenny Hill. 'German election: A hollow victory for Angela Merkel'. *Bbc.com.* 25 September 2017.
100. Harvey Gavin. 'EUROPE'S CRISIS: EU facing 'serious strain' as Austria coalition to cause reform NIGHTMARE'. *Express.co.uk.* 18 October 2017.
101. Griff Witte, Luisa Beck 'For Austria's Muslims, country's hard-right turn signals an ominous direction'. *Washingtonpost.com.* – *The Washington Post.* 20 October 2017.
102. Peter Kreko. 'MERKEL MUST KEEP EASTERN EUROPEANS OUT OF PUTIN'S CLUTCHES'. *Newsweek.com – Newsweek.* 3 October 2017.
103. Vincent Tremolet De Villers. 'Alain Finkielkraut: 'Il se s'agit plus, en votant, de choisir, mais d'obéir". *Le Figaro. Page 16.* 2 April 2017.
104. Vincent Tremolet de Villers. 'Michel Onfray: 'Cette étrange perversion qui consiste à nourrir le monstre Le Pen qu'on prétend combattre". *Lefigaro.fr – Le Figaro.* 24 April 2017.
105. Charles Jaigu. 'Emmanuel Macron, philosophe de la surface?'. *Le Figaro Magazine. Pages 32–36.* 19 May 2017.
106. Ivan Rioufol. 'L'election de Macron, farce démocratique'. *Le Figaro. Page 17.* 12 May 2017.
107. Hank K. '4 raisons pour lesquelles à 25 ans, je vote Front National'. *Huffingtonpost.fr.* 20 May 2017.

108. Ivan Rioufol. 'La révolte des oubliés de la démocratie'. *Le Figaro. Page 17.* 16 June 2017.
109. Eugènie Bastié, Alexandre Devecchio, 'Eric Zemmour-Emmanuel Todd: globalisation ou retour des nations?'. *Le Figaro. Page 18.* 12 September 2017.
110. Dalibor Rohac. 'Meet the Other Emmanuel Macron'. *The Wall Street Journal. Page A10.* 17 May 2017.
111. Nicolas Baverez. 'Emmanuel Macron: le sursaut ou le sursis'. *Le Figaro. Page 29.* 8 May 2017.
112. Nicolas Barotte. 'Woilfgang Schauble: 'Je m'imagine faire davantage avec la France'. *Le Figaro. Page 4.* 15 May 2017.
113. Pascal-Emmanuel Gobry. 'Why 'More Europe' Won't Solve Europe's Fiscal Quandary'. *Bloomberg.com.* 31 August 2017.
114. Clive Crook. 'Germany's Enthusiasm for Macron Won't Last'. *Bloomberg.com.* 9 May 2017.
115. 'Macron défend son action à la tête d'un pays « pas réformable »'. *Lefigaro.fr – Le Figaro.* 25 August 2017.
116. Anne de Guigné. 'Le déficit commercial, inquiétant talon d'Achille de l'économie française'. *Le Figaro. Page 22.* 9 November 2017.
117. Éric Verhaeghe 'La France en pleine hécatombe industrielle'. *Atlantico.fr.* 12 April 2017.
118. 'In 2014, civil Service employment was still on the rise but slowed down'. *Insee.fr.* 15 December 2015.
119. Cecile Crouzel. 'Dette, chomage: Macron hérite d'une France en piteux état'. *Le Figaro. Page 16.* 8 May 2017.
120. 'La France en panne de compétitivité". *Le Figaro. Page 1.* 9 November 2017.
121. Martin Wolf. 'Macron and the battle for the eurozone'. *Financial Times. Page 11.* 17 May 2017.
122. Nicolas Barotte. 'Wolfgang Schauble: 'Je m'imagine faire davantage avec la France'. *Le Figaro. Page 4.* 15 May 2017.
123. Nicolas Baverez. 'Emmanuel Macron: le sursaut ou le sursis'. *Le Figaro. Page 29.* 8 May 2017.
124. Juliette Mickiewicz. 'Chute d'Emmanuel Macron dans les sondages, d'une ampleur quasi inédite'. *Lefigaro.fr – Le Figaro.* 3 August 2017.

6

Ensuring the Survival of a 'Europe of Values'

> How can Europe deal with these challenges while remaining true to its ideals?

Clarity of Purpose

The title of this chapter includes two important words: 'survival' and 'values'. These words embody the key criteria that need to be taken into account in finding solutions to the challenges described so far in this book. If Europeans cherish their open societies, a solution that does not effectively contribute to the protection and perpetuation of these open societies is not a solution—just as a solution that works from a practical standpoint but requires a substantial rejection of the core values that underpin these open societies is not a solution. To some extent 'survival' and 'values' can be perceived as pulling in opposite directions yet this is not a zero-sum game. A delicate balance needs to be reached. This is no easy task yet Europeans have to bite the bullet at some point because the conclusion that emerges from our study is that the clock is ticking and the current trajectory can lead to chaos.

Europe is at a crossroads and needs to decide what it stands for and act firmly to defend it. The choice is between a courageous and comprehensive change in attitudes and policies or a new future that—in some places at least—may be characterized by growing social instability and insecurity, a deterioration of intra-communal relations, a fragmentation of physical and social space, the return of nationalism and the rolling back of the European project. Clarity of purpose and pragmatism need to drive the effort to avoid such a future. When self-preservation is at stake, measures that may appear drastic and unsavoury under normal circumstances may need to be taken where necessary and for as long as necessary. There is no shame in this. Setting limits on what is acceptable in terms of immigration and minorities' self-assertion, and taking reasonable steps to preserve a country's identity and security within its borders does not mean being intolerant, self-centred or racist. It is the natural right (if not duty) of any state and is necessary to maintain internal peace and to ensure the stability of the diverse societies that compose modern Europe. Tolerance is not in question; tolerance is one of the core values of modern European civilization and should remain so. But more and more Europeans have been asking what sense there is in building a free, prosperous, diverse and open society if a hostile alien ideology is allowed to undermine it in the name of tolerance? What sense is there in welcoming masses from abroad if they can't be cared for properly, can't be afforded, can't contribute to and end up disrupting society? What is the future of Europe if home-made totalitarian ideologies that brought disaster in the past end up being resuscitated in the vain hope that they will provide solutions this time around? No perfect solutions exist to these very complex questions and every solution necessarily involves some pain and some trade-offs. Yet measures that make reasonable sense and protect open societies while upholding the core values that make Europe what it is today exist and must be explored.

UMI: Solutions Exist!

No one can stay indifferent in the face of human tragedy. Author Yuval Noah Harari *(Homo Deus; Sapiens)* bluntly lays out the moral dilemma: 'Does preserving polka, bratwurst and the German language justify leaving millions of refugees exposed to poverty and even death?'[1] Choices are certainly not easy. Yet the choices recently made by Europe were not the only possible ones. A more pragmatic Europe would have developed pro-active measures aimed at helping the needy *outside* Europe, as close as possible to where they come from, while shutting down its external frontiers to all but the most pressing humanitarian cases, however unpleasant such a trade-off may be. In an interview with German newspaper *Welt am Sonntag*, Microsoft founder Bill Gates—who has provided billions in aid to Africans—recognized that Germany's open door policy to migrants would overwhelm Europe. Warning that the generosity of European leaders would only encourage more to come 'the more generous you are, the more word gets around about this—which in turn motivates more people to leave Africa', he urged Europeans to 'make it more difficult' for Africans to reach the continent via current routes and suggested instead spending more money on foreign aid.[2]

Under the 1951 Refugee Convention, and EU regulations, Europe must offer protection to people who can prove they are fleeing war or persecution, that is, 'refugees'. There is no obligation however to take any 'economic migrants', that is, people who come to find a better life. Yet the reality on the ground is that close to 60% of all migrants reaching Europe are economic migrants and most come from the African continent.[3] The law says these unwanted economic migrants cannot stay in Europe and should be repatriated. Yet, as we have previously seen, Europe has not had the heart to round them up and send them back home en masse—a situation that has, however, been recently changing with the enactment of deportations in various countries as we have previously pointed out, albeit to a very limited extent. We also pointed out that the economic and social costs of UMI in today's configuration are very substantial and likely to be unsustainable. Belgium's outspoken Migration Minister Theo Francken (member of the Flemish nationalist N-VA party) was adamant that Europe must not accept African migrants who pay people smugglers to cross the Mediterranean, but turn them back. He said 'taking a ticket on a smuggler boat does not give you free entrance into the European continent'. He also decried an 'inhumane' system in which criminal people-smuggling networks enrich themselves at the expense of people dying on the high seas and where absurd EU laws forbid European rescue vessels from sending migrants back to Libya.⁴ To Francken, migrants intercepted in the Mediterranean should be turned back or disembarked in other African states like Morocco, Tunisia, Egypt and Algeria. 'Do it for two weeks and it stops immediately.' he said, 'Nobody will pay thousands of euros to end up in Tunisia, Egypt or Morocco [...] The rumour with spread quickly that it has finished.'

If Europe wishes to welcome some economic migrants, it should do so on the basis of annual quotas reflecting actual needs for labour and interviews should take place in the applicants' home countries. For those already in, Europe has little choice but to send those it doesn't actually need back home yet owes it to them and to itself to do so in a humane way, in line with its values. A constructive solution to this conundrum could be the following: unwanted economic migrants already in Europe should be enrolled in six month mandatory training programmes during which they are taught a skill (and possibly also a language). At the end of the programme the economic migrant should automatically be sent back to his or her country of origin, perhaps with a little bonus in the pocket to help start a new life back home. The skills gained should, as much as realistically possible, respond to the most pressing needs of the area the migrant comes from. The economic migrant should, from day one, be given the choice of either going through the programme or being immediately sent back home. An added twist could be European governments giving incentives to European enterprises to invest in the migrants' countries of origin, ideally prioritizing the use of these 'returnees'.

Regarding genuine 'war refugees', asylum interviews for new applications should first of all be conducted only in existing refugee camps close to war zones. For those who are already in Europe, the option of sending them back to countries at war is repulsive. Europe needs to turn its attention to refugee camps in areas close to conflict zones and ensure that these camps become safe, liveable and sustainable, in order for refugees to be safely sent back to them. Europe may need to closely cooperate with institutions such as the UNHCR and some NGOs, and perhaps also incentivize the countries that actually host these camps (such as Jordan, Lebanon and Turkey). Life in these camps needs to become 'attractive' enough so that Europe can, with a good conscience, relocate refugees there. The ultimate goal would be that they return to their home countries safe and sound once war is over. The refugee camp in Kilis, Turkey, was reported in 2014 to be an example of a very well-run refugee camp, clean, safe, and with schools and good amenities. The credit for the success of Kilis, which sheltered 14,000 residents, goes to the Turkish authorities, who funded and managed it.[5] Whether or not Kilis's success was engineered as a showcase by Turkey for political reasons, Kilis proves that a refugee camp can actually be liveable if properly funded and run. To preempt the next human tsunami, Europe should pay close attention to warnings, such as the declaration made in March 2017 by Saad al-Hariri, Lebanon's prime minister, to the effect that his country was at breaking point. Lebanon had spent more than 18 billion USD taking care of over 1.5 million Syrian refugees on its soil. Al-Hariri requested that the international community should increase its aid from 1000–1200 USD per year per refugee to 10,000–12,000 USD.[6] As an additional measure, programmes could be put in place to provide schooling for children in these camps and to teach adults skills that they could take back to their countries post-conflict, contributing positively to reconstruction efforts.

Programmes such as those suggested above require careful assessment, budgeting and planning, and their viability needs to be established. They would inevitably carry a substantial economic cost and their implementation is likely to be challenging. Efforts should be undertaken to raise funds worldwide, yet the economic burden may well fall mainly on the European taxpayer. It is, however, likely that the cost of implementing this type of solution will be lower than the cost of carrying on with today's absurd situation. Running an economic migrant through a six month skills-building programme before sending him or her back home and ensuring the sustainability of refugee camps abroad, will probably cost less than supporting these same masses year after year—with no end in sight, no end-game and no purpose—on European soil. Not to mention the adverse effects on host societies and domestic security. Europe is better off funding initiatives that keep people safe and provide decent living conditions close to refugees' countries of origin and in actively investing abroad to help create jobs in countries that people flee for economic reasons than importing these problems onto its soil and then attempt to deal with them.

A common European policy for immigration and refugees should replace the patchwork of a different policy for each country that exists today. This policy needs to recognize that Europe cannot afford UMI and must firmly defend its external frontiers. Meant to ease Europe's plight when it comes to the issue of unwanted immigrants already on the continent and to do so in a humane fashion, the above proposals only make sense if Europe effectively shuts down its external frontiers. Otherwise there is no end to the problem, there being a reservoir out there of tens of millions of desperate souls who long to reach Europe. The first four months of 2017 saw an increase in migrants arriving in Italy from Africa of over 36% compared with the previous year.[7] According to the Australian political journalist Julia Baird, Australia's harsh policies that involve the Navy in turning back any migrant boat arrival and indefinitely detaining migrants under tough conditions on the remote islands of Manus and Nauru have 'worked'. The number of arrivals by sea—which had reached over 5000 in 2012—has dropped to almost nothing.[8] But Australians themselves pay a heavy price: they are morally torn apart and the country suffers from a lot of adverse publicity. Is this what is in store for Europe too or are there alternative solutions in the quest for safer external frontiers? Defending external frontiers needs to be as much as possible a proactive and pre-emptive enterprise. Defence needs to begin as close as possible to the actual sources of migration. This could only happen with the close cooperation (and incentivizing) of countries such as Libya from where migrants embark when travelling by sea, however difficult a task it may be. NGOs undertaking rescue operations at sea may be motivated by humanitarian principles but they have often ended up facilitating the task of human traffickers and should be controlled.[9] Migrants should ideally be turned back at, or as close as possible to, the start of their journey. An added benefit would be that human trafficking networks would see the economic incentives of their trade disappear, causing them to dismantle. The closer the line of defence is to the point of origin of migration, the better for Europe and for the migrants themselves. Again, there is no perfect solution, there is not even a 'pleasant' solution. There are only trade-offs to achieve an objective that represents a lesser evil.

Fighting the War at Home

When it comes to the march of Islamization in Europe, french author Philippe De Villiers, who wrote about the Islamisation of France, foresees three possible outcomes, all of them unpalatable. In the first instance the state yields and some areas are virtually abandoned to the Islamists, who then rule them as sort of independent mini-states with their own laws (i.e. the 'Bantustanization' of the country, as discussed in Chap. 5). The second outcome is one of massive re-migration (i.e. the mass exodus of Euromuslims). The third outcome which De Villiers foresees is a painful and lengthy 'Reconquista' (i.e. the physical re-conquest and 'clean-up' of Islamicized territories).[10] De Villiers' mass re-migration and re-conquest outcomes may seem outlandish speculations. But, to his credit one cannot ignore the fact that territorial fragmentation along ethno-religious lines is already happening in some areas. It can be inferred that the real danger of Islamization is not the unrealistic scenario that an entire European country would succumb to this ideology. Mass conversion of Europeans to Islam—let alone radical Islam—is not going to happen, as we earlier pointed out. The real danger of Islamization in countries with significant minorities is that it could theoretically lead to the fragmentation, partition or even disintegration of the state.

In confronting the creeping Islamization of European societies, Europeans first need to decide what they are ready to tolerate and where to draw the line. Different countries are affected in different ways. Each country has its own history, mentality, and tolerance levels. The size of the minority and extent of Islamization may also greatly differ and influence attitudes. As a result, the perception of the challenge may vary greatly from country to country, making a coordinated European response elusive. The political establishment has so far mostly adopted a strategy of laissez-faire, which in extreme cases can result in a country losing its cohesion, as we have seen. If Europeans do not want to see mini Islamic states or cities appearing within their countries, host populations and the moderates within the minority need to make a concerted effort. The minorities must be seen to unequivocally share the same basic European values as the mainstream. Both sides need to be prepared to stand side by side to do whatever it takes to defend these shared values against the offenders.

In order to achieve this alliance mainstream Europeans need to come to terms with one fact of life: whether they like it or not, settled Euromuslim minorities are now as European as they are and are here to stay. There will not be mass emigration of these established minorities and there is no turning back the clock. At the same time, Euromuslim minorities need to come to terms with the fact that they are, after all, newcomers in mature host societies. They shouldn't lose their own heritage but they must adapt and live by the values, customs and laws of their host societies. Aggressive assertions of separate identities—particularly in opposition to host societies values—or the desire to carve a separate space for their communities, will only lead to rejection and confrontation. Both sides need to accept these realities and make the best of them. Better still, they could embrace each other, because their destinies are intertwined. There needs to be an open debate between the two communities to define how they want to live side by side and how they want to confront the radicals. Countries must remain firm in defending their unique identities and values lest they lose any sense of themselves and leave an open space for disruptive alien ideologies. A proper compromise needs to be found between the natural right for a country to retain its unique identity, values and culture and the space given to minorities to express their own unique character, which cannot be in opposition to a host society's values and customs. If mainstream Europeans and the moderate majorities of their Euromuslim communities join forces to define and firmly defend a shared vision for a multicultural society that takes all this into account, then radical ideologies won't stand much of a chance and Europe as a whole will emerge stronger and more cohesive from this crisis.

To the question 'How do you defeat terrorism?' Salman Rushdie had a very simple answer: 'Don't be terrorized'.[11] Behind this seemingly jocular response hides a pearl of wisdom: terror resides in the mind of the terrorized and Europeans have everything to gain by keeping a cool mind and doing what needs to be done to eradicate the scourge. When it comes to hard-core radicals, unless Europeans are willing to accept increased insecurity, violence, and self-apartheid on European soil, there can be no compromise and nothing short of zero tolerance will work. Religious tolerance is a core European value. However, tolerating Islam is one thing and tolerating Islamism and radicals is another. The first is a religion and, as such, deserves respect, the other is an alien totalitarian ideology of conquest and subjugation that has contrarian values and leads to unacceptable outcomes. Europe does not need to make space for such an ideology in order to prove to itself and the world that it is tolerant. Europe needs to recognize the clear and present danger the ideology poses and cannot continue to wage an asymmetrical war in which it is absurdly shackled by rules of its own making. Europe's open societies can't survive if self-apartheid is tolerated and people intent on destroying a country and what it stands for are allowed to enjoy freedom as normal citizens. More and more Europeans feel that every radical represents a potential danger to the population. More and more Europeans feel that extraordinary circumstances call for extraordinary measures and that Europe has little choice but to compromise with its lofty ideals, at least for a while, in order to give itself the means to rid itself of this danger. One of the core values of modern Europe has been the elimination of the death penalty, something every European feels proud of. Questions have nevertheless been timidly raised in some quarters as to the appropriateness of reviving the death penalty in the case of convicted terrorists. Opponents argue, first of all, that such a measure goes firmly against the values of modern Europe and that in any case it would carry little deterrent value since Jihadists are willing to sacrifice their lives to their cause. Advocates of such a measure argue that it would carry great symbolic value, showing that Europe is willing to cross the Rubicon to fight the scourge. In truth, the death penalty has not really been eliminated in Europe: police forces carry lethal weapons which they are authorized to use to kill Jihadists at home during an assault, and European troops have been involved in lethal operations abroad resulting not only in the death of declared enemies but also at times of civilians in what is callously called 'collateral damage'. None of this elicits any protests. In truth, Europe still administers the death penalty, albeit selectively and in certain circumstances. The only novelty is that it does not apply it as a result of a judicial process, even in the case of a terrorist convicted of slaughtering scores of women and children. How far are we from a revival of this debate?

In respect of prevention, little can be done in the case of people who are skilfully hiding their radical views, except stepping up intelligence and surveillance operations. But people who are known or strongly suspected to be radicals (as has been the case with most of the perpetrators of terror attacks) should be physically removed from society, if not from European soil. The political class and the authorities, whose first duty is to protect the citizens (who, after all, pay their salaries), are guilty of dereliction and criminal negligence by failing to do so. Logic has it that anyone who harbours radical Islamist ideas or even sympathizes with them has to be considered a ticking bomb capable of exploding at any time, and has no business continuing to live in Europe's open societies. This holds whether they are a student, preacher, doctor, shop owner, unemployed or a housewife, old or young, and is independent of their degree of radicalization. French presidential candidate Nicolas Dupont-Aignan advocated measures aimed at the 2–300 most dangerous radicals known in the country. In the case of Jihadists returning to France from Syria, he proposed to preventively ship them out or lock them up in detention centres and penitentiaries to be established in remote French territories such as the Kerguelen islands in the Indian Ocean.[12] From a legal standpoint his proposal was a step towards preventive justice. However, his call for a kind of French 'Guantanameau' received no traction from a political class that is still in denial. Yet, more and more people feel that proposals aimed at preventively and physically removing such threats from the public social space deserve serious consideration. They feel it is absurd that known dangerous radicals remain free to mingle with a population they intend to harm. Fighting radical Islam in Europe cannot, however, just be confined to increased judicial and security measures. Such measures are necessary to try to contain the problem, but far from sufficient to eradicate it. The radical ideology itself needs to be rooted out and replaced by a 'sanitized' and controlled version of the faith. The spread of the radical ideology must first of all be stopped and there should be zero tolerance for any of its vectors.

Keeping the Stork Busy

Openness to the rest of the world is one of Europe's core values and should remain so. Yet issues such as labour mobility and broad demographic decline deserve to be taken more seriously because they indirectly feed the pro-immigration narrative that contributes to the destabilization of Europe. Intra-European labour mobility should be promoted in order to minimize the temptation to import cheap labour from afar. It would also make for a stronger and more cohesive Europe. How much sense does it make for Germany to import labour from the Middle East at a time when tens of millions of European citizens remain unemployed? Similarly, how much sense does it make that an unemployed Southern European can comfortably collect unemployment benefits at home while job opportunities exist in Germany? German Finance Minister Wolfgang Schäuble himself recognized that it is absurd to have unfilled training positions in Germany at the same time as there are unemployed youths in France.[13] Why not unify the European labour market? Individual states and the EU must develop incentives, training and language programmes, regulations and other measures to promote labour flows from high to low unemployment areas within Europe.

Europe should also take a close look at the causes of its demographic decline and put in place the right incentives to try to reverse it. For some countries, such as Italy, it is perhaps already too late. Yet, in a country with such a dismal economy, where many young married people can't afford to move away from their parents' homes, substantial financial incentives are likely to motivate people to have children. If budgetary constraints amount to a zero-sum game, the question ought to be framed in terms of Europe having to decide whether it makes more sense to spend tens of billions a year taking care of migrants or to spend the same sums incentivizing its own citizens to have more children. If so, these incentives should be looked at as investments in a country's future, perhaps the most important investment which can be made by the state. The notion that indiscriminate immigration is the natural solution to declining birth rates carries some merits but needs to be taken with a grain of salt. Is it the only solution? In *The Strange Death of Europe*, Douglas Murray argues that, instead of importing young people, European governments should first 'work out whether there are policies that could encourage more procreation among their existing populations'.[14] The reality is that pro-natalist policies, for instance (in particular subsidized childcare and nurseries), have not necessarily been tried to the fullest extent everywhere. Where they have been tried they generate positive results in increasing birth rates. According to a study by *The Economist*: 'Decent, affordable nurseries make it easier for women to combine work and motherhood. They seem to be the main reason France and Sweden have robust fertility rates. If a country wants more babies, it should spend more money on nurseries. And this is probably the best policy any government can pursue.'[15] If this is the case, perhaps the more than 20 billion euros Germany now spends every year caring for refugees and migrants in Germany could have been used to incentivize Germans to have more babies. Logic would have it that immigration is a drastic remedy that should be considered as a last resort, only if the strongest natalist policies do not work. In this case, governments owe it to their citizens to optimize the qualitative and quantitative aspects of such immigration, taking into account the impact of cultural and other differences on social cohesion.

The Value of Values

Italian essayist Oriana Fallaci warned that 'The moment you give up your principles, and your values, you are dead, your culture is dead, your civilization is dead. Period.' Europeans do not question the fundamental values on which their societies are built and they wish for these values to remain the bedrock on which their lives and those of their descendants are built. And so should they. Values must be upheld because they define a society and its DNA. Yet they may need to be compromised from time to time to some extent to ensure their own survival. Refusing such compromises outright is, paradoxically, tantamount to condemning these values to extinction. Apathy is a choice but not one that generates a desirable outcome. By failing to defend what they stand for and what they and their forebears have achieved, Europeans may be threatening the sustainability of their cherished way of life. The line dividing political correctness from cowardice is thin as a hair and has been crossed too many times by an inept political class bred in ideology and by a subservient fourth estate; and by the people who elect the politicians, uninterested in defending a way of life they take for granted. If the 'free world' wants to remain so, it must first muster the will to fight and win its first battle at home, where the real enemy is found looking in the mirror.

Notes

1. Yuval Noah Harari. 'Homo Deus'. *Harvill Secker.* 2016. *Page 250.*
2. Chris Pleasance. 'Bill Gates warns that Germany's open door policy to migrants will overwhelm Europe and urges leaders to 'make it more difficult for Africans to reach the continent via current routes''. *Dailymail.co.uk.* 4 July 2017.
3. Laurence Norman. 'Growing Percentage of People Arriving in EU Are Economic Migrants, Commission Says'. *Wsj.com – The Wall Street Journal.* 26 January 2016.
4. Robert-Jan Bartunek, Gabriela Baczynska 'INTERVIEW-Europe must turn back migrants on smugglers' boats – Belgian minister'. *Reuters.* 11 May, 2017.
5. Mac McClelland. 'How to Build a Perfect Refugee Camp'. *The New York Times Magazine.* 13 February 2014.
6. 'Réfugiés: le Liban 'Au point de rupture''. *Lefigaro.fr – Le Figaro.* 31 March 2017.
7. 'Fausto Biloslavo. 'E l'invasione dalla Libia continua Quasi 37mila arrivati in soli 4 mesi'. *Il Giornale. Page 2.* 27 April 2017.
8. Julia Baird. 'Australia's gulag archipelago'. *International New York Times. Page 8.* 31 August 2016.
9. Jean-Jacques Mevel. 'Migrants: l'UE veut accroître les contrôles au large de la Libye'. *Lefigaro.fr – Le Figaro.* 5 July 2017.
10. Philippe De Villiers. 'Les cloches sonneront-elles encore demain?'. *Editions Albin Michel.* Page 225.
11. Salman Rushdie. Step Across This Line: Collected Nonfiction 1992–2002.
12. 'Dupont-Aignan veut envoyer les Jihadistes sur les îles Kerguelen'. *Lepoint.fr – Le Point.* 16 March 2016.
13. Nicolas Barotte. 'Wolfgang Schaeuble: 'Je m'imagine faire advantage avec la France''. *Le Figaro. Page 4.* 15 May 2017.
14. Michael Rosen. ''The Strange Death Of Europe' Says Europe's Decline Is A Choice'. *Thefederalist.com.* 29 September 2017.
15. 'Breaking the baby strike'. *Economist.com – The Economist.* 25 July 2015.

Part II

A Brief History of How to Mess Things Up

7

The Island That Couldn't Get Far Enough

Brexit and its consequences across various dimensions

After Tea Time, a Little Surprise

Following the publication of *The Decline and Fall of Europe* I found myself invited to give speeches and interviews in the USA and Asia. I adopted the habit of using the analogy of geology's plate tectonics to describe Europe's fragmentation. Here was a southern European plate slowly sinking. There was a central European plate made of Germany and its satellites holding steady (at the time). France had a foot on both plates but was losing its footing on the central European plate. In the north a Scandinavian plate was mostly detached from the affairs of the rest of the continent was blissfully rising. To the West was the British plate, all by itself, trying its best to drift away from the continent. This was back in 2012. Little did I suspect that a mere four years later the island would detach itself from the continent and float away.

Brexit was not meant to happen. To silence opposition to the EU in his own conservative camp British Prime Minister David Cameron launched a referendum on EU membership. It was supposed to be a walk in the park and to silence these Eurosceptics forever. Cameron chose, however, to ignore the 'law of unintended consequences' as well as the history of past popular referenda on matters concerning Europe which seem inevitably to end badly. Referenda end up being used by ordinary citizens as means to vent their frustrations concerning all sorts of matters not necessarily related to the referendum topic. They can be hijacked easily by eloquent populists advocating simple demagogic answers to complex issues. Many people resent being stuck with what they perceive as an EU that behaves as a super-state dictating everything and every rule. They see it as a faceless, monstrous, Brussels-based bureaucracy they can't identify with. They feel that the EU is mismanaged, unable to protect them, unable to solve their problems. They are increasingly frightened by the denial and dilution of national identity and their roots implicit in the European project, a project that has not been replaced by an alternative vision with popular traction. When it comes to a loss of identity markers, or to broad issues such as UMI (unwanted mass immigration) or terrorism, citizens are frightened by the open borders implicit in the European project and don't see any concrete solutions coming from Brussels. They long for the protection of the traditional nation-state. European governing elites chose to close their eyes to the grievances of this 'populace'. When confronted with the popular vote of referenda related to European matters, they stumbled from one failure to the next. The Danes voted 'no' in 1992 and 2000; the Irish voted 'no' in 2001 and 2008; the French voted 'no' in 2005; the Dutch voted 'no' in 2005; the British finally voted 'no and farewell' on 23 June 2016. The result of the British vote was not disputable: 33.5 million people, representing 72% of eligible voters, participated and 52% of them voted for Brexit.

The British vision of the EU, shared by the Dutch, was traditionally one of a trading zone long on free trade and short in terms of regulatory power or interference from Brussels. It went against the French and German visions which were more intrusive. The UK's economy had been doing relatively well, although its success was concentrated in London which had become a worldwide hub-city decoupled from the rest of the country. Outside the eurozone, the UK was largely immune from the currency crisis. As long as the only arguments of British nationalists centred on Brussel's inadequacies, they didn't stand much chance of winning the referendum. This is despite the serious misgivings many British citizens had concerning the EU. But then German chancellor Angela Merkel handed nationalists the perfect issue to exploit when she opened the floodgates to migrants and subsequently pushed for Europe-wide immigration quotas. Writing for the *New York Times*, Jochen Bittner, political editor for German weekly *Die Zeit*, explained that Brexit was very much a vote of the old against the young. Only 35% of the older generation (those between 50 and 64) wanted to remain in the EU versus 64% of the younger generation (those 18 to 24). Yet, he added, 'predictably, the German chancellor Angela Merkel's welcome mat policy to refugees, and her insistence that Europe follow her lead, will be blamed for much of the momentum behind the Leave vote. And that's fair'.[1] To British historian Robert Tombs, the roots for the 'leave' vote go deeper and wider than the immigration issue. Tombs points out a fundamental difference between France, where 34% of citizens were favourable to transferring more power to Brussels, and the UK, where the percentage (prior to the Brexit referendum) was only 6%.[2] The historian thinks this wide difference reflects the rejection of European federalism by British citizens, who have more confidence in, and are more attached to, their own institutions and governance. Britain's national confidence grew steadily after the 1980s, according to Tombs. Added to this, the fact that commercial exchanges between the UK and the EU have been declining for the past decade, while they have been growing with the rest of the world, and the fact that the UK was not in the eurozone, contributed to make it 'easier' for the public to vote for an exit. Tombs reminds us that Pew Research Center surveys showed the EU was as unpopular in the UK as it was in Germany and Holland and was even less popular in France or Greece than in the UK. In other words, EU unpopularity is widespread in Europe and is not specific to the UK. But, leaving the EU was a little 'easier' for a country that had one foot out already, was self-confident in itself and its institutions and saw its future in terms of the world rather than the EU. Arguments have also been heard to the effect that Brexit was a vote against immigration in general (including intra-European immigration) by those who feared that the very generous British welfare system cannot even support the wave of legal immigration. This argument flies in the face of evidence that, despite some well-publicized abuses, legal migrant workers have, in aggregate, been net contributors to the system. Whatever the causes of the 'leave' vote may have been, Brexit came as a total surprise and its consequences will probably reverberate for decades.

Disagreeing to Disagree

Whatever the causes of Brexit may have been, the calendar is now in the driving seat. Britain voted to leave Europe in June 2016. British Prime Minister Teresa May invoked Article 50 of the EU's Lisbon Treaty in March 2017 effectively transforming the referendum's result into reality. Brexit talks officially began on 19 June 2017 and Britain will officially leave Europe on Friday, 29 March 2019. The invocation of Article 50 launched a highly complex and risky two-year process in which both sides must enact a formal exit. It became obvious from day one that this process would be far from orderly and friendly. Negotiations quickly got stalled by a fundamental difference in the approach of both sides. The UK's main interest was in keeping privileged access to the EU market, so it wanted to sort out trade issues first. The EU, on the other hand, was losing an important budget contributor and wanted to recoup some of these losses before agreeing to anything else. Unsurprisingly, the UK's Brexit Secretary, David Davis, warned that negotiations would be turbulent. The one thing he and his EU counterpart Michel Barnier agreed on was that the size of the 'divorce bill' remained a sticking point.[3] EU concerns actually extended beyond the settlement of British liabilities and included complex issues such as the rights of European citizens in the UK. Adding a further layer of complexity is the fact that a solid majority of Scottish voters wanted to stay in the EU. As a result, Scotland and Northern Ireland may both decide to leave the UK and stay in the EU, something which would please Brussels but deeply worry London. The trickiest issue may be that of the 310 mile land border between Northern Ireland and the Republic of Ireland. Norther Ireland is part of the UK and the Republic is in the EU. Once the UK leaves the EU—and given its desire to control its borders—there needs to be a border between the two, constituting the only physical border between the UK and the EU. However, thanks to today's open border, trade flows between the two Irelands exceed 1 billion euros per week. A hard border may hit local economies hard and jeopardize peace in a region that saw sectarian violence for decades. Junior Brexit Minister Robin Walker conceded that 'the government absolutely recognizes that we want to ensure that there is no return to those borders of the past'.[4] It will be interesting to see how the conundrum of a border that needs to remain open and shut at the same time will be resolved. The following two years will be a race against the clock to resolve these and myriad other issues: a bitter and divisive race that will mobilize a great deal of energy and attention on both sides. For the UK, first at stake was its 600 billion euros per year trading relationship with the EU. Around 44% of all British exports go to the EU, without tariffs or customs procedures.[5] Pro-Brexiters quickly pointed out that the net result of this trade relationship has been, after all, a deficit of over 60 billion euros per year for Britain, and that, since Britain bought 20% of all cars made by German companies, Germany had an interest in the trade relationship with Britain remaining friendly.[6] Yet, should London not manage to strike a trade deal with the EU, 'this would almost certainly involve the immediate imposition of tariffs across a range of sectors' warned a Parliamentary report.[7] At stake was also the huge 'divorce bill' estimated at between 25 to 73 billion euros, which London may have to pay in relation to previous commitments for EU pension schemes and future projects already approved.[8] Needless to say, British voters were not happy with having to foot such a bill, particularly given that 'the average Eurocrat's pension is double Britain's average household income'.[9] Nevertheless they wouldn't find sympathy on the other side of the English Channel where, 'If there is one thing net payers and net recipients agree on, it is to make the bill for Britain as high as possible.'[10] The self-inflicted defeat of Prime Minister Teresa May in June 2017 (politicians never seem to learn lessons, do they?) meant the UK government would, at least in the short term, be a weak and divided partner for the EU to negotiate with, something likely to make things even more complicated. Given the chasm dividing both sides and the degree of acrimony characterizing the negotiations, a scenario in which no deal is reached between the EU and Britain is not entirely impossible. This scenario would mean the country would, from one day to another, find itself facing tariffs and trade restrictions just like any other country outside the Union, seriously impacting exports.

Waking Up with a Hangover

One consequence of Brexit that took everybody by surprise is that London has been caught completely unprepared for the enormous complexity of what comes next. On some issues, British and European positions seemed to be intractably opposed. This was the case with London's desire to keep access to the European market while at the same time restricting migration, even from European jobseekers. The *Financial Times* recognized that 'Mrs. May's overwhelming priority in Brexit has been control over immigration and British law'.[11] The new commercial treaty Britain sought with the EU would require the approval of the parliaments of each and every one of the remaining 27 members of the Union, no simple feat. Aside from the main, well publicized issues—such as the divorce bill and the treatment of the 3.2 million EU citizens living in the UK and the 1 million British citizens living in the EU—the British EU negotiator and expert Steve Bullock, for one, was adamant that British politicians and the public did not understand the daunting task awaiting the UK. He said it was confronted with literally hundreds of very complex technical issues, severing links with all sorts of EU organizations, agreements and agencies. The UK has to reformat itself, pick up the slack and do so within the short time left before it effectively leaves the Union in 2019. In the case of the airline sector, for instance, Bullock pointed out that the UK will no longer be able to certify people who fix planes or certify maintenance facilities as it leaves the European Aviation Safety Agency. Airlines such as Ryanair may need to relocate some activities and assets to the EU as the UK leaves the Open Skies Agreement, he added. And EasyJet may need to get established in all of the EU's countries. In the case of the nuclear industry sector, Bullock said that nobody thought about the consequences of leaving Euratom, the EU agency on which Britain's nuclear industry is highly dependent (remaining part of EU agencies would mean accepting the European Court of justice, a no-no for the British side). In addition, a new customs IT system would have to be established. Speaking for the many British experts whom he felt have been largely ignored, Bullock wondered 'How will the UK remain in the EU's internal energy market post-Brexit as it looks to import more energy from the EU, and what are the implications if it doesn't? What about the

Emissions Trading System? Patents and intellectual property rights? Food standards? Medicine approvals? Europol? The list goes on and on.' He concluded: 'Brexit would have been a terrible idea even if done as well as possible, but for the Government to blithely march the country towards consequences that they don't even themselves understand is an appalling dereliction of duty.'[12]

The date is inexorably set, there will be no going back. Aside from the practical issues related to the exit, the natural question is: what does this new reality mean for the UK and for Europe? To the British actor Hugh Grant, the response is very straightforward: 'Brexit is a perfect example of a nation shooting itself full in the face.' In truth, the first consequence is that Europe is politically weaker and more divided than ever since the fall of the Berlin Wall. For former British Prime Minister Tony Blair, the immediate impact of Brexit will be economic but the lasting effect will be political. It will go beyond British shores as populist movements in other countries will gain momentum, he believes.[13] British historian Timothy Garton, shocked by the vote result wrote 'Vladimir Putin will be rubbing his hands in glee' and 'the unhappy English have delivered a body blow to the West, and to the ideals of international cooperation, liberal order and open societies to which England has in the past contributed so much'.[14] Garton was correct that Brexit undoubtedly damages the Western institutional unity that has maintained stability and peace since the end of the Second World War. Britain's traditional position as the USA's privileged partner in Europe, not only with regard to security issues but also as a vector of US influence on the continent, was also dealt a severe blow with Brexit. As Britain becomes less 'useful' to the USA (especially if Britain's commitment to European security decreases), London's position in Europe and the world is likely to weaken. The USA may henceforth attach more importance to its relationship with Germany than that with Britain. Following Brexit, Germany's position as Europe's leader is stronger, it now only has to contend with a very weak France. On the other hand Brexit poses a new, unwanted challenge to Germany because Berlin will need to provide even more leadership to a dislocating Europe. Brexit is also bad news for the remaining members of the EU as it eliminates the main driving force behind pushes for much-needed reform in the Union. Additional complications may arise with the spectre of new hard frontiers separating the rest of the UK from Scotland and Northern Ireland which express a desire to remain in the EU.

When it comes to assessing the economic impact of Brexit, nobody really knows how this very complex saga will play out, except that it will be painful to both sides. Some prominent economists and politicians as well as institutions such as the IMF predicted economic catastrophe. Others, such as the former head of the Bank of England Mervyn King, felt such dire predictions were exaggerated. To American economist and Nobel laureate Paul Krugman speaking to *The Independent* at a conference in London organised by the Centre for Economic Policy Research in September 2017, the writing was on the wall: 'I don't think there's any plausible case that Brexit is a good thing for the British economy as a whole.' This view was shared by economists from the London School of Economics, who estimated that the UK could lose up to 9.5% of its GDP if it left the EU without a free trade deal, a view diametrically opposed to that of a fringe group of Brexiters called Economists for Free Trade, who predicted Brexit could boost Britain's GDP by as much as 4%.[15] Former London Mayor Boris Johnson (who became Foreign Secretary after Brexit) was adamant the UK had everything to gain by opting out. Perhaps Johnson didn't fully grasp the extent to which the fate of the City of London—Europe's financial heart and a key driver of the British economy—and the future of legions of financial sector jobs would be in question in a post-Brexit world. Among others, London accounts for over a third of all wholesale banking between large companies, institutions, governments and pension funds, and for close to 80% of EU foreign exchange transactions. This is not to clearing, multi-trillion-pounds-a-day derivatives market, three-quarters of which is executed in London. 'The current model of using London as a gateway to Europe is likely to end' predicted Dr Andreas Dombret, executive board member for the Bundesbank (Germany's central bank).[16] It is difficult to envision euro clearing remaining in London since the thousands of contracts that are signed on a daily basis in this business are based on acceptance of the European Court of Justice (ECJ), an institution Britain is adamant it will do away with. Unsurprisingly, Dombret saw 'strong arguments for having the bulk of the clearing business inside the euro area'.[17] What the City may lose, Frankfurt seems best positioned to win. Large institutions such as Morgan Stanley, Citigroup and Standard Chartered, are moving their European base to Frankfurt. Others, such as Goldman Sachs and UBS, are moving some of their operations in an exodus that could take up to 100,000 jobs away from London.[18] What seems to be a zero-sum game has no clear winners. Continental Europe may be gaining some jobs but according to the *Financial Times* 'The restructuring of the EU's banking landscape would not only be inefficient but could also add to risk.'[19] As of 2017 there was little sign of London losing its pre-eminence in the world of finance as it was ranked a very solid first (ahead of New York, Hong Kong and Singapore) in the global financial centres index (GFCI), that takes into account infrastructure and the quality of manpower.[20] Aside from financial services, London would lose, among others, EU agencies along with the highly skilled jobs, prestige and the lavish funding from Brussels that comes with hosting them. Assessing the full impact of Brexit remains an elusive task.

The UK has prospered in recent years despite being part of a flawed EU. Those advocating a Brexit basically made a bet that the UK would do even better by leaving it. In truth it is difficult to envision the UK or Europe being better off after Brexit. The outcome is, at the very least, uncertain. There will inevitably be negative consequences as investors, markets and businesses don't like uncertainty of any kind. The Bank of England cut its growth forecasts from 1.9% to 1.7% for 2017 and from 1.7% to 1.6% for 2018 (at a time when eurozone economies were growing an average 2.2%). Mark Carney, the Bank's Governor, recognized that Brexit uncertainty was affecting business confidence and hitting investment levels and wage negotiations across the country.[21] Weak wage growth, combined with rising inflation (a weakening Pound made imports more expensive) resulted in a lowering of household spending power. Reduced consumer confidence and falling spending on cars, consumer goods, and an increase in consumer debt followed. The UK, previously perceived as a beacon of stability and prosperity, will henceforth carry an element of risk at the very least until the dust settles, which could take years. To Dutch Premier Mark Rutte, Brexit means 'game over' for the UK. He warned: 'Britain has collapsed: politically, economically, monetarily and constitutionally.'[22] Will Rutte's prediction come true, or will the country successfully defy the odds as it has done time and again through history?

Finding Meaning in the Afterlife

There are many ways to interpret the significance of Brexit. To most Eastern European countries Britain was the champion of free markets and of the light version of the EU which they favour. Its departure is bad news since they are left to contend with Germany and France who do not espouse such views. For jubilant French far-right anti-EU leader Marine Le Pen, Brexit was 'by far the most important historic event known by our continent since the fall of the Berlin Wall'.[23] For *The Economist*, Brexit was brought about by angry voters (such as the 'Somewheres' mentioned in Chap. 5 of this book) who feel they have been left behind. The stakes go way beyond Europe as 'The triumph of the Brexit campaign is a warning to the liberal international order', and may mark 'the start of an unravelling of globalisation and the prosperity it has created'.[24] Perhaps. But I believe that, from a European standpoint, the real big-picture significance of Brexit is that it marks the end of an age of innocence in Europe that lasted over 60 years. During this age it was assumed that, despite its problems, the European project would inevitably move in only one direction, that of more and more integration. Brexit 'strikes at the very idea of a union, rather than its shoddy or misguided implementation'.[25] It has now dawned on Europeans that the disintegration of the EU is now a real possibility. More and more things seem to oppose European nations than unite them. For the first time since the Second World War, centrifugal forces seem to have the upper hand. Pessimists see Brexit as marking the formal beginning of this unravelling process. Is it so? Aside from formal exits *à la* Brexit, what about disintegration of the eurozone, for instance? Would it lead to disintegration of the EU or just a return to the status quo before the single currency was launched? If disintegration is a distinct possibility, how should it be contained or prevented? If it happened anyway, how should it be managed? Nobody really knows. To some extent 'disintegration' is not new in European history, witness the disintegration of the Habsburg empire, or more recently that of the Soviet empire or of Tito's Yugoslavia. Bulgarian political scientist Ivan Kratsev pointed out that in 18 of the 27 post-Brexit members of the Union, one or more political parties demanded a popular referendum on the EU. The position of some anti-establishment parties from the right and left alike shows that the disintegration of the Union could lead to the disintegration of some individual states (the UK with Scotland, Spain with Catalonia etc.). Even more ominously, they point to the disintegration of the democratic political system itself.[26] To Kratsev, moves towards a smaller but more functional EU could have the effect of speeding up the disintegration process instead of containing it. The biggest risks come from opportunistic 'elites' leveraging on the crisis to promote their own agendas. These 'elites' could launch disintegration processes from within the heart of the EU, rather than angry populists operating from the political periphery. In this context Kratsev feels the Union can only be saved by those who advocate more flexibility within the existing framework.

Who is heading for the door next? Poland has been in a deepening dispute with Brussels and EU governments over various issues since the ultranationalist, eurosceptic Law and Justice (PiS) party came to power in 2015. In particular, the EU opposes PiS moves to place the courts and judges under tighter government control. By early 2017, the EU was getting close to giving Poland and Hungary an ultimatum on accepting their quotas of migrants or leaving the EU. A few months later the EU executive was getting ready to ratchet up the pressure on the judicial issue with unprecedented punitive measures being considered. In Europe, the ghosts of history assumed to be buried often lurk just below the surface. It is not entirely surprising that—after taking heat from Germany and France over the quota refusal and for its perceived shift away from democratic rule and judicial independence—Poland's right-wing government brought out the old question of German reparations from the Second World War. Interior Minister Mariusz Blaszczak hinted that Warsaw could claim one trillion USD from Germany.[27] As it was straying from core European ideals and resisting European pressure to open its doors to migrants, Poland was turning into a serious challenge for the EU. It seemed the country was 'testing the limits of Europe's 70-year-old experiment in conferring peace and democracy on this once bloody continent by the soft power of cooperative integration'.[28] Will Poland remain in the EU or is it heading for the door? Surveys showed 70% of Polish citizens wished to remain in the Union yet the PiS's fiercely nationalist leader, Jaroslaw Kaczynski, seemed to have different ideas.[29]

If the challenge of what to do with Poland and other 'unruly' members of the Union had one positive side, it was that it brought to the table the issue of what sort of Europe was desirable. After a rapid expansion fuelled by Brussel's proselytizing zeal the EU had 28 members and had become clearly unworkable. France and Germany hinted that a 'multi-speed' or *à la carte* Europe might be more desirable. Italy and Spain warmed to the idea. Poland feared it would 'lose sway in the EU if a core group of countries, such as those sharing the euro, decided to integrate further' while it struggled 'to find allies who want to dilute the powers of EU institutions and give national parliaments more say, especially as the bloc's hitherto biggest advocate of a looser union—the UK—is negotiating its exit from the club'.[30] Polish Prime Minister Beata Szydlo was quick to say that Poland would never entertain such an idea.[31] Some observers then warned that 'If the EU does not improve on its ability to expand the political inclusion of countries in Central and Eastern Europe, the already crumbling trust between Brussels and these members will entirely collapse, and its newest members will end up quitting.'[32] To some extent 'Europe is already a multi-speed Europe, but Eastern and Central European countries are wary of becoming second-class Europeans' and 'the course of least resistance is to once again muddle through'.[33] The 'multi-speed' notion remains vague and nothing less than a complete rethinking of how to organize Europe across its many dimensions is needed: a herculean task. Dutch politician Frans Timmermans, first vice president of the European Commission, warned that 'Either we prepare for the future, or we become obsolete'.[34] I won't tire of repeating that, for all the problems with the EU (and God knows they are plenty), the European continent has been a battlefield between competing nations, empires, city states and the like for most of the past two millennia. It is only after the Second World War, as a result of the European integration process, that Europe has enjoyed seven decades of peace and prosperity. Seventy years are a mere drop in the ocean of the troubled history of Europe and one has every reason to believe that the natural default position of a fragmented Europe is one of competing states. From this historical perspective Brexit moves Europe back into a direction that the entire region may come to regret.

Back to Basics

If Brexit has one virtue, it is that of forcing a rethink of what the EU should be. If the EU does not want to be entirely rejected by the people and see more 'exits', Europe needs to be reinvented and become more representative of its people and less intrusive. The euro means countries do not have control over their currencies or their budgets. The primacy of EU laws over national ones mean countries do not have full control of legislation on their territory. EU decision makers in Brussels are perceived as 'foreign' bureaucrats with too much power of intrusion in the domestic affairs of countries that didn't elect them. Measures such as replacing the European commission with a council of European heads of state, ensuring that the European parliament is composed of delegates of the various European parliaments and ending the primacy of EU laws over national laws in certain cases would be steps in the right direction. The current bureaucratic and faceless European super-state is not what people want. It has shown its limitations and needs to be replaced by a platform in which nations actually interact with other nations. There is, however, little chance of any of this happening since any changes in treaties require the assent of each and every one of the 28 nations that form the club today.

The BBC's Nick Bryant reported that a senior EU diplomat summarized the mood on the continent in this way: 'Britain has shot itself in one foot. We intend to shoot you in the other.'[35] This attitude can partly be explained by a desire to ensure that no other state will follow Britain's example and leave the Union. But retribution is not constructive and damages both sides. Britain would find itself in a pickle but may retaliate by turning itself into the 'Singapore of Europe' with low taxes and liberal regulations (both measures are anathema to authorities on the continent) in order to lure financial and other businesses away from the EU. 'If the EU chooses to stand there and watch, the likely outcome is no agreement, a disorderly exit as the clock on talks runs down, maximum economic dislocation, and years of bitter recrimination all around—terrible for the UK, but no picnic for the EU, either'.[36] If France and Germany really feel that 'there is little to lose by pushing Britain hard' they will be committing yet another historical mistake.[37] For one, despite British Defence Minister

Michael Fallon's declaration that London will stick to protecting Europe no matter what,[38] why should London make good on its NATO commitments and protect European countries hell-bent on hurting British interests? Brexit does not change the reality that Britain and Europe need each other. Britain remains geographically attached to Europe and will undeniably continue to share many interests, commercial, security, strategic and otherwise, with the rest of Europe. So why not take a constructive approach instead, make the 'best' of what has happened and try to invent a new type of 'positive' partnership between the EU and some countries outside the EU? Could such a format be perhaps applied to, besides the UK, Ukraine, Turkey and others? Wouldn't that make more sense than focusing on 'making the UK pay the price'? German Foreign Minister Sigmar Gabriel seemed to think as much: 'If we get a smart agreement with Britain regulating relations with Europe after Brexit, that could be a model for other countries – Ukraine and also Turkey.'[39]

Could Brexit have been avoided? Perhaps. It is amazing that at no time in the final weeks before the referendum vote, as the anti-EU camp looked increasingly likely to win, did a European politician say 'time out, let us all sit down around a table and talk seriously about reforming the Union'. The only rhetoric coming from the continent was one of retribution: if the Brits left Europe, Europe would ensure that they would pay a high price. In this respect, the similarities with Catalonia's failed independence bid in 2017 are striking. Aside from the fact that in both cases the separatists did not have a plan for after the vote, how is it possible that the Spanish central government and the separatists were not able to sit down and work out a modus vivendi? Is the art of compromise a thing of the past in Western societies? Brexit is the latest proof of the chronic mismanagement of the European project by a mediocre European political class on both sides of the English Channel. Can Brexit be reversed at this stage? Few think so, but former Labour Cabinet Minister Lord Adonis is one of them. Recognizing once more that immigration is at the centre of British concerns in this saga, Adonis felt that 'if France and Germany agree that the UK can take control over immigration while staying in the EU single market' Brexit could possibly be reversed (through another referendum). He added 'Why might Macron and Merkel make this offer? Partly because—in Macron's case—he (rightly) doesn't believe that unrestricted free movement of labour is integral to the single market. Partly because many other EU leaders agree with him. And partly for the big strategic reason—which weighs on strategic thinkers in Berlin—that, if Britain leaves the EU, 80% of NATO resources will then be outside the EU, which is hardly a recipe for European security and stability if you are looking across at the Russian and Chinese bears.'[40] Adonis' views were in line with those expressed by none less than Tony Blair, the former British prime minister, who also thought such a deal might be possible.[41] Can London have its cake and eat it? Is this wishful thinking or would it represent, after all, the most reasonable course of action for both sides?

Notes

1. Jochen Bittner. 'Brexit and Europe's Angry Old Men'. *Nytimes.com – The New York Times.* 24 June 2016.
2. Robert Tombs. 'Non, le Brexit n'est pas seulement l'expression du nationalisme anglais'. *Le Monde. Page 23.* 23 November 2017.
3. Brexit: UK 'must not allow itself to be blackmailed'. *Bbc.com.* 1 September 2017.
4. Nic Robertson. 'Theresa May's final Brexit hurdle looks a near impossible leap'. *Cnn.com.* 30 November 2017.
5. Simon Shuster. 'The Fall of Europe'. *Time. Page 11.* 11–18 July 2016.
6. Chris Grayling. 'Pro Brexit: Leaving the EU gives Britain the freedom to thrive'. *Time. Page 14.* 11–18 July 2016.
7. Jon Stone. 'Brexit: What happens if talks collapse and there's no deal?'. *Independent.co.uk – The Independent.* 19 September 2017.
8. 'Time to pick up the tab'. *The Economist. Page 8.* 11 February 2017.
9. 'Time to pick up the tab'. *The Economist. Page 8.* 11 February 2017.
10. 'From Brussels with love'. *The Economist. Page 21.* 11 February 2017.
11. 'A Queen's Speech to reflect a sombre Britain'. *Financial Times. Page 8.* 22 June 2017.
12. Steve Bullock. 'As a British EU negotiator, I can tell you that Brexit is going to be far worse than anyone could have guessed'. *Independent.co.uk – The Independent.* 25 July 2017.
13. Tony Blair. 'Brexit's Stunning Coup'. *Nytimes.com – The New York Times.* 24 June 2016.

14. Timothy Garton Ash. 'As an English European, this is the biggest defeat of my political life'. *Theguardian.com – The Guardian*. 24 June 2016.
15. Ben Chu. 'Brexit: 'Zero chance' leaving EU will make Britons better off, Nobel laureate economist Paul Krugman says'. *Independent.co.uk – The Independent*. 25 September 2017.
16. Kamal Ahmed. 'Germany warns the City over Brexit risk'. *Bbc.com*. 10 February 2017.
17. Kamal Ahmed. 'Germany warns the City over Brexit risk'. *Bbc.com*. 10 February 2017.
18. Joe Miller. 'Frankfurt is winning the battle for Brexit spoils'. *Bbc.com*. 29 August 2017.
19. Patrick Jenkins. 'How the City finally raised its voice over Brexit'. *Financialtimes.com*. 3 October 2017.
20. John O'Donnell, Andrew MacAskill. 'London stays world's top finance center despite Brexit'. *ca.reuters.com*. 11 September 2017.
21. 'Carney warns Brexit uncertainty is building'. *Bbc.com*. 3 August 2017.
22. Alex Barker, Jim Brunsden. 'EU unity masks fragile foundations'. *Financial Times. Page 4*. 22 June 2017.
23. 'An aggravating absence'. *The Economist. Page 19*. 2 July 2016.
24. 'The politics of anger'. *The Economist. Page 12*. 2 July 2016.
25. 'An aggravating absence'. *The Economist. Page 19*. 2 July 2016.
26. Ivan Kratsev. 'Le scenario noir d'une désintégration de l'UE'. *Le Monde. Page 24*. 12 July 2016.
27. 'Poland wants talks with Germany on WWII payout: minister.' *AFP*. 4 September 2017.
28. Elizabeth Pond. 'How Poland is testing the limits of the EU 'experiment". *Csmonitor.com – The Christian Science Monitor*. 30 August 2017.
29. Vanessa Gera. 'Open conflict triggers concern Poland might leave EU next'. *Associated Press*. 5 August 2017.
30. Marek Strzelecki, Konrad Krasuski. 'Poland to EU: No Second-Class Members (and Mind Your Own Business)'. *Bloomberg.com*. 5 September 2017.
31. Le Figaro.fr, AFP. 'La Pologne refuse l'UE 'à plusieurs vitesses". *Lefigaro.fr – Le Figaro*. 10 March 2017.
32. Bill Wirtz. 'Forget Frexit, the EU's next threat comes from the East'. *Newsweek.com*. 5 February 2017.
33. Gavin Hewitt. 'Europe's future: Small steps rather than big dreams?'. *Bbc.com*. 7 March 2017.

34. Charles Riley. 'Europe is falling apart. Saving it won't be easy'. *Money.cnn.com*. 20 January 2017.
35. Nick Bryant. 'The end of the Anglo-American order?'. *Bbc.com*. 9 June 2017.
36. 'What Europe Should Do About Britain'. *Bloomberg*. 12 June 2017.
37. Alex Barker, Jim Brunsden. 'EU unity masks fragile foundations'. *Financial Times. Page 4*. 22 June 2017.
38. 'Brexit: Londres prêt à une coopération 'étroite' et 'sans condition' avec l'UE'. *Lefigaro.fr – Le Figaro*. 12 September 2017.
39. 'Brexit deal could be template for EU ties to Ukraine, Turkey, Germany's Gabriel says'. *Reuters*. 6 December 2017.
40. Toby Helm. 'EU immigration offer could lead to Brexit reversal, claims Adonis'. *Guardian.co.uk – The Guardian*. 9 September 2017.
41. Arj Singh. 'Brexit could be reversed if EU agrees to immigration deal, Tony Blair says'. *Guardian.co.uk – The Guardian*. 10 September 2017.

8

Uber Alles? Not So Fast!

Why Germany is not all that it seems and can't lead Europe

A Benign Hegemon

It is difficult not to admire Germany. Germany gave us Bach, Einstein, Beckenbauer, Mercedes-Benz, Oktoberfest and Schiller, and won yet another soccer World Cup in 2014. It makes the world's best cars, managed the impossible feat of absorbing its poorer Eastern half and reformed itself to embrace globalization and become the world's number one exporter. It enjoys a 'feel-good economy that's proved more egalitarian than its European peers'.[1] It is an economic powerhouse dwarfing the rest of Europe and batting in the same league as the USA and China. A benign power and a moderate democracy championing soft power, Germany seems to excel at everything it does. Its strength and reputation stem from various sources including stability, a moderate stance in world affairs, the general perception that Germans are serious, reasonable, disciplined and have their heads on their shoulders, and, most of all its economic prowess. The 'German Question' has, however, haunted European politics since Bismarck unified Germans into a nation-state in the late nineteenth century. It was larger, more populated and more powerful than any of its neighbours. Alluding to the Cold War reality that saw Germany divided by the infamous Berlin Wall into a western and an eastern half, François Mauriac joked that he loved Germany so much that he was happy to have two of them. A cosy *pas de deux* featuring France and Germany used to define the post-Second World War European agenda, with France hiding its weakness behind Germany and Germany hiding its strength behind France. This state of affairs provided some form of balance and stability to European matters. Today this paradigm is no more. Due to its own success as much as to the rapid decline of France and the recent British estrangement, Germany is alone in the driving seat. Former US Secretary of State Henry Kissinger who famously complained he didn't know which number to dial if he needed to 'call Europe' finally has his answer: +49. The new reality of German hegemony is already shaping the future of Europe and not necessarily for the better. That much became obvious from two monumental challenges Europe found itself confronted with in recent times, the eurozone crisis and the refugee crisis. In the course of both crises Germany made decisions and everyone else fell into place, with results that were far from satisfactory. In all fairness let us keep in mind a simple fact: there are no pan-European politicians. Germany has its own interests just like any other nation-state. The German Chancellor is elected by Germans and, while the rest of Europe is doubtlessly important to German hearts, the Chancellor's job is first to promote what she or he perceives as the interests of Germany itself. Germany's position is firmly entrenched as the dominant European power and the EU 'centre' is weak (not weak enough said the British). Brussels' politicians are, after all, mostly glorified bureaucrats with a small EU budget to play with and the power of utmost legislative nuisance, which they wield with great pleasure. Consequently for the foreseeable future the de facto leader of Europe will be elected by the German people.

For all its prowess Germany has recently used its dominant European position to dictate key European policies, often with disastrous results. Germany's diagnosis that the eurozone crisis was of a fiscal nature was plain wrong. It led to the imposition of severe austerity measures across the board in troubled countries. As a result they were condemned to depression, high unemployment and ever-rising debt burdens. The refugee crisis was another instance of Germany unilaterally exercising its hegemonic power with dire consequences for itself and the rest of Europe. As we have seen, Germany's generous offer to take in masses of migrants turned out to be a hasty, emotional decision that was not well thought out. It precipitated a crisis with side-effects that included Brexit and the death of Schengen. What emerges from these examples is a Germany that may not necessarily relish its newfound leadership yet no longer shies away from asserting its power and imposing its views on others, and not necessarily with good results.

Annoying Details

The myth of German rectitude was spectacularly debunked by the revelation of vast cheating operations at the iconic company Volkswagen and at another icon, Deutsche Bank. Germany claimed the moral high ground throughout the eurozone crisis, proclaiming loud and clear that the Greeks deserve to suffer because they cheated. Well, sorry to break the news, Angela, but Volkswagen and Deutsche Bank have been caught cheating on a large scale, and they are not exactly Greek. The giant German car manufacturer that owns brands such as Volkswagen, Audi and Porsche was hammered with some 22 billion USD worth of fines for having equipped its diesel cars with software purposely designed to deceive US emission and pollution controls. As a result, over 600,000 cars were recalled in the USA.[2] In 2017, Volkswagen was poised to recall another 281,000 cars in the USA, this time for purely technical reasons related to malfunctioning fuel pumps.[3] Merkel herself recognized that the auto sector has 'seen a great loss of trust'.[4] One could be excused for finding the recent criticism of the country's car industry voiced by Merkel and other government figures a bit hypocritical, given the very cosy historic relationship between Germany's two main political parties (Merkel's CDU and Schulz's SPD) with the car industry. Also given that Merkel (who had anointed herself with the title 'automobile chancellor' before her 2013 re-election and whose political party received a 700,000 euro donation from the Quandt family, who happens to own part of BMW) fought in Brussels against a ceiling on gas emissions proposed by the EU. Also given that no concrete measures have been proposed to rein in the auto industry[5] which employs over 800,000 people in Germany alone.[6]

Deutsche Bank's woes were known for quite some time. Falling income due to low lending revenues in an age of low interest rates may have contributed to the institution's increasingly adventurous posture abroad. The massive hiring of risk-prone investment bankers in its US operations two decades ago may have compounded the problem. Yet, not only did the bank embark in questionable, high risk operations but it knowingly defrauded investors for years and on a large scale. Among the many criminal lawsuits it was faced, Deutsche Bank pleaded guilty in 2015 to charges of rigging Libor, resulting in a 2.5 billion USD fine from authorities in the USA and the UK.[7] It was given another 14 billion USD fine from the US Justice Department a year later, due to the bank's fraudulent practices in relation to mortgage backed securities.[8] Yet in the financial industry crime often pays and in the USA Deutsche Bank was bailed out by US taxpayers during the latest financial crisis with assistance loans aggregating over 350 billion USD: about twice what Lehman Brothers received. The bank's profitability in recent years has been dismal. It lost almost 7 billion euros in 2015.[9] It 'posted a net loss of 1.9 billion euross in the final quarter of 2016 as legal costs for past misdeeds weighed heavily on results'.[10] Its stock price crashed and the IMF warned in 2016 that the institution had become the 'world's most important net contributor to systemic risks in the global banking system'.[11] With 1.8 trillion euros in assets (equivalent to almost 60% of Germany's GDP) and more than 100,000 employees,[12] the bank was obviously too big to fail. Some observers said that Germany could be expected to rescue the bank in which case it would be doing what it has prevented other European countries from doing with their own failing banks. During 2016, speculation was rife. Rumours ranged from a possible merger with the partly state-owned Commerzbank to Berlin's potential use of a loophole according to which a state can recapitalize a bank as a 'preventive measure' with public money if the bank fails a stress test (which could be a fake test). Germany has insisted in the past that the bondholders and depositors of banks in Europe should be hit before any state aid is allowed and pushed for this policy to be enshrined in EU Bank Recovery and Resolution Directive rules. Yet, if it feels it would serve its own interests, Germany is likely, once more, to break the rules. This would be to the great pleasure of other troubled countries who would finally feel free to do the same, signifying the end of any serious efforts to improve a financial sector badly in need of reform all over the continent. Berlin's immediate priority was, unsurprisingly, to put pressure on the USA to reduce the huge fine. At the end of 2016 the bank announced that it had reached a settlement with the US Justice Department at 7.2 billion USD. In 2017 the bank seemed to be slowly improving its position. It was poised to downsize some of its operations yet remained plagued by serious problems. For a country that prides itself on following rules and being the epitome of rectitude it seems Germany is on its way to be *Uber Alles* at the top of the podium for receiving the world's biggest fines for cheating and breaking rules.

It Isn't All that It Seems to Be

In recent years German leaders have been trumpeting the success of the German economic model. There are ample reasons to rejoice. Germany has achieved the remarkable feat of absorbing its much poorer eastern half following the fall of the Berlin Wall. It injected over 2 trillion euros which resulted in a remarkable convergence of living standards between West and East although a gap remains. Interestingly enough it is between the North and the South that the gap is now growing. The German south is becoming richer and its north poorer (the northern states collectively have 371 billion euros of debt and annual exports worth 391 billion euros; the southern states collectively have 170 billion euros of debt and annual exports worth 559 billion euros).[13] This worrisome trend led Demographic Risk Atlas, a study of population trends, to suggest that Germany's north-south divide could become larger than Italy's.[14] To its credit, Germany enjoys an almost full employment economy (3.9% unemployment only), its GDP has kept growing since 2005 (by mid-2016, the economy had grown 2.1% year-on-year),[15] its total debt level in 2017 is the same as it was in 2005 and its fiscal position shows a positive balance.[16] The German economy is the envy of many. Its economic success is to a great extent a reflection of the success of the *Mittlestandt*: a universe of well-run family enterprises that restructured themselves to jump on the globalization train and propelled the country to become the world's number one export machine (with no little help from an undervalued euro). Yet it is easy to forget that—despite its commendable AAA rating—prior to its respectable growth performance, Germany had effectively seen little GDP growth since just before the financial crisis in 2007. Its average growth rate (adjusted for inflation) of only 0.8% from 2007 to 2015 led American economics Nobel laureate Joseph Stiglitz to say 'this is not the performance of a champion!'. It is also easy to forget that German productivity growth has continuously declined over the past 20 years (just as it has done in France and Italy), while capital expenditure as a percentage of GDP has also been declining (again, the same goes for France and Italy).[17] The infrastructure investment rate is the lowest of any big developed economy (*The Economist* blames the Merkel 'government's obsession with balanced books' which 'has led it to invest too little').[18] None of these facts are good news for the future direction of economic competitiveness. Germany's arcane tax code, one of the most complicated on the planet, contributed to its ranking behind Macedonia in the 2015 World Bank country classification of 'Ease of doing business'. German rankings in the World Economic Forum's global competitiveness survey for road quality, railway quality and internet bandwidth visibly worsened from respectively 5th, 4th and 12th in 2010–11 to 16th, 11th and 29th in 2017.[19] The German service sector, representing 60% of the economy, remains mired in the past and 'an insecure, low-wage service sector is growing'.[20] It comes as a surprise that, according to Eurostat, 9.7% of the German employed population was living below the poverty line (defined at approximately 940 euros per month) in 2014 (an increase compared to 2006's 7.5%): above the European average of 9.5%.[21] Since Angela Merkel assumed power in 2005 the percentage of the population below the poverty line (established at 60% of median income) has more than doubled in ten years.[22] According to *The Economist*,

> 'The lowest-paid 40% of German workers are earning less in real terms than 20 years ago. Food-bank use is up. The rate of investment has been dropping since 2012. Bridges creak and potholed roads challenge even the best-engineered suspensions' […] Dirty coal is filling some of the gap left by the

closure of the country's nuclear plants as part of an 'energy transformation'; the country's carbon-dioxide emissions are up [...] Mrs Merkel bears a good bit of the blame for all this [...] after her 12 years as chancellor the tax system remains strikingly unprogressive and state governments' ability to invest in infrastructure or anything else is limited by an excessively rigid 'debt brake'.[23]

The German economy is on one hand the envy of the world yet remains, in certain respects, a myth that rests in no small part on depressed wages and on an undervalued currency. Disciplined German workers have stomached wage restraint for more than a decade (wage restraint acts like an artificial internal devaluation, making German goods even more competitive and, by the way, Germany was quick to criticize Ireland's 'tax dumping' but will not tolerate its wage restraint being labelled as 'salary dumping'). Similarly, the euro will probably remain undervalued for Germany, helping its exports. These factors can be expected to continue fuelling growth for the foreseeable future: Germany seems to be living through a magic moment.

The Missing Goods

Legitimacy of leadership in international affairs derives not just from economic or military power, but also from the delivery of 'international public goods': initiatives and actions that bring obvious benefits to other nations. After the Second World War, the USA led the free world and gained legitimacy because it delivered international public goods. These included the Marshall Plan that helped rebuild Europe, a credible military protection umbrella and acting as the architect of institutions such as the IMF and the World Bank. What about Germany today? In the Trump era, some commentators ventured that 'Merkel could oversee a truly consequential change in foreign affairs, a shift from Pax Americana to Pax Germania', with Germany becoming the guardian of the 'liberal world order'.[24] They said a fourth mandate would see Merkel 'preside over the creation of a newly powerful Germany'[25] and become 'leader of the free world'.[26] Perhaps. What is more certain is that Merkel's steadfast, reliable and polite style of leadership, her advocacy of international alliances and European unity (under German leadership of course) contrasted with that of a US leadership that seems erratic under Trump. Merkel has given the impression of injecting a dose of much needed stability into a world in turmoil. But what international public goods does Germany concretely deliver beyond what benefits itself? On the security front Germany, today a pacifist nation *par excellence*, has always been happy to allow France and the UK to lead. Moreover, a 2015 Pew Research Center poll showed that a 58% majority of Germans are unwilling to use force to defend a NATO ally under attack, the highest such proportion in Europe.[27] NATO members are supposed to spend 2% of their GDP on defence (the target was agreed by NATO members in 2006). In reality, the USA covers about 70% of all NATO allies' defence expenditure and only four other NATO members (Estonia, Greece, Poland and Britain) abide by the 2% target.[28] France spends close to 2%, while some spend more, such as Greece which spends 2.5% (due to the threat it perceives from Turkey). Some spend less, such as Germany which spends only 1.2%.[29] The better Germany has been doing, the less it seems to have been willing to spend on defence. In 1989, West Germany was spending 2.7% of GDP on defence, a figure which had dropped down to 1.4% by the year 2000, after reunification, where it remained until 2013, decreasing then to 1.2% by 2016.[30] The USA pushing Germany and others to spend more on defence is nothing new and is not a 'Trump thing'. Robert Gates, the Defence Secretary during Barack Obama's presidency declared: 'The blunt reality is that there will be dwindling appetite and patience in the US Congress, and in the American body politic writ large, to expend increasingly precious funds on behalf of nations that are apparently unwilling to devote the necessary resources.'[31] The consequences of Germany's cavalier attitude in respect of NATO's military readiness are real, they are not American inventions: German forces used broomsticks instead of machine guns during a NATO exercise a few years ago because of a shortage of equipment; not a single German submarine was deployable in the autumn of 2017; German military pilots have been 'using choppers owned by a private automobile club to practice because so many of their own helicopters are in need of repair.[32] As reported by Reuters in 2016, Merkel herself recognized that 'In the 21st century, we won't be getting as much help as we got in the 20th. We need to greatly increase the Bundeswehr budget to get from 1.2 to 2%' (a goal she set for 2024). Her Minister of Defence Ursula Von der Leyen admitted that other NATO members saw Germany was 'doing so well economically' and she recognized that 'we must bear a larger, fairer, share of the burden for trans-Atlantic security'.[33] In all fairness to Germany defence spending by Europeans in general has usually matched the overall perception of threat. It steadily declined after the end of the Cold War, but Europe sought to reverse the falling trend after Russia annexed Crimea in 2014.[34]

Is change in the air? Many in Europe would like to see Germany substantially expand its military forces and get more involved in European defence. But if there is change it is likely to be marginal as there is little appetite for it in Germany. German Foreign Minister Sigmar Gabriel made it clear that the 2% NATO target was neither 'reachable nor desirable' for Germany.[35] In all fairness, one is entitled to question the validity and wisdom of this 2% 'magic number', which does not rest on anything solid and reduces the complex issue of defence to a quantitative parameter. In the case of Ukraine, for instance, Europe outspent the USA ten to one on its non-military responses to Russian actions in recent years—through foreign assistance, trade deals, sanctions, energy policy, and more—so in a sense Merkel can be excused for calling the 2% spending standard 'narrow-minded'.[36] But if so, then one can also question the 3% eurozone rule on deficits that Germany insists on every country respecting and which does not rest on any economic theory either. Another case of Berlin sticking by the rules when it suits its situation and ignoring them otherwise. As a result of lack of traction for serious defence spending, initiatives such as the Framework Nations Concept launched in 2013—a clever way for Germany to share resources with smaller European countries in exchange for the use of their troops so as to avoid real military expansion while showing more involvement—will have a marginal effect.[37] Recent declarations by Berlin and Paris to the effect that they are working together toward a European security force, viewed by some as a reaction to Trump's prodding (these initiatives actually go back a lot further),[38] are also likely to have a marginal effect on overall European defence. Why has rich Germany been spending so little in recent times? First of all because after the fall of the Soviet Empire Germany does not perceive any direct existential threats to its security. Secondly because it can get away with it. Just as Germany was the first country to break the rules of the euro when it was in difficulty in 2003 and got away with it.

What about delivery of international public goods on the economic front? Here too Germany fails the test. Germany's solidity underpins the euro but it has been unwilling to allow more symmetrical adjustments or measures such as Eurobonds or a softening of austerity measures to help stimulate weaker European economies. The same 'selfishness' applies to current-account surpluses. In February 2017, Germany reported the world's largest current-account surplus: a monumental 270 billion euros. (compared with a 60 billion euro deficit for France).[39] Chronic features of the German economy, these surpluses are testimony to its success. They are, however, controversial, because they create imbalances with Germany's European partners as well as with the rest of the world. They represent distortions which have been criticized, among others, by the IMF, the US Treasury Department and the OECD. These surpluses are the result of several factors including wage growth restraint coupled with the fact that Germany invests little and saves more than it invests (excess savings end up as funds that Germany lends or invests abroad). If Germany was serious about lowering its surpluses (and stimulating weaker European economies) it would take measures to raise domestic wages faster, invest more at home and run deficits. But newfound German fiscal orthodoxy has it that deficits are anathema to the extent that a famous 'debt brake law' was enshrined in the constitution, capping structural borrowings at 0.35% of GDP (well below the 3% limit set by eurozone rules) from 2016 on, to prevent the temptation of using the Keynesian remedy of deficits. Germany is a nation of savers. Public opinion has latched on to the dogma of fiscal orthodoxy and German voters are loath to spend hard-earned cash on directly or indirectly helping other European countries. As a result, the wilful correction of structural current-account imbalances is just as unlikely to become reality as are any meaningful concessions aimed at making the eurozone more workable or helping weaker economies. French President Macron's desire to reform the EU and the eurozone will probably flounder on the reality that nothing of substance will happen without Berlin's approval; Berlin is unlikely to make concessions on anything substantial (even less so after the far-right AfD entry to the *Bundestag* in the fall of 2017) and Merkel's weakened political position at home. Supremely confident and practical, Germany will first see to what it perceives as its own interests. The lack of international public goods emanating from Germany means the legitimacy of its de facto leadership only rests on the relative economic power it enjoys today compared to other European nations.

In all fairness one would be remiss not to consider the German point of view. Germany is not a nation of risk takers or big spenders. It is a nation of conservative and hard-working savers. Moreover it spent a lot on its reunification after the fall of the Berlin Wall. Unlike Southern Europeans Germans have had the merit of recognizing the need for painful structural reforms at home. They bit the bullet and undertook these reforms years ago. Reforms require sacrifices so Germans rightly ask: 'Why, after all the sacrifices that got us where we are today, do we have to pay for others who refuse to undertake similar reforms? Moreover, we know that whenever we help them we take away the incentives for them to reform as we did?' How do you think Germans would feel about helping a country, such as France, where people retire years earlier? Or one, such as Italy, where a woman has been known to get paid leave from her job because her dog was sick?[40]

The Joys of Becoming More 'Normal'?

Angela Merkel's popularity reached high levels as she ruled during a period in which everything seemed to blissfully go Germany's way. The *Kanzlerin* projected an image of stability, sobriety and sound moral principles that endeared her to her constituency who fondly called her *mutti*. Yet history may remember her one day as the most divisive German Chancellor since the end of the Second World War. It is not just that, as Foreign Policy magazine put it, 'After 11 years in power, Merkel's CDU has run out of ideas'.[41] Many feel that Berlin's newfound unilateralism and assertiveness have severely damaged the European edifice. Under Merkel's watch Germany's handling of the eurozone crisis ended up firmly dividing Europe into creditors and debtors and contributed to economic collapse and massive unemployment in most of southern Europe. Her handling of the recent immigration crisis—unilaterally deciding to open the doors to a human tsunami and subsequently impose quotas—resulted in Brexit, the death of Schengen, an East–West cleavage and walls between countries, something Europe had not seen for a long time. Her decision to ignore the Dublin agreements in the case of Syrian migrants was taken without the consultation of her European partners. While it may have been partly motivated by commendable humanitarian concerns, it was doubtlessly also taken with the narrow interests of Germany's demographic predicaments in mind. In Germany itself, her open-door immigration policies created profound divisions. They resulted in a palpable worsening of the country's domestic security and stability and paved the way for the emergence of the far right. As a result, the AfD, founded only in 2014, accessed the *Bundestag* (parliament) in 2017: a first in postwar Germany. With its 13%, the far right is not about to assume power in a country where 80% of the people say they are centrist (compared to 51% in France).[42] Germany is likely to continue being a 'beacon of moderation and stability', yet 'one in eight voters supported a party that said Germans should be proud of the soldiers who fought in the Nazi army.'[43] With the CDU/CSU (*Christlich Demokratische Union Deutschlands/Christlich Soziale Union in Bayern*) coalition of Christian democrats that traditionally governed German politics achieving its worse score in many years in 2017, the *Kanzlerin* faced the need to establish alliances comprising smaller, untested parties. The AfD intends to make itself heard loud and clear in the *Bundestag* and so a 'noisy and fractious edge' will be introduced 'to a legislature previously marked by a relatively calm and collegiate tone'.[44] According to World Politics Review columnist Frida Ghitis, 'Merkel has vowed to regain the votes of those who backed the AfD. That will likely end plans for closer ties to the European Union, and it means German politics and policies will need to move to the right […] We can now say goodbye to sedate and predictable politics in Germany.'[45]

Autumn 2017 saw another important thing happen for the first time since the end of the Second World War. Following the failure of coalition-building negotiations in the aftermath of the September elections, Germany was, for the first time, without a government. On 20 November 2017 the world woke up to the reality that Germany—the exception, the epitome of stability—was starting to look a bit more like a 'normal' country by the day as the spectre of a new election loomed and the future of the *Kanzlerin* was in question. In an article ominously entitled

'Germany Has Plunged Into Unprecedented Political Chaos', *Foreign Policy* reported the words of University of Hannover sociologist Detlev Claussen: 'It's an ideal situation for the AfD, which will paint the mainstream parties as bumbling elites ready to compromise everything and waste taxpayers' money [...] The AfD will look all the more respectable now. It's very likely that come fresh elections we'll see a further shift to the right. This would be extremely bad for Germany—and for Europe, too. Now there'll be in less room for negotiating EU reforms, and Germany-first sentiment will be all the louder.'[46] Having a few months earlier praised the virtues of Germany observers and the media now concurred that Europe ran the risk of losing this pillar of stability, especially in a post-Merkel era. Having praised Merkel as the new 'leader of the free world' in a February 2015 article by journalist Jochen Bittner, *The New York Times* warned of 'serious uncertainty for all Europe and the West' in November 2017. The first casualty would be French President Macron's grand plans for further integration and reform of the EU and the eurozone, for which he needed Berlin's full attention and cooperation. Germany would, instead, probably be thinking 'Germany first' even more and would be busy licking its wounds. Brexit talks would be further complicated by a weakened Berlin. 'The European Union, mired in the severest crisis since its founding, was counting on Merkel and a new German government to deliver, in tandem with France's President Emmanuel Macron, the energy and vision for far-reaching reforms to deepen European integration' wrote *Foreign Policy* 'But now everything, including the EU's prospects, is up in the air'. On the other hand, Macron would probably see a weakening of Germany as an opportunity to reassert more leadership from France on the continent and a rebalancing of the Paris-Berlin partnership was not all that bad for Europe. According to former Italian Premier Enrico Letta, the few months following the German election amounted to the last chance for France and Germany to join hands in order to undertake much needed European reforms.[47] Scenarios of political instability in Germany are, however, easy to overdramatize. Extreme scenarios—such as the far right coming to power, or a succession of Italian-style short-lived, unstable governments—are entirely out of the question. In all likelihood, the prudent Germans will work something out that will take the country not too far from its current trajectory. Nevertheless, a slightly more divided and less stable

Germany, where the AfD could gain slightly more power, would mean an even more self-centred Germany. The paradox, from a EU perspective, is that the only thing worse than a strong Germany is a weak Germany. CNN warned that 'The EU is mired in its gravest crisis since its founding, shaken by Brexit, the stubborn eurozone crisis, lack of unity, and the rise of a far right in its midst. Donald Trump's erratic international policies have dramatically underscored the need for the Europeans to get their act together on security and foreign affairs [...] This is why the EU needs and expects a strong Germany—now more than ever [...] The EU is stuck in a holding pattern as long as the German crisis persists.'[48]

The point of this section is not that Germany is 'bad'. Far from it. One can only admire this country's undeniable successes across in many fields. It has been a pillar of European construction, stability and order. It is arguably the most successful post-modern power at the dawn of the twenty-first century. Yet, in order to better understand the world around us, a little debunking about German myths is in order. The point is that for all its prowess Germany is not infallible. It can make mistakes: small as well as big. Despite being Europeanist, Germany roots for Germany—and will continue, mostly unopposed, doing what it perceives as being in its self-interest—and why should it be any different? Whether it wanted it or not, Germany has found itself firmly *Uber Alles*, in the position of de facto leader of Europe, unchecked, and in control of the European agenda. All the more since the rest of Europe has been unable to get its act together. Yet, Germany's reluctance to see beyond its narrow self-interest, its self-righteousness, its fixation on economic orthodoxy and its tendency to exercise its hegemonic position with scant regard for its European partners, mean Germany is unfit to lead Europe.

Notes

1. Rainer Buergin. 'Germany's Success Could Wreck Martin Schulz's Bid for Power'. *Bloomberg.com – Bloomberg*. 16 August 2017.
2. 'USA/dieselgate: peine de prison pour un ex-ingénieur de Volkswagen'. *Lefigaro.fr – Le Figaro*. 25 August 2017.
3. 'USA: Volkswagen rappelle 281.000 voitures'. *Lefigaro.fr – Le Figaro*. 29 August 2017.

4. Oliver Sachgau. 'Merkel Cites 'Trust' Problem With German Carmakers'. *Bloomberg.com*. 9 September 2017.
5. Michelle Fitzpatrick. 'Les mensonges de l'automobile au coeur de la campagne électorale allemande'. *France24.com*. 15 August 2017.
6. Oliver Sachgau. 'Merkel Cites 'Trust' Problem With German Carmakers". *Bloomberg.com*. 9 September 2017.
7. Ben Protess, Jack Ewing. 'Deutsche Bank to Pay $2.5 Billion Fine to Settle Rate-Rigging Case'. *Nytimes.com – The New York Times*. 23 April 2015.
8. Arno Schuetze. 'Deutsche Bank to fight $14 billion demand from US authorities'. *Reuters.com – Reuters*. 16 September 2016.
9. Jack Ewing. 'Deutsche Bank Announces $7 Billion Yearly Loss as Legal Issues Weigh on Results'. *Nytimes.com – The New York Times*. 20 January 2016.
10. 'Deutsche Bank prepares 8 billion-euro capital increase'. *Reuters.com – Reuters*. 3 March 2017.
11. L. Shapiro, Lili Bayer. 'Signs of Trouble for Deutsche Bank'. *Geopoliticalfutures.com*. 1 July 2016.
12. Mark Thompson, Paul R. La Monica. 'Deutsche Bank: Does it need a bailout?'. *Money.cnn.com*. 30 September 2016.
13. J.C. 'Explaining the Munich miracle. On almost every indicator, Germany's south is doing better than its north'. *The Economist*. 20 August 2017.
14. 'The beautiful south. Germany's new divide'. *The Economist*. 19 August 2017.
15. Rida Husna. 'Germany GDP growth rate'. *Tradingeconomics.com*. 15 August 2017.
16. Mathilde Golla, Clémentine Maligorne. 'Sous Merkel, l'économie allemande s'est imposée comme moteur de l'Europe'. *Lefigaro.fr – Le Figaro*. 24 September 2017.
17. Dr. Philip Ehmer. 'Labour productivity of large euro area countries drifts apart – Italy falling behind'. *Kfw.de*. 26 July 2016.
18. 'Why Angela Merkel deserves to win Germany's election'. *Economist.com – The Economist*. 9 September 2017.
19. 'The Germany that doesn't work'. *The Economist. Page 25*. 17 June 2017.
20. J.C. 'German politics is about to tip rightwards'. *Economist.com – The Economist*. 17 September 2017.
21. Estelle Peard. 'Dans la Ruhr, la désespérance des travailleurs allemands pauvres'. *AFP*. 11 May 2017.

22. Mathilde Golla, Clémentine Maligorne. 'Sous Merkel, l'économie allemande s'est imposée comme moteur de l'Europe'. *Lefigaro.fr – Le Figaro*. 24 September 2017.
23. 'How Angela Merkel is changing, and not changing, Germany'. *Economist.com – The Economist*. 9 September 2017.
24. Johanna Scbuster-Craig. 'Angela Merkel, Donald Trump and the free world: is the stage set for a strong German leader to eclipse America?'. *Newsweek.com – Newsweek*. 11 July 2017.
25. Jacob Heilbrunn. 'Will Pax Germania replace Pax Americana?'. *Latimes.com – Los Angeles Times*. 9 February 2017.
26. Johanna Scbuster-Craig. 'Angela Merkel, Donald Trump and the free world: is the stage set for a strong German leader to eclipse America?'. *Newsweek.com – Newsweek*. 11 July 2017.
27. 'Many NATO Countries Reluctant to Use Force to Defend Allies.' *Pewglobal.org*. 8 June 2015.
28. 'Germany rebukes Tillerson over call for Nato allies to boost defense spending'. *Theguardian.com – The Guardian*. 31 March 2017.
29. 'Military spending by NATO members'. *Economist.com – The Economist*. 16 February 2017.
30. Elizabeth Braw. 'Germany Is Quietly Building a European Army Under Its Command'. *Foreignpolicy.com – Foreign Policy*. 22 May 2017.
31. Doug Bandow. 'Is Germany Serious About Defending Itself, Europe, And The West? Time For Europeans To Run NATO'. *Forbes.com – Forbes*. 2 May 2017.
32. Rick Noack. 'Afraid of a major conflict? The German military is currently unavailable'. *Washingtonpost.com, Washington Post*. 24 January 2018.
33. Doug Bandow. 'Is Germany Serious About Defending Itself, Europe, And The West? Time For Europeans To Run NATO'. *Forbes.com. Forbes*. 2 May 2017.
34. Gabriela Baczynska. 'Defense spending by European NATO allies inches up in 2016'. *Reuters*. 13 March 2017.
35. 'Germany rebukes Tillerson over call for Nato allies to boost defense spending'. *Theguardian.com. The Guardian*. 31 March 2017.
36. Zeeshan Aleem. 'The epic Trump-Merkel feud, explained'. *Vox.com*. 1 June 2017.
37. Elizabeth Braw. 'Germany Is Quietly Building a European Army Under Its Command'. *Foreignpolicy.com – Foreign Policy*. 22 May 2017.

38. Jefferson Chase. 'German, French defense ministers talk new European security force'. *Dw.com – Deutsche Welle.* 1 June 2017.
39. 'Surplus war'. *The Economist. Page 20.* 11 February 2017; Alexandre Devecchio. 'Les Français ne se sont pas prononcés pour une politique européiste'. *Le Figaro. Page 20.* 29 September 2017.
40. 'Italie: son chien est malade, elle obtient des congés'. *Lefigaro.fr – Le Figaro.* 12 October 2017.
41. Matthias Mattijs. 'The West Should Hope That Merkel Loses'. *Foreignpolicy.com – Foreign Policy.* 21 December 2016.
42. J.C. 'German politics is about to tip rightwards'. *Economist.com – The Economist.* 17 September 2017.
43. Frida Ghitis. 'We can say goodbye to a stable Germany'. *Cnn.com.* 25 September 2017.
44. J.C. 'German politics is about to tip rightwards'. *Economist.com – The Economist.* 17 September 2017.
45. Frida Ghitis. 'We can say goodbye to a stable Germany'. *Cnn.com.* 25 September 2017.
46. Paul Hockenos. 'Germany Has Plunged Into Unprecedented Political Chaos'. *Foreign Policy.* 20 November 2017.
47. Enrico Letta. "Pour l'Europe, on est dans l'avant-match". *France Inter.* 18 September 2017.
48. Paul Hockenos. 'Europe will pay a high price for Germany's paralysis'. *Cnn.com.* 29 November 2017.

9

The More It Changes, the More It Stays the Same

> Nothing much has happened with the euro in the past few years and this is worrying

The Wrong Stuff

In this chapter we shall look at the euro in the aftermath of the eurozone crisis. The reader is entitled to wonder why we are now embarking on this particular journey, as nothing really dramatic has happened to the euro since 2012 and since, after all, the eurozone is still alive and kicking. But that's precisely the point: nothing has been done to prepare for the next, inevitable crisis. Granted, the currency was stabilized and the eurozone crisis seems to be behind us. But nothing has substantially changed in the architecture of the single currency union. None of the profound structural reforms and improvements needed following the last crisis have been undertaken. The single currency construct continues to be plagued by the same fundamental structural flaws as it was before. The policy of 'muddling through', which Europeans have perfected into an art form, is still the norm. As a result, the next crisis is likely to hit just as hard or could even be fatal.

As I pointed out in *The Decline and Fall of Europe*, the euro started as a political project. As such it was not underpinned by a compelling economic rationale. In the 1990s, the French agreed to German re-unification on the condition that Germany would be tied even more to Europe's destiny by means of a common currency. Germany accepted abandoning its beloved deutschmark on condition that the new common currency would follow some fundamental rules and, in particular, that the deficits and public debt levels of member countries would be tightly controlled and the European Central Bank's (ECB) mandate would be limited to controlling inflation unlike the American Federal Reserve—which enjoys a broader mandate, enabling it, for instance, to take growth and unemployment into account in devising policies. When they joined the eurozone individual countries knowingly gave up their economic independence. For one, the 3% limit on budget deficits imposed by Maastricht Treaty rules removed some of the most effective Keynesian instruments that governments could use to fight unemployment or respond to a crisis. A single currency also meant a fixed exchange rate and a single interest rate for everybody. Eurozone member countries could no longer control interest rates at home, they could not freely run deficits to stimulate their economy, nor could they devalue their currencies to stimulate exports. Given all this, how do you make everyone happy when the economies of the various member countries are so different and require different medicine at different times? Economics Nobel Prize laureate Robert Mundell— who was considered by some as one of the spiritual fathers of the euro and who wrongly predicted in 2000 that the euro would cover 50 countries before 2010[1]—recognized that the economies of the eurozone were too diverse for a common currency to be easily shared.[2] There would be problems sooner or later. The architects of the euro chose the easy route: they simply assumed that if all eurozone countries adhered to the Maastricht debt and deficit limits (the 'magic numbers' set at respectively 60% and 3% of GDP), their diverse economies would sooner or later miraculously converge—that is, would become similar. Given these assumptions, there would be no need for solidarity mechanisms (i.e. helping countries in need) and the same interest rate and the same fiscal rules would work for all. If ever there was a seriously unrealistic set of assumptions, this was it. According to Joseph Stiglitz, another Nobel Prize laureate in economics, the belief that by having countries strictly adhere to the Maastricht debt and deficit limits and by having the ECB only focus on inflation, things would work out all right was based on simplistic ideology, not economic science; and Europe had created a divergent system while it thought it was creating a convergent one, losing track of financial stability.[3] As a result, the euro's architecture was fundamentally flawed.

Post-Mortem

Supposed to cement the unity of European nations, the single currency has instead exacerbated differences and generated deep divisions between creditors and debtor nations. It has not promoted economic convergence as the ECB itself recognized in a 2015 report: 'There has been no process of real convergence among the 12 countries that adopted the euro in 1999 and 2001'.[4] The shortcomings of the single currency construct became obvious when Greece, which represented only 2.3% of eurozone GDP pre-crisis, threatened to bring the whole edifice down. Lacking key institutional features and resting on the utopian hope of convergence, the common currency project never made much sense the way it was put together. Eurozone integrity rested on the politics of solidarity for adjustments that would become necessary sooner or later, yet solidarity was not part of the blueprints and was conspicuously absent when needed. To British historian Mark Mazower, the Greek debt saga revealed the lack of any sense of political solidarity across the continent and the limits of EU political institutions. Mazower pointed out that the euro could theoretically have worked despite divergences: regional disparities are just as great in the USA (where more than 50 states share the dollar), but 'two things exist across the Atlantic that are absent in Europe. One is a sense of common political allegiance to the federal system—to be American means something, to be European much less. And the second, which contributes to the first, is that there are mechanisms for redistributing wealth and influence across the country as a whole.'[5] Mazower could have added that, compared with the USA, Europe does not enjoy the same labour mobility, that its central budget, standing at just 1% of total GDP, is far too small to help a country in crisis, and that it still lacks a common banking system.

The global financial crisis of 2008 morphed into the eurozone crisis. When the crisis hit, the Troika (the ECB, EC and the IMF), pushed by Germany, imposed a series of across-the-board austerity and other measures which resulted in a substantial contraction of GDP, an explosion of unemployment, a massive contraction of credit to SMEs (small and medium-sized enterprises) and of demand and output, as well as a worsening of debt-to-GDP ratios for affected countries. Before the crisis, Ireland and Spain had low levels of national debt and were running surpluses. The debt ratio of Ireland, for instance, exploded from a pre-crisis 24% to 95% of GDP post-crisis. Austerity means government cutbacks and those hardest hit are the poorest, the many middle- and lower-class people who depend the most on government programmes and public services. According to Stiglitz, 'the convergence criteria were intended to help the countries converge, and the austerity imposed was intended to reduce the fiscal deficit, typically, the effects were just the opposite' and 'as one program after another unfolded each country that followed the Troika's program went into a deep downturn and the Troika was always surprised by these outcomes … the Troika's grasp of the underlying economics was abysmal', concluding that 'Greece's depression wasn't because Greece didn't do what it was supposed to; it was because it did … it is shocking that Germany and the Troika have demanded that Greece and other crisis countries maintain large primary surpluses'.[6] Stiglitz's judgement of Germany is particularly harsh: 'Germany's stance is predicated on the belief that profligate government spending leads to crises-and that it led to the current eurozone crisis. That is simply wrong … Germany's suggestion that the failures of the countries in the eurozone are due do their profligacy seems so out of touch with economic reality, so demonstrative of a total lack of analysis.'[7] In other words, not only was the eurozone's architecture flawed to start with, but the diagnosis was wrong and the medicine imposed at Germany's insistence—long on ideology and short on pragmatism—largely contributed to transforming the crisis into an unmitigated disaster. Groucho Marx was spot on when he said that 'Politics is the art of looking for trouble, finding it everywhere, diagnosing it incorrectly and applying the wrong remedies'. According to Stiglitz, the eurozone's performance on all accounts has been worse than that of the countries in Europe that did not belong to the eurozone.[8]

When the eurozone crisis exploded, the hardest hit countries found themselves stuck. They couldn't even get out of the euro because, as at a 'Roach Motel', one could get in but not get out. The IMF itself, former champion of austerity policies, admitted that austerity doesn't work because when a government contracts spending, the economy contracts too. Yet the medicine imposed was austerity. Affected countries had, moreover, borrowed in euro which was effectively a foreign currency since they had no control over it. One does not need to be a genius to figure out that when the crisis hit, in order to limit the damage, a surplus country such as Germany should have at the very least stimulated its own economy to help others. Troubled countries should have been allowed to run deficits to jump-start their economies. The exact opposite was done at the creditors' insistence, with no solidarity and no easing of constraints. The ECB carries part of the blame, having twice raised interest rates in 2011 in the thick of the crisis. ECB head Jean-Claude Trichet 'will be remembered for his colossal misjudgements, in particular rising interest rates at moments when the economy was contracting' says Stiglitz.[9] Rate hikes had the double effect of choking economies and causing the euro to be too strong. As a result of wrong diagnosis and wrong policies, weak economies were ravaged and the eurozone came close to collapse. The situation was stabilized at the cost of a series of huge bailouts (the real purpose of which has been to repay German and foreign lenders to preserve the integrity of their own banks), of a deep divide between creditor and debtor nations, and of millions upon millions of people losing their jobs. In autumn 2016, as output in 11 EU countries still remained below 2007 levels and per-capita income had fallen, *The Economist* pointed out that 'what Europe desperately needs is growth. Yet Europeans train their sights on the sources of growth and shoot them down one by one.'[10] To Stiglitz, the euro system is broken, having led to an increase in inequality and divergence, with the weaker countries becoming weaker and the stronger countries becoming stronger.

The Missing Link

The mood of northern creditor countries facing their hapless southern partners was summarized by an off-the-cuff comment by Jeroen Dijsselbloem, the Dutch head of eurozone finance ministers: 'I can't spend my money on liqueurs and women then ask for help'.[11] This is the sort of stereotype that *Foreign Policy* magazine labelled 'a populist refrain that touted the Continent's northern saints and southern sinners',[12] and which, as can be expected, earned him the wrath of southern European politicians. This sort of attitude of European creditor nations towards debtors led Stiglitz in the past to say that 'there is an element of vindictiveness' in the way northerners have reacted to the plight of southerners. Led by Germany, creditor countries are convinced that the causes of the eurozone crisis lay in the laziness, profligacy and lack of fiscal discipline of their southern 'partners'. According to this mantra, had these countries followed the Maastricht rules they wouldn't be in trouble—ergo they brought it upon themselves and don't deserve to be helped. Aside from being a self-serving attitude this is a wrong assessment of the causes and realities of the eurozone crisis. As a result of this assessment creditor countries led by Germany do not want to take any meaningful measures such as more symmetrical adjustments or the mutualization of debt, or any measures that smack of 'paying for others' and their electorates firmly agree. In a sense, who can blame them? Why should countries that are doing well help countries that are in trouble, especially if the trouble is perceived to come from their own fault? The answer is that without such solidarity measures the eurozone simply can't work because it is made of a patchwork of very disparate economies that will never really converge. Germany, moreover, is conveniently oblivious to the fact that the euro, reflecting the average health of the various economies that compose the eurozone, is grossly undervalued compared to where a 'pure' deutschmark would be. The IMF estimates that the undervalued euro results in a 15% advantage to Germany while, for instance, giving a 6% burden to France, thus providing a substantial and chronic competitive advantage to Germany's export machine.[13] Debtor countries such as Italy, on the other hand, dislike the euro because it is overvalued for them for the same reasons, thus hurting exports, in addition to which it shackles them.

'Solidarity' means the stronger countries of the eurozone should have taken measures to assist their weaker partners. 'Asymmetrical adjustments', which has been the norm in the eurozone, means the contrary: only the affected countries are required to adjust, in other words: make an effort. Many measures implying some form of solidarity could have been taken. Stiglitz, for one, reminds us that an efficient and natural way to adjust would have been for Germany to let its wages and prices rise so that the value of the euro would have fallen and the countries in crisis would have been more competitive. But instead, Germany ensured that 'all of the burden of adjustment rest on their poorer 'partners'[14]; moreover, 'Germany has a surplus, that means the rest of the Eurozone *must* have a deficit' and 'the surplus countries-Germany in particular-can even be thought of being a fundamental cause of the fiscal and trade deficits and the unsustainable credit expansion in other countries of the zone'.[15] According to Stiglitz, as Germany refused to back off from a required primary fiscal surplus of 3.5%—a number virtually guaranteed to continue depression in Greece—and as it was suggested that Greece should be deprived of its voting rights in the EU, the attitude of creditor countries towards Greece could be summarized as: 'accept the conditions or your banking system will be destroyed, your economy will be devastated, and you will have to leave the euro'. Such lack of solidarity and democratic deficit inevitably fuels the rise of extremist parties.[16] Ngaire Woods, dean of the Blavatnik School of Government at Oxford, recognized that 'The eurozone crisis really did split the EU into creditors and debtors, and destroyed a certain solidarity that was holding it together', and 'This has shown that it's almost impossible to continue with a deepening integration on fiscal affairs.'[17]

The main problem of the euro today, the one with the deepest sociopolitical implications, is that of 'asymmetrical adjustments' pointed out earlier, which basically means 'lack of solidarity'. In order to fend off or at least limit the impact of the next eurozone crisis, the first thing that should have happened is for some symmetry to be introduced. But Germany has steadfastly rejected this notion and is even more likely to stick to its guns after the September 2017 electoral earthquake. Mazower is adamant that 'if the euro survives it will do so in a continent of different political traditions and economic performance, and that means that a system of redistribution from surplus to deficit countries needs to become part of the culture', warning that 'if the euro is run as before, whether or not Greece remains will not be the point. The single currency will generate the same kind of problem over time, and the kinds of politics it embodies will weaken the popularity of the idea of a united Europe still further'.[18]

Bad Students and Good Students

The euro has undoubtedly brought about benefits. To be fair, the likes of Italy are quick to forget that the euro brought inflation under control and resulted in cheap money. Italian investment bank Mediobanca lamented, however, how the country ended up with the worst of all worlds: no growth for this third-largest economy of the eurozone, an overvalued currency hurting exports and ever-increasing levels of debt.[19] Unsurprisingly, a February 2017 Eumetra survey found that 64% of the Italian population felt it had been a mistake to enter the eurozone. Yet, a majority of 53% preferred to stay in because of the unfathomable costs and consequences of getting out (interestingly enough, the proportion of those wanting to stay in decreased by 10% in six months, reflecting growing despair).[20] This sort of ambivalence is common throughout Europe these days. Complaints from then Italian Prime Minister Matteo Renzi that Spain's deficit was double that of Italy, that France's own deficit was beyond eurozone authorized limits and that Germany itself was in default on its commercial surplus (which stood at almost 9%, against an authorized eurozone ceiling of 6%), and that the final communiqué of the September 2016 European summit in Bratislava failed to include a single word on immigration issues greatly affecting Italy echoed the daily *Corriere Della Sera*'s complaints that austerity was a failure because rules were not applied evenly.[21] Broadly speaking, such complaints fell on deaf ears and are testimony to Italy's newfound irrelevance and impotence as a marginal power in today's Europe.

Not all southern countries, however, share the plight of Greece and Italy. One country enacted courageous and decisive structural reforms immediately after 2012, which included tackling its banks' bad debts head-on, making the labour market less rigid and trimming deficits (which fell from 10.6% in 2012 to 4.3% in 2016), and with exports replacing construction as a driver of growth. As a result, Spain has been heralded as the most remarkable eurozone recovery story. Spanish GDP growth exceeded 3% for the third year in a row in 2017, and by now Spain the fastest-growing economy in Europe, creating 500,000 jobs per year.[22] Wage bargaining was brought down to company level (a reform Macron successfully pushed in France). Overall unemployment dramatically fell from 26.1% in 2013 to 19.6% in 2016 and keeps falling.[23] Yet, in Stiglitz's view 'the eurozone downturn has lasted 8 years and the slightest sign of growth of or unemployment fall are trumpeted as the harbinger of the long awaited recovery'.[24] Spain remains stuck with youth unemployment levels at over 40%,[25] most new jobs are of a temporary nature, public debt crept up to 100% of GDP, real wages are back to the levels of about a decade ago and Podemos, a far-left political party, obtained 21% of the vote in 2016, reflecting broad discontent. Spain is not yet out of the woods as Stiglitz points out: 'Even what Europe celebrates as a success signifies a failure: Spain's unemployment rate has fallen ... but one out of two youth remain unemployed, and the unemployment rate would be even higher if so many of its most talented young people had not left the country to look for jobs elsewhere'.[26] Whether or not one agrees with this assessment, the truth is that Spain is in better shape than a few years ago. Spanish 'recovery' is testimony that, for all of Berlin's misplaced adamancy on austerity measures in time of crisis, its insistence on troubled countries biting the bullet and enacting structural reforms to improve their fundamentals has merit. Structural reforms have worked for Germany and they are working for Spain. The problem is that some countries can't bring themselves to enact profound structural reforms as a result of which the euro remains a feature of the European landscape that people end up loving just as much as they hate it. It comes as no surprise that 7 February 2017, the 25th anniversary of the Maastricht Treaty which gave rise to the single currency, turned out to be a non-event: nobody felt like celebrating.

In recent years, the ECB has kept interest rates near zero and bought over a trillion euro of sovereign debt with the primary purpose of stimulating troubled economies in what has been called 'quantitative easing'. This monetary stimulus kept troubled economies alive but has been criticized by some creditors as taking away the urge to reform these economies. A bout of controlled inflation would also have been helpful if only to decrease the real cost of debt repayment. Yet if Germany has reluctantly let quantitative easing happen it has been dead set against any inflationary measures. Having said in a radio interview that she was delighted that eurozone inflation rebounded to 1.8% in January 2017, ECB executive board member Sabine Lautenschlager came under intense fire in Germany. Berlin, always critical of the ECB, sees such measures as subsidies to profligate southern European economies at the expense of German savers.[27] They are not entirely wrong in this assessment but, as we said before, this is only half of the story and ignores two key facts: without solidarity, the eurozone is not sustainable, and Germany is effectively the greatest beneficiary of the euro's status quo. Peter Navarro of the US National Trade Council bluntly told the *Financial Times* that Germany has been using a 'grossly undervalued' euro to 'exploit' its trading partners and former German finance minister and fiscal hawk Wolfgang Schäuble himself acknowledged that the euro is too weak for Germany, laying the blame with the ECB's quantitative easing policies.[28] French President Macron himself, not particularly prone to criticize Germany, recognized that 'a part of German competitiveness is due to the dysfunctionalities of the eurozone, and the weakness of other economies'.[29] Furthermore, according to Stiglitz, Germany's decision to constrain wages has been a form of competitive devaluation.[30] If there is a winner in this saga, there is little doubt who it is…

Never Missing an Opportunity to Miss an Opportunity

Sir Winston Churchill's wise advice that one should never let a good crisis go to waste seems to have been lost on Europeans when it comes to the single currency. Lessons should have been learned from the crisis and the past few years should have been put to use to enact serious structural reforms in order to improve eurozone stability and resilience. It didn't happen. As a result, the eurozone remains fragile, an accident waiting to happen. The situation today is hardly encouraging as evidenced by investors' deepening lack of confidence. Back in 2012, during the presidential election that resulted in Francois Hollande's victory, France was borrowing for ten years at 2.91% compared to Germany's 1.96%—reflecting a risk premium spread between the countries of roughly 50% (lower borrowing rates reflect a lower perception of risk by the market). Granted, by February 2017, five years later, with the (first) eurozone crisis mostly over, borrowing rates were substantially down in absolute terms, yet the relative risk premium was triple that of 2012 as France now borrowed at 1.02%

against Germany's 0.31%, reflecting France's worsening deficits—by now the worse public deficits in the eurozone. Investors' perception of the relative difference in risk between countries doing well and those not doing well has also visibly worsened in the last few years.[31] By early 2017 yields on ten-year Italian notes had doubled to 2.3% compared to the previous autumn and Greece's went from 6.7% to 8%, reflecting the worsening debt burdens of these countries compared to 2012 (Italian debt grew from 123% of GDP to 133% and Greece's from 159% to 183%—clear proof, by the way, that austerity measures have had the opposite effect than expected, at least when it comes to debt[32]). The single currency's fiscal constraints, evidenced by austerity measures, mean that these economies have very little chance to significantly grow in the near future. It is thus unrealistic to assume that they will be able to repay their debts. In order to survive, they either will have to restructure debt to dramatically reduce its burden to affordable levels or they will have to get out of the eurozone. The mere declaration by Angela Merkel at the end of the informal February 2017 Malta Summit, suggesting that Europe, unmanageable with 28 members, might end up as a 'two-speed' Europe (effectively a Europe à la carte with different levels of integration for different members), led to an alarmed Unicredit bank warning that Italy may effectively need to abandon the single currency, thus starting the disintegration of the eurozone.[33] In the case of Italy, most the debt issued so far is governed by Italian law, making it easier to restructure than Greece's debt which is more often than not governed by foreign law. Most of the debt raised by Italy in the past few years was bought by the ECB and by sick Italian banks, reflecting market distrust. Recently, only the ECB has had the courage to buy new Italian bonds—to the tune of 247 billion euro over two years, a clear sign of problems with the Italian banking system and of the market's loss of confidence. The August 2017 ruling by Germany's constitutional court in Karlsruhe, pressed by Germany's far-right AfD party, to the effect that the ECB has been acting outside its mandate and should stop quantitative easing got the edgy Italians worried that by cutting this lifeline Germany was going to provoke Italy's failure.[34] In early 2017, at a time when eurozone economies were in aggregate growing at a respectable 2.2% annualized rate, Italy's growth remained the worst of the pack at 1.5% and should the ECB lifeline be curtailed, Italy would be stuck mostly on its own and as the only G20 country with a GDP still below that of pre-crisis level.[35] Italy and the eurozone have failed to muster the courage to enact meaningful structural reforms and may soon come to regret this missed opportunity.

The Mishandling of Greece

Only a fool would deny Greece's widely publicized dysfunctionalities, the extent of the corruption plaguing it or the need for profound reforms of the country's governance, economy, work ethics, institutions and mindset. Yet, popular views blaming the crisis solely on Greek tax avoidance, laziness and trickery are gross oversimplifications. The flawed architecture of the euro, the misdiagnosis of the eurozone crisis and the erroneous policies that were imposed thereafter are in no small part responsible for the morphing of the eurozone crisis into a disaster of epic proportions as far as Greece is concerned. Stiglitz reminds us that during the last two decades in which Greece had its own currency (the drachma) before adopting the euro, the country grew much faster and with lower unemployment than during the almost two decades following its switch to the euro, and that 'the allegedly lazy Greeks worked almost 50 percent more hours than the allegedly hard-working Germans in 2014'.[36] Today's situation is as much Greece's fault as it is the fault of its lenders—European banks and institutions who failed to do their homework and were happy to lend money to Greece way beyond its means, not unlike American institutions did with subprime customers. Greece's application to join the eurozone had first been rejected because it didn't meet entry criteria. Sure enough, the crafty Greeks re-applied with numbers that worked, *et voila!*. Everybody in Europe knew they had cooked the books yet not only was Greece let in but once it got in European banks and institutions launched themselves into an orgy of lending, entirely oblivious of country risk. German surpluses, after all, need to be recycled somewhere. A single currency means fixed exchange rates, doing away with currency exchange rate risks, but it does not mean country risk has been eliminated and foreign banks failed to keep this in mind. There are no innocent parties in this tragedy.

As a result of measures imposed by the Troika, Greek GDP dramatically collapsed, its debt burden shot up and unemployment reached unbearable levels. There is no way that Greece will be able to repay its debts—ergo, nothing short of substantial debt relief will work, a reality that the IMF itself finally recognized. Yet Germany, who calls the shots, persisted in its idea that as long as Greece would stick to austerity measures and keep spending tight, it would be able to repay its debts. This is lunacy because Greece has cut down its expenses to the extent that it is now running budget surpluses—yet its debt keeps rising. Bailouts have not been as much about saving Greece as they have been about saving the foreign (and German) lenders who recklessly lent to Greece in the past, saving the euro from itself and salvaging the last remnants of unity in a Europe divided between lenders and borrowers. Hardliners choose to ignore that no economic recovery plan can work unless it enlists the Greek people and gives them some hope. This can't happen as long as Greeks see that no matter how much themselves, their children and grandchildren toil and sacrifice, there will be no end to the suffering. Alexis Tsipras may have been an inexperienced and radical populist firebrand but he was democratically elected in an act of despair by a population that had lost all hope. Unless debt is cut to a level that it is clearly sustainable for what is left of the Greek economy and unless measures are taken to enable the people to regain dignity one day, there will just be last minute deals to avert the next catastrophe, to buy yet a bit more time against more austerity measures, and bailout N will inevitably be followed by bailout N+1.

In dealing with the Greek situation, a newly assertive Germany, conveniently forgetting that it was itself the first country to break eurozone rules in 2003, has committed historical mistakes:

- The first was the imposition of very harsh austerity measures, a badly conceived programme that made matters worse, resulting in the dramatic and sudden 25% contraction in Greek GDP mentioned before and an explosion of debt from under 110% of GDP before the crisis to close to over 185% and rising.[37] (Naturally at parity of debt level a contraction of GDP results in debt representing a higher percentage of remaining GDP). It is difficult to understand how the additional harsh measures attached to new bailouts such as tax increases and pension cuts were expected to revive the economy, which should have been the priority. High tax rates were imposed even on low-income people and small businesses, who, adding insult to injury, were required to pay their taxes ahead of time, with total disregard for the destruction of the economic fabric of a country which largely comprised small businesses. Public sector pensions were drastically slashed, throwing many people into poverty. Chatting with a taxi driver during a recent trip to Greece I was told that in Athens it was close to impossible to find a job and that if one were lucky enough to find one it would only be temporary and the average temporary job salary would be around 600–800 euro per month, while the average rent for a flat was around 300 euro per month (*Trading Economics* data show full-time employment average salaries in Greece had fallen to 1092 euro/month by April 2016). How are families expected to survive at such levels of income? The solidarity many Europeans have proudly shown towards migrants from Africa and the Middle East is nowhere to be seen when it comes to Greeks who are, after all, Europeans. Mazower pointed out that 'the consequences for continental solidarity have been toxic' and that the remedy to the crisis 'has too often been presented as just a question of signing up to rules, as if central bankers and not the elected representatives of member nations should make the fundamental decisions in any kind of democratic confederation'.[38]

- The second mistake has been to refuse to cancel a substantial portion of Greece's debt, even though the IMF itself, echoed by the ECB, finally came out of the closet and declared that Greece's current debt level was 'highly unsustainable' and would reach 275% of GDP by 2060 if it was not restructured.[39] Germany's refusal to restructure Greek debt means that Greeks are condemned to never-ending hell. Having been dragged into this crisis by Germany, the IMF made it clear it would not be party to any future assistance devoid of a substantial haircut. European leaders are still in complete denial of the basic reality that no matter how much the Greeks tighten their belts, they will never be able to repay their pile of debt—now standing at over 326 billion euro.[40] The Eurogroup's estimate that Greece would reach and maintain a budgetary surplus of 3.5% of GDP by 2017 and use it to repay its debts over 30 or so years was simply outlandish.[41] Germany's newfound posture of financial rectitude and refusal to forgive Greek debt was labelled 'a joke' by Nobel economics laureate Thomas Piketty, who pointed out that the London Treaty of 1953 forgave 60% of Germany's external debt, enabling its postwar recovery.[42] A massive haircut is a necessity and, in order to keep the Greeks honest in their implementation of structural reforms, debt relief could be enacted in tranches tied to their implementation.

- The third mistake, a political one, was for Germany to publicly ask for Greece to be kicked out of the eurozone if they didn't reform as required.[43] Granted, the hard-working German taxpayer, who absorbed the tremendous costs of German reunification, suffered through painful labour market and other reforms and remarkably came out on top, works hard and saves, is entitled to be loath to pick up the lion's share of the bill for yet another Greek bailout. But the first responsibility of any de facto leader of Europe is a historical one: to maintain the integrity of the European Project. Perhaps the euro should never have been launched but it was launched, Europe is stuck with it and today a Grexit would not just encourage financial markets to attack the countries next in line, it would, after Brexit, be another significant step towards the disintegration of Europe. A collapse of Greece could, moreover, result in an economic, social and humanitarian catastrophe that would likely be blamed on Germany, reviving ghosts of the past. The question I asked in my previous book: 'Are there any Europeans in Europe?' is one that better not be asked these days.

We pointed out earlier that Greek bailouts have been little more than disguised bailouts of German, French and other foreign banks who had been recklessly lending to Greece in the past. Stiglitz reminds us that 'of the total lent to Greece, less than 10 percent ever got to the Greek people' and 'Greece has ... paid a high price to preserve other countries' banking systems', concluding that 'for German politicians it was easier to vilify Greece and provide indirect assistance to German banks through a bailout loan called a "Greek bailout"'.[44] Greece was taken advantage of in many other ways by the dominant countries of the eurozone, who seem to have had few scruples in advancing their own business interests. For instance, in 2014 the Troika forced Greece to drop the label 'fresh' on it truly fresh milk and extend allowable shelf life, clearly in the interest of their competitors, Dutch and European milk producers 'who would like to increase sales by having their milk transported over long distances, [and] appear to be as fresh as the local product'.[45] In another instance, while taxes were required to be raised across the board, it is interesting to note that 'the only tax that the Troika demanded to be eliminated was the withholding tax on money sent from Greece to foreign investors'.[46] Such measures imposed by Greece's European 'partners' clearly and shamelessly benefitted these partners' own business interests while damaging Greek ones, in a clear conflict of interest and a travesty of solidarity.

The Problem with Being on the Wrong Continent

Back in June 2013 Greece was officially demoted from 'developed market' to 'emerging market' by index provider MSCI.[47] 'Emerging' may be too idealizing a word for a country whose trajectory seemed to point straight down, but here we are: Greece was now an emerging market, just as Ghana, Sierra Leone, Nicaragua or Myanmar. At the same time, however, the World Bank ranked Greece number 38 in the world for development, with a 2014 per capital GDP of 21,682 USD, far ahead of Russia (12,735 USD) and Brazil (11,612 USD), and way above the 11,905 USD limit below which it would qualify as a 'Developing Country'.[48] Greece is thus both wave and particle, an emerging market stuck in Europe where it is considered a developed country gone astray. The European Commission estimates total development assistance provided by the EU and its member states to Africa between 2007 and 2013 alone at 141 billion euro in addition to which 28 billion euro in grants were to be provided in the following five years,[49] and these figures do not take into account bilateral assistance from individual EU member states. None of this assistance carried the harsh terms attached to Greek rescue packages. Despite catastrophic levels of unemployment, Greece has, for more than seven years now, gone through successive increases in taxes and severe pension cuts imposed by its creditors. In May 2017 it had to slash pensions again and enact yet more austerity measures, hitting citizens with incomes just above the poverty line.⁵⁰ The people most affected by these creditor-imposed measures are the weakest elements of society: the elderly and the poor. European solidarity was spectacularly absent. Greece's main problem is perhaps one of geography: it is stuck on the wrong continent. Had Greece been located in Africa, the dysfunctionalities that secured it a place among emerging markets would likely have earned it the sympathies of Germany and of the likes of Bob Geldof and Bono, whose efforts contributed to wiping out some 100 billion USD of African debt from international creditors in recent times.⁵¹ Sadly, Greece is paying the full price for being stuck in Europe. Location, location, location…

The Show Is Not Over

Summer 2017 seemed to bring some good news regarding Greece as an agreement was finally reached enabling the release of the third tranche of the country's 86 billion euro bailout. The agreement had, incidentally, been delayed by a feud pitting the IMF—advocating debt relief—against an intransigent Germany, with the result that the IMF decided to not participate in any further rescues of Greece.⁵² One can only wonder why, on one side, Germany insists on the IMF being part of Greek rescue packages if, on the other side, Germany refuses to abide by the recommendations of this same IMF. In any case Greece's creditors granted 8 billion euro in aid payments and in July 2017 Greece sold 3 billion euro worth of new bonds to the market, the first time since 2014 it had done so—a sign of investor confidence slowly returning.⁵³ In another piece of goods news the eurozone was, by the summer of 2017, posting an average yearly growth rate of 2.2%, the highest since 2007, prompting ECB chief Mario Draghi to say of the recovery: 'It's robust, it's broad-based, and it was recalled that six million jobs were created since 2013.'⁵⁴ Propelled by low interest rates, low oil prices and close to 60 billion euro per month of bond-buying by the ECB, eurozone recovery seemed to set in. The ECB was poised to start dialling down its quantitative easing measures but would likely do so slowly given that inflation remained below target and the euro had been appreciating with respect to the dollar. Is the eurozone crisis a thing of the past?

Authors of a report on concrete measures to reinforce the eurozone (the report had the rare honour of being approved by the European Parliament in early 2017) Pervenche Berès and Reimer Böge are adamant that another eurozone crisis is inevitable.[55] Stiglitz warns that 'the euro crisis is far from over', a view shared by many experts. Another eurozone crisis may thus be waiting around the corner and in the absence of firebreaks could hit just as hard as the previous one. It could come from escalating debt pressure in Italy and Greece, from weak Italian banks (despite the recent success of UniCredito bank in shedding its portfolio of toxic loans, Italy remains far from having addressed its non-performing loans—NPL—problem which is close to a 174 billion euro challenge[56]) or from some unexpected, exogenous direction. If a country such as Italy gets in very serious trouble the eurozone would be hit by a problem orders of magnitude larger than Greece ever was.

Free Willy

Certain experts see some 'exits' or re-dimensioning of eurozone membership as solutions to the union's woes. Some suggest that the troubled countries of the south should get out of the eurozone, others that Germany itself should leave and go back to the deutschmark. Stiglitz explored the possibility of a southern euro (a currency grouping southern countries) and a northern euro (grouping northern countries)—in other words, separate currency groupings reflecting the realities of their respective members, resulting in adjustments by de facto devaluation in the first case and revaluation in the second. He even proposed the use of an electronic currency in the case of a Grexit: 'with electronic money, leaving the euro can, in principle, be done smoothly, assuming there is cooperation with other European authorities'.[57] Whether or not these solutions are concretely workable, a disintegration of the eurozone would likely mean the political end of Europe. To its credit, the euro is unlikely to disappear so easily. It remains underpinned by a strong German economy, which is by now the world's foremost export machine. It has brought good things to Europeans, such as low inflation, low interest rates and has eliminated intra-European exchange risk. For the time being Germany insists on maintaining austerity and the status quo and weak countries simply have no choice. They can't get out and they can't devalue the currency, so they are condemned to what economists call 'internal devaluation', that is, lowering wages and standards of living to remain competitive (become poorer). In 2016, the world's largest central banks held an average of close to 20% of their currency reserves in euro (down from a peak of 28% in 2009).[58] To the outside world, such as China, survival of the euro is important because it represents a means to diversify away from the American dollar. The fact that following the last crisis nothing substantial was done to prevent a new crisis from hitting the eurozone hard is remarkable and many could soon come to bitterly regret this lost opportunity. Europeans are likely to continue doing what they have successfully done since 2008: wait for the last minute to do the bare minimum needed to avoid catastrophe. There is, so far, much talk but little or no consensus on any fundamental reforms, just the usual muddling through in the hope of a miracle.

To Stiglitz, the greatest urgency is to fundamentally reform eurozone structure, policies and institutions, a priority even before the reform of individual countries. There needs to be a common fiscal framework and a banking union with common rules and supervision, a common deposit insurance and a common resolution framework (to deal with defaulting banks), as in the USA. Some form of mutualization of debt is needed, as well as solidarity in time of crisis including a stabilization fund and a facility for lending to SMEs in times of trouble. The ECB's mandate should be expanded to include growth and unemployment considerations and the ECB should allow for some inflation to reduce the real burden of debt. The excessive influence of Germany should be curbed and Germany and others should shed their misguided economic ideology, their obsession with deficits. The Maastricht debt and deficit rules should be abandoned because, according to Stiglitz, they are 'automatic destabilizers'. He reminds us that 'the European project is too important to be sacrificed on the cross of the euro' and that muddling through will not work: there should either be 'more Europe', *i.e.* Europe needs to take a big step forward and become more like the USA, or the euro should be abandoned altogether, because the current halfway position is not sustainable.[59] Berès and Böge proposed, among others, measures aimed at promoting economic convergence, the creation of a ministry of finance for the eurozone, the transformation of the European Monetary System (the rescue fund which currently enjoys a mostly unused borrowing capacity of up to 700 billion euro) into a permanent European Monetary Fund (EMF)—a sort of eurozone IMF, and to have some kind of a central budget to assist countries in crisis. The EMF idea is not new, having been proposed by Schäuble in 2010, although his intent was for the EMF to act as a pure enforcer of orthodoxy tasked with imposing austerity programmes and debt restructuring, with no solidarity mechanisms.

September 2017 saw two major speeches outlining visions of Europe by two genuine Europeanists, French President Emmanuel Macron and EU Commission President Jean-Claude Juncker. Macron's speech at the Sorbonne outlined his bold vision for reforming Europe to the delight of Europeanists such as German Foreign Minister Sigmar Gabriel who labelled it 'a passionate plea against nationalism and for Europe'.[60] Calling for deeper integration, Macron was, as far as the eurozone was concerned, advocating a substantial central budget (funded by new taxes and overseen by a eurozone finance minister) and a fund to pre-emptively help troubled countries. The eurozone was, to Macron, the central piece of the European edifice. Macron's vision amounted to a 'multispeed' union led by core eurozone countries. It gave countries the choice of staying out and losing clout in Brussels or joining the club while leaving economic sovereignty at the door, a proposal that did not endear him to Eastern European countries such as Poland, which is still outside the eurozone and whose economy has, by the way, been doing well. During his upbeat state of the union speech, Juncker on the other hand advocated no less than complete political and institutional integration, resulting in a sort of United States of Europe led by a powerful central president. His more ambitious plan called, among others, for all European countries to join the eurozone as well as Schengen and do so on an equal basis. This bold, egalitarian and single-speed vision of a federal Europe got Juncker a standing ovation, yet, coming at a time when centrifugal forces have the upper hand and fragmentation is the new trend, it is simply unworkable and was not taken seriously by many. Moreover, 'Britons who voted to leave the EU will feel vindicated' said a commentator, adding that 'this is the superstate of which they never wanted to be part'.[61]

The proposals from Stiglitz, Macron, Berès and Böge and most other experts interested in reinforcing the eurozone call for roughly similar sets of measures. There is thus broad agreement from all quarters on what needs to be done. The problem is that all of the remedies imply more solidarity, more of a transfer union, more symmetrical adjustments. This is after all what is needed to make the eurozone work. But at the end of the day it may result in Germany picking up the lion's share of the bills, a notion that remains anathema to German voters (and, again, who can blame them?). Had Merkel won a resounding victory in the September 2017 general election, she might have had a bit more room to manoeuvre in order to make a case at home to support such ideas, at least partially. But her victory was marginal and given that her CDU/CSU coalition didn't garner enough votes to govern she would have to form a shaky coalition with smaller parties, likely including the FPD which was dead set against any eurozone concessions. According to Reuters, 'Such a coalition, unprecedented at the national level, is likely to face opposition in the Bundestag when it comes to any major EU reform idea.'[62] It was thus not surprising that the *Kanzlerin* reacted coolly to Macron's speech, declaring: 'It is not about the slogans but what lies behind them',[63] while an even blunter Alexander Lambsdorff (FDP member in the European Parliament) Tweeted 'You don't strengthen Europe with new pots of money… The problem in Europe is not a lack of public funds, but the lack of reform. A eurozone budget would set exactly the wrong incentives.'[64] Given the new divisions in Europe and the new political realities in Germany it is unlikely that any substantial reforms of the EU or the eurozone will see the light of day. Merkel's new coalition government, as shaky as it may be, will be keeping a tough line in dealing with the likes of Greece and rejecting any reform proposal that may result in bills presented to German voters. As a result, eurozone tensions will persist and concrete integration is unlikely for the foreseeable future. Stiglitz ventured that 'as a political forecaster, I would … place my bets on a course of muddling through'.[65] My response to the often-heard question of whether the euro has a future is as follows: should there be a new, very major crisis (such as one coming from Italy, or even an exogenous one), then the eurozone could potentially implode if pushed hard, because its architecture remains nearly as flawed as it was when the previous crisis hit. But barring such a major crisis, the euro is here to stay, for the long term and likely in more or less its current form. The reason is simply that the way the euro is set today suits the interests of Germany and Germany is, by far, the dominant power in the eurozone. Berlin's self-interest is in keeping things as they are now, as far as eurozone architecture is concerned. Germany enjoys an undervalued currency and the lowest relative borrowing rates without being burdened by significant solidarity costs. Since Germany calls the shots, under normal circumstances no major reforms of the eurozone can be expected soon. When it comes to the euro, muddling through works perfectly well for Germany, and, barring a major crisis, Germany will ensure that the euro stays as it is today. The more it changes, the more it stays the same.

Notes

1. Robert Mundell. *Wikipedia.*
2. Joseph E. Stiglitz. 'The Euro and its threat to the future of Europe'. *Allen Lane. Page 87.* 2016.
3. Joseph E. Stiglitz. 'The Euro and its threat to the future of Europe'. *Allen Lane. Page 123.* 2016.
4. Tony Barber. 'Widening economic divide stretches case for further integration'. *Financial Times. Page 2.* 14 September 2014.
5. Mark Mazower. 'Why the eurozone crisis is just part of our long struggle for peace'. *Guardian.co.uk—The Guardian.* 12 July 2015.
6. Joseph E. Stiglitz. 'The Euro and its threat to the future of Europe'. *Allen Lane. Pages 183,187.* 2016.
7. Joseph E. Stiglitz. 'The Euro and its threat to the future of Europe'. *Allen Lane. Page 245,81.* 2016.
8. Joseph E. Stiglitz. 'The Euro and its threat to the future of Europe'. *Allen Lane. Page 65.* 2016.
9. Joseph E. Stiglitz. 'The Euro and its threat to the future of Europe'. *Allen Lane. Page 165.* 2016.
10. 'Unshrinking the continent'. *The Economist. Page 29.* 10 September 2016.
11. 'Fury at eurozone chief Dijsselbloem's 'racist' remarks'. *Bbc.com.* 22 March 2017.

12. Matthias Mattijs. 'The West Should Hope That Merkel Loses'. *Foreignpolicy.com—Foreign Policy*. 21 December 2016.
13. Jean-Pierre Robin. 'L'euro est trop fort de 6% pour la France et trop faible de 15% pour l'Allemagne, selon le FMI'. *Lefigaro.fr—Le Figaro*. 3 August 2016.
14. Joseph E. Stiglitz. 'The Euro and its threat to the future of Europe'. *Allen Lane. Pages 18, 20*. 2016.
15. Joseph E. Stiglitz. 'The Euro and its threat to the future of Europe'. *Allen Lane. Page 118*. 2016.
16. Joseph E. Stiglitz. 'The Euro and its threat to the future of Europe'. *Allen Lane. Pages 60, 61*. 2016.
17. Charles Riley. 'Europe is falling apart. Saving it won't be easy'. *money.cnn.com*. 20 January 2017
18. Mark Mazower. 'Why the eurozone crisis is just part of our long struggle for peace'. *Guardian.co.uk—The Guardian*. 12 July 2015.
19. Landon Thomas Jr. 'Debts raise new worries about future of the euro'. *The New York Times. Page 11*. 10 February 2017.
20. Renato Mannheimer. 'La moneta unica? Un errore Pentiti due Italiani su tre'. *Il Giornale. Page 10*. 4 February 2017.
21. Maria Teresa Meli. 'L'austerity europea é un fallimento, sono gli altri a violare le regole'. *Corriere della Sera. Page 2*. 18 September 2016.
22. 'Stamp of approval'. *The Economist. Page 22*. 17 June 2017.
23. 'Cécile Crouzel. 'Dette, chomage: Macron hérite d'une France en piteux état'. *Le Figaro. Page 16*. 8 Mai 2017.
24. Joseph E. Stiglitz. 'The Euro and its threat to the future of Europe'. *Allen Lane. Page 179*. 2016.
25. 'Unshrinking the continent'. *The Economist. Page 29*. 10 September 2016.
26. Joseph E. Stiglitz. 'The Euro and its threat to the future of Europe'. *Allen Lane. Page xi*. 2016.
27. Tom Fairless. 'ECB Official Under Fire for Praising Inflation'. *The Wall Street Journal. Page A3*. 22 February 2017.
28. Tom Fairless. 'ECB Official Under Fire for Praising Inflation'. *The Wall Street Journal. Page A3*. 22 February 2017.
29. 'Macron urges greater euro zone convergence, presses Germany to act'. *Reuters.com*. 13 July 2017.
30. Joseph E. Stiglitz. 'The Euro and its threat to the future of Europe'. *Allen Lane. Page 41i*. 2016.

31. Jean-Pierre Robin. 'La protection de l'euro devient de plus en plus illusoire'. *Le Figaro. Page 17.* 10 February 2017.
32. Landon Thomas Jr. 'Debts raise new worries about future of the euro'. *The New York Times. Page 1.* 10 February 2017.
33. Noam Benjamin. 'La Merkel uccide l'Euro: Europa a due velocità'. *Il Giornale. Pages 1 and 11.* 4 February 2017.
34. Rodolfo Parietti. 'I tedeschi ci riprovano: 'Draghi oltre i compiti il bazooka va fermato'. *Il Giornale. Pages 1 and 3.* 17 August 2017.
35. Antonio Signorini. 'Il Pil mette il turbo ma siamo ancora gli ultimi in Europa'. *Il Giornale. Page 2.* 17 August 2017.
36. Joseph E. Stiglitz. 'The Euro and its threat to the future of Europe'. *Allen Lane. Page 274, 72.* 2016.
37. 'OECD Data. Selected Indicators for Greece.' *Data.oecd.org.*
38. Mark Mazower. 'Why the eurozone crisis is just part of our long struggle for peace'. *Guardian.co.uk—The Guardian.* 12 July 2015.
39. Viktoria Dendrinou. 'IMF Assesses Greek Debt as "Highly Unsustainable"'. *Wsj.com—The Wall Street Journal.* 27 January 2017.
40. 'National debt of Greece'. *Nationaldebtclocks.org.* 21 August 2017.
41. Silvia Aloisi, David Lawder. 'IMF, euro zone say need more time to reach Greek debt relief deal'. *Reuters.com.* 12 May 2017.
42. Georg Blume. 'Deutschland hat nie bezahlt'. *Zeit.de—Die Zeit.* 27 June 2015.
43. Helena Smith. 'Greece must reform or leave eurozone, says German minister'. *Theguardian.com—The Guardian.* 4 December 2016.
44. Joseph E. Stiglitz. 'The Euro and its threat to the future of Europe'. *Allen Lane. Pages 203, 207, 310.* 2016.
45. Joseph E. Stiglitz. 'The Euro and its threat to the future of Europe'. *Allen Lane. Page 218.* 2016.
46. Joseph E. Stiglitz. 'The Euro and its threat to the future of Europe'. *Allen Lane. Page 191.* 2016.
47. Charles Sizemore. 'Greece Downgraded To 'Emerging Market,' But Will It Ever Emerge?'. *Forbes.com.* 20 June 2013.
48. 'GDP per capita (current US$)'. *Data.worldbank.org.*
49. 'Africa-EU continental cooperation'. *ec.europa.eu—European Commission.*
50. Hélène COLLIOPOULOU. 'Greek families left struggling after successive cuts'. *AFP.* 11 June 2017.
51. Tosin Sulaiman. 'Analysis: Decade after debt relief, Africa's rush to borrow stirs concern'. *Reuters.com.* 18 March 2014.

52. 'IMF to participate for 'last time' in Greek bailout: Schaeuble.' *AFP.* 1 July 2017.
53. Viktoria Dendrinou, Nikos Chrysoloras. 'Crisis-Plagued Europe Sees a New Dawn After Greek Market Return'. *Bloomberg.com – Bloomberg.* 26 July 2017.
54. 'Eurozone set for fastest growth since 2007, says ECB'. *Bbc.com.* 7 September 2017.
55. Jean Quatremer. 'Zone euro: 'Si on ne bouge pas rapidement, on va vers la catastrophe'. *Liberation.fr.* 16 May 2017.
56. Thomas Hale, Dan McCrum. 'Italy's bad debt problem refuses to go away'. *Ft.com—Financial Times.* 8 May 2017; 'The world this week'. *The Economist. Page 9.* 16 September 2017.
57. Joseph E. Stiglitz. 'The Euro and its threat to the future of Europe'. *Allen Lane. Page 276.* 2016.
58. Richard Leong, Anirbarn Nag. 'Dollar gains share of global FX reserves, euro shrinks'. *Reuters.com.* 31 March 2016.
59. Joseph E. Stiglitz. 'The Euro and its threat to the future of Europe'. *Allen Lane. Page 32.* 2016.
60. Ingrid Melander, Richard Lough. 'After German election, France's Macron paints sweeping vision for Europe'. *Reuters.* 26 September 2017.
61. Garvan Walshe. 'Juncker pulls Europe away from Brexit Britain'. *Cnn.com,* 13 September 2017.
62. Noah Barkin, Jean-Baptiste Vey. 'Merkel strikes reserved tone ahead of Macron's Europe speech'. *Reuters.com.* 25 September 2017.
63. Noah Barkin, Jean-Baptiste Vey. 'Merkel strikes reserved tone ahead of Macron's Europe speech'. *Reuters.com.* 25 September 2017.
64. Noah Barkin, Jean-Baptiste Vey. 'Merkel strikes reserved tone ahead of Macron's Europe speech'. *Reuters.com.* 25 September 2017.
65. Joseph E. Stiglitz. 'The Euro and its threat to the future of Europe'. *Allen Lane. Page 326.* 2016.

10

The Gas Wars

The perils of Europe as a pawn in the big game

New Kid on the Block

After the Second World War, the USA and Russia, moved by two mutually exclusive ideological visions of the world, competed everywhere, at all levels. The resulting Cold War set the tone for most of what happened on the planet. Following the collapse of the Soviet empire and the fall of the Berlin Wall in 1990, the reasons for ideological competition between the two superpowers vanished or should have done. A weakened Russia could hardly harbour imperial ambitions anymore and what it perceived as its vital interests became restricted to its traditional imperative to control its 'near abroad'—that is, the ring of countries bordering Russia itself. The one thing Russia would not tolerate under any circumstances was Western (and in particular NATO) encroachment into this zone, an issue on which Moscow has always been paranoid. Vladimir Kozin, a veteran Russian arms control specialist, summed up the sentiment when he said that Russians saw themselves being encircled by NATO; that of the 16 countries bordering Russia, eight had anti-Russia sentiments; and that the US military budget was 12 times greater than that of Russia and increasing.[1] Aside from this, not only was Russia no longer a rival of the USA in ideology or in empire-building, but its economy is marginal in terms of the world stage. Russia was not even close to being a competitor of the USA in the business or financial sphere or in markets abroad. On the geopolitical front Russia could only act as an intermittent spoiler of Washington's ambitions. It still harboured ambitions of playing a geopolitical role here and there and longed to be 'respected', backed by a military machine that remained awesome, but it couldn't afford much more. There was a priori little of real substance that should have opposed these two superpowers at the dawn of the new millennium.

Ranking only as the world's 13th largest economy, Russia has relatively little to offer abroad besides natural resources and military hardware.[2] The export of oil and gas represents Russia's lifeline today, accounting for 70–75% of total exports and 50–60% of federal budget revenues.[3] For Russia, this is clearly a sector in which it can ill afford to lose markets to competitors, especially in a low oil prices environment. Moscow can be expected to go to great lengths to protect its interests in this respect. In this context, the European gas market is one that 'Gazprom considers as its own backyard' according to the *Financial Times*,[4] and in 2016 Russia accounted for a very significant 34% of European oil imports and 30% of its gas imports.[5] Russia's biggest market, Europe, and its most promising market, China, are just 'next door', enabling most deliveries to take place by the relatively simple and cheap route of land pipelines. Worldwide the biggest demand for natural gas has recently come from Europe, up 6% to 28 billion cbm (cubic meters) and China is in second place with 16 billion cbm.[6] Moreover, when it comes to exports of natural resources, the USA is not a significant player in these markets. Thus it makes sense that Moscow has emerged as a leader in the European market for natural resources. Over time, however, an eager and divided Europe has become over-dependent on Russian supplies, giving Moscow increasing political leverage—something that has got Washington and Brussels increasingly worried.

A new development has rocked the boat, helping push the strategic relationship between the USA and Russia towards a more confrontational path. A precise date can be attached to this new development: 24 February 2016, when the first shipment from the Sabine Pass terminal (located at the border between Texas and Louisiana) marked the beginning of American liquefied natural gas (LNG) exports to Europe.[7] Recent advances in fracking technology have propelled the USA to being the world's largest producer of gas, a position it has held since 2011.[8] On balance, the USA still remains a net importer, recently importing close to 10% of its total use,[9] but this was set to change in 2016/2017 with the USA becoming a net exporter for the first time. Global shipments of American gas, starting from marginal quantities, were projected to rise year after year up to anywhere between 114 to 130 billion cbm (estimates depend on projected levels of crude oil prices) by 2040,[10] a significant amount considering the 163.8 billion cbm exported by Russia to Europe in 2016[11] where total demand is stable around 400 billion cbm per year.[12] The USA has embarked on the building of expensive LNG (liquefied natural gas) port terminals, including some in the East Coast, positioning itself as a major potential exporter to, among others, Europe where LNG imports, currently standing at around 10% of total gas imports,[13] are projected to almost quadruple by 2030 according to some sources.[14] In fact, the USA is expected to have the capacity to export 10–12 billion cubic feet per day of LNG to the world by 2020, representing is one third of the current global market.[15] The State Department's Bureau of Energy Resources was established in 2011 to turn the USA's newfound energy bonanza into a geopolitical tool. The USA's position was clearly illustrated by the Trump administration's desire to 'unleash America's 50 trillion USD in untapped shale, oil, and natural gas reserves'.[16] The man chosen by Donald Trump as Secretary of State was Rex Tillerson, former CEO of oil giant ExxonMobil. Positioning itself to get a slice of this global market has become important to Washington. The USA is suddenly a new contender in the huge European gas import market, pitting it directly against Europe's traditional main supplier, Russia.

T. Boone Pickens boasted that 'The cheapest natural gas in the world is in the United States'; yet, when it comes to delivering natural gas to Europe the USA is at a clear disadvantage compared to Russia because nothing less than an ocean separates it from Europe. While, as mentioned, Russian natural gas can be cheaply delivered in gas form through land pipelines, American gas needs to be compressed and liquefied. Expensive new terminals need to be built in the East Coast in order for LNG to be shipped by special pressurized container ships to terminals on Europe's western coast. It has been estimated that the additional cost of doing all this results in American LNG costing around 6USD per MMBtu (summer 2017 prices), against European market prices of 5USD or so for piped gas.[17] Some observers have ventured that 'U.S. LNG is so desired in Europe that some nations have offered to accept higher prices for it, willing to lose money to lower the reliance on Russia',[18] while, according to Platts, 'evidence so far suggests that southern Europe has been able to attract some American LNG—though in limited volume—but its appeal in northwest Europe has yet to emerge where competition from pipeline suppliers Norway and Russia is fierce … Gazprom has repeatedly dismissed the economic viability of American LNG in Europe given the current low gas prices in Europe and its own low production costs.'[19] Moreover, however encouraged they may be by Washington to export to Europe, American LNG exporters are private companies, and they will generally tend to ship to where prices are higher, and that is currently not Europe. Prices are higher in Asia-Pacific and South America due to a glut of supplies being piped from regions close to Europe, a reality unlikely to change in the near future. 'The start of American LNG exports has brought an unexpected burst of gas onto markets, clobbering prices for the foreseeable future and forcing producers into concessions. Demand in rich countries such as Japan and much of western Europe appears to be in long term decline'—so wrote *The Economist*, adding that 'LNG producers are increasingly reliant on small developing countries'.[20] LNG (the American stuff) by itself will not replace piped gas (the Russian stuff), but the simple fact that American LNG is now available, even at a higher price than piped gas from Russia, can be taken advantage of by European countries. First, it can be used as leverage in their negotiations with Russia's Gazprom to push for lower prices, given that Gazprom doesn't want to lose market share. Second, it represents a source of diversification that should be used in any case to lower dependence on a Russia that has not shied away from using energy supplies for political ends in the past (disruption of supplies of Russian gas to Ukraine following Russia's annexation of Crimea in 2014 are still fresh in European minds). According to the European Commission: 'LNG can give a real boost to the EU's diversity of gas supply and hence greatly improve energy security'.[21] A few things happened in the autumn of 2017 that prompted Russian Foreign Minister Sergei Lavrov to accuse the USA of efforts to 'elbow Russia out of energy markets'.[22] The US House of Representatives passed the National Defense Authorization Act, clearly aimed at countering Russia's influence in European energy markets, and Polish Oil and Gas Co. signed 'a five-year contract to secure LNG from the Sabine Pass terminal in Louisiana, the first mid-term contract of its kind', prompting a Louisiana senator to praise the deal that 'will also be playing an important role in reducing Russian President Vladimir Putin's ability to bully Europe'.[23]

Seizing the Opportunity

Given that diversification of energy supplies is good news for Europe, the reader is entitled to ask at this point 'So what's the problem?'. The problem is that in this new, high-stakes contest between Russia and the USA market share in European energy markets, a weak and divided Europe finds itself as a pawn, dragged into a dangerous geopolitical confrontation well above its punching grade. As the USA was having difficulty competing with Russian gas on purely commercial terms, it needed something else to crack open the European market. On 14 March 2014, Russia annexed the Ukrainian territory of Crimea. This event was a game-changer in the relationship between Europe and Russia. Conspiracy theorists on both sides see Washington as having engineered the crisis, provoking Moscow's reaction with calls that Ukraine (part of Russia's near abroad) join the EU and NATO, and adding that the Ukrainian *coup d'état* was prepared by Washington. American journalist William Pfaff wrote of 'a bungled and essentially American attempt to annex Ukraine to NATO and the European Union, and to undermine the domestic political position of President Putin', wondering 'Why else were the State Department official in charge of Europe and Eurasian Affairs, Victoria Nuland, together with officials of the European Union and a number of intelligence people present, in company with the "moderate" Ukrainians programmed to take over the government after the planned overthrow of the corrupt (but elected) President Viktor Yanukovych.'[24] Whether the Ukrainian crisis was effectively masterminded by Washington, and if so, whether access to the European gas market was a key reason behind it, we don't really know—and these understandings may or may not be far from reality. But the crisis represented at the very least the perfect opportunity for Washington to spook Europeans into reconsidering their ever-closer ties with a Russia always prone to promote the fragmentation and weakening of Europe and to diversifying away *en masse* from Russian gas supplies, thus lessening Moscow's geopolitical leverage on the continent, and opening up the European market to American LNG imports. The USA may still be a very marginal supplier to Europe today but its position with respect to the long-term game has dramatically improved as a result.

The Ukrainian crisis brought important strategic changes to the European continent. First of all NATO, a key instrument of American influence, having found itself out of a job following the end of the Cold War, was suddenly back in business and with it Washington's strategic influence over a weak and divided Europe was revivified. Second, despite being Moscow's largest customer for gas, a politically fragmented Europe had become increasingly dependent on a Russia only too happy to use supplies to advance its geopolitical interests and skilful at dividing European nations that were incapable of opposing a truly united front in negotiations. This rapprochement, which had been seen with dismay by the USA—and by Eastern European countries that joined the EU and NATO after the Cold War as an insurance policy against Russia—now lay in ruins. These developments represented major strategic gains in favour of Washington, and, together with a dramatic fall in oil prices, were a decisive blow to Russian ambitions to 'construct a new world order' as Vladimir Putin himself had laid out it in his Valdai speech in Sochi in October 2014. It may all be a coincidence but one may be excused for thinking that, at the very least, Washington took advantage of the crisis and played its cards masterfully, driving a solid wedge between Europe and Russia and achieving these gains at little cost since, contrary to Europe, the USA had not much trade with Russia and was thus largely unaffected by sanctions subsequently imposed to Russian trade. Checkmate.

Promoted by Washington, the sanctions game continued unabated and its aims became increasingly obvious as the *Financial Times* reported in the summer of 2017 that 'Fresh US sanctions against Russia signed into law by Mr Trump ... over alleged meddling in the US presidential election could directly target energy export pipelines that Washington fears will increase Moscow's influence over Europe's gas supplies'.[25] Europe was, to say the least, not eager to play ball with the USA on this one, with EU chief executive Jean-Claude Juncker commenting in July 2017 that the American sanctions 'could have unintended unilateral effects that impact the EU's energy security interests', reported the European Commission. These sanctions targeted the controversial Nord Stream II project for a new pipeline directly linking Russia to Germany under the Baltic Sea; yet, as the EU put it in a documents prepared for EU commissioners in July 2017 and seen by Reuters, 'the impact would in reality be much wider', hindering upkeep of the pipeline network that goes through Ukraine and fulfils over a quarter of EU needs, as well as threatening projects crucial to European energy diversification goals, including the LNG plant on the Gulf of Finland (in which Shell is partnering with Gazprom), Eni's 50% stake in the Blue Stream pipeline from Russia to Turkey, or the CPC (Caspian Pipeline Consortium) pipeline bringing oil from Kazakhstan to the Black Sea.[26] In other words, sanctions unilaterally imposed by Washington did not cost the USA anything and played into its own hands but carried a substantial cost to Europe in terms of diversity and stability of energy supplies as well as in terms of regional security risks from an increasingly angry Russia. Europe is, however, not united in such matters. Having invested over 1 billion USD in an LNG terminal on the Baltic Sea in Swinoujscie, directly competing with Russian piped gas, Poland has been trying to stop the Nord Stream II pipeline project and is eagerly positioning itself to become a long-term buyer and distributor of American LNG.[27] Encouraged by Washington, Warsaw is not just interested in reducing its own overdependence on Russian energy but is also eager to use its new Baltic terminal to develop a pipeline infrastructure in the region, which makes strategic sense.[28] In this context, Trump's shot from the hip during a meeting in Warsaw—'If one of you needs energy, just give us a call'—was music to Polish ears and to Eastern European leaders worried about their dependence on Russian energy.[29]

Do You Know When to Stop?

The question remains whether Washington will show restraint and defuse the situation or continue to press for advantage, further humbling Russia, with the risks that such a choice would entail for Europe and the rest of the world. A debate has been raging in the USA between partisans of increased military support and aid to Ukraine and those advocating de-escalation. A resolution passed by Congress in December 2016, authorizing 350 million USD in military aid to Kiev,[30] followed a year later by a decision to sell lethal weapons to Ukraine such as Javelin anti-tank missiles for the first time,[31] seemed to indicate that the Trump administration had opted to press on, perhaps moved by a combination of truculence, belief that the bear needed to be defanged or at least kept on its toes, and conviction that, for all his military posturing, Putin's options were effectively very limited. This last assumption flew in the face of Putin's domestic popularity ratings standing at around 80% and of well-known Russian paranoia about the *Rodina* (motherland) being encircled by the West by means of NATO penetration of its near abroad. Moscow didn't hesitate to annex part of Georgia in 2008 when it became clear that Tbilisi was getting too close to the West and to NATO and took over Crimea when it emerged that Ukraine was now embarking on a similar path, which would have also resulted in Russia losing its military base in Crimea and with this its only warm water port of Sevastopol. Given these realities, declarations by Ukrainian President Poroshenko that Ukraine would seek closer ties with NATO and similar hints by Georgia were likely to be perceived by Moscow as further provocations. This perception was reinforced by the presence of US Defense Secretary James Mattis and of 230 soldiers from the USA and other NATO countries marching alongside Ukrainian forces during the 24 august 2017 Ukraine National Day military parade in Kiev. Mattis' statement, 'Have no doubt the United States also stands with Ukraine in all things', after American approval of an additional 175 million USD of military aid to Kiev, left little doubt in Russian minds as to Washington's intentions.[32]

In reply to Western reactions following its annexation of Crimea and proxy fighting in Ukraine, Russia's reactions have initially been confined to displays of military machismo and to Russia doing its own pivot east and south, which saw it land in the arms of China—an uneasy *pas de deux* but one that could gain China access to valuable military technology and possibly to some form of support in the context of its own regional ambitions in Asia. Needless to say, Beijing has been paying close attention to the way Washington has swiftly marginalized rival superpower Russia. Yet, if pushed into a corner the Russian bear can lash out. Its military may not be what it was during Soviet times but it learned valuable lessons in Georgia and remains a lethal force with global power capabilities. Russia is a nuclear superpower, has allies abroad, can cause trouble and has proved that it can call the shots in Syria. Nobody, least of all Ukraine and Europe, stands to gain anything by testing how far the bear can be cornered. If Washington's goal is to humble Moscow to the extent of trying to provoke regime change, what next? The lesson from Iraq is that the law of unintended consequences is hard at work in such matters and that chaos can follow regime change, with unfathomable consequences. A destabilized Russia at Europe's doorstep would be a disaster for Europe. What more could the USA reasonably expect to gain by pressing on? The rewards from here on would be unclear whereas the potential risks, for Europe and for others, from Washington overplaying its hand would be immense. In 2016, former NATO deputy commander, British General Sir Alexander Richard Shirreff published *2017: War With Russia*, a book (published by Coronet in 2016) arguing that conflict was inevitable and would begin in 2017, with Russia seizing territory in eastern Ukraine, opening up a land corridor to Crimea and invading the Baltic states in order to escape encirclement by NATO, then threatening nuclear action to deter NATO from intervening.[33] In case of conflict, it seems the Baltic states would be the first to pay the price, and American think-tank Rand Corporation warned that NATO's forces in the Baltics are very mismatched with Russia's, 'inviting a devastating war, rather than deterring it', with Russia set to conquer the Baltics within 36 hours (NATO has been taking steps to move additional forces into the Baltic region).[34] These scenarios seem far-fetched and nothing of the sort happened in 2017, but why take more risks than necessary?

Being the Ball in the Ballgame

It comes as no surprise that a fragmented and weak Europe ended up as a pawn of large powers in a big game played way above its weight. Europe frequently found itself in the position of reluctant junior partner in new US-led adventures, Batman's eternal Robin. Granted, an additional energy supplier in the form of the USA is welcome and it is about time Europe took real steps to diversify its sources of gas away from an increasingly assertive Russia. But let's be realistic: geography has it that Europe needs Russian markets for its finished goods (ask the many German and Italian firms whose exports dramatically suffered as a result of sanctions) and needs Russian gas and natural resources. Sanctions imposed on Russia are causing substantial damage to some European economies still barely recovering from the worst economic crisis since the Second World War. The Vienna Institute for Economic Studies reportedly estimated the EU to have lost 44 billion euros worth of exports and 90,000 jobs in the last few years due to Russian sanctions.[35] Lastly, Europe has little stomach for a further disastrous escalation of tensions that could end up at its doorstep.

Russia is paying the price of more than a decade of neglect of its economy. The impact of sanctions on a dysfunctional economy overly dependent on oil and gas has been brutal, initially sending the ruble into freefall and carrying direct costs estimated at hundreds of billions of dollars—to which must be added the impact of tumbling oil prices on the country's budget. It will be a long time before confidence between Europe and Russia can be restored, if ever, so prospects are not particularly bright. For Moscow, a military escalation of the crisis is not a viable option as it would turn Russia into a pariah state, compel Europe to enact further sanctions that would reduce trade with Russia to a trickle, send Moscow's economy crashing and destabilize the country. It is clearly also in Russia's own interest to cool things down. For the bear to retract its claws, it must, however, obtain something. The annexation of Crimea (which was arguably Russian territory to start with), however unsavoury, has to be seen as an irreversible fact on the ground (seriously, is the West ready to start the Third World War over Crimea?), and while neither the West, let alone Ukraine, can officially condone this annexation, they will have to live with it. Broadly speaking, how could an EU plagued by its own intractable economic, social and political problems even consider absorbing Ukraine, yet another relatively large, poor, dysfunctional country? There are concrete ways in which Europe can help Ukraine, short of making empty, unrealistic and provocative promises. It is also difficult to take seriously the idea of NATO enlarging its membership (or expanding beyond its current borders) gaining any traction among Western European members concerned with lowering the threshold triggering Article 7 (by which all members of NATO have to come to the help of a member under attack). Realpolitik dictates that Russia and the West should work out an understanding, following which the West will not press for additional countries bordering Russia to formally join NATO or the EU and Russia will respect their territorial integrity. Blessed with huge natural and human resources and being second to none when it comes to technological prowess, Russia has everything to gain by moving its focus away from superpower rivalry and into reforming its economy and unleashing its full potential lest it be increasingly isolated and left behind in the twenty-first century.

The war in Ukraine has first of all been a human tragedy, with an estimated 10,000 killed so far.[36] The biggest loser in this conflict has obviously been Ukraine, with the country effectively partitioned. While the worst of the Ukrainian conflict seems over, for Kiev a return to the status quo ante is not realistic. Some experts have ventured that the only viable option to put a definite end to the military conflict may be some form of federalization of the country. Granted, it would enshrine some form of Russian influence in the Eastern parts, but if this is the only way to keep the country in one piece, put an end to the tragedy and give Ukraine the opportunity to slowly rebuild its economy and society, it should be seriously explored. Putin's hint in autumn 2017 that a UN peacekeeping force could perhaps be interposed between the warring parties might have come from a desire to prevent Ukraine from gaining access to more and more American weapons, but it also signalled Moscow's general weariness—which could bring about a cooling down of the conflict. For Ukraine, the road to mending fences internally and with its omnipresent neighbour will be long and fraught with uncertainty. With shrewd management, Kiev could ideally turn the situation to its advantage by fostering a climate in which the West and Russia would compete to invest in and help develop their respective zones of commercial (rather than military) influence, for the overall benefit of the country, but that is a very long shot. At the end of 2014, Robert Fico, Prime Minister of Slovakia at the time, warned of a 70% probability that the Ukrainian situation would degenerate into an open military conflict that could extend beyond Ukraine (read 'to Europe').[37] Thankfully, this didn't happen. Yet, the crisis is not over. Europe should forge a united front based on a pragmatic approach. It has everything to gain by rebuilding its bridges with Moscow and reopening access to the Russian market while securing supplies of natural resources and won't gain anything by getting dragged into new rounds of sanctions against Moscow or partaking in provocative invitations for Russia's neighbours to join the EU or NATO. At the same time Europe has much to gain by welcoming the USA as an additional supplier of gas, making it possible to diversify sources even more, for the benefit of the European consumer. Europe should muster the courage to play suppliers against each other to secure better terms. Instead of being kicked around as a football by the two super-contenders, Europe should look after its own interests while remaining a firm ally of Washington and reopening trade links with Russia. I like occasionally to mention Pulitzer Prize-winner Barbara W. Thuchman's book *The March of Folly: From Troy to Vietnam*, an impressive study of how some governments pursue foolish policies against their own interests that lead to useless wars that could have been avoided despite obvious alternatives. It is up to the leaders of the USA, Russia, Ukraine and Europe to choose either to be remembered as those who led a new march of folly or as the wise people who pulled it all back from the brink.

Notes

1. Rick Sterling. 'Gorbachev Warns of Growing Danger'. *Consortiumnews.com*. 15 May 2017.
2. *Atlas.media.mit.edu*. Russia.
3. Jude Clemente. 'More U.S. Oil And Natural Gas Exports Buffer Russia'. *Forbes.com*. 16 July 2017.

4. David Sheppard, Henry Foy. 'US and Russia step up fight to supply Europe's gas'. *Ft.com – The Financial Times*. 3 August 2017.
5. Jude Clemente. 'More U.S. Oil And Natural Gas Exports Buffer Russia'. *Forbes.com*. 16 July 2017.
6. Kenneth Rapoza. 'Trump's LNG Plans For Poland Won't Beat The Russians'. *Forbes.com – Forbes*. 18 July 2017.
7. Agata Łoskot-Strachota. 'Great expectations: LNG on the European gas market'. *Osw.waw.pl*. 13 April 2016.
8. Linda Doman. 'United States remains largest producer of petroleum and natural gas hydrocarbons'. *Eia.gov – U.S. Energy Information Administration*. 23 May 2016.
9. John Krohn, Nicholas Skarzynski, Katie Teller. 'Growth in domestic natural gas production leads to development of LNG export terminals'. *Eia.gov – U.S. Energy Information Administration*. 4 March 2016.
10. Michael Ford. 'Projections show U.S. becoming a net exporter of natural gas'. *Eia.gov – U.S. Energy Information Administration*. 28 April 2015.
11. 'Delivery statistics. Gas supplies to Europe'. *Gazpromexport.ru*.
12. 'Liquefied Natural Gas and gas storage will boost EU's energy security'. *Europa.eu – European Commission*. 16 February 2016.
13. 'Liquefied Natural Gas and gas storage will boost EU's energy security'. *Europa.eu – European Commission*. 16 February 2016.
14. Beatrice Petrovich and Howard Rogers, OIES, Harald Hecking, Simon Schulte & Florian Weiser, ewi Energy Research & Scenarios 'Future European Gas Transmission Bottlenecks in Differing Supply and Demand Scenarios'. *Oxfordenergy.org – The Oxford Institute for Energy Studies*. June 2017.
15. Jude Clemente. 'U.S. Set To Rival Russia In Oil And Natural Gas Exports'. *Forbes.com – Forbes*. 25 February 2017.
16. Jude Clemente. 'U.S. Set To Rival Russia In Oil And Natural Gas Exports'. *Forbes.com – Forbes*. 25 February 2017.
17. David Sheppard, Henry Foy. 'US and Russia step up fight to supply Europe's gas'. *Ft.com – The Financial Times*. 3 August 2017.
18. Jude Clemente. 'U.S. Set To Rival Russia In Oil And Natural Gas Exports'. *Forbes.com – Forbes*. 25 February 2017.
19. Stuart Elliott, Alisdair Bowles. 'Feature: US LNG makes negligible impact on European gas market'. *www.platts.com*. 27 December 2016.
20. 'Think smaller'. *The Economist*. Page 57. 16 September 2017.

21. 'Liquefied Natural Gas and gas storage will boost EU's energy security'. *Europa.eu – European Commission*. 16 February 2016.
22. Daniel J. Graeber. 'U.S. sees LNG as a way to contain Russia'. *Upi.com*. 15 November 2017.
23. Daniel J. Graeber. 'U.S. sees LNG as a way to contain Russia'. *Upi.com*. 15 November 2017.
24. William Pfaff. 'America Started This Ukraine Crisis'. *Ronpaulinstitute.org – Ron Paul Institute*. 10 August 2014.
25. David Sheppard, Henry Foy. 'US and Russia step up fight to supply Europe's gas'. *Ft.com – The Financial Times*. 3 August 2017.
26. Alissa de Carbonnel. 'EU warns U.S. it may respond swiftly to counter new sanctions on Russia'. *Reuters*. 26 July 2017.
27. Kenneth Rapoza. 'Trump's LNG Plans For Poland Won't Beat The Russians'. *Forbes.com – Forbes*. 18 July 2017.
28. Wojciech Moskva, Marek Strzelecki 'Trump Urges East Europe to Loosen Russia's Grip With U.S. Gas'. *Bloomberg*. 6 July 2017.
29. Wojciech Moskva, Marek Strzelecki 'Trump Urges East Europe to Loosen Russia's Grip With U.S. Gas'. *Bloomberg*. 6 July 2017.
30. 'H.R.2029 – Consolidated Appropriations Act, 2016'. *www.congress.gov*.
31. Josh Lederman. "Officials: US agrees to provide lethal weapons to Ukraine". *Associated Press*. 21 December 2017.
32. Daniel Brown. 'A scene from Putin's worst nightmare just unfolded in Ukraine'. *Business Insider*. 25 August 2017.
33. Ewen MacAskill. 'West and Russia on course for war, says ex-Nato deputy commander'. *Theguardian.com – The Guardian*. 18 May 2016.
34. Adam Withnall. 'Russia could overrun Baltic states in 36 hours if it wanted to, Nato warned'. *Independent.co.uk – The Independent*. 28 October 2016.
35. Laura Cavestri. 'Russian sanctions have cost Italy €4 billion'. *Italy24. ilsole24ore.com – Il Sole 24 Ore*. 8 February 2017.
36. Carl Bildt. 'Putin's new Ukraine gambit suggests a shift in the Kremlin'. *Washingtonpost.com – The Washington Post*. 7 September 2017.
37. John Boyd. 'PM Says 70 percent Chance of Regional Military Conflict'. *Thedaily.sk*. 3 December 2014.

11

The Trump Card

The Trump presidency and its effect on Europe

Reshuffling the Deck

Since the end of the Second World War, Europeans have been able to leave key geopolitical and security issues—and most related expenses—to Washington, a comfortable arrangement that enabled them to 'invest in butter instead of guns' and improve their livelihoods to an extent they could never have dreamed. Under the new paradigm of *Pax Americana*, NATO—the Western military alliance underpinned by American power—offered advantages to both parties. To Washington it represented the ultimate instrument of control over Europe and to Europe it represented a convenient way to latch on to the ready-made and all-powerful US military umbrella and concentrate on achieving bliss and prosperity. The USA was happy playing Mars while Europe embraced the role of Venus.

The first crack in this edifice came with the fall of the Berlin Wall in 1990. The 'clear and present danger' from the East having suddenly disappeared, NATO found itself out of a job. The transatlantic alliance remained the linchpin of the Western world order but its main raison d'etre became less compelling, affecting transatlantic cohesion. NATO attempted to keep itself relevant by participating in police operations beyond its shores and responding with a 'yes' when Washington needed to shroud some of its muscular foreign policy endeavours in the cloak of a coalition. The USA's attention shifted to Asia, attracted by promising new markets, because it felt compelled to counter China's rising power and because there seemed to be no more direct and credible threat to Europe. The second shock came with the Trump election. If Trump was elected on a protectionist and 'America first' platform and if his interest in the transatlantic relationship was as marginal, practical and not ideologically driven as he advertised, it raised an important question for Europeans: was this a mere blip and Europe just had to sit tight and wait for the storm to be over in four (or eight) years; or was this a new paradigm, a strategic re-alignment of America that would last well beyond the Trump presidency, forcing Europe to increasingly fend off for itself?

The Joy of Working Against Yourself

Contrary to popular belief the change in American attitudes is not just a 'Trump thing'. It started some time ago and is difficult to comprehend since it is American-made and seems at times to go against Washington's own interests. Future generations of historians may scratch their heads figuring out why the USA, whose leadership position in the world was solidly entrenched, started giving it all up, all by itself, not compelled by anyone else to do so. As pointed out in our analysis of Germany's hegemony in Chap. 8, in modern times legitimacy in world affairs comes not just from raw military and economic power but rests to a great extent on the delivery of what other nations perceive as 'public goods' from which they can benefit. The point is that while the USA is still the leading economic and military power of the world, it has, in recent times—and, many in the USA say, with good reason—visibly renounced supremacy in the delivery of such international public goods, consequently affecting its legitimacy as world leader. While the Trump presidency appeared to epitomize this new reality, the process of self-imposed decline in leadership started well before Trump's ascent to the White House. Back in 2015, Lawrence Summers, who had been US Treasury Secretary during Bill Clinton's presidency, had already warned that the tendency towards more ideological rigidity and unilateralism was weakening America's position on the world stage.[1] Trump merely brought this to a new, more visible level. His very public abandonment of the climate change treaty (known as the Paris Agreement) in 2017 is a case in point, having clearly cost America a lot of goodwill around the world. Several years before that, America's reluctance to adopt IMF reforms handed China—the world's rising superpower eager to fill the vacuum and establish its own legitimacy—an easy victory. Beijing created the Asian Infrastructure Investment Bank in 2015, headquartered in Beijing and comprising up to 80 countries, with the notable exception of the USA, which was invited to join but declined. Similarly, the Trump administration's decision to abandon the Trans-Pacific Partnership trade agreement negotiated by his predecessor Barack Obama with the objective of getting the USA closer to its Asian allies became another instance of the USA renouncing a multilateral approach, handing China yet another golden opportunity to fill its shoes by proposing attractive commercial agreements to the 11 countries concerned (excluding, once more, the USA). In all fairness, Americans are no fools and it may be that a deeper analysis of what was contained in these proposed reforms, treaties and initiatives would show that, as the Trump camp claims, they go against the USA's narrow self-interest or that it ends up footing most of the bills for no clear returns. But this is immaterial to the point being made here, which is that every time the USA puts a dent in these multilateral institutions and initiatives, every time it trumpets the 'America first' slogan, every time it is perceived as renouncing the delivery of international public goods, the result is more de-legitimization of American leadership in the world especially in a Europe obsessed by multilateralism. This de-legitimization profits competing powers as in a sort of zero-sum game and generates instability in the world order (the reader will have picked up the interesting analogy with Germany's reluctance to provide international public goods in Europe mentioned in Chap. 8).

Tweets and Fits

This de-legitimization of American leadership among many Europeans took a visible turn for the worse with the ascent of Trump to the US presidency. The new president personified the 'Somewheres', the nationalists, the isolationists and the reactionary right at a time when European 'elites' (and a substantial part of the public) were firmly in the camp of the 'Anywheres', internationalists and liberals. Aside from deep ideological differences, to many Europeans the shoot-from-the-hip and crude antics of the new US president conveyed the image of a loose cannon unfit to lead the free world and they didn't shy away from showing their distaste. European 'elites' perceived Trump's conduct at the May 2017 NATO and G7 summits as blatantly uncooperative if not adversarial or downright insulting. Among others, his refusal to give the traditional public endorsement of Article 5 of the NATO charter (which states that an attack on one member of the military alliance is viewed as an attack on all, requiring a collective response), his public recriminations against European nations spending less than NATO's required 2% of GDP on defence, and his refusal to endorse the Paris climate deal didn't exactly ingratiate him to European leaders. In the aftermath of these summits the usually self-restrained Merkel confessed during her famous 'beer tent' speech in Munich: 'I can only say that we Europeans must really take our fate into our own hands—of course in friendship with the United States of America, in friendship with Great Britain and as good neighbours wherever that is possible also with other countries, even with Russia… But we have to know that we must fight for our future on our own, for our destiny as Europeans'.[2] German foreign minister, Sigmar Gabriel, piled it on, saying:

> The short-sighted policies of the American government stand against the interests of the European Union. The West has become smaller, at least it has become weaker… the Trump administration wants to terminate climate agreements, wants to enforce military action in crisis regions and won't allow people from certain religious circles to enter the US … if the Europeans are not resolutely opposing to this right now, the migration flow to Europe will continue to grow. Those who do not oppose this US policy are guilty.[3]

He later added: 'There are things that cause great concern that the United States start a trade war with Europe'.⁴ Not one to stand down, Trump responded to Merkel's criticism on May 30 with his usual Tweeter-in-chief style (he recognized that he was 'the Ernest Hemingway of 140 characters'): 'We have a MASSIVE trade deficit with Germany, plus they pay FAR LESS than they should on NATO & military. Very bad for U.S. This will change'.

Remarkably, this very public and virulent feud was not the consequence of a crisis opposing allies but was all about incompatible personal styles and differing ideologies. Granted, Trump had made himself not particularly likeable during his visit to Europe. But he was, after all, the US president-elect, speaking for the majority of his constituency, even if this constituency was very polarized. His shoot-from-the-hip style may be unsettling, his view of the world unsophisticated and his ideas controversial and diametrically opposed to those of European 'elites' in many matters. Yet, for Europeans to believe that everything Trump says or thinks is outlandish and merely represents his own, personal views, is a gross, dangerous and counterproductive oversimplification. A vast swath of the American public backs Trump. For one, didn't he have a right to ask, in the name of the American people, that Europeans do more? Did the *Kanzlerin* have to so publicly show her dislike of the new president? Was she playing to her voters in light of the upcoming September elections given that Trump was widely disliked in Germany? To Gideon Rachman, chief foreign affairs commentator of the *Financial Times*, 'Merkel has also behaved irresponsibly—making a statement that threatens to widen a dangerous rift in the Atlantic alliance into a permanent breach', adding 'It is a mistake to allow four months of the Trump presidency to throw into doubt a Transatlantic alliance that has kept the peace in Europe for 70 years… It may come to that. But it is also possible that Mr Trump is an aberration and will soon be out of office.'⁵ Merkel's swift and emotional reaction was in sharp contrast to French President Macron's personal invitation to Trump and his wife to attend July 14th, France's national day, in Paris. Was Macron trying to mend fences in the name of Europe or to take advantage of the Merkel–Trump feud by reinforcing France's own transatlantic relationship? Was he attempting to regain the traditional diplomatic center-stage role for France that was lost during

François Hollande's presidency? Perhaps. The key question, however, was whether the mutual dislike between Trump's America and most of Europe was going to remain confined to the level of words or whether there would be consequences in terms of policy. Former American ambassador to NATO Ivo Daalder warned that 'Rhetoric is not unimportant', adding: 'The relationship, particularly NATO, is at its bottom a relationship based on trust, based on confidence that when necessary you can count on your other partners.'[6] In other words, if this sorry spectacle happened when there was no compelling reason for it to, one wonders what could arise in case of a real crisis.

The damage was done and a wedge had been very publicly driven between the USA and its allies—to the delight, of course, of Moscow and Beijing. According to Asia scholar Angela Stanzel at the European Council on Foreign Relations: 'The election of Trump has facilitated China's aims in Europe … Trump facilitates China's narrative of being the new defender of multilateralism and especially global free trade, and China sees Germany as defending that, too, as a kind of sidekick … it fits into the Chinese idea of creating an alternative leadership to the United States'.[7] Broadly speaking, Europe's trade with China, Japan, India, Australia, South Korea and Southeast Asia already exceeds its trade with the USA by about 300 billion USD per year—a gap likely to expand if Europe grants China 'market economy' status or signs free trade agreements with Japan, India and others, as is currently in the cards. Labelled the largest coordinated infrastructure investment programme in history, Beijing's Belt and Road Initiative 'could easily generate $2 trillion per year in trade between Europe and Asia' and 'Washington may soon realize that Europe is the swing superpower between the United States and China—and is leaning toward Eurasian connectivity'.[8]

Pay or Pray

From a security standpoint, there exists no credible European deterrent outside the US military umbrella. While Europeans have been talking for years about creating a joint defence compact outside NATO (i.e. outside American control), nothing concrete has really come of it and nothing that is game-changing is likely to materialize. At a time when budgets are being slashed across most of the continent and few countries allocate the required 2% of GDP to defence, and in a post-Brexit world where European cohesiveness is at a low, it is difficult to envision a credible, common European defence initiative. US defence spending in 2016 stood at 3.61% of its GDP compared to 1.47% for NATO's European allies.[9] To some observers, Trump's 'claim that 23 of 28 nations in NATO don't fulfill their formal obligations to spend 2 percent of their GDP on their militaries was accurate. And his refusal to back Article 5 wasn't pure sadism—it was a bid to compel them to ramp up their spending.'[10] His criticism of the alliance as 'obsolete' and suggestions that America's commitments to European security were conditional on Europeans paying their 'fair share' shook the tree a bit. The General de Villiers saga, during which President Macron 'fired' his military chief of staff for budget reasons, laid bare the simple reality that the days when France could marshal the economic resources to keep its powerful military machine in working order are over. Any independent European defence project would need to be bankrolled by the likes of Germany, something the German public wouldn't tolerate. In the wake of Merkel's commitment in the summer of 2017 to raise Germany's defence spending to 2% of GDP by 2024, an unhappy Sigmar Gabriel complained that 'It would be simply insane for us to follow Trump's goal and start investing 2 percent of our annual economic output on defence', adding with regard to the upcoming September 2017 elections in Germany that 'This election is among other things a decision if we're going to submit to Trump or not'. His views were shared by Social Democrat heavyweight Manuela Schwesig, who commented: 'We don't need rearmament, we don't need to spend an additional 20 billion euros a year on weapons. We want to spend that money instead on education and better equipment at our schools.' as reported by the *Los Angeles Times* in mid August 2017. Trailing behind Angela Merkel in polls, her main competitor, SPD's Martin Schulz, latched onto Germany's widespread dislike of Donald Trump, becoming his most vocal critic and making defence spending a key issue of the election.[11] Schulz went a step further, leveraging fears of a possible US–North Korean conflict following Trump's harsh rhetorical exchanges with Kim Jong-Un, declaring that he would remove US nuclear weapons from German soil if he became chancellor—a surprising position, designed to endear him to a pacifist German public that saw Trump as a loose cannon.¹² Against this backdrop, Trump's hint that America would not necessarily come to the aid of a NATO ally under attack—unless the ally had properly contributed economically to the alliance—meant he was 'prepared to ditch the postwar internationalist tradition inside the Republican party in favour of an approach to foreign affairs that hinged solely on American economic interests'.¹³ If Germany feels that the USA's decoupling from Europe is for real, Berlin will be compelled to forge a closer relationship with France, for one, especially on security issues, and particularly after London has waved goodbye. Fears of such a decoupling may also, paradoxically, push Germany closer to Moscow and Beijing. To Eastern European countries who rushed to join Europe after the fall of the Berlin Wall, largely because they wanted to become part of NATO and enjoy the protection of the US military umbrella, Brexit was a cold shower and any weakening of US security commitments to Europe results in sleepless nights. Yet, in all fairness, the average American citizen is entitled to ask why he/she should fund most of Europe's security (i.e. indirectly fund European welfare) with his/her taxes.

Messiah or Devil?

It has been said that Trump's 'America first' presidency could either make Europe or break it. It could push Europeans closer to each other and force more integration or it could have a centrifugal effect, pushing individual European nations to forge their own opportunistic alliances and even to look East, to the detriment of Western cohesion. In the aftermath of Trump's 2017 European tour, leading German security journalist Julia Weigelt told broadcaster *Deutsche Welle*: 'With Trump's last tour, it became clear that he's not just "America first" but "America only and we don't care about the rest." People may have thought that he was just making campaign promises, but more and more of them are waking up.' And Christian Mölling of the German Council on Foreign Relations opined: 'There's a long-term shift in US interests, and the trans-Atlantic relationship has changed… It's become harder to define common interests between Americans and Europeans.'¹⁴ Perhaps. But can Europe play the 'big game' by itself in the world arena? Tasked with monitoring the use of nuclear technology, the International Atomic Energy Agency confirmed for the eighth time that Iran was complying with the Joint Comprehensive Plan of Action (JCPOA) nuclear agreement. But Trump could decide to decertify Iranian compliance, pull out of JCPOA and reapply sanctions targeting Iran as well as other countries that do business with Iran. David O'Sullivan, EU ambassador to the USA made it clear that Europe would resist such a move and protect its business interests 'with all the means at our disposal'.[15] In *The Decline and Fall of Europe*, I wrote that 'whatever little power is left for Europe to wield on the geopolitical scene is turning softer by the day, melting like snow under the sun and cementing the continent's growing geopolitical irrelevance ... Europe's destiny is to be prey to the forces of history instead of shaping them'.[16] In the case of Iran, would Europe be ready and equipped to go to bat directly against the USA to defend its own views and interests? To CNBC senior columnist Jake Novak:

> 'President Trump is the first US president since World War II who is willing to tell Europe that America can't keep backing it up even as Europe adds to its costs by refusing to budge on its open border policies and its expensive and economically damaging focus on climate change ... this is the only responsible course of action for any American president presiding over our own nation's spiralling welfare state costs and changing public priorities ... for the reality deniers that include Merkel, Macron, and even Britain's Theresa May, President Trump is indeed a nightmare. But for the European people, he may be their last best hope.'[17]

For better or for worse, the Trump presidency is shaking Europeans when it comes to security and geopolitics and Europe's place in the world. The winners are likely to be found in Beijing and Moscow.

Notes

1. Moisés Naím, Micha Cziffra. 'La mort annoncée de la superpuissance américaine'. *Slate.fr.* 3 June 2017.
2. Joern Poltz, Tatiana Jancarikova, Michael Nienaber, Susan Thomas. 'After summits with Trump, Merkel says Europe must take fate into own hands'. *Reuters.com.* 29 May 2017.

3. James Masters. 'Trump's actions have 'weakened' the West, German foreign minister says'. *Cnn.com*. 29 May 2017.
4. 'Germany worried U.S. could start trade war with Europe: Gabriel'. *Reuters.com*. 6 July 2017.
5. Gideon Rachman. 'Angela Merkel's blunder, Donald Trump and the end of the west'. *Ft.com—Financial Times*. 29 May 2017.
6. Zeeshan Aleem. 'The epic Trump-Merkel feud, explained'. *Vox.com*. 1 June 2017.
7. Dominique Mosbergen. 'With America No Longer A 'Friend,' Angela Merkel Looks To China As New Partner'. *Huffingtonpost.com—The Huffington Post*. 6 July 2017.
8. Parag Khanna. 'Macron and Merkel can make Europe great again'. *Cnn.com*. 8 August 2017.
9. Gabriela Baczynska. 'Defense spending by European NATO allies inches up in 2016'. *Reuters*. 13 March 2017.
10. Zeeshan Aleem. 'The epic Trump-Merkel feud, explained'. *Vox.com*. 1 June 2017.
11. Erik Kirschbaum. 'Trump's demand that Germany increase its military defense spending enters German election campaign'. *Latimes.com – Los Angeles Times*. 15 August 2017.
12. Erik Kirschbaum. 'German rival of Chancellor Merkel vows to remove U.S. nuclear weapons from the country'. *Latimes.com – Los Angeles Times*. 23 August 2017.
13. Justin McCurry. 'Trump says US may not automatically defend Nato allies under attack'. *Theguardian.com – The Guardian*. 21 July 2016.
14. Jefferson Chase. 'German, French defense ministers talk new European security force'. *Dw.com—Deutsche Welle*. 1 June 2017.
15. Jessica Schulberg. 'Europe Considering Blocking Iran Sanctions If US Leaves Nuclear Deal, EU Ambassador Says'. *Huffingtonpost.com—The Huffington Post*. 26 September 2017.
16. Francesco M. Bongiovanni. 'The Decline and Fall of Europe'. *Page 7. Palgrave Macmillan*. 2012.
17. Jake Novak. 'Trump is threatening Europe…with the truth'. *Cnbc.com*. 31 May 2017.

12

Conclusion

'The stars are aligning for Europe to reclaim a central role in the global strategic balance. Merkel and Macron are reminding their peers of the region's timeless strengths: world-class infrastructure, efficient midsize cities, social-democratic politics, locally rooted businesses, low inequality and rich cultural traditions. Take a deep breath: The 21st century will be neither the American nor the Chinese. Europe is going to do whatever it can to remain at the center of the map.'[1]

So wrote the international relations expert Parag Khanna in the summer of 2017. 'The wind is back in Europe's sails', added European Commission President Jean-Claude Juncker in his September 2017 State of the Union speech, contrasting with his remarks the previous year in which he spoke sombrely of Europe's 'existential crisis'.[2] Juncker lauded the recent recovery trend of Europe's economies, pointed out that EU member states 'chose unity' and that the Union was 'slowly but surely gathering momentum'[3] and praised Europe's progress on migration and on the protection of its external borders. Brushing Brexit aside, he suggested that Europe should seize this positive momentum, strike new trade deals (such as its recent ones with Canada and Japan and upcoming deals with Mexico and South America) and forge a stronger union in which every European country would join the eurozone and the Schengen free-travel area on equal terms, with more integration and centralization, including a 'pan-European campaign' to elect a strong EU president. He continued: 'To understand the challenges of his or her job and the diversity of our member states, a future president should have met citizens in the town halls of Helsinki as well as in the squares of Athens.' In other words, for Juncker things were looking good and the time was right to push for a United States of Europe.[4] Khanna's and Juncker's words are beautiful, bold and inspiring. The problem with them is that they do not match the reality on the ground, for the reasons outlined in this book.

We have seen that the main preoccupation of Europeans nowadays has evolved from jobs and the economy to an existential one far more related to identity, values and the presence of others. We have seen that an ideologically biased traditional political class has failed to address these and other challenges, leading on one side to a question mark hanging over the sustainability of Europe's open societies model and, on the other, to the rise of an untested alternative political class that could further divide Europe and take it into uncharted waters. We have seen that Brexit, a reversal of the direction of the European integration project, unthinkable until very recently, has now become reality. We have seen that disastrous, ideology-driven migration policies are generating profound social changes and instability as well as a deep East–West divide that complements the North–South fracture caused by flaws in the single currency architecture and in the mismanagement of the eurozone crisis. We have seen that in recent times Europe has been dominated by a Germany that is not all that it seems to be, one that is focused on its narrow self-interest and is prey to ideological biases that render it inept at assuming the mantle of a real leader among European nations. We have seen that this same Germany may now be entering an era of political instability. And we have seen that there is little chance that grand European integration plans à la Macron or à la Juncker will come to fruition. In view of these and other observations that we have made throughout our journey of discovery, it is difficult to give credence to Khanna's or Juncker's words. Granted, the eurozone crisis of 2008 has not resulted in the complete meltdown we all feared. Yet, given the breadth, depth and intractability of the additional set of challenges that have emerged in the very recent past—some of which were known to be simmering while others came as complete surprises—it is impossible to conclude that Europe is better off today or that its prospects have improved since 2012, when *The Decline and Fall of Europe* was published. Apart from hints of economic recovery, all indicators point to a markedly worse, if not alarming, situation. Most of these scourges, incidentally, Europe saw coming and brought upon itself through a combination of denial, being blinded by ideology, being ensconced in a world of comfort and privilege that comes from the (unsustainable) Civilization of Entitlements, being ruled by mostly inept and ideologically blinded 'elites' and having learned to content itself with mediocrity. The absence of true pan-European politicians means every politician in Europe promotes and defends the interests of his or her own country, as can be expected and as a consequence of which there is no real cohesive political vision of Europe and no real solidarity except as a matter of give-and-take during negotiations. Perhaps when European heads of state sit at a table for a meeting, having placed themselves behind the signs displaying their countries' names, they should be asked to leave the signs in place and move a seat or two to the left or right in order to gain some understanding of what it means to be in another country's shoes. Having pointed out some of the new challenges facing Europe, we have seen that solutions exist—although the clock is ticking. In facing these difficulties, a divided, fragmented and bewildered Europe has so far mostly remained passive. Will Europeans in general be able to collectively muster the political will to do what it takes to reverse or at least contain the negative trends we have outlined? Will common sense and pragmatism prevail against ideology? Highly desirable yet highly unlikely. This leads me to reiterate that today's Europe is effectively in worse shape than it was five years ago, and to infer that it is today in better shape than it likely will be five years from now. It goes without saying that nothing would please me more than to be proven wrong.

A sliver of hope comes from an important change that has taken place in the collective European psyche in the last few years: Europeans are not burying their heads in the sand to the extent they used to do. Subjects that were taboo until recently are now increasingly openly discussed. Everything is being laid out on the table for the first time, at least to some extent. Europeans have come to realize that for a long time they have lived in an age of innocence, blissfully insulated from most of the major challenges plaguing the rest of the planet and oblivious to problems that were building up in their own backyard. As a result, they have been able to achieve a degree of well-being their forefathers could never have dreamed of. They have, however, now begun waking up to the fact that challenges they used to look at from afar are now becoming part of their world and their daily lives, and that they will have to deal with them one way or another. Unless they are willing to let go of their open societies and their cherished way of life, Europeans are going to have to confront reality, decide what they stand for, what kind of Europe they want their children to inherit and make hard decisions. Martin Luther King, Jr. said: 'A nation or civilization that continues to produce soft-minded men purchases its own spiritual death on the installment plan.' The age of innocence that Europeans were used to is over. Welcome to the real world.

Europe is not about to disappear into a hole nor will it sink into chaos tomorrow morning. It is still relatively strong, rich and stable. In all fairness some comfort can be taken from the fact that the European economy in general is doing broadly better than five years ago and is picking up speed. Let us not forget, though, that five years ago Europe was in the throes of its worst economic crisis since the end of the Second World War, and that it is still playing catch-up today, assisted by near-zero interest rates, low oil prices and tons of money thrown into the system by the European Central Bank—factors that are bound to disappear or go into reverse sometime soon. The reality is that Europe is in deep decline and trouble. Possibly in more trouble today than it has ever been since the end of the Second World War. Social and political instability, perhaps the most worrisome of all the issues now, are reaching levels unthinkable less than a decade ago. Forecasting the medium- to long-term trajectory of Europe these days has become an impossible task; uncertainty has become the norm. There are so many new fault lines, running in all directions and going deep. What will Europe look like five years from now? Ten years from now? Will the E.U. still be around? If so, in what shape and form? Will portions of some countries have become part of another civilization and Europeans forgotten the words of American theologian Reinhold Niebuhr: 'There are historic situations in which refusal to defend the inheritance of a civilization, however imperfect, against tyranny and aggression may result in consequences even worse than war.' Will the euro still exist? Will people and goods still freely move around the continent? Will NATO, for that matter, still be a going concern? How will the UK really fare in the years to come? It is all very difficult to predict. Thankfully, the purpose of this book is not to predict what will happen. Its ambition is limited to sharing with the reader the journey of discovery I undertook in order to achieve a better understanding of what is going on in Europe today. I hope this book does so, and, to some extent does it in an understandable, informative, entertaining and balanced way. More importantly, it is now up to you to draw your own conclusions.

Notes

1. Parag Khanna. 'Macron and Merkel can make Europe great again'. *Cnn.com*. 8 August 2017.
2. 'Brexit: UK will 'soon regret' leaving EU argues Juncker'. *Bbc.com*. 13 September 2017.
3. 'EU: Juncker sees window of opportunity for reform'. *Bbc.com*. 13 September 2017.
4. Leonid Bershidsky. 'Juncker Wants a U.S. of Europe. Does Anyone Else?'. *Bloomberg.com*. September 13, 2017.

Sources and Acknowledgements

Proper analysis rests on proper information. The reliability and credibility of sources of information is a delicate subject, especially where controversial issues—such as some of those that we have been exploring during our journey of discovery—are concerned. Information is available and plentiful. Its availability is not a problem. Indeed, in today's media-filled and internet-based world the quantity of information is overwhelming. Finding robust, unbiased, reliable information is, however, an entirely different matter. Everybody seems to want to put a spin on things. Doctored, biased and fake news has become the norm. One needs to be careful and discerning. In conducting my own research, I had to navigate this sea of information, steering away from the dangerous shoals of obviously biased media, fake news and the like—of which there is an overabundance. I have tried to avoid biased sources except when necessary to extract factual information or when useful explicitly to expose a specific point of view. Allow me to paraphrase something I wrote in *The Decline and Fall of Europe* as it applies to *Europe and the End of the Age of Innocence* and I couldn't find better words to express myself:

This book is the result of personal reflexions but also of conversations with government officials, experts and scholars, businessmen, ordinary people and, yes, taxi drivers. It is also the result of going through many books as well as countless articles from newspapers and magazines from various countries in various languages for news, opinions, information, data, ideas and inspiration. I have been jolting down reams of notes, learning and borrowing from these works with the objective of trying to connect the dots they represented to see patterns emerge in order to form my own ideas ... This book will inevitably contain material from these works and I humbly acknowledge my debt to their authors and rights holders including to those not explicitly credited herein, if they have been overlooked or where I have lost trace of the source.

As was the case with *The Decline and Fall of Europe*, this book was written during my free time and I researched and mined facts and figures without the benefit of any staff or resources. Any shortcomings are thus my own. I should like to take this opportunity to thank all the people who knowingly or unknowingly contributed to my journey and to the making of this book by providing ideas, facts, opinions or inspiration. I should like to thank the people who had the patience to read the draft of the book and who provided advice, reviews, comments or endorsements, as well as to express my gratitude, in advance, to those who will do so in the future. Last but not least, I should like to thank my publisher, Palgrave Macmillan, who gave me yet one more opportunity to express my views in *Europe and The End of the Age of Innocence* and share them with you.

Bibliography

Beneton, Philippe, *Le déreglement moral de l'Occident* (CERF, 2017)
Bongiovanni, Francesco M., *The Decline and Fall of Europe* (Palgrave Macmillan, 2012)
De Villiers, Bernard, *Les cloches sonneront-elles encore demain?* (Albin Michel, 2016)
Dos Santos, José Rodrigues, *Furie Divine* (Pocket, 2017)
Harari, Yuval Noah, *Homo Deus* (Harvill Secker, 2016)
Houllebecq, Michel, *Soumission* (Flammarion, 2015)
Huntington, Samuel P., *Who Are We? The Challenges to America's National Identity* (Simon & Schuster, 2004)
Mishra, Pankaj, *Age of Anger: A History of the Present* (Penguin Press, 2017)
Murray, Douglas, *The Strange Death of Europe* (Bloomsbury, 2017)
Onfray, Michel, *La parole au people* (Editions de l'aube, 2017)
Ravet, Bernard, *Principal de collège ou imam de la République* (Editions Kero, 2017)
Remadia, Nadia, *Comment j'ai sauvé mes enfants* (Calmann-Lévy, 2016)
Shirreff, General Sir Richard, *2017 War with Russia* (Coronet, 2016)
Stiglitz, Joseph E., *The Euro and Its Threat to the Future of Europe* (Allen Lane, 2016)
Tribalat, Michèle, *Les yeux grands fermés – L'immigration en France* (Denoel, 2010)
Tuchman, Barbara W., *The March of Folly* (Knopf, 1984)

Index

A

Aalberberg, Pieter-Jaap, 126
Abdeslam, Salah, 110
Abedi, Salman, 112
Accommodation, illusion of, 119–120
Adonis, Lord, 220, 221
Afghani Pashtuns, 64
Afghanistan, 53
Africa, 6, 37, 39–41, 54, 57, 65, 71, 84, 97, 196, 256, 258, 259
Agren, Peter, 158
Agricultural Revolution, 42
Aguirre, Eduardo, 113
Ahmed, Quanta A., 107
AKP, 48, 93–94
Akrap, Doris, 55–56
Algeria, 70, 176, 194
Alighieri, Dante, 7–8
Allons Enfants, 96–101
Al-Qaeda, 91

Alternative für Deutschland (AfD), 17, 57, 62, 144, 159, 161, 163–165, 168, 172, 173, 234, 236–238, 253
Alyah, 104
American Federal Reserve, 244
American LNG, 272, 274, 275
American Muslims, 42
Amnesty International, 62
Amri, Anis, 13, 112, 115, 122
Angry citizens, 141–142
Ankara, 48, 49, 63, 71
Anti-capitalism, 163
Anti-EU movements, 145, 161, 164, 169, 174, 220
Anti-euro movements, 164
Anti-immigration nationalist parties, 160
Anti-racism, 148, 151
Anti-Russia sentiments, 270
Anti-Schengen movement, 164

Index

Anti-Semitism, 105, 123, 162
'Anywheres', 143, 144
Apartheid regime, 44, 87, 89, 125, 169, 170
Apathy, 114, 202
Arab Christians, 151, 157
Arab-Germans, 44
Arab-Israelis, 117
Arab Spring, 88
Archbishop of Canterbury, 109
Archipelago, 83–87, 170
Article 5 (NATO charter), 286
Article 50 (Lisbon Treaty), 210
Asia, 2, 4, 41, 207, 277, 284
Asian Infrastructure Investment Bank, 285
Asylum seekers, 13, 15, 52, 53, 56, 65, 69, 160
Asymmetrical adjustments, 182, 248–249
Asymmetric war, 117–119
Audi, 227
Austerity, 6, 26, 62, 142, 145, 161, 168, 178, 180, 226, 234, 246, 247, 250, 251, 253, 255, 258, 261, 262
Austria, 15, 40, 47–49, 66, 67, 69, 161, 163, 168, 169, 172, 173, 175

B

Babis, Andrej, 173
Bainville, Jacques, 154
Balkans, 33, 34, 54, 67, 106
Baltic Sea, 275
Baltic states, 277
Bank of England, 214, 215

Banlieues, 102, 103, 105, 119, 121, 148
al-Banna, Hassan, 99
Bantustanization, 169, 170, 183
Barbarians, 83–130
Barcelona, 114, 115
Barnier, Michel, 210
Bataclan massacre, 13, 14
Baverez, Nicolas, 183
Beijing, 277, 285, 288, 290, 291
Belt and Road Initiative, 288
Bénéton, Philippe, 125
Beppe Grillo's Movimento Cinque Stelle, 142, 161
Berès, Pervenche, 260
Berlin, 6, 13, 18, 20, 35, 44, 48, 51, 52, 62, 113, 115, 120, 122, 159, 179–180, 213, 221, 228, 229, 233–235, 237, 251, 264, 290
Berlin Wall, 213, 216, 226, 229, 235, 269, 283, 290
Bernardini, Giuseppe, 89
Bertelsmann Foundation, 35
Bésson, Eric, 98
bin Laden, Osama, 107
Birmingham, 94, 109, 120, 122
Bismarck, 225
Bittner, Jochen, 159, 209
Black Sea, 275
Blair, Tony, 213, 221
Blaszczak, Mariusz, 217
Blavatnik School of Government, 249
Blue Stream pipeline, 275
Böge, Reimer, 260
Boistard, Pascale, 121
Boko Haram, 152
Borjas, George J., 40

Bouhlel, Mohamed Lahouaiej, 13
Bouvet, Laurent, 158
Bradford Muslims, 44
Brexit, 5, 16, 18, 27, 33, 144, 150, 153, 165, 207–221, 227, 236–238, 290, 293, 294
British security services, 112
Brookings Institution, 86, 98
Bruckner, Pascal, 20, 25
Brussels, 13, 26, 55, 66, 110, 145, 164, 168, 173, 208–210, 215, 217–219, 226, 227, 262, 270
Bruxelles, 110
Bryant, Nick, 219
Bulgaria, 49
Bullock, Steve, 212
Bundestag (parliament), 165, 234, 236
Bundesverfassungsschutz, 112
Bundeswehr budget, 233
Burka, 85, 92, 109, 119, 126
Bush, George W., 163
Butt, Khuram, 112

C

Calvar, Patrick, 92, 97
Cambrils, 114, 115
Cameron, David, 146, 207
Carney, Mark, 215
Casey, Dame Louise, 94
Cash allowance, for refugee, 59, 62, 63
Central Council of Jews, 162
Cheurfi, Karim, 111
China, 7, 46, 143, 152, 225, 261, 270, 277, 284, 285, 288
Chirac, Jacques, 161
Chomsky, Noam, 24
Choudary, Anjem, 110

Christendom–Islam dispute, 49
Christian Democrats (CDU) party, 16
Christianity, 20, 89, 106
Christian Patrol, 171
Christians, 22, 89, 92, 99, 106, 121, 123, 151, 157, 170
Citigroup, 214
Civilization, 7, 8, 23, 35, 91, 100, 103, 109, 119, 123, 126, 174, 192, 202, 296, 297
Civilization of Entitlements, 2, 26, 27, 35, 41, 57, 149, 169, 180, 295
Civil liberties, 111, 129
Civil war, 97, 170
Clarke, Peter, 94
Claussen, Detlev, 237
Clientelism, 147
Clinton, Bill, 285
Clinton, Hillary, 147
Closed factories, 144
Cold War, 20, 117, 226, 233, 269, 274
Collateral damage, 199
Collett, Elizabeth, 69
Cologne (Germany), 14, 25, 50, 51, 53, 85, 151, 155, 158, 160, 171
Colosseum, 23
Columbus, Christopher, 22
Commerzbank, 228
Common sense, 124–125, 129
Communism, 23, 93, 148
Communist Party, 164
Conseil d'Etat (State Council), 92, 109
Conspiracy of silence, 155–160
Consumer debt, 215

Conventional wisdom, 26, 154, 162, 167
Corriere Della Sera, 250
Corruption allegations, 177
Coulibaly, Amedy, 110
Coussedière, Vincent, 154
Criminal negligence, 116, 200
Critical Debates on Counter-Terrorist Judicial Review, 119
Crouch, Melissa, 87
Czech Republic, 37, 55, 173

D

Daalder, Ivo, 288
Dagens Nyheter, 156
Danish immigration policies, 66
Dansk Folkeparti (Danish People's Party), 160
Daoud, Kamel, 87, 93, 101
Dark-skinned suspect, 156
Davis, David (UK's Brexit Secretary), 210
Davis, Julienne, 91
de Maizière, Thomas, 49, 100
de Moliner, Christian, 170
de Montbrial, Thibaud, 100
Death penalty, 199
Deaton, Angus, 144
Debtor countries, 145, 248
Debt ratio, 246
Debt-to-GDP ratios, 246
Decline and Fall of Europe, The, 1, 2, 4, 6, 8, 35, 45, 83, 87, 207, 244, 291, 295, 299, 300
De-construction of nations, 144
De facto devaluation, 260
Defrauded investors, 228

Del Sol, Chantal, 153
Delmas-Marty, Mireille, 129
Democracy, 24, 26, 87, 88, 118, 124, 217
Democratic elections, 118
Demographic decline, 31, 35, 36, 200, 201
Demographic Risk Atlas, 229
Demographics, 27, 31, 35–38, 40, 85, 200, 201, 236
Demonization, 175, 177
Denmark, 56, 66, 67, 117, 160
Deportations, 19, 56–58, 61, 113, 116, 169, 193
Der Spiegel, 47, 51, 59, 160
Deutsche Bank, 227–229
Deutschmark, 244, 248, 260
Developed market, 258
Developing Country, 258
De Villiers, Philippe, 89, 99, 105, 121, 122, 124, 147, 170
DGSI security services, 111
Dhimmis, 89
Die Welt, 49, 67, 157
Die Zeit, 209
Dijsselbloem, Jeroen, 247
Discrimination, 42, 43, 102, 149
Diverse sociocultural identities, 21
Diversity, 45, 58, 94, 125, 147, 153, 273, 275, 294
Divorce bill, 210–212
Diyanet, 49
Djaziri, Adam, 111
d'Iribarne, Philippe, 43
Dombret, Andreas, 214
Domestic terrorism, 114, 128
Dos Santos, José Rodrigues, 105, 106
Draghi, Mario, 259

Dublin agreement, 34, 236
Duisburg, 122
Dupont-Aignan, Nicolas, 200

E

East–West fracture, 55
EasyJet, 212
Economic incentives, 196
Economic migrants, 15, 18, 19, 32, 37, 57, 61, 64, 65, 68, 169, 193–195
Economic patriotism, 163
Economic solidarity, 6
Economist, The, 16, 25, 36, 56, 108, 109, 151, 164, 201, 216, 247, 272
Economists for Free Trade, 214
Efficient midsize cities, 293
Egalitarian principles, 92, 98, 100
Egypt, 23, 96, 194
Elab survey, 166
Eldorado, 35, 63
Electoral geography, 144
El Haski, Hassan, 110
El-Rhazoui, Zineb, 105
Elysées, 111
Emerging market, 143, 258, 259
Emissions Trading System, 213
En Marche! in France, 142, 176
ENA (École nationale d'adminstration), 176
Energy transformation, 231
English Channel, 211, 220
Enslavement of women, 109
Erdogan, Recep Tayyip, 48, 93
Ergo, 52, 98, 248, 255
Eritreans, 36, 65

Ethiopians, 65
Eumetra survey, 250
Euratom, 212
Euro, 35, 146
  in Europe, 243–264
Eurobarometer, 16
Eurobonds, 179, 182, 234
EuroJihadists, 87, 90
Euromuslims, 5, 17, 43, 46, 84, 86–93, 97, 102, 104, 106–108, 147, 197, 198
Europe, 1, 2, 6–8, 14, 15, 17, 23, 24, 26, 27, 35, 36, 38, 41, 46, 62, 65, 66, 68, 71, 83–88, 93, 98, 104, 105, 110, 124, 126
  alternative political movements in, 141–183
  euro currency, 243–264
  gas wars, 269–280
  Germany (European partner), 225–238
  Trump presidency and its effect, 283–291
  UMI, 192–196
European Aviation Safety Agency, 212
Europe and the End of the Age of Innocence, 4, 9, 299, 300
European elites, 40, 148
European Central Bank (ECB), 244, 245, 247, 251, 253, 259, 261, 296
European Commission, 66, 69, 219, 258, 273, 293
European Council on Foreign Relations, 288
European Court of Justice (ECJ), 55, 71, 212, 214
European elites, 40, 286

Europeanization of Islam, 87
European market prices, 272
European Monetary Fund (EMF), 262
European Monetary System, 262
European troops, 199
European Union (EU), 273
    Bank Recovery and Resolution Directive rules, 228
    integration, 143
    regulations, 193
European Union Agency for Fundamental Rights (FRA), 43
Europe of values, 191–202
Europol, 127, 128
Eurostat, 230
Eurozone, 5, 27, 146, 168, 183, 208, 294
    bailout, 164
    crisis, 40, 145, 226, 227, 243
EU–Turkish agreement, 49
Exceptionalism, 17, 120
Existential crisis, 293
ExxonMobil, 271
Eyes Wide Shut, 39–41

F

Fallaci, Oriana, 18, 202
Fallon, Michael, 220
Fascism, 93
Faymann, Werner, 66
Federal Criminal Police Office (BKA), 52, 112
Federal parliament, 164
Ferry, Luc, 109
Fertility rates, 202
Fichés S radicals, 111, 157

Fico, Robert (Prime Minister of Slovakia), 280
Fillon, François, 99, 177
Financial incentives, 70, 201
Financial Times, 182, 212, 215, 270, 275, 287
Finkielkraut, Alain, 175
Fiscal austerity, 6
Fiscal deficit, 246
Fiscal federalism, 182
Fixed exchange rate, 244, 254
Fleeing war, 193
Flemish nationalist N-VA party, 193
Fondation Concorde, 166
Forbes, 171, 173
Forced integration, 44
Ford, Henry, 21
Foreign investors, 166, 167
Fracking technology, 271
Framework Nations Concept, 233
France, 24, 37, 43, 59, 67, 84, 88, 96–100, 104, 110, 117, 127, 146
    2017 presidential election, 145
    mainstream media, 158
Francken, Theo (Migration Minister), 193
Frankfurter Allgemeine Zeitung (conservative daily), 144
Franklin, Benjamin, 129
Free markets, 216
    reforms, 162
Free radicals, 108–114
Free-trade, 143
Freiheitliche Partei Österreichs (FPO), 161
French courts, 157
French Jihadists, 14, 113

French labour laws, 181
French security service (DGSE), 113
Friedman, George, 5
Friedman, Thomas L., 42
Friedrich, Hans-Peter, 156
Frisch, Max, 47
Front National (FN), 146
Fundamentalists, 87–89
Furedi, Frank, 24

G

G7 summits, 286
Gabriel, Sigmar, 55, 220, 233, 262, 286
Gaddafi Blues, 68–71
Garton, Timothy, 213
Gas wars, 269–280
Gates, Bill, 193
Gates, Robert, 232
Gauland, Alexander, 165
Gazprom, 270, 272, 275
Geert Wilders, 161, 168
General de Villiers saga, 289
Geneva airport, 116
Gentiloni, Paolo, 39–40
German Council on Foreign Relations, 161, 290
German security services, 112, 113
German Turks, 47, 48, 50
German–Turkish relations, 54
Germany, 5, 6, 17, 31, 32, 35, 37, 38, 47, 50, 51, 56, 59–61, 65, 66, 85, 98, 109, 112, 115, 120, 146, 225–238
  caring for refugees, 202
  economic powerhouse, 225
  euro, common currency, 244–245

Framework Nations Concept, 233
giant German car manufacturer (Volkswagen, Audi, and Porsche), 227
Jews in, 162
living standards, 229–231
third largest political force, 164
winner of soccer World Cup 2014, 225
Ghetto, 33, 43, 47, 63–65
Ghitis, Frida, 236
Global financial centres index (GFCI), 215
Globalization, 20, 141, 143–145, 149
Global Villagers, 144
Goldman Sachs, 215
Goldnadel, Gilles-William, 25
Good conscience, cost of, 58–63
Goodhart, David, 143, 144, 151
Grant, Hugh, 213
Great Immigration Debacle, 31–33
Greece
  agreement with IMF, 259–260
  in eurozone crisis, 254–258
  in MSCI index, 258–259
Grillo, Beppe, 161
Guantanameau, 200
Guardian, 94, 128, 156, 159
Gulen, Fethullah, 49

H

Hadiths, 88
al-Hariri, Saad, 195
Hajek, Peter, 15
Hamburg cell, 113
Habsburg empire, 216
Harari, Yuval Noah, 91, 118

Hard-core radicals, 198
Hard power, 20
Hare Krishna, 148
Helsinki, 294
Heston, Charlton, 7
Hidalgo, Anne, 99
High tax rates, 256
Hizbut Tahrir, 86
Hizmet, 49
Hofer, Norbert, 161, 168
Hollande, Francois, 118, 252
Holocaust, 164
Homo Deus, 118
Houllebecq, Phillippe, 3
House arrest, 157
How I Saved My Children, 104
Hubbard, Glenn R., 163
Human rights, 20, 21, 24, 107, 148
Human traffickers, 53, 64, 65, 70, 196
Human trafficking networks, 69, 196
100 Billion Euro Gamble, 50–54
Hungary, 33, 36, 37, 55, 56, 66, 173, 217
Huntington, Samuel P., 152

Imam of Bordeaux, 102
IMF, 214, 228, 231, 234, 247, 248, 255, 256, 259, 262, 285
Immigration, 40, 45, 58, 83, 84, 141, 143, 192, 202
Imperialism, 37
Independence Party (UK), 163
India, 143, 152, 288
Inhumane system, 193
Insecurity, 192, 198
International Atomic Energy Agency, 291
International public goods, 6, 231, 232, 234, 235, 284, 285
Intolerance, 24, 123, 141
Intra-European labour mobility, 38, 39, 201
Intra-European migration, 83
Intra-European minorities, 83
IPSOS survey, 17
Iraq, 23, 113, 116, 277
Ireland, 97, 98, 106, 211, 231, 246
ISIS, 14, 23, 96, 98, 111, 117, 145
Islam, 13, 15, 17, 23, 49, 52, 86, 87, 89, 91, 93, 94, 97, 99, 103, 105–107, 110, 112, 114, 148, 173, 197, 198, 200
Islamic Caliphate, 44
Islamic garb, 92
Islamicized communities, 120, 123, 125
Islamism, 86–88, 90, 91, 93, 94, 96, 101, 103, 107, 125, 198
   Wikipedia, definition, 86
Islamization, 2, 3, 5, 15, 16, 18, 27, 85, 87–90, 93, 95, 96, 104, 105, 119, 121, 122, 125, 126, 141, 146, 148, 151, 153, 197
Islamofascist ideology, 90
Islamo-leftists, 147
Islamophobia, 21, 25, 87, 95, 123, 148, 158, 170
Islamosphere, 95
Isolationists, 286
Israeli-Palestinian conflict, 165
ISTAT, 36, 40
Italy, 34, 37, 39, 40, 61, 146
   African migrants, 196
   debtor country, 248

J

Jamali, Naweed, 42
Javelin anti-tank missiles, 276
Jean Luc Mélanchon
   (France Insoumise), 177
Jean Marie Le Pen, 161
Jews, 61, 104, 123, 162
Jihadism, 18, 19, 27, 86, 87,
   89–91, 95, 96, 103, 110,
   125, 141, 146, 157
Jihadis Next Door, The, 112
Jihadists, 5, 15, 16, 52, 90, 95–97,
   106, 110, 113–114, 116,
   118, 123, 125, 127–129,
   154, 171, 199, 200
Jobs, Steven, 45
John Paul II (Pope), 22
Johnson, Boris, 214
Joint Comprehensive
   Plan of Action (JCPOA)
   nuclear agreement, 291
Juncker, Jean-Claude, 67, 262, 275,
   293, 294
Jungle of Calais, 64
Justice and Development Party
   (AKP), 93

K

Kaczynski, Jaroslaw, 217
Kaffir, 88, 89, 124
Kanzlerin, 54, 235, 236, 263, 287
Karoui, Hakim El, 103
Kelek, Necla, 48
Kemalization, 47
Kerguelen islands, 200
Keynesian instruments, 244
Khanna, Parag, 293, 294
Kilis, Turkish refugee camp, 195

Kim Jong-Un, 289
King, Martin Luther, Jr., 296
King, Mervyn, 214
Kissinger, Henry (former US
   Secretary of State), 226
Kolakowski, Leszek, 22
Koran, 88, 106, 123
Koranic schools, 92, 120
Kozin, Vladimir (veteran Russian
   arms control specialist), 269
Kratsev, Ivan (Bulgarian political
   scientist), 216
Krichbaum, Gunther, 51
Kristian, Bonnie, 97
Krugman, Paul (American economist
   and Nobel laureate), 214
Kurdi, Aylan, 35
Kurds, 65

L

Labour market, 181, 250, 257
Labour mobility, 38, 39, 200,
   201, 245
Lagarde, Christine, 166
Laicité, 93, 121
Laissez-faire, 197
Lambsdorff, Alexander, 263
Laurence, Jonathan, 98
Lautenschlager, Sabine, 251
Lavrov, Sergei, 273
Law of unintended consequences,
   208, 277
Le Figaro, 97, 151, 166
Le Pen, Marine, 5, 177, 216
Leave vote, 209, 210
Lebanon, 34, 195
Lehman Brothers, 228
Lehne, Stefan, 169

Leitkultur, 100
Les cloches sonneront-elles encore demain, 121
Les Republicains En Marche (LREM), 177
Lethal weapons, 199, 276
Letta, Enrico (Italian Premier), 237
LGBT (lesbian, gay, bisexual and trans) electorates, 147
Liberal elites, 143
Liberal paradigm, 20, 21
Liberal universalist elites, 153
Libor, 228
Libya, 32, 34, 39, 68–71, 152, 194, 196
Life expectancy, 144
Lilla, Mark, 147
Liquefied natural gas (LNG), 271
Lisbon Treaty, Article 50, 210
LNG (liquefied natural gas) port terminals, 271
Lodhi, Faheen, 118
London Bridge terror attack, 112
London School of Economics, 214
London Treaty of 1953, 257
Lone wolf terrorist attacks, 15, 157
Longworth, Richard C., 43
Lower Saxony, 51, 57
Low inequality, 293
Lügenpresse ('lying press'), 159
Lusa, 106
Lynching, 152

M

Maastricht debt and deficit limits, 244, 245
Maastricht debt and deficit rules, 261
Maastricht deficit criteria, 166
Maastricht Treaty, 244, 251
Mabrouk, Sonia, 102, 147
Macron, Emmanuel, 99, 110, 142, 165, 173, 262
Maio, Luigi di, 69
Maisano, Leonardo, 142
Maktouf, Lotfi, 86
Maktouf, Samia, 104
Malta Summit 2017, 253
Manchester massacre, 90
Manchester terror attack, 107
Manus island, 196
March of Folly: From Troy to Vietnam, The, 280
Market economy, 288
Marsaud, Alain, 158
Marshall Plan, 231
Martel, Charles, 99
Marx, Groucho, 246
Masood, Khalid, 114, 120
Mass emigration, 198
Mass sexual assaults, 14, 50, 151, 155
Mattis, James, 276
Matussek, Matthias, 157
Mauriac, François, 226
May, Theresa, 107, 146, 210, 291
Mazower, Mark, 148, 245
Mea culpa, 20, 25
Mechkah, Abderrahman, 115
Mediobanca (Italian investment bank), 250
Mental illness, 157
Merah, Mohamed, 104–105
Merkel, Angela, 5, 16, 31, 62, 66, 67, 157, 174, 209, 227, 230, 289
Mexican immigration, 152
Mexican migrants, 153

Mexico, 152, 293
Minorities' self-assertion, 192
Minority communities, 93, 148
Minority leaders, 148
Minority-Indian Muslims, 152
Mishra, Pankaj, 36, 145
Mittlestandt, 229
Moderation, price of, 102–105
Molenbeek, 110, 124
Mölling, Christian, 290
Moral nihilism, 22
Moseley, Clare, 64
MoVimento Cinque Stelle (M5S), 142, 161
Mueller, Gerd, 54
Muezzin, 122
Multiculturalism, 45, 91, 119, 149, 151, 155
Mundell, Robert, 244
Murray, Douglas, 40, 58, 155, 201
Muslim–American migrant, 42
Muslim Brotherhood, 91, 121
Muslim Bumiputra, 45
Muslim Council of Britain, 108
Muslims, 42–44, 84, 85, 90, 92, 94, 97, 102, 103, 105–108, 122
  immigrants, 162
  minorities, 18, 83, 85, 115, 152, 153
  neighbourhood, 171
Muslim Xinjiang Province, 152

N

National debt, 179, 246
National Defense Authorization Act, 273
National Geographic study, 32

National identity, 15, 17, 21, 24, 32, 46, 98–101, 141, 146, 148, 151, 153, 160, 162–164, 167, 169, 175, 177, 208
National Review, 118
National socialism, 23, 148
Nation-state, 42, 147–150
NATO, 269, 273, 283, 286, 288, 297
  relationship with Turkey, 48
Nauru island, 196
Navarro, Peter, 252
Nazis, 48, 157, 164, 236
Nemmouche, Mehdi, 110
Neo-colonial leftist, 158
Neo-Nazi Soldiers, 171
Netherlands, the, 49, 146, 168
New York Times, 209, 237
Niebuhr, Reinhold, 296
Nigeria, 40
9/11, 107, 113, 153
Ninth Symphony, 148
Non-Christian minorities, 22
Non-Muslim intra-European minorities, 83
Non-white ethnic groups, 169
Nordic countries, 155, 160
Nord Stream II pipeline project, 275
Normal delinquency, 157
North Africa, 34, 43, 65
North America, 2
North Rhine-Westphalia, 60
Norway, 67, 98
Novak, Jake (CNBC senior columnist), 291
Nuland, Victoria, 273
Nurseries, 201, 202

O

Obama, Barack, 285
Oberhausen, 60
Omertà, 158
Onfray, Michel, 148, 158, 175
Open-door immigration policies, 236
Open door policy, 57, 193
Open Skies Agreement, 212
Open trade, 144, 146
Optimism, 8
Orban, Viktor, 36, 55
Organe de Coordination Pour l'Analyse de la Menace' (OCAM), 88
Organisation for Economic Co-operation and Development (OECD), 31, 181, 234
O'Sullivan, David (EU ambassador), 291
Oubrou, Tareq, 102

P

Pan-European politicians, 295
Paris Agreement, 285
Paris–Berlin axis, 179
Paris–Berlin partnership, 237
Partij voor de Vrijheid (Party for Freedom), 161, 168
Pax Americana, 231, 283
Pax Germania, 231
Pegida, 86
People media, 159
Persecution, 151, 193
Perussuomalaiset (True Finns), Finland, 160
Petry, Frauke, 161
Pew Forum, 84
Pew Research Center, 42, 209, 232
Pfaff, William (American journalist), 273
Pfeiffer, Christian, 51
Philosophical digressions, 23
Pickens, Boone T., 271
Piet, Remi, 165
Piketty, Thomas, 257
Pina, Céline, 119, 120
Pipes, Daniel, 93, 94, 96, 103, 107
Pirincci, Akif (Turkish origin), 158
Podemos
  far-left political party, 251
  in Spain, 142
Poland, 173, 217, 218, 262, 275
Polish Oil and Gas Co., 273
Political elites, 66, 85
Political correctness, 7, 19–24
Pollack, Detlef, 49
Polony, Natacha, 143
Popular vote of referenda, 208
Populism, 55, 154, 161, 163, 169, 173
Populists, 142, 153, 208, 217
Porsche, German car manufacturer, 227
Portugal, 97, 98
Pound, 215
Poverty, 19, 122, 143, 193, 230
Pragmatism, 8, 23, 192, 246, 295
Predictive justice system, 129
Primary fiscal surplus, 249
Pro-Brexiters, 211
Pro-EU, 142, 173, 177, 179
Pro-free trade country, 168
Pro-globalization, 142, 176, 177
Pro-immigration policies, 164
Pro-minority agenda, 147, 151
Pro-multiculturalism, 176, 177

Pro-natalist policies, 201
Protectionism, 144, 163, 174
Psota, Georg, 157
Public outrage, 35
Pulitzer Prize, 280
Pupponi, François, 121
Pure 'lone wolf' attacks, 114
Putin, Vladimir, 174, 213, 273, 274

Q

al-Qardawi, Youssef, 89
Quandt family, 227

R

Rachman, Gideon, 287
Racial purity, 36
Radev, Rumen, 49
Radial Islam, 13, 91, 93, 110
Radical Islamism, 101
Ramadan, Tariq, 99, 104, 123
Rand Corporation, 277
Randers (Denmark), 160
Rasmussen, Lars Løkke, 66
Ravet, Bernard, 95, 123
Reconquista, 197
Refugee Convention 1951, 193
Refugees, 14, 34, 65, 193
    boats, 157
    camps, 157, 194, 195
    crisis, 32, 67, 226–227
Refuseniks, 57, 61
Religious convictions, 147
Religious tolerance, 198
Remadna, Nadia, 104
Re-migration, 197
Renzi, Matteo, 62, 250
Replacement migration, 39

Retirement age, 163, 166, 181
Rettig, Jan, 162
Returnees, 194
Revenge voting, 144
Rich cultural traditions, 293
Rioufol, Ivan, 149, 153
Rizzuto, Isola di Capo, 62
Roach Motel, 247
Rodina (motherland), 276
Rogers' neighbourhood, 120–124
Rohingya, 152
Rooted businesses, 293
Rothschild investment banker, 176
Rouhani, 85
Rowley, Mark, 112
Rubicon, 199
Rushdie, Salman, 198
Rutte, Mark, 171, 215
Ryanair airlines, 212

S

Sabine Pass terminal, 271, 273
Salafism, 113
Salafists, 87, 88, 97, 112, 120, 122
Salary dumping, 231
Salzgitter, 57
Sansal, Boualem, 90, 91, 121
Sapin, Michel, 59
Sarcelles, 121
Sarkozy, Nicolas, 99, 128
Satty, Abdelbaki Es, 115
Saudi Arabia, 85, 88
Scandinavian plate, 207
Schäuble, Wolfgang, 16, 55, 59, 179, 182, 201, 252
Schengen, 5, 19, 27, 33, 34, 65–68, 70, 115, 169, 227, 262, 294
Schira, Jean-François, 144, 145

Schulte, Joachim, 47
Schultz, Martin, 67
Schulz, André, 156
Schulz, Martin, 289
Schuster, Stefan, 162
Schwartzer, Alice, 15, 25
Schweitzer, Albert, 154
Schwesig, Manuela, 289
Scottish voters, 210
Second-generation migrants, 101
Second law of human thermodynamics, 42
Second World War, 162, 213, 216–218, 235, 236, 269, 278, 296
Self-apartheid, 92, 121, 198, 199
Self-ghettoization, 46, 101, 123
Separatist forces, in Catalonia, 150
Sevastopol, water port, 276
Sevran, 121
Sex assaults, 156, 159
Shahin, Mariam, 44
Sharia, 107, 109, 123, 170
  law, 102, 109
  patrols, 92
Sharrouf, Khaled, 117
Shirreff, Alexander Richard (NATO deputy commander, 277
Simcox, Robin, 97
Singapore, 46
Single currency, 2, 6, 7, 65, 146, 166, 182, 216, 243–245, 249, 251–254, 294
Slaughtering, 199
Slave markets, in Libya, 152
Social Democrats, 100, 160, 173, 289
Social instability, 183, 192
Social media, 4, 13, 35, 159

Social-democratic politics, 293
Socio-cultural homogenization, 142
Socio-cultural liberalism, 144
Socio-economic realities, 27
Soft power, 20, 173, 217
Soini, Timo, 160
Solidarity, 6, 27, 34, 37, 40, 54, 67, 69, 244, 245, 247–249, 252, 256, 258, 259, 261–264, 295
'Somewheres', 143, 144, 151, 176, 177, 216, 286
Soul of Europe, changing, 142–147
Southern European plate, 207
Soviet empire, 216, 269
Spain, 2, 34, 37, 63, 115, 142, 150, 217, 218, 246, 250, 251
Stanley, Morgan, 162
Stanzel, Angela, 288
State Department's Bureau of Energy Resources, 271
Stiglitz, Joseph (American economics Nobel Prize Laureate), 143
Stojberg, Inger, 66
Strange Death of Europe, The, 41, 201
Strasbourg, 110
Summers, Lawrence, 285
Sunna, 88
Sunni Islam, 94
Supremacism, 103
'Survival', 191
Sustainability, 41, 57, 202
Sweden, 19, 43, 53, 65, 85, 120, 146
Sweden Democrats, 155, 158, 160
Swedish Migration Agency, 61
Switzerland, 49, 53, 86, 97, 98, 126
Syria, 23, 45, 68, 112, 113, 116, 120, 200, 277
Syrian conflict, 32, 169

Syrian migrants, 236
Syrian refugee crisis, 34
Syrian refugees, 34, 46, 48, 49, 52, 57, 61, 195
Syrian war, 68
Syriza party, 142
Szydlo, Beata, 218

T

Target rich environment, 156
Tax dumping, 231
Taxpayers, 52, 61, 70, 228
Telegraph, 146
Tempel, Sylke, 161
Terrorism, 94, 208
Terrorist attacks, 18, 111, 113, 117, 118, 120, 157, 171
Thrall, Trevor, 98
Thuchman, Barbara W., 280
Tillerson, Rex, 271
Timmermans, Frans, 69, 218
Tinguely Machine, 2
Titanic scraping, 3
Todd, Emmanuel, 100, 177
Tombs, Robert, 209
Totalitarian ideology, 23, 93, 107
Traditional political forces, 143
Trans-atlantic alliance, 283–284, 287
Trans-atlantic relationship, 290
Trans-Pacific Partnership trade agreement, 285
Trappes, 120, 121
Trappistan, 121
Treaty of Westphalia, 42
Tribalat, Michèle, 40
Trichet, Jean-Claude (ECB head), 247
Trilogy, 5–7, 16, 18, 19, 26, 141, 142, 146, 153, 162, 174, 183
Trojan Horse Enquiry, 94
Trotignon, Yves, 113
True Finns, 160, 172
Trump, Donald, 153, 163, 283–291
Tsipras, Alexis, 142, 255
Tsunami, 19, 31–71
Tunisia, 13, 32, 70, 194
Turkey, 34, 46, 47, 49, 50, 68, 71
Turkish *gastarbeiter*, 45
Turkish–Islamic Union for Religious Affairs, 49
Turkish nationalism, 48
Tusk, Donald, 67
Twitter, 159

U

UAVMT, 127
Uber Alles, 229
UBS, 215
Ukraine National Day military parade, 276
Ukrainian crisis, 7, 274
Ummah, 88
Unfair competitors, 144
UNHCR, 61, 194
Union of European-Turkish Democrats (UETD), 48
Universalism, 148
University of Bremen, 162
University of Hannover, 237
UN peacekeeping force, 279
Unwanted mass immigration (UMI), 5, 6, 16, 18, 19, 32, 34, 40, 52, 57–59, 61–64, 67, 68, 70, 125, 141, 146, 192–196, 208

USA
  conflict with North Korea, 289
  election, 147
  emission and pollution
    controls, 227
  income of male worker, 143
  Justice Department, 228, 229
  LNG exports, 270–271
  National Trade Council, 252
  nuclear weapons, 289
  Somewheres,
    class of people in, 144
  Treasury Department, 234
US Congress, 232

V

Valls, Manuel, 104, 109, 110
Victim of oppression, 158
Vienna Institute for Economic
  Studies, 278
Voice of the people, 150–155
Volkswagen, German car
  manufacturer, 227
Von der Leyen, Ursula, 233
Vote of anger, 144

W

Wage bargaining, 250
Wahhabism, 44
Waintraub, Judith, 95
Walker, Robin (Junior Brexit
  Minister), 211
Wall Street Journal, 97, 178
War refugees, 18, 19, 32, 37,
  61, 68, 194
Wars of moralization, 7
War zones, 194

Washington Post, 69, 127, 173
Weigelt, Julia, 290
Welt am Sonntag (German
  newspaper), 193
Wendt, Rainer, 51
Western civilization, 7, 8, 23, 109
Western military alliance, 283
Western world, 3, 7, 56, 143, 284
White House, 22, 285
White middle lower class, 144
Wikileaks, 113
Willkommenskultur, 26, 27, 54,
  57, 120, 156
Wir schaffen es!, 50, 54–58
Wolf, Martin, 182
Wolfe, Tom, 23
Woods, Ngaire, 249
World Bank, 230, 231, 258
World-class infrastructure, 293
World Economic Forum, 230
World War II, 55, 291
Wrath of God, The, 105

X

Xenophobia, 21, 155
Xenophobic violence, 152

Y

Yanukovych, Viktor, 274
Yusanto, Ismail, 86

Z

Zagury, Daniel, 157
ZDF, 156
Zeman, Milos, 37
Zemmour, Eric, 97, 99, 147

GPSR Compliance

The European Union's (EU) General Product Safety Regulation (GPSR) is a set of rules that requires consumer products to be safe and our obligations to ensure this.

If you have any concerns about our products, you can contact us on

ProductSafety@springernature.com

In case Publisher is established outside the EU, the EU authorized representative is:

Springer Nature Customer Service Center GmbH
Europaplatz 3
69115 Heidelberg, Germany

www.ingramcontent.com/pod-product-compliance
Lightning Source LLC
LaVergne TN
LVHW040732250326
834688LV00031B/261